Frontispiece. The Theatre of Dionysus

THE THEATRE
OF DIONYSUS IN
ATHENS

BY

A. W. PICKARD-CAMBRIDGE

D.Litt., LL.D., F.B.A.
HON. FELLOW OF BALLIOL COLLEGE

OXFORD
AT THE CLARENDON PRESS

Oxford University Press, Amen House, London E.C. 4

GLASGOW NEW YORK TORONTO MELBOURNE WELLINGTON
BOMBAY CALCUTTA MADRAS KARACHI CAPE TOWN IBADAN

Geoffrey Cumberlege, Publisher to the University

FIRST EDITION 1946

REPRINTED LITHOGRAPHICALLY IN GREAT BRITAIN
AT THE UNIVERSITY PRESS, OXFORD
FROM SHEETS OF THE FIRST EDITION
1956

PREFACE

AFTER the death of my friend Mr. A. E. Haigh, I was entrusted with the revision of his work, *The Attic Theatre*, for a third edition, which was published in 1907. At that time I shared the view, which was then common to most English scholars, that the theatre of the Classical epoch included a stage, raised above the level of the orchestra which the chorus occupied, and that the actors in tragedy and comedy performed almost entirely on this higher level. But as the result of a number of visits to Athens and of much further study of the subject, I became convinced that as regards the drama of the fifth century Dörpfeld was right in rejecting the raised stage, though as regards later periods I could not always agree with him. I greatly regret that, owing to the war, I have been unable to go through the present volume on the spot, as I had hoped to do, but thanks to a fairly accurate visual memory, refreshed by the extremely good illustrations of other scholars, I trust that I have had the remains of the theatre fairly clearly in my eye.

The work of Dörpfeld and Reisch, *Das griechische Theater*, published in 1896, is still the necessary foundation of all study of the subject. But two other works of great importance have appeared since. The first is the *Untersuchungen an griechischen Theatern* of H. Bulle (assisted by K. Lehmann-Hartleben and other distinguished scholars). This, published in 1928, embodies the results of several months' work and excavation in the Theatre of Dionysus, and though it is often over-venturesome and unconvincing, it has raised important questions and contributed materials for the solution of these and others. The second work is the monograph of E. Fiechter, *Das Theater in Athen*, published in three parts in 1935 and 1936, and based on exhaustive work, carried out in the years 1927 to 1929 and 1933, in all parts of the theatre except a portion of the auditorium and its walls. Fiechter's work is of first-rate importance owing to his minute and careful examination of the extant remains, stone by stone, the exactness of his records, and the lucidity of his exposition. His drawings and descriptions (when a few slips and inconsistencies have been corrected) must be the basis of all future work, and I have therefore adopted, in the plan and text of this volume, his lettering and numbering in place of those of Dörpfeld, which most scholars have followed hitherto. At the same time, his work aims at being, not a critical history, but a *Quellenausgabe*, an exhaustive account of the facts upon which such a history must be founded, and when he does draw historical conclusions, I have sometimes had to differ from him.

I must also mention with gratitude the work of two American scholars, Professors Roy Flickinger and J. T. Allen, whose studies have shown that accurate and comprehensive results in this region of scholarship are not the monopoly of the German people. For students who desire to see the theatre in its proper relation to the Greek Drama as a whole, Flickinger's *Greek Theater* (fourth edition, 1936) is of the highest value.

The flood of controversy which followed the publication of the great work of Dörpfeld and Reisch in 1896 continued unabated for many years, and did not cease until Dörpfeld's death at Leukas in 1940. While not afraid to change some of his opinions, if he thought the evidence sufficient, Dörpfeld maintained most of his views unaltered and remained a doughty fighter to the end. The Bibliography at the end of this volume will enable those who desire to do so to follow the course of the controversy. In addition to the countless articles contributed to periodicals by many scholars, more substantial studies were produced by O. Puchstein, A. Müller, F. Noack, and A. Frickenhaus, and by Fiechter himself in his earlier work on the architectural development of the Greek theatre. The articles in Pauly–Wissowa's *Real-Encyclopädie*, s.v. *Skene* by A. Frickenhaus and s.v. *Theatron* by C. Fensterbusch are also important. Dr. Margarete Bieber laid all students of the subject under a debt of gratitude by the publication in 1920 of her *Denkmäler zum Theaterwesen im Altertum*, with its admirable illustrations. This is unfortunately out of print, and its place is only imperfectly filled by her *History of the Greek and Roman Theater* (1939). Problems raised by the Athenian theatre have often been discussed by A. von Gerkan, both in his fine book on the theatre of Priene (1921) and in reviews and articles.

The present volume is almost entirely confined to the theatre of Dionysus in Athens, and other theatres are mentioned only for purposes of comparison or illustration. I have made no attempt to discuss the classification of the many ancient theatres under types; this would need a very thorough and critical description of each theatre, and the discussion has not so far produced very illuminating results. But a comprehensive work on the Greek and Roman theatres of which remains are extant is much needed.

Nor have I attempted to include in this volume many matters of great interest which are treated in Haigh's *Attic Theatre*. On some of these—the Dionysiac festivals, the inscriptional records, the costumes of the actors, and other subjects—Haigh is now out of date. I hope to write of these in a later work, if life and strength are given me; but at the age of 73 one must not expect too much. In this volume I have thought of the buildings of the theatre mainly as a setting for the drama, and have not entered into all of the endless arguments about such minute details of the material structures as could have little or no human interest. The continuance of such disputes by architectural specialists for over fifty years is itself some indication that no conclusions are to be expected. Further, I have not always thought it necessary to refer to arguments raised in the course of the controversy and then discussed and dropped. But I have tried to state the evidence fairly on every point which appeared to be worth consideration.

I fear that my critics will complain that I have too often been content—or, as I should say, compelled—to state my conclusions in the form of probabilities or possibilities, instead of drawing such definite and detailed pictures as others have often confidently produced. I could not honestly do otherwise, though I may envy others their gifts of imagination.

In studying the writings of scholars on this subject, I have found certain assumptions continually (though not always explicitly) made, which seem to me to be mere superstitions, and contrary to what we know of human nature and freedom—such as these:

that variations in structure always take place in a logical order, and that the chronological order can be inferred from the logical;

that careless work in stone is only possible at late periods, and that whatever is to be ascribed to the Classical age must have been relatively perfect (even when buried underground);

that any structure which is found in stone must previously have existed in wood;

that no artist (or architect) ever thought of anything for

himself, but that whatever any artist embodies in his structures or paintings or reliefs must have been 'derived' from someone else.

But as the questioning of this last assumption might encourage a sceptical attitude towards much that is dear to Archaeology and *Entwicklungsgeschichte*, I had better not pursue the subject.

Whenever I have been conscious of an obligation to earlier writers, I have tried to acknowledge it, but I cannot always distinguish the points which in the course of fifty years have been suggested by others and those which have occurred to me independently. I hope I shall be forgiven if the conditions of a time of war have prevented me from obtaining formal leave to insert every one of the illustrations which have been drawn from many sources. Wherever it has been possible, the source has been acknowledged, and I hope that the invariable generosity of authors and publishers (of all nations) in this field has not led me to presume too far in a matter in which, under other conditions, I should have been very scrupulous. In regard to the illustrations generally I am greatly indebted to Professor J. D. Beazley for advice and help, and for the careful drawing of a number of Plans my gratitude is due to Dr. Bruno Ahrends, a distinguished architect who has been a welcome guest in this country during the war.

A. W. P.-C.

29 September 1946

CONTENTS

LIST OF ILLUSTRATIONS

D.R. = Dörpfeld und Reisch, *Das griechische Theater* (Barth und von Hirst).
Fiechter, i, ii, iii = Fiechter, *Das Dionysos-Theater in Athen*, i, ii, iii (Kohlhammer).

SOME ABBREVIATIONS

(Most of the abbreviations used will need no explanation, or, at most, a reference to the Bibliography; but the following list may be a convenience to some readers.)

Am. J. Arch. = *American Journal of Archaeology.*

Arch. Ztg. = *Archäologische Zeitung.*

Ath. Mitt. = *Mitteilungen des deutschen archäologischen Instituts, Athenische Abteilung.*

Berl. Phil. Woch. = *Berliner philologische Wochenschrift.*

B.C.H. = *Bulletin de Correspondance Hellénique.*

C.I.G. = *Corpus Inscriptionum Graecarum* (Boeckh), 1828–77.

Dith. Trag. Com. = Pickard-Cambridge, *Dithyramb, Tragedy, and Comedy* (1927).

Dittenb. *Syll.*³ = Dittenberger, *Sylloge Inscriptionum Graecarum,* ed. 3.

D.R. = Dörpfeld und Reisch, *Das griechische Theater.*

'Εφ. 'Αρχ. or 'Εφημ. 'Αρχ. = 'Εφημερὶς 'Αρχαιολογική.

Fiechter, i, ii, iii = Fiechter, *Das Theater in Athen,* vols. i, ii, iii.

Fiechter, *Baugesch.* = Fiechter, *Die baugeschichtliche Entwicklung des griechischen Theaters.*

Furtw.–Reich. = Furtwängler und Reichhold, *Griechische Vasenmalerei.*

G.G.A. or *Gött. Gel. Anz.* = *Göttingische gelehrte Anzeigen.*

I.G. = *Inscriptiones Graecae,* 1877–90.

*I.G.*² = *Inscriptiones Graecae,* ed. minor, 1924 onwards.

Jahrb. Arch. = *Jahrbuch des deutschen archäologischen Instituts.*

J.H.S. = *Journal of Hellenic Studies.*

Pauly–W. = Pauly–Wissowa, *Real-Encyclopädie der classischen Altertumswissenschaft.*

Philol. or *Philolog.* = *Philologus.*

Philol. Woch. = *Philologische Wochenschrift.*

Rh. Mus. = Rheinisches Museum.

Röm. Mitt. = *Mitteilungen des deutschen archäologischen Instituts, Römische Abteilung.*

Sitz. bayr. Akad. = *Sitzungsberichte der bayrischen Akademie zu München.*

Woch. Klass. Phil. = *Wochenschrift für klassische Philologie.*

I

THE THEATRE BEFORE LYCURGUS

I. THE PRECINCT OF DIONYSUS

THE precinct of Dionysus Eleuthereus, in which the theatre of Dionysus was situated, occupied the eastern portion of the southern slope of the Acropolis rock; the lines of the precinct wall, whether marked by existing remains or traced by conjectures which cannot be far wrong, are given in Plan I.[1] At its lowest point the southern boundary of the precinct is about 276 feet above sea-level. In the fourth century B.C., when the auditorium had attained its fullest extent, it met the perpendicular rock above it at about 401 feet, i.e. about 125 feet above the lowest point of the precinct.[2]

FIG. I. Coin showing Odeum of Pericles

It is practically certain that in the fifth century B.C. the principal entrance to the precinct was on the east side. In the year 415, so Andokides relates,[3] a certain Diokleides, standing close to the Propylaeum, or entrance portico, of the precinct of Dionysus, saw the supposed mutilators of the Hermai coming down from the Odeum into the orchestra. Now that the position of the Odeum and part of its outline have been determined by excavation (Fig. 2),[4] it is clear that a Propylaeum in the east wall of the

---

[1] Based on Dörpfeld and Reisch, Taf. I, but with necessary modifications and changes of lettering.

[2] There is some reason for thinking that the precinct of Dionysus in the strict sense—the sacred τέμενος—may not have included the ground on which the auditorium was built; see Judeich, *Topogr. v. Athen*², p. 316.

[3] Andok. i. 38 ἐπεὶ δὲ παρὰ τὸ προπύλαιον τὸ Διονύσου ἦν, ὁρᾶν ἀνθρώπους πολλοὺς ἀπὸ τοῦ Ὠιδείου καταβαίνοντας εἰς τὴν ὀρχήστραν.

[4] P. Kastriotis, Ἐφ. Ἀρχ., 1922, pp. 25–38; Welter, *Ath. Mitt.* xlvii (1922), pp. 72–7. The remains excavated are those of the building as reconstructed by Ariobarzanes II of Cappadocia, after the destruction of the Odeum of Pericles by fire in the first Mithridatic War (86 B.C.). Of Pericles' building only layers of ashes and a few nails and stones remain (Judeich, op. cit., p. 307). But there is no reason to think that the outline of the restored Odeum differed from that of

precinct (if this wall ran roughly as Dörpfeld outlined it) would afford such a view of the orchestra and the descent from the Odeum, particularly if, as will be shown to be almost certain, there were at this date no permanent stage-building of sufficient height to obstruct the vision. It is some confirmation of this that

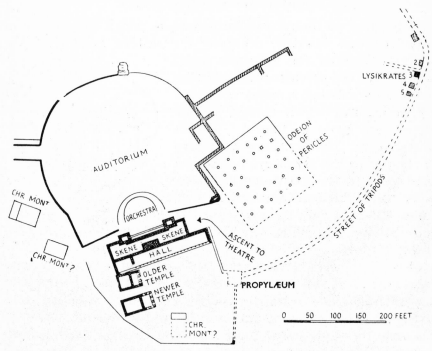

FIG. 2. Plan showing position of Odeum

in the second century A.D. Pausanias evidently entered the precinct from the east by the Street of the Tripods,[1] the course of which has been approximately made out[2] and is shown in Fig. 2. There is no reason to think that the position of the Propylaeum had changed in the intervening centuries. The exact spot where Pericles' building, which must have been finished by 443 B.C., when Cratinus, in his Θρᾷτται (fr. 71 K) compared Pericles' helmet—which, being made to suit the unusual shape of his head, was a curious as well as a familiar sight—to the Odeum with its remarkable roof. (See Judeich, pp. 78, 97.) The line of the south wall of the Odeum has not yet been certainly determined.

[1] Paus. I. xx.

[2] A. Philadelpheus, 'Εφ. 'Αρχ., 1921, p. 85. Unfortunately a great part of this street, along which the tripods erected by victorious choregi were erected, is covered by modern buildings; but its general course is certain.

it stood cannot be determined in the absence of remains; but it is natural to suppose that the road which passed through it into the precinct led originally to the Older Temple of Dionysus, the oldest building in the precinct and the chief object of religious interest, and that the Propylaeum was placed conveniently for this purpose. From the Propylaeum the ground would have risen gradually to the level of the orchestra as this level was in the fifth century (and still is, with little or no alteration), and this ascent would meet a descent from the Odeum towards the same spot. In the earliest period, before the construction of permanent theatre-buildings, the road from the Propylaeum, after passing the Older Temple, probably turned gradually to the right and gave access to the level ground of the earliest orchestra.[1] Whether at this time or later there was an entrance to the precinct from the west is unknown.

II. THE OLDER TEMPLE OF DIONYSUS

1. The earliest building of which remains exist within the precinct of Dionysus is the *Older Temple of Dionysus*. It was obviously older than the long hall, at the south-west corner of which (where it meets the north-west corner of the temple) the stones of the hall encroach upon the temple step but are carefully arranged so as to leave the wall of the temple uninjured; and had the temple been the later building it would have been easy to place it a little farther south, so as not to interfere with the hall. But further, the combination of the materials used and the masonry of the remains of the temple prove it to be of a date anterior to the Persian Wars and almost certainly of the sixth century B.C. The foundations were of the hard bluish limestone of the Acropolis rock; the step resting upon them and running round the temple was of limestone from Karà (at the foot of Hymettus), and the main building was of poros; the outer surface of the upper existing layer of stone was well finished on the outside, but within this the masonry is of a polygonal type, and the shape of the iron clamps used points to a very early date. These characteristics are found in other buildings of the Peisistratean epoch.[2] Pausanias[3] speaks of this as the oldest Temple of Dionysus

[1] See pp. 5 ff. [2] D.R., p. 15.

[3] I. XX, § 3 τοῦ Διονύσου δέ ἐστι πρὸς τῷ θεάτρῳ τὸ ἀρχαιότατον ἱερόν. δύο δέ εἰσιν ἐντὸς τοῦ περιβόλου ναοὶ καὶ Διόνυσοι, ὅ τε Ἐλευθερεὺς καὶ ὃν Ἀλκαμένης ἐποίησεν ἐλέφαντος καὶ χρυσοῦ.

in Athens, and although (as is shown by Thucydides[1]) the temple ἐν Λίμναις must have been older, this had probably disappeared by the time of Pausanias. Pausanias mentions in the same passage the Later Temple, in which the statue of Dionysus in gold and ivory, the work of Alkamenes, was housed. He mentions also the image of Dionysus Eleuthereus (to whom the theatre precinct belonged), and although he does not expressly say where it stood, he does state[2] that the ancient ξόανον of Dionysus had been brought to Athens from the temple at Eleutherai, and it may safely be conjectured that this was the image which stood in the Older Temple. The transfer of the statue from Eleutherai to Athens (where at first it was not well received) was ascribed[3] to a legendary Pegasos of Eleutherai, and the temple may either have been built quite early in the sixth century to receive it,[4] or may have been one of several temples built or begun by Peisistratus; this would be in keeping with the policy followed by the tyrants of encouraging popular festivals, and especially those of Dionysus, and with the fact that Thespis competed at the first state-organized performances of tragedy in or about 534 B.C. No nearer dating is at present possible.

2. The plan of the remains as given by Dörpfeld[5] (Fig. 3) was drawn when some of the stones were in better condition than they are now. The temple was of the type known as *in antis*, and consisted of two portions, the cella, and to the east of it a pronaos, probably rather smaller. Dörpfeld calculates that, if the normal proportions of such structures were observed, the temple must have been about 44 feet long by 26 ft. 3 in. wide externally, and 21 ft. 7 in. wide internally. Fiechter,[6] on the other hand, thinks an external width of about 21 ft. 8 in. more likely. There would probably have been two columns between the *antae*. Various fragments found in the neighbourhood of the temple have been conjecturally ascribed to it, among them part of a poros tympanum[7] bearing two satyrs and a maenad in relief, and also some fragments of fluted columns, the head of one of a pair of *antae* and some bits of triglyphs;[8] but there is no certainty in these ascrip-

---

[1] II. xv.   [2] I. xxxviii, § 8.
[3] Paus. I. ii, § 5 and schol. on Aristoph. *Ach.* 242.
[4] See Farnell, *Cults of Greek States*, v, pp. 227–8.   [5] D.R., p. 14, fig. 1.
[6] iii, p. 66.   [7] Described by Studniczka, *Ath. Mitt.* xi (1886), p. 78, pl. II.
[8] D.R., pp. 17, 18.

tions, and it is not possible to reconstruct the appearance of the temple.

III. THE EARLIEST ORCHESTRA

1. There is no reasonable doubt that the provision made for performances, dramatic or lyric, in the Dionysiac precinct, must

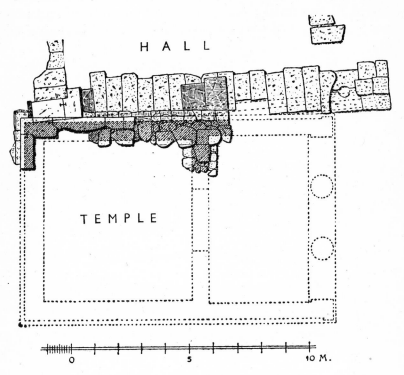

HALL

TEMPLE

Fig. 3. The Older Temple of Dionysus

at first have consisted of an orchestra or dancing-ground, for which a level area must have been made in the sloping hill-side by terracing and levelling, or by cutting into the slope, or both. The only certain traces of all this work consist of a fragment of the base of a supporting wall, SM 1 in Plan III. This consists of six stones (a seventh which was seen by Dörpfeld having now disappeared) set in a curved line nearly 14 feet long. The masonry is polygonal, and this implies an early—at latest a sixth-century —date. The outer surface of the stones was finished in a way which shows that it was intended to be exposed to view. The

inner surface was left rough, and within it (on the inner side of
the curve) the first investigators found a filling of smaller stones,
which have now disappeared. The stones of SM I are on the
natural soil, about 6 ft. 6 in. below the level of the later orchestra.
They are evidently part of the base of the supporting wall of
some kind of embankment, and it was believed for many years
by Dörpfeld and until a few years ago by practically all investigators in the present century that they formed part of a circle,

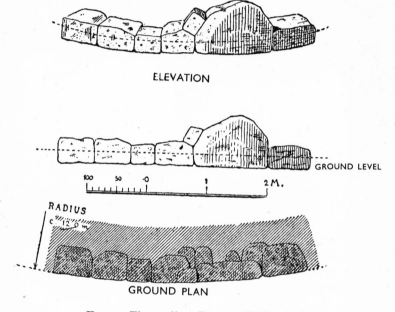

ELEVATION

GROUND LEVEL

RADIUS
c 12 0 m

GROUND PLAN

Fig. 4. The earliest Terrace Wall (1896)

the diameter of which was from 85 to 88 feet. (There were several
slightly different calculations, which it is not necessary to record;
the condition of the stones is in any case not such as to admit of
very exact reckoning.) The dimensions of such a circle would be
very nearly the same as those of the later orchestral circle,[1] and

---

[1] The best exposition of this theory is given by J. T. Allen, *The Greek Theater
of the Fifth Century* (1919), with the corrections made in *The Orchestra Terrace of
the Aeschylean Theater* (1922). The 'later orchestral circle' in question here is
the 'larger orchestra circle' (Allen, *Orch. Terr.*, p. 127), i.e. the circle inscribed
within the lowest tier of seats in the fourth-century theatre, not the orchestra
in the narrower sense of the circle actually used for dancing by the chorus.

FIG. 5. The Earliest Terrace Wall (1923)

it was not unnaturally supposed that the stones belonged to the circular supporting wall of an 'earlier' orchestra of approximately the same size as the later, but situated somewhat to the south-south-east of it. A good deal of imaginary history was re-constructed on this hypothesis. The hypothesis was further supported by the observation of other supposed traces of the wall, which, when the imaginary circle was plotted (it is marked by a

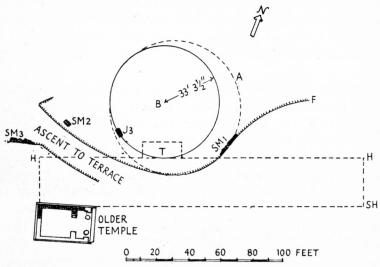

FIG. 6. The earliest Orchestra Terrace

broken line in Fig. 6), were found to lie on its circumference. One of these was a fragment of wall, J 3, lying under a rectangular stone of later date. The other consisted of some signs of altera-tion in construction underneath the eastern parodos of the theatre (as it was at a later date) at a point (A) which would also lie on the circumference of the imaginary circle. These Dörpfeld took to be evidence of an original cutting in the rock in the form of the segment of a circle—a cutting forming part of the cir-cumference of the supposed earliest orchestra. It all seemed to fit in exactly. But further investigation has shown that the fragment of wall at J 3 is of quite different material and masonry from SM 1, and is in fact a section, not of a curve, but of a straight line, its date and purpose being so far undeterminable,[1] and that the cutting has no clear direction and no plainly formed

[1] Fiechter, i, pp. 39, 40; iii, pp. 58, 67.

sides, and cannot be regarded as part of a circle.[1] As to SM 1 itself, this could be a part of any supporting wall which at that point was curved, and, in fact, its curve (so far as the condition of the stones permits any judgement on the matter) has not quite the regularity of the segment of a circle, the curvature being stronger at one end than at the other. It may be added that the hypothesis under discussion asks us to suppose that the supporting wall of the orchestra terrace coincided with the extreme edge of the circular orchestra itself, with no allowance for any margin between the latter and a drop of (probably) between 6 feet and 7 feet, and of course with no convenient space for the use of actors, if there were any.[2]

2. But it is still probable that the six stones formed part of the supporting wall, not of the orchestra itself, but of a terrace which was larger than the actual orchestra, and on which, at a little distance inwards (i.e. northwards) from the edge of the terrace, the first circular orchestra lay. The exact size and position of this orchestra cannot be determined; but it may perhaps be assumed, in default of evidence to the contrary, that it was of the same size as the later orchestra—not the larger circle within the lowest tier of seats, but the orchestra actually used for dancing—and that it lay in the same line from north to south—a line which was probably determined by the conformation of the hill-side, and which itself determined at a later date the position of the centre of the stage buildings. At the point where the six stones lie, the terrace, though not forming the segment of a circle, must have been curved in outline, and Fiechter[3] imagines it as (e.g.) bow-shaped (see Fig. 6). He supposes that the immediate approach to the terrace level was on the west side, the way to this, from the Propylaeum, passing upwards between the terrace wall and the Older Temple. (This agrees with what was said above.) Some stones, SM 3 in Fig. 6 and Plan III, consisting of a fragment of polygonal masonry differing very little in technique from the six stones,[4] may be part of the supporting wall of this rising way, or

---

[1] Fiechter, i, p. 39.

[2] Dörpfeld himself virtually gave up this 'earliest orchestra', based on the assignment of SM 1 and J 3 (R and Q in his Plans) to the same circle, in 1923 (*Philol. Woch.* xliii, pp. 442–3), and though Allen, Flickinger, and others adhered to it after this date, Flickinger abandoned it in the fourth edition of his *Greek Theater*, p. 362.   [3] Fiechter, iii, Abb. 29 and Taf. 16.

[4] Ibid. i, p. 84; iii, p. 59. In the latter place F. shows conclusively that slight

possibly of the same wall as the six stones (SM 1), which may here have run almost parallel to the Older Temple, only breaking into a more pronounced curve farther east.[1] Fiechter's view, while not susceptible of proof, is as probable as any yet advanced.

3. It is impossible to assign a precise date to the wall SM 1 and the orchestra which lay on the terrace supported by this work, but it has already been noticed that the polygonal masonry of SM 1 and SM 3 cannot be later than the sixth century, and may go back to a time earlier than Peisistratus. It is quite possible that there was a dancing-ground on this site from very ancient times.[2] The temple, the date of which is equally uncertain, may have been constructed at the same time as this orchestra, or later. Nor can the exact height of the terrace wall and the level of the first orchestra be determined; but there is no reason why this level should have been much, if at all, lower than that of later times, particularly as the solid rock is not very far below the surface a very little way northwards, where the orchestra is likely to have lain.

4. It seems most probable that an altar stood in the centre of the orchestra[3]—probably resting on a step forming a low plat-form, which may have been occupied by the flute-player who accompanied the choruses, and possibly by the leader of the chorus, if he separated himself from the rest and held dialogue with them. (Some such arrangement probably dates from Thespis, and may go back as far as 560 B.C.[4]) This central altar persisted throughout the history of tragedy, for it is misleading to speak (as more than one writer does) as if a suitable speaking-place for actors were formed by the removal of *this* altar to the

differences in masonry do not necessarily prove that the two fragments cannot belong to the same structure. [1] Cf. von Gerkan, *Gnomon*, 1938, p. 238.

[2] Whether the first orchestra was originally a threshing-floor, as was conjectured by Dr. E. A. Gardner (*Ancient Athens*, p. 123), may be doubted. Threshing-floors are still used for dancing by simple people in many lands; but it is hardly likely that a high terrace, supported by a very substantial wall, would have been built to support a threshing-floor, when there was plenty of fairly level ground not far off, whereas the hill-side would offer great advantages to the spectators of performances in an orchestra.

[3] The existence of a central altar in the fifth (and *a fortiori* in the sixth) century is denied by Robert (*Hermes*, xxxii, 1897, pp. 438–47) and Bethe (ibid., xxxvi, pp. 597–601); but see Dörpfeld's reply (ib. xxxvii, pp. 249–57) and below, pp. 34, 71, 131–2. [4] See my *Dith. Trag. Com.*, pp. 107–10.

southern edge of the orchestra, where the actors stood around or on it. The central altar and the later speaking-place for actors are to be kept distinct, and the former retained its position. Still less is there any ground for ascribing the supposed removal to Thespis, as Bulle does.[1]

5. Any stage buildings in this early period (the lower limit of which must be considered later, but which may be taken as including about the first third of the fifth century) must have been of a purely temporary character, erected for each festival and adapted as required for each play—possibly a background of wood or canvas, and a tent or hut as a dressing-room at some convenient point. When the evidence of the extant plays is considered in the next chapter, it will be seen that the earliest of these, the *Suppliants* of Aeschylus, does not require the presence of any building,[2] but only of a great altar in the open air, with statues grouped about it, either just inside or (more probably) just outside the orchestral circle on the south side. The next two plays, the *Persians* in 472 B.C. and the *Seven against Thebes* in 467 B.C., require at most a very simple building with a single door; this would naturally stand at a tangent, or on a line parallel at a short distance to a tangent, to the orchestral circle. Even the *Oresteia* in 458 B.C., though requiring more elaborate arrangements, could quite well have been acted with temporary stage-buildings. But this trilogy and, with it, the fact that scene-painting is said to have been introduced by Aeschylus, raise questions which will be more conveniently discussed later.

IV. THE SPECTATORS IN THE EARLIEST PERIOD OF THE THEATRE

1. It may be assumed that spectators of the performances in the earliest orchestra at first stood on the levelled terrace, or sat

---

[1] *Untersuch.*, p. 221. The supposed trace of the foundations of the stage of Thespis, which Bulle uses to confirm his argument, has been shown to be of much later date; see Fensterbusch in Pauly–W. V A II, col. 1389 (art. *Theatron*).

[2] The argument by which Fiechter attempts to prove the existence of a permanent stone background and stage building as far back as the sixth century, viz. that they must have been required by Thespis for his plays and for a dressing-room, rests on a mere assumption. Whether for Thespis or for Aeschylus, some temporary provision may quite well have served (as it does for open-air performances of Shakespeare to-day). We do not know what background the two other plays of the Danaid trilogy may have required, but it is likely to have been quite simple. See below, p. 35.

and stood on the sloping ground above, but wooden seats supported on stands (ἴκρια) had certainly come into use at a very early date in the fifth century B.C.

The evidence in regard to these, however, is not altogether free from difficulty, and must be set out in some detail. It consists almost entirely of quotations from lexicographers and scholiasts, but two passages of the Old Comedy show that the seats in the theatre were called ἴκρια after the middle of the fifth century. It is disputed whether in some passages the word indicates the boards on which the spectators sat, or the upright supports (when there were any) of the whole structure known comprehensively as τὰ ἴκρια, but the word very rarely refers to the uprights alone.

Aristoph. *Thesmoph.* 395, 6 ὥστ' εὐθὺς εἰσιόντες ἀπὸ τῶν ἰκρίων
ὑποβλέπουσ' ἡμᾶς.

(He has been speaking of the effect on the spectators of the performances of Euripides, and the reference must almost certainly be to the theatre of Dionysus. The play was produced at the Dionysia in 411 B.C.)

Schol. ad loc. ὡς ἔτι ἰκρίων ὄντων ἐν τῷ θεάτρῳ καὶ ἐν ταῖς ἐκκλησίαις ἐπὶ ξύλων καθημένων. πρὶν γὰρ γενέσθαι τὸ θέατρον, ξύλα ἐδέσμευον καὶ οὕτως ἐθεώρουν.

Cratinus, fr. incert. 323 (K) χαῖρ', ὦ μέγ' ἀχρειόγελως ὅμιλε ταῖς ἐπίβδαις,
τῆς ἡμετέρας σοφίας κριτὴς ἄριστε πάντων,
εὐδαίμον' ἔτικτέ σε μήτηρ ἰκρίων ψόφησις.

(Whatever the meaning of the passage, the reference is clearly to ἴκρια in the theatre where comic poets presented their plays.)

Hesychius, s.v. ' αἰγείρου θέα': αἴγειρος ἦν Ἀθήνησι πλησίον τοῦ ἱεροῦ, ἔνθα, πρὶν γενέσθαι θέατρον, τὰ ἴκρια ἐπήγνυον.

Id., s.v. ' παρ' αἰγείρου θέα': ἴκρια ἐστὶν ὀρθὰ ξύλα, ἔχοντα σανίδας προσδεδεμένας οἷον βαθμούς, ἐφ' αἷς ἐκαθέζοντο, πρὸ τοῦ κατασκευασθῆναι τὸ θέατρον.

Id., s.v. ' ἴκρια': καὶ τὰ ξύλινα οὕτως ἐλέγοντο Ἀθήνησιν, ἀφ' ὧν ἐθεῶντο, πρὶν τὸ ἐν Διονύσου θέατρον γενέσθαι.

(In the first of these passages, τοῦ ἱεροῦ is unexplained, and some scholars would emend to τῶν ἰκρίων, but this does not seem justifiable.)

Photius, s.v. ' ἴκρια' (= Eustathius, *Od.* iii. 350): ἴκρια· τὰ ἐν τῇ ἀγορᾷ ἀφ' ὧν ἐθεῶντο (τὸ παλαιὸν) τοὺς Διονυσιακοὺς ἀγῶνας πρὶν ἢ (κατα)-σκευασθῆναι τὸ ἐν Διονύσου θέατρον.

Bekk. *Anecd.* 354, 25 (= Photius): ʽαἰγείρου θέα καὶ ἡ παρ' αἰγείρου θέα'·

Ἀθήνησιν αἴγειρος ἦν, ἧς πλησίον τὰ ἴκρια ἐπήγνυτο εἰς τὴν θέαν, πρὸ τοῦ θέατρον γενέσθαι.

Suidas, s.v. ' αἰγείρου θέα ': αἴγειρος ἦν Ἀθήνησι πλησίον τοῦ ἱεροῦ, ἔνθα πρὶν γενέσθαι τὸ θέατρον τὰ ἴκρια ἐπήγνυον· ἀφ' ἧς αἰγείρου οἱ μὴ ἔχοντες τόπον ἐθεώρουν.

(This practically reproduces Hesychius.)

Id., s.v. ' ἀπ' αἰγείρου θέα ': ἡ ἀπὸ τῶν ἐσχάτων· αἴγειρος γὰρ ἐπάνω ἦν τοῦ θεάτρου, ἀφ' ἧς οἱ μὴ ἔχοντες τόπον ἐθεώρων.

Id., s.v. ' ἴκρία ': ὀρθὰ ξύλα ἢ σανιδώματα τῆς νηός· καὶ τὰ τῶν θεάτρων, ἃ ἦσαν καὶ ἐν ταῖς ἐκκλησίαις· ἐπὶ ξύλων γὰρ ἐκάθηντο. πρὶν γένηται [leg. γενέσθαι] τὸ θέατρον, ξύλα ἐδέσμευον καὶ οὕτως ἐθεώρουν. (Quotation from Aristoph. *Thesm.* follows.)

Id., s.v. ' Πρατίνας ': . . . ἀντηγωνίζετο δὲ Αἰσχύλῳ τε καὶ Χοιρίλῳ ἐπὶ τῆς ἑβδομηκοστῆς Ὀλυμπιάδος [i.e. 499–496 B.C.], καὶ πρῶτος ἔγραψε σατύρους. ἐπιδεικνυμένου δὲ τούτου, συνέβη τὰ ἴκρια ἐφ' ὧν ἑστήκεσαν οἱ θεαταὶ πεσεῖν, καὶ ἐκ τούτου θέατρον ᾠκοδομήθη Ἀθηναίοις.

Id., s.v. ' Αἰσχύλος ': φυγὼν δὲ εἰς Σικελίαν διὰ τὸ πεσεῖν τὰ ἴκρια ἐπιδεικνυμένου αὐτοῦ, χελώνης ἐπιρριφείσης αὐτῷ ὑπὸ ἀετοῦ φέροντος κατὰ τῆς κεφαλῆς, ἀπώλετο.

2. Many of the above notices obviously come from one source, which may have been Eratosthenes.[1] There is a general agreement that a collapse of ἴκρία led to the construction of a θέατρον. Photius says that the ἴκρία were in the market-place, and Hesychius' notices are consistent with this. Various passages, not quoted above,[2] speak of a single poplar-tree (αἴγειρος) in the market-place, which must surely be identical with the αἴγειρος close to the ἴκρία—the tree from which those who could not get seats used to watch performances.[3] This implies that there *were* performances in the agora at a very early date, and Photius expressly says that Διονυσιακοὶ ἀγῶνες took place there; there is no further evidence of this, but it is possible that the Lenaean contests were held there before (at a date about which there is no agreement among scholars) they were transferred to the theatre of Dionysus, and ἴκρία, in the sense of stands with upright supports, would be more necessary in the relatively level market-

[1] See Wilamowitz, *Hermes*, xxi, 1886, p. 597, who (less convincingly) finds a second source in the lexicographer Pausanias.

[2] References are given by Frickenhaus, art. Ἰκρίον in Pauly–W., col. 993.

[3] Some tradition of the struggle for seats in early days seems to be preserved by the scholiast on Lucian, *Timon* 49 μήπω δὲ τοῦ θεάτρου διὰ λιθίνων κατεσκευασμένου καὶ συρρεόντων τῶν ἀνθρώπων ἐπὶ τὴν θέαν καὶ νυκτὸς τοὺς τόπους καταλαβόντων ὀχλήσεις τε ἐγένοντο καὶ μάχαι καὶ πληγαί.

place than on the slope of the Acropolis. But the evidence that there were also ἰκρία in the theatre of Dionysus is unmistakable, and if the collapse occurred when tragedies were being produced either by Pratinas or by Aeschylus it is more likely that it happened in the theatre of Dionysus.[1] The assertion of von Gerkan[2] that the Athenians would not have been so stupid as to erect wooden stands on a sloping hill-side is quite unconvincing. It may have been just because they were so stupid that the calamity took place, or the slope may not have given a sufficiently good view for a great number without stands. But the localization of the disaster is unimportant, as a disaster in the market-place might well lead to precautions being taken in the precinct of Dionysus as well.

3. These precautions are described as the provision of a θέατρον. The word θέατρον is found used in two senses. It might refer to the whole group of buildings connected with the production of plays, including the stage buildings as well as the auditorium,[3] or (perhaps more commonly) to the place of the θεαταί, i.e. the auditorium itself.[4] The latter is probably the meaning here, and the tradition recorded by the lexicographers and scholiasts was evidently the construction of a safe auditorium—not of a stone structure (which seems to be out of the question as early as this), but at least of suitably shaped earthen embankments, on which wooden planks or benches—still called ἰκρία through most of the fifth century—could safely rest.

4. As to the date of the disaster, Suidas gives two accounts, but the second, which connects it with Aeschylus' final departure to Sicily in (or just before) 456 B.C., is absurd in itself; the poet

[1] In Plato, *Laws* 817 c, tragic poets are forbidden to set up σκηναί and give performances in the agora, but the passage cannot be used to prove anything as regards Athenian customs. There was no regular theatre in the Ideal State of the *Laws*, so that visiting poets could only set up temporary stages, if they were allowed to enter at all. The use of such temporary stages was regular in Magna Graecia, as Plato must have known.

[2] *Gnomon*, 1938, p. 238.

[3] E.g. *I.G.* xi. 2. 199 A, l. 96 τὸ παρασκήνιον τὸ ἐν τῷ θεάτρῳ, and probably Thucyd. viii. 93 εἰς τὸ πρὸς τῇ Μουνυχίᾳ Διονυσιακὸν θέατρον ἐλθόντες . . . ἐκκλησίασαν.

[4] It was used of the place of the spectators in other buildings than theatres, e.g. Xen. *Hellen.* vii. iv. 31 τοῦ τῆς Ἑστίας ἱεροῦ καὶ τοῦ πρὸς ταῦτα προσήκοντος θεάτρου, and Dittenb. *Syll.*³ 970 θέατρον τὸ ἐπὶ τοῦ σταδίου (at Eleusis); and see below, p. 73.

could not in any case be held responsible for the seating arrangements. In his other account, the disaster is said to have happened when Pratinas was giving a performance. It is not said
that (as some scholars have assumed) this was the performance in
the 70th Olympiad (499–496 B.C.), when Pratinas was contending
against Aeschylus and Choirilos; and it may have been any
performance of a play by Pratinas before his death, which probably occurred shortly before 467 B.C. when his son Aristias
brought out one of his plays posthumously. (The absurd notice
s.v. Αἰσχύλος shows at least that Suidas' authorities were not
committed to the 70th Olympiad as the date of the calamity.)
Accordingly the date may have been any year in the first three
decades of the fifth century.[1]

5. Excavations carried out by Dörpfeld in 1889[2] in the middle
region of the extant ruins of the auditorium showed that the
height and the steepness of the auditorium had twice been increased by the heaping up of earth, and that the first operation,
which we may safely identify with the work carried out after the
accident, must have been fairly early in the fifth century, because hardly any of the potsherds found in this earlier mass of
piled-up earth were later than 500 B.C. This combines with the
literary evidence just considered to show that at this time, during
which Aeschylus was producing his plays, an earthen auditorium
was constructed, less steep than that which is visible to-day, and
probably sloping farther southwards than the auditorium of later
times, so as to approach and overlook the first orchestra, which
was also somewhat farther south than the later. This first auditorium probably consisted of successively rising terraces of earth,
on which the wooden planks or benches (still called ἴκρια) were

---

[1] Bulle, *Untersuch.*, p. 71, still thinks that there may have been *two* disasters,
the second of which led to the construction of the stone auditorium soon after
458 B.C. The inner western supporting wall of the (extant) stone auditorium
bears, thrice repeated, a peculiar form of Α, as a mason's mark, which is said
to be not much later than this. He may be right in thinking that the absurdity
of the reason given does not disprove the fact: but the use of stones bearing these
mason's marks would be equally possible even if the stone auditorium were part
of the 'Periclean' reconstruction, a few years later (see below). The suggestion
that the date of the disaster may have been that of Aeschylus' earlier visit to
Sicily in 472 B.C. was bound to occur to more than one mind, but is hardly
convincing; it is unlikely that the disaster had anything to do with his visit.

[2] D.R., pp. 30, 31.

laid—not so rigidly fastened as to prevent a good deal of noise (Cratinus' ἰκρίων ψόφησις) when the spectators moved about. No traces of supporting walls for such an auditorium have been found.[1] If they existed, they would inevitably have disappeared when a larger and steeper auditorium was constructed in connexion with an orchestra lying rather farther northwards than the original, as part of a replanning of the whole area which may be called 'Periclean'. To this we may now pass.

V. THE 'PERICLEAN' THEATRE

1. The comprehensive reconstruction[2] which we are now to consider is conveniently named after Pericles, because it was closely connected with the Odeum built by him and completed by 443 B.C.[3] The new plan consisted in the first place in the removal a slight distance northwards of the whole scene of dramatic performances. The auditorium was banked up to a steeper slope, and was rendered secure and its lines fixed by the construction of substantial supporting walls on the south, east, and west, the conformation of the eastern wall being made to accord with that of the walls of the Odeum. The orchestra was moved northwards, though without changing its north and south axis. (It is no longer possible to say exactly how far it was moved, or how nearly its site coincided with that of the Lycurgean orchestra, which obliterated all traces of its predecessor.[4]) By this means more room was afforded for the performance of the actors and for scenery, as the internal development of the drama in the hands of Sophocles and, later, of Euripides demanded. The

[1] Dörpfeld (*Jahrb. Arch.* xi, 1925, *Anz.*, col. 311–13) thought that he had found such traces in the fragments marked b[1] and b[2] in Plate III; but Fiechter (i, pp. 77, 87; iii, pp. 58, 59) shows that this is impossible, since the masonry of both is of late date, and b[1] must be later than the supporting wall a A (see below) of the 'Periclean' auditorium. With this von Gerkan agrees (*Gnomon*, l.c.). It is a very probable conjecture that the auditorium in the time of Aeschylus did not rise northwards beyond the line of the road which ran across the later auditorium from east to west.

[2] The 'Periclean' reconstruction, more or less on the lines here indicated, was accepted by Dörpfeld, *Ath. Mitt.* xlix (publ. 1926), p. 89.

[3] See above, p. 1.

[4] Some suppose that the Periclean orchestra was actually in the same position as the Lycurgean; this is not impossible but less probable. On the bearing upon this question of the history of the channels which drained the orchestra, see below, pp. 25–6.

southern boundary of the terrace was entirely remodelled, and instead of the old curved supporting wall, of polygonal masonry, a long straight wall of large breccia blocks was built to hold up the terrace, the level of which, especially on the east and west, must have been made up to suit the new needs.[1] Somewhat later, fitting closely against the southern face of this new wall through

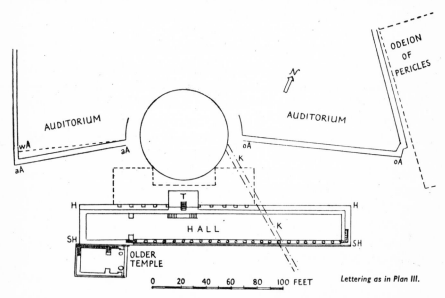

FIG. 7. Sketch-plan of Periclean Theatre
(For explanation of symbols, see p. 287)

its whole length, there was built the long hall, the south wall of which, in its western portion, encroached upon the step surrounding the Older Temple of Dionysus.[2] A new Temple of Dionysus was built a little south of the old, and its lines and those of the hall were parallel to one another. In the new temple was placed the statue of the god in gold and ivory made by Alkamenes.[3]

2. As regards the date of this 'Periclean' reconstruction as a

[1] The orchestra terrace supported by the new wall must have been roughly on the same level as the extant orchestra, or possibly, as Schleif thinks (*Jahrb. Arch.* 1937, *Anz.*, col. 26 ff.), a little higher (e.g. 8 inches), as the rough masonry of the existing wall would not have been left visible from the orchestra.

[2] That the hall was part of the same plan as the terrace wall, though only built later, is shown by the fact that, though not masonically tied together at any higher point, both rest on a common foundation of conglomerate blocks. See Fiechter, i, pp. 15–17.   [3] See above, p. 4.

whole, the opinion of most archaeologists was, until recently, that the buildings involved in it, of which the foundations remain, could not be so early. The supporting walls of the auditorium had breccia (conglomerate) foundations; so had the terrace wall and the hall which backs on to it, and the construction of the hall above the foundations shows considerable use of Hymettian marble. It used to be supposed that the use of these materials pointed to the fourth century; but Dörpfeld, who maintained this opinion,[1] ultimately retracted it[2] in view of the evidence that breccia foundations were occasionally laid as far back as the first quarter of the fifth century and were not uncommon in the last half of the century, while the Later Temple of Dionysus, which shows the combination of materials supposed to have been late, must almost certainly have been a fifth-century structure, as Alkamenes' last recorded work was executed for Thrasybulus in 403 B.C. The attempt of Fiechter to date the hall as far back as the latter part of the sixth century seems to be disposed of by the finding of fifth-century potsherds below the foundations of its north wall. The whole 'Periclean' reconstruction was probably carried out by stages covering most of the second half of the fifth century. Pericles himself died in 429, but the Peace of Nikias, 421–416 B.C., suggests itself as a time when extensive building operations may well have been undertaken, and some writers have thought that the period from 410 to 404 B.C., when Kleophon was influential and there was certainly some architectural activity in Athens, may have been a time of constructive work in the theatre.[3]

3. The lines of the auditorium walls of this period have been fixed with reasonable certainty. On the east they were determined, as has already been noticed, by the Odeum.[4] The eastern supporting wall of the auditorium was separated, in its southern section, from the wall of the Odeum by an interval of about 4 ft. 7 in., and the two walls were connected (at a point about 15 ft. 5 in. from the south-east corner of the auditorium) by a

---

[1] D.R., p. 12.

[2] Πρακτικά, 1925–6, p. 25 f. Breccia (conglomerate) foundations did not come into *common* use till the last half of the century (cf. Judeich, *Topogr. Athen.*², pp. 3, 4; Fiechter, iii, p. 58; Bulle, *Unters.*, p. 53).

[3] See Allen, *Gk. Theat.*, p. 18. It was at this time that the Erechtheum was completed.   [4] See Fig. 7.

cross-wall.[1] The east wall itself consisted of large blocks of breccia. The south walls of the 'Periclean' auditorium are marked a A (west of orchestra) and o A (east of orchestra) in the plans. (Of these the former, a A, was demolished at the time of the Lycurgean reconstruction, when the new supporting wall w A was built.) The wall o A, which is considerably longer than a A was, consists of breccia blocks faced with poros. All that remains of a A is part of the breccia foundations, the blocks of which closely resemble in size those of the new terrace wall and the hall. It will be noticed that a A and o A do not lie symmetrically in relation to the north and south axis of the auditorium, and it would be natural to expect that there was originally a 'Periclean' wall in front of o A, corresponding more exactly with a A (in which case o A would have to be considered as 'Lycurgean', like the corresponding wall w A). But the most careful exploration has discovered none, and it must be supposed that the line of o A, like the position of the south-east corner of the auditorium, on which the direction of o A depends, was due to the desire to conform with the Odeum. The Lycurgean builders corrected the want of symmetry by building w A to correspond with o A.[2] The extant remains of a A were below the ground in the 'Periclean' building,[3] and it is not possible to say how high a A and o A originally were, nor what exactly was the slope of the auditorium which they supported, nor how far northwards the regularly terraced earthen embankments may have run.

The western supporting wall of the 'Periclean' auditorium is the inner of the two parallel walls, of which considerable remains are extant. It is of large breccia blocks, and at a later date was supported by buttresses (partly extant) and an outer wall of poros blocks. These may have been part of the original 'Periclean'

[1] What remains of this is marked in Plan I. See Fiechter, i, pp. 80–3, Abb. 70–3; he regards the Odeum and the east wall as contemporary.

[2] Fiechter (i, p. 77) proves that a A is earlier than w A (as against Bulle, who thought that they were contemporary and part of one plan) by showing the irregularity of the junction between w A and the short cross-wall by which a A is connected with it.

[3] When w A was built, the space between it and the levelled a A was filled up with stones of Acropolis rock and levelled off. Fiechter's suggestion (i, p. 76) that a A was now used to support a terrace for the reception of monuments is disproved by von Gerkan (*Gnomon*, 1938, p. 242). For Schleif's theory of the Periclean supporting wall, see below, p. 26.

design, though only executed later, perhaps by degrees, and not completed before the fourth century.

4. The seats in the 'Periclean' auditorium were probably of wood—they are still called ἰκρία by Aristophanes[1] in 411 B.C.—and though the plan *may* have included some stone seats, these were perhaps introduced very gradually, and there was not a complete stone auditorium before Lycurgus.[2] There may possibly have been some special seats of stone for particular persons. Some scholars, at least, have conjectured that such was the original use of certain stones bearing inscriptions, that were later used for repairing the channel which drained the orchestra; others suppose that these stones were the stone foundations on which wooden seats reserved for such persons were placed;[3] while others, with perhaps greater probability, think that these stones indicated areas in the theatre reserved for particular classes of spectators. That there were such reservations is indicated by the mention in Aristophanes' *Birds* 793-5 of a part of the auditorium called τὸ βουλευτικόν, and Pollux (iv. 122) mentions an ἐφηβικὸν μέρος (at what date is not stated).

[1] See above, p. 11. It is suggested by J. T. Allen (*Univ. Calif. Class. Publicns.* i, pp. 173 ff.) that stone seats were at once introduced at the time of the building of the Odeum; he argues that the masts and yard-arms of the Persian ships, which were used in the Odeum (Vitruv. v. ix), must have been *somewhere* for the preceding thirty years, and he can think of no more likely place than the theatre, in which they may have been hurriedly adapted for use as ἰκρία after the (supposed) destruction of the theatre by the Persians, so that, when they were removed, the theatre would have to be reseated. But this is wholly unsupported by evidence. The destruction of the theatre by the Persians is nowhere recorded; there was probably not much to destroy. That the masts, &c., were used in the theatre is a mere guess, and the fact that Vitruvius ascribes their use in the Odeum to *Themistocles* throws suspicion on the whole story.

[2] Pollux iv. 122 has sometimes been quoted in support of the belief in wooden seats: τὸ μέντοι τὰ ἑδώλια ταῖς πτέρναις κατακρούειν πτερνοκοπεῖν ἔλεγον· ἐποίουν δὲ τοῦτο ὁπότε τινὰ ἐκβάλοιεν. But this method of showing displeasure might be used even with stone seats, and we do not know of what time or what theatres Pollux is speaking. Wooden seats were used at a comparatively late date in some Greek theatres.

[3] Lehmann-Hartleben ap. Bulle, *Untersuch.*, pp. 61 ff.; Fiechter, i, p. 78; iii, p. 72. The former treats the inscribed stones as part of the stone step or foundation of a prohedria (a front row of seats of honour), in which priests, or at least the priest of Dionysus, sat. This is only conjecture, and a further conjecture finds a seat for the hierophant. But the seats themselves would be of wood, standing on these stone bases.

Some of these inscriptions are single letters, possibly used as numbers; the letters are certainly pre-Euclidean, and may go back to the middle of the fifth century. Others formed parts of words, and of these IEPE and ETON may be the remains of ἱερέως or ἱερέων and ὑπηρετῶν. A stone, subsequently built upside down into the outer western wall of the auditorium (where it may now be seen) bears the inscription BOΛHΣ YΠHPETON in characters which date it late in the fifth century, and this in its original use must have reserved a place for the Council staff in the 'Periclean' auditorium.[1] (The characters in this inscription are partly pre-

FIG. 8. Stones in W. Wall of Auditorium

Euclidean, partly post-Euclidean, but characters of the latter type may well have been in frequent use before the official recognition of the Ionic alphabet in the archonship of Eucleides, 404 B.C.) The inelegance of the inscription suggests to Bulle that it may have been the work of the Council's servants themselves. Some letters on the stone, serving as mason's marks, indicate a use of the stone later than the date of the longer inscription. Other stones in the western wall also bear letters of a form not likely to have been used very long before the official recognition of the Ionic alphabet. (The letter Ω in particular belongs to this alphabet.) A stone with the unexplained inscription OKEPYON has been conjectured to belong to the auditorium of the fifth century—possibly reserving a place for heralds—but as it was not actually found in the theatre, it is not certain whether it belonged there at all. In front of the two southern supporting walls of the auditorium, a A and o A, ran the eastern and western entrances

---

[1] Bulle thinks that the stone is too large to have come from the auditorium itself; but if the lower part of it were set rather deeper in the earth it would not necessarily have been discordant with other stones.

to the orchestra, later called *Parodoi*,[1] which also gave the spectators access to the auditorium itself.

5. The new supporting wall of the whole remodelled and extended terraced area—hereafter called the 'terrace wall', H in the Plans—is (in what remains of it) about 204 feet long, and is built of a single row of breccia blocks laid longitudinally; it is about 2 feet wide. It seems to have been built before the northern wall of the hall, which runs back to back with it, but is not tied to it by any cross-masonry, though the fact that the two rest on a common foundation shows that they are part of the same design. At a point about 68 feet from the west end of this terrace wall there projects northwards to a distance of about 9 feet a solid foundation (T in the Plans) which is structurally tied to the wall and must have been built at the same time.[2] It is about 26 feet long and is made of breccia blocks, of which five layers remain, the lowest resting upon the natural rock. Its upper surface, when it was perfect, may have risen up to the ground-level of the terrace on which the orchestra lay. This ground-level must have been higher than the present top of the terrace wall,[3] and was probably very nearly the same as that of the Lycurgean orchestra—about 2 ft. 7½ in. above the present surface of T—since there is no reason to suppose that the 'Periclean' orchestra was on a lower level than the Lycurgean. At the back of T was an opening in the terrace wall, which, when the hall was built, was carried also through the wall of the hall; this opening was originally about 23 ft. 3 in. wide, i.e. almost the full width of T, though later alterations in the wall have obliterated part of it.[4]

In the surface of T are two holes (which were found filled with earth, stones, and potsherds), one about 2 ft. 3½ in. square, the other about 4 feet long by 2 ft. 3½ in. wide. In the north face of the terrace wall H are eight vertical grooves or cuttings in the wall, each from 13½ to 15½ inches across and set at approximately, but not exactly, equal distances, and there can be little doubt that there were originally ten—five on either side of T. (All ten are marked in Fig. 7.) The two missing grooves must have dis-

---

[1] They are termed εἴσοδοι, 'entrances', in Aristoph. *Clouds* 326, *Birds* 296. The term πάροδοι does not occur in this sense in the fifth century. It is found in Plutarch and in Pollux iv. 126, and in the schol. on Aristoph. *Knights* 149.

[2] Fiechter, i, p. 15.   [3] See above, pp. 9, 16.

[4] Fiechter, i, p. 17.

appeared in some reconstruction, perhaps in the Roman period, and the original stones in the face of the wall in this part have in fact been partly replaced by substitutes.[1] The grooves were evidently intended to hold stout posts, doubtless to support scenic structures,[2] and the depressions in T may also have had some purpose in connexion with the scenery. They may all have been cut as soon as the terrace wall was built ; the fact that the position of the grooves stands in no fixed relation to the joints of the masonry is no argument to the contrary, since what remains of them is all below ground-level, where such aesthetic considerations would not matter. These grooves and the holes in T are the only extant material evidence of the wooden scenery of the fifth century. For any further light on its character it is necessary to consult the plays which have come down to us. (See Chapter II.)

6. There is no evidence to prove the original height of the terrace wall, but it probably rose little above the level of the orchestra terrace which it supported. In that case the posts set in the grooves would have stood free above ground, and would have been more useful as parts of the framework of a temporary skené of wood (or as the supports of an upper floor) than they would have been if the terrace wall had risen to a considerable height (such as that of the hall which was afterwards built against it), with the posts partially embedded in grooves in the wall all the way up. What seems most likely is that when necessary a temporary wooden skené (representing, e.g., a palace or temple), forming the background for the actors, was built out in front of and partly supported by these posts, as well as by others of which no trace remains, and that this normally included and concealed the foundation T. The opening at the back of the latter

---

[1] Fiechter, i, p. 16. This is sufficient answer to Petersen's denial (*Jahrb. Arch.*, xxiii, 1908, p. 44) that the missing grooves ever existed. Versakis (*Jahrb. Arch.*, xxiv, 1909, pp. 223–4) thinks that the grooves were made to receive stone ribs for the internal strengthening of the structure in the Lycurgean period; Dörpfeld (ibid., p. 226) points out the technical impossibility of this, and Bulle (*Unters.*, p. 50) agrees. See also Dörpfeld in *Ath. Mitt.* xxxii, 1907, p. 251, where he suggests that the grooves held posts for the support of a wooden skené. Bulle's idea that T rose to the height of the first story of the stage building is very inadequately supported.

[2] Similar holes for posts are found in the theatres at Elis (*Jahrb. Arch.* xxxi, 1914, *Anz.*, col. 139), Oropos (Fiechter, *Das Theater in Oropos*, p. 12, Taf. 3), and elsewhere.

afforded the entrance to a staircase leading down into the hall[1] when the latter was built; but T may from the first have served as a foundation for mechanical devices used for stage purposes, such as the mechané or the ekkyklema if it was used. In appearing before the audience the actors must have used doorways in the temporary wooden skené (dotted in Fig. 7) opening on to the orchestra level. This temporary skené, with its front, before which the actors would perform, would have obvious advantages. It would not only improve the acoustic conditions, but would set off the figures of the actors, whose importance as elements in the play, and probably in the eyes of the public, was greater in the later than in the earlier part of the fifth century, and it would still be possible to change the scenes of wood and canvas from day to day or between play and play; and as scene-painting had come into vogue in the last days of Aeschylus, a wall, if only of wood, and the structures connected with it, would be useful and even necessary for the reception of the painted scene.[2]

That the main stage buildings were of wood down to about the middle of the fourth century (and therefore in the earlier period) seems to be implied in passages of Xenophon's *Cyropaedia*, the date of which was not later than 362 B.C.,[3] and in Demosthenes' speech *Against Meidias* in 348 B.C. Xenophon[4] speaks of a mov-

---

[1] The form of the staircase leading down from T into the hall (the floor of which lay about 8 ft. 2 in. below the level of the orchestra) is discussed by H. Schleif (*Jahrb. Arch.* lii (1937), *Anz.*, cols. 30, 31). Steps are inserted in Fig. 7 in accordance with his conjecture.

[2] There is no satisfactory ground for ascribing to the Periclean age the erection of a stone skené and massive paraskenia, as Fiechter (iii, pp. 72 ff.) appears to do, though he admits that it is impossible to tell what they were like. He seems to be influenced by the dating in this period of the first theatre buildings at Eretria, but as that dating is at least in part based on the supposed resemblance of these buildings to those of Athens, the argument is a circular one. (The other reasons for the dating of the Eretrian theatre are quite inconclusive. See Bulle, *Untersuch.*, p. 86 f., and Fiechter, *Das Theater in Eretria*, pp. 39, 40; also below, pp. 198–9.) At Athens the first stone skené and paraskenia seem more probably to have been begun soon after the middle of the fourth century, as part of the general reconstruction afterwards completed by Lycurgus.

[3] As shown by references in VIII. viii, § 4.

[4] τοῦ δὲ πύργου ὥσπερ τραγικῆς σκηνῆς τῶν ξύλων πάχος ἐχόντων (*Cyrop.* VI. i, § 54). The language suggests the existence of stock 'sets' made of wood, the construction of which would be familiar to those who saw them set up and taken down annually or oftener.

able tower, the timbers of which were as thick as those of the tragic skené, and Demosthenes[1] of Meidias barricading the παρα-σκήνια and so *nailing up* public property. If the παρασκήνια were part of the stage building, they must have been something into which nails could be hammered.

7. The long hall, the wall of which was in contact with the supporting wall of the terrace and rested upon a common foundation with it, is represented by remains of which the two lowest strata consist each of a double row of breccia blocks. These foundations are about 6 ft. 6 in. wide in the north, east, and south walls of the hall, about 4 ft. 4 in. wide in the west wall. Resting upon these two strata was a layer of hard poros blocks, which ran level with the floor of the hall, this being about 8 ft. 2 in. lower than the surface of the orchestra terrace. The upright walls which stood on these poros blocks were of Hymettian marble, and some fragments of these remain.[2] Against the outer side of the east wall of the hall ran a supporting wall of breccia blocks, serving (like the terrace wall, at right angles to which it ran) to resist the thrust of the soil. The columns ranged on the south side of the hall probably stood above three broad steps running the whole

---

[1] *in Meid.* § 17 τὰ παρασκήνια φράττων, προσηλῶν ἰδιώτης ὢν τὰ δημόσια. But what these παρασκήνια were, the old commentators were uncertain; see Harpocr. s.v. ' παρασκήνια '· Δημοσθένης ἐν τῷ κατὰ Μειδίου· ὡς καὶ Θεόφραστος ἐν εἰκοστῷ Νόμων ὑποσημαίνει, ὁ παρὰ τὴν σκηνὴν ἀποδεδειγμένος τόπος ταῖς εἰς τὸν ἀγῶνα παρασκευαῖς· ὁ δὲ Δίδυμος τὰς ἑκατέρωθεν τῆς ὀρχήστρας εἰσόδους οὕτω φησὶ καλεῖσθαι. Ulpian's commentary agrees with Didymus and says that Meidias' object was to oblige the chorus to enter by the entrance 'from outside', i.e. by the public parodos, instead of by the entrances on each side of the λογεῖον (ὀρχήστρας being equated with λογείου, as sometimes in late writers); but if so, Didymus is ascribing to the early theatre an arrangement which only came into existence much later. A. Müller (*Untersuch.*, p. 59) thinks that the reference is to the doors in the *scaenae frons* to right and left of the centre; these could conceivably be called εἴσοδοι on to the skené—in the sense of 'scene of action'; but there is no parallel to this, or to the application of the name παρασκήνια to doorways. Theophrastus (Demosthenes' junior contemporary) is most likely to be right; and if so, the παρασκήνια were side-wings (whether projecting or not) used as store-rooms for stage-properties, &c. The chorus were probably intended to assemble in these for entry direct on to the orchestra, and the action of Meidias obliged them to go round by the public parodoi, and so to appear on the scene late and bring discredit upon Demosthenes as choregus. For the conventional use of the word 'paraskenia', see pp. 169–70.

[2] Fiechter's ascription of these fragments to a period later than that of the original building of the hall is quite inconclusive.

length of the building, except where it was in contact with the Older Temple. At the south-east corner of the hall are some complications not so far explained, but probably due to alterations at some later period; and from this corner a wall ran southwards not quite in a line with the east wall of the hall and not yet fully explored. At some very late date a cistern was constructed inside the hall at the east end.

The total external length of the hall was about 204 feet, its breadth internally about 22 feet. It was divided internally by a cross-wall, which meets the south wall at the point where the latter reached the Older Temple and ceased to bear columns as it did for the rest of its length. In this way a smaller chamber at the west end was cut off from the much longer main hall, the former being about 34 feet long internally, the latter about 156 feet. The south wall of the smaller chamber and the westernmost extremity of the south wall of the main hall encroach upon the steps of the temple; but whether at some period there were some structural alterations at or close to the point of encroachment does not appear certain.

8. Underneath the hall, towards its eastern end, there ran (roughly speaking from north-north-west to south-south-east) a water channel, which drained the higher ground to the north, on which the orchestra lay, and which, when the hall was built, had to be accommodated to the sudden drop from the orchestra-terrace to a depth below the floor of the hall. The adaptations are traceable in the north wall of the hall,[1] and after passing under the floor, the channel, a little over 2 feet wide, ran though the breccia foundations of the south wall of the hall, which (as the remains show) were cut to receive it at the time when this wall was built. At this point Hymettian marble is employed along with the breccia and poros.

This channel must obviously have drained the 'Periclean' orchestra, and it was connected in the fourth century with the circular channel running round the 'Lycurgean' (and still partly existing) orchestra. But what exactly was its early history depends upon whether the 'Periclean' orchestra occupied practically the same position as the 'Lycurgean'. Those who believe that it did so think that the connexion between the circular channel of the 'Lycurgean' orchestra and what may for brevity

---

[1] See Fiechter, i, pp. 18–20. The channel is KK in Fig. 7 above.

be called the north-and-south channel simply continues the arrangements of the 'Periclean' theatre. This, according to Fiechter,[1] seems to have been Dörpfeld's latest view, as against, for example, that of Wrede,[2] and it is strongly defended by Schleif.[3] But the assumption that the position of the 'Periclean' orchestra was the same as that of the 'Lycurgean' is not free from difficulty. If it were so, then, since the position of the auditorium partly depends upon that of the orchestra, the southern supporting wall of the auditorium must have been in the same place in both periods, and in the 'Periclean' period, no less than in the 'Lycurgean', it must (in its western half) have followed the line w A, instead of a A, which has been treated as the line of the 'Periclean' wall in an earlier part of this chapter.[4] Schleif accepts this, and regards a A as the relic of some pre-Periclean attempt, of which nothing else is known, to provide a supporting wall for the auditorium. But this seems very speculative, and he does not really meet the proofs given by Wrede, from a careful study of the stones, that the north-and-south channel is older than the circular channel of the 'Lycurgean' orchestra, and therefore, as naturally follows, began its career as a drainage channel for the Periclean orchestra, which may have lain a little farther south than the Lycurgean. How exactly the north-and-south channel was connected with whatever channel or gutter may have run round the Periclean orchestra, there are no remains to show. But there seems to be no need to change the views expressed earlier in this chapter, though the slender evidence does not justify a dogmatic attitude either way. Comparative certainty only begins with the Lycurgean orchestra and its water channel. All that can be said is that the section of the north-and-south channel which passes under the hall must have already existed in the 'Periclean' epoch and that the channel must have been modified to enable it so to pass.

9. There must have been an opening in the north wall of the hall, corresponding to the opening in the terrace wall at the back of T and giving access across T to the orchestra through any stage buildings which may have been employed. There is nothing left to show what other openings there may have been, whether doors or windows: the south side was almost certainly open, with col-

[1] Fiechter, iii, p. 55, n. 1.
[2] In his contribution to Bulle's *Untersuch.*, pp. 55–60.
[3] *Jahrb. Arch.*, lii (1937), *Anz.*, col. 32 ff.   [4] p. 18.

umns resting on poros slabs and supporting the roof, and it is at
least likely that there was an entrance at the west end giving
access from outside to the smaller chamber. Nor is there any
evidence as to the character of the roof of the hall or the possibility of making use of it for the purposes of the drama.

10. Different opinions have been expressed as to the date of
the hall, but it seems most probable that it was part of the
general plan of the 'Periclean' lay-out, though it may have been
one of the last executed elements in the plan. It runs parallel, as
has already been noticed, to the Later Temple of Dionysus, which
must be dated in the last third of the fifth century,[1] and it resembles it in the material of its foundations. The discovery of
potsherds of the fifth century underneath the north wall of the
hall seems to dispose of Fiechter's attempt to date the hall as far
back as the latter part of the sixth century.[2] Fiechter's further
opinion that the hall was originally a great store-room in which
were kept scenery, stage properties, and the scaffolding and other
woodwork used for seating the audience, also seems insufficiently
grounded. If his view were correct, we should have to suppose
that the hall was enclosed by a wall (not a colonnade) on the south
side, as well as on the other three. But there seems to be no
reason why the hall should not from the first have been the long
portico or stoa referred to by Vitruvius[3] and designed as a place
of refuge from sudden storms and a promenade for spectators not
watching the plays. It is true that the form of the poros blocks
in the stratum of the south wall immediately above the foundations is somewhat different from that of the corresponding blocks
of the same material in the north wall, but this difference is as
likely to be original, if these blocks were intended to bear a row of
columns instead of a wall, as to be due to a transformation of the
south wall for that purpose.

Fiechter's attempt[4] to reconstruct the appearance of the hall
from some architectural fragments lying about inside it is open
to grave doubt, and von Gerkan[5] denies that these fragments
belong to the hall at all, the clamps used in them being of a
different pattern from those found in the marble remains in the
hall. This is, perhaps, not a very strong argument; but it is clear
that the materials for a convincing reconstruction do not exist.

[1] See pp. 17, 18.   [2] Fiechter, iii, p. 47.   [3] v. ix. 1.   [4] iii, p. 19.
[5] *Gnomon*, 1938, p. 239.

28

11. The special purpose of the smaller chamber at the west end of the hall, which was enclosed all round where it runs close to the Older Temple, is unknown. Frickenhaus thinks that it was the archon's dining-room, on the strength of a fragment of Hypereides[1] quoted by Pollux in a section referring to the theatre; but the passage is only quoted to show that αὐλαία was an occasional synonym of παραπέτασμα, and *need* not itself refer to the theatre, though it may do so. The chamber may well have been a theatrical store-room.

12. The Later Temple of Dionysus seems certainly to belong to the last third of the fifth century. Nothing is now left but the breccia foundations, which run parallel (as has already been noticed) to the hall and the connected terrace wall, not to the Older Temple. Pausanias[2] implies that the statue of Dionysus in gold and ivory was made for this temple by Alkamenes, whose last recorded work was executed for Thrasybulus in 403 B.C. The temple, which was about 72 ft. 6 in. long by 31 ft. 4 in. wide, was divided into cella and pronaos; the basis on which the statue stood in the cella is partly preserved, but the reconstruction of the pronaos is very uncertain.[3]

13. Whether the wall-paintings which Pausanias describes just after his mention of the two temples were in the Later Temple itself or, as some scholars suppose, in the hall, is quite uncertain. (The paintings depicted the bringing back of Hephaistos to heaven by Dionysus, the punishment of Pentheus and of Lycurgus for their hostility to Dionysus, and the sleeping Ariadne, with Theseus putting out to sea and Dionysus preparing to carry her off; the four groups of figures must have been of considerable size.) Pausanias' language is ambiguous; τοῦ Διονύσου δέ ἐστι πρὸς τῷ θεάτρῳ τὸ ἀρχαιότατον ἱερόν· δύο δέ εἰσιν ἐντὸς τοῦ περιβόλου ναοὶ καὶ Διόνυσοι, ὅ τε Ἐλευθερεὺς καὶ ὃν Ἀλκαμένης ἐποίησεν ἐλέφαντος καὶ χρυσοῦ. γραφαὶ δὲ αὐτόθι Διόνυσός ἐστιν ἀνάγων Ἥφαιστον, κτλ. The word αὐτόθι may merely mean 'within the precinct', or may mean 'in the same place as Alkamenes' statue'; there is no mention of the hall and no reference to the theatre buildings until a later chapter, but the hall was of course within the precinct, and would probably have been a better place for the display of wall-paintings

[1] fr. 139 (Kenyon) ap. Poll. iv. 122 οἱ δὲ ἐννέα ἄρχοντες εἱστιῶντο ἐν τῇ στοᾷ, περιφραξάμενοί τι μέρος αὐτῆς αὐλαίᾳ.   [2] I. xx, § 3.

[3] Dörpfeld attempts it very tentatively (D.R., pp. 20, 21; fig. 4).

than the temple. Dr. Bieber[1] notes that vases in the best red-figured style of the late fifth century presented striking paintings of two of the subjects mentioned by Pausanias (the return of Hephaistos and the desertion of Ariadne), and suggests that the vase-painters may have taken their treatment from the newly executed wall-paintings in the Dionysiac precinct, and that if so, the date of the temple or the hall, whichever it was, would be confirmed.

14. Dörpfeld[2] identified the Later Temple with the monument mentioned by Plutarch as erected by Nikias (ὁ τοῖς χορηγικοῖς τρίποσιν ὑποκείμενος ἐν Διονύσου νεώς).[3] The temple was certainly not erected as a base for tripods, but if tripods were subsequently erected on its roof, Plutarch might refer to it in these terms to distinguish it from the Older Temple, on which there were no tripods. This cannot be taken as certain, though it is perhaps more probable than the view of Furtwängler,[4] who imagines that Plutarch has wrongly ascribed to the famous Nikias of the fifth century the choragic monument of a younger Nikias for a victory in 320 B.C.; fragments of the latter monument were much later (perhaps in the second century A.D.) built into the 'Beulé' gate of the Acropolis. Reisch[5] and Bulle[6] prefer to identify the dedication of Nikias with a rectangular foundation of breccia blocks,[7] of about the same date as the Later Temple and about 40 feet south-east of it. This monument was about 38 ft. 8 in. long by 12 feet wide, and, apart from this conjecture, its nature is unknown.

---

[1] *Denkmäler zum Theaterwesen*, p. 15; cf. von Salis, *Jahrb. Arch.*, 1910, pp. 134 ff., and Buschor in Furtw.–Reich. iii, 144 f. (text to pl. 145).

[2] D.R., p. 22: *Ath. Mitt.* xxxvi (1911), pp. 62 ff., where some impossible suggestions of Versakis are disposed of; cf. Judeich, *Topogr. Ath.*², p. 283, n. 12.

[3] Plut. *Nik.* iii. 3.   [4] *Sitz. bayr. Akad.*, 1901, p. 413.

[5] *Eranos*, 2.   [6] *Untersuch.*, p. 73.   [7] D.R., p. 23.

II

THE THEATRE BEFORE LYCURGUS: EVIDENCE OF THE PLAYS

In the present chapter it is proposed to consider the evidence of the extant tragedies and comedies of the fifth century B.C. as regards the character of the scenery employed and of the temporary wooden buildings which, when present, formed the background for the action. It will be necessary to discuss in this connexion the questions whether, as was generally supposed until about half a century ago, there was a stage for the actors raised to a moderate or a considerable height above the level of the orchestra in which the chorus danced, and whether the temporary buildings included paraskenia or side wings projecting from each end of the background. In regard to these two points archaeological evidence is wholly wanting for the fifth century; the evidence of certain vase-paintings as regards the fourth century will be considered in its place.[1] Certain special questions regarding (*a*) the employment of a porch projecting from the background (i.e. from the front wall of the palace or temple represented by the wooden stage building), (*b*) the use of a device termed ἐκκύκλημα, (*c*) scene-painting and changes of scenery, will be reserved for a later chapter.

A. AESCHYLUS

1. The plays of Aeschylus belong to a period before the date at which the 'Periclean' reconstruction of the theatre described in the last chapter can have begun, though his later plays, as will be seen, require arrangements such as that reconstruction must have made much easier, especially as regards the provision of the framework for a normal type of background and of the painted

---

[1] See below, pp. 170–2. The argument of Fiechter, iii, p. 69, that the existence of stone paraskenia at a later period in Athens implies an earlier stage of development in which such structures existed in wood, as in certain Italian theatres (whose arrangements are reflected in the vases), is manifestly inconclusive. Fiechter himself points out that the Italian vases represent an Italian style of building, and that the Athenian paraskenia of the fifth century are not likely to have been so slight in structure. In fact no inference is possible from the Italian vases to the Athenian theatre of nearly a century earlier.

scenery which was introduced in the poet's later years; and it may have been his requirements, and those of Sophocles, who began to exhibit plays in 468, that gave the impetus to the improvement of the theatre.

Unfortunately scholars are far from being agreed as to the inferences to be drawn from the plays, and there may always remain differences of opinion on the fundamental question of the amount of illusion which an Athenian audience expected. Did they require a considerable degree of realism in the representation, or were they content to take a good deal for granted, and to see only with the mind's eye much of what the poet described or hinted at, just as in vase-painting and sculpture a very few figures might stand for many, and much might be conveyed by very simple symbols? This question must inevitably complicate the discussion at many points.

2. The problem as it affects the *Suppliants* (which, whatever its date—and scholars range in their dating over three decades—must certainly be regarded as the earliest extant play) is further complicated by the dispute as to the size of the chorus. Were all the fifty daughters of Danaus there, or was Aeschylus content (as he was in the *Oresteia*), with a chorus of twelve? (It may be assumed that each of the other plays of the Danaid trilogy must have had the same number of choreutae as the *Suppliants*, whatever the number was.) Each of the Danaids was accompanied by a handmaid (l. 978), and in the last scene these handmaids form a supplementary chorus. They were probably present—perhaps grouped near the entrances to the orchestra—throughout the action; otherwise the full understanding of the situation, which their lyrics show, would be less natural; so that, if there were fifty Danaids, room had to be found for at least a hundred women. Further, there was a band of Egyptian ruffians, who came with the Herald to carry the Danaids off, and who (according to the most probable view) joined in an excited lyric altercation with them. Perhaps there need not have been as many as fifty of these, but the number cannot have been much less; and there must have been room at the same time for enough Argive soldiers to overpower them when Pelasgos returned to the rescue. There must, in short, on this hypothesis have been room for nearly two hundred persons, all in active movement, and for this an orchestra of very large dimensions would have

been necessary. It seems at least possible that Aeschylus allowed twelve Danaids with twelve attendants to stand for fifty of each. The fact that a dithyrambic chorus of fifty performed in the orchestra affords no argument; they had neither attendants nor opponents, nor did their performance involve violent action; and the supposition that the tragic chorus was 'derived' from the dithyrambic and was therefore originally a chorus of fifty is one which I have elsewhere tried to disprove.[1] But even if it were so derived, and if Pollux[2] is correct in saying that the tragic chorus was originally one of fifty, it still does not necessarily follow that it was so in this play. Indeed the statement of Pollux may itself be an inference from the fact that legend spoke of fifty Danaids. The smaller number is not ruled out by the fact that Aegyptus is described in passing[3] as πεντηκοντάπαις, for this does not necessarily imply that all fifty sons appeared in the chorus of the *Aegyptii*. Further, there is a passage[4] in which the Danaid chorus threaten to hang themselves on the images of the gods before which they have taken sanctuary. There were certainly several images; there may have been a dozen, but surely not enough to afford gallows for fifty? There are therefore strong arguments in favour of a chorus of twelve, and the chorus, in fact, never speak of themselves as fifty. On the other hand, it is argued that Aeschylus may well have indulged his lifelong fondness for scenic display in the *Suppliants*, as he probably did in the *Persae*; that the first orchestra may have been big enough to allow the larger numbers to perform without difficulty, and may only have been reduced at a later date to a smaller size; and that this reduction may have been due to his decision to reduce his chorus to twelve for the future. A chorus of fifty, especially with supplementary choruses, would have been a heavy burden on a choregus, and this might also have suggested the supposed reduction. The question cannot be absolutely decided, and with it the size of the orchestra required must be left unsettled. The site would have allowed an orchestra considerably larger than that of later times, if it was demanded.

There is, fortunately, less uncertainty about the other external requirements of the play. The scene is a sacred precinct at a little distance from Argos. After an ode sung in the orchestra, the chorus, at the bidding of Danaus, take refuge at the common

---

[1] *Dith. Trag. Com.*, pp. 87 ff.   [2] iv. 110.   [3] l. 321.   [4] l. 465.

altar¹ of the ἀγώνιοι θεοί of Argos. Behind the altar, perhaps in a semicircle, were statues of a number of these gods—βρέτη,² probably archaic images of wood. There must have been a considerable number of these, and they must have been of some size, if (as at l. 885) the Danaids could all cling to them, and if (whether there were twelve maidens or fifty) they could contemplate hanging themselves from them. The gods mentioned by name, or indicated as those whose images or symbols are visible,³ are Zeus (though this is not quite certain), Helios, Apollo, Poseidon with his trident, and Hermes. (There is no indication of separate *altars*, but only of a joint altar and of images.) The whole precinct is conceived of as on a height, e.g. in l. 189 πάγον προσίζειν τόνδ' ἀγωνίων θεῶν, and Danaus uses the altar, or its steps, as a lookout post giving a view of the shore in the distance (l. 714). The conditions would be satisfied if, at a tangent to the orchestra, on the side farthest from the audience, there were an erection of considerable size representing the κοινὸς βωμός, mounted on one or two broad steps—large enough to accommodate the chorus—with the images grouped about it, and affording free passage to and from the orchestra. The whole action of the play requires this freedom; there cannot possibly have been a raised stage, as both Danaus and the chorus pass freely between the orchestra, which is described as a level precinct (λευρὸν ἄλσος), and the altar. (The verb προσίζειν presents no real difficulty—the chorus as suppliants settle themselves against, or leaning upon, the altar and its steps.) The appearance of height (πάγος) would be enhanced by the fact that the orchestra must have been on a terrace of which the edge must have been just behind the altar, so that it there showed a sudden drop. (It is just possible that, as some scholars have conjectured, the altar and statues may have been just within the orchestra circle, instead of at a tangent to it; but there seems no reason why the later arrangement as regards

---

¹ l. 222 πάντων ἀνάκτων τήνδε κοινοβωμίαν: cf. l. 423 ἐξ ἑδρᾶν πολυθέων ῥυσιασθεῖσαν. The word κοινοβωμία is probably abstract, 'fellowship in a common altar', but of course it implies a κοινὸς βωμός. A joint altar of a number of gods was not an unfamiliar thing in Greek religion; but (as Reisch, Noack, and others have suggested) Aeschylus would have been particularly familiar with the altar of the Twelve Gods in the agora at Athens, erected, probably in his own lifetime, by the younger Peisistratus.

² l. 429. ³ ll. 207 ff.

the normal position of the actors should not have existed from the first.)

Was there any background? The action requires none, and dressing accommodation could be provided by a tent at any convenient point on the approaches to the orchestra. Wilamowitz supposes that when (ll. 145–6) the chorus appeal to Artemis— ἐπιδέτω Διὸς κόρα, ἔχουσα σέμν᾽ ἐνώπι᾽ ἀσφαλῶς (or ἀσφαλέα)—it is implied that they are *looking at* the σέμν᾽ ἐνώπια, and that these —the façade of her temple—formed the background. But the supposition is quite unnecessary, and there is no indication what Temple of Artemis the chorus may have had in mind. There *may* have been a Temple of Artemis Orthia close to Argos; there can certainly be no reference to a Temple of Artemis supposed (very doubtfully) to be visible from the theatre *at Athens*; but the whole expression is probably intended simply to contrast the security of Artemis in her abode with the peril of the wandering Danaids, and need not refer to any particular temple.[1]

There appears to be no reason to accept two other suggestions of Wilamowitz, (1) that there was a high stage (*Chor-podium* or *Oberbühne*) erected in the orchestra to hold the great chorus and supplementary choruses,[2] (2) that the erection was composed of or based on a high mound of earth, with a slope of earth leading up to it. The orchestra itself was provided for the chorus to dance in, and it is difficult to see what is gained by the monstrous device suggested. All that the play requires is a great altar raised on broad steps to a sufficient height above that of the orchestra—the height need not be great to symbolize a πάγος sufficiently well—and the structure is most likely to have been of wood, so that it could easily be removed or changed between plays, whereas a mound or bank of earth might be very tiresome to shift.

Flickinger and others suppose that the access to the orchestra

---

[1] The passage is fully discussed in Vürtheim's edition, pp. 83 ff. He entirely disproves the theory of Wilamowitz, that the scenery of the play included a walled precinct of Artemis, identified with Hekaté.

[2] *Hermes*, xxi, p. 597. See Reisch in D.R., pp. 195–6, and Bulle, *Untersuch.*, p. 222. There probably was an altar of Dionysus as the god of the festival in the centre of the orchestra from the first, as there was later; but this was in no sense a 'stage-property'; and it seems probable that the erections in Aeschylus' earliest plays, which afterwards developed into stage buildings, should have been roughly where the stage buildings were later, viz. at a tangent to the orchestra on its south side. See pp. 9, 71, 131–2, 147.

terrace being originally on the west, the altar and images were exactly opposite this on the east side of the orchestra—roughly where the later eastern parodos entered. This, however, would require an entirely different orientation of the seating arrangements from that of later years, and one which would not conform so well to the slope of the hill-side. Otherwise we should have to suppose that the greater part of the play was acted at the side of the field of action (from the point of view of the audience) and not centrally, and this seems very improbable.

There is no reason to think that there was any background. In the other plays of the trilogy the scene must have been laid in the city of Argos and probably in an open place or agora in the city; the houses in which the Danaids were lodged (μονόρρυθμοι δόμοι, *Suppl.* 961) need not, so far as we know, have been represented. But if any background was required, it may have been very simple and easily erected either before or after the performance of the first play.[1]

3. The arrangements required by the *Persians* are fundamentally the same as those of the *Suppliants*. On the far side of the orchestra from the audience, probably just outside the circle, instead of the great altar, is an erection representing the grave of Darius, sufficiently high to conceal (inside or behind it) an actor who in due course rises up out of or above it (l. 659 ἔλθ᾽ ἐπ᾽ ἄκρον κόρυμβον ὄχθου). How far this erection was made to resemble an ὄχθος, a mound of earth, it is impossible to say. It is disputed whether there was any background behind this. At l. 140 the chorus of Persian elders—their number is nowhere indicated—describe themselves as τόδ᾽ ἐνεζόμενοι στέγος ἀρχαῖον to discuss the crisis. The στέγος ἀρχαῖον is supposed by some scholars to be the tomb of Darius; but it is a strange description of a tomb, and that a recent tomb, for Darius was but lately dead; and it is also strange that if it were their king's tomb, the chorus should give no hint of it. Accordingly it seems more natural to think that some simple background represented the Council Chamber, which might well be a στέγος ἀρχαῖον, on the step or entrance of which they took up their position. But it is never mentioned again,

---

[1] The artistic advantage of the definition of the scene of action by even the simplest background is obvious. Aeschylus must undoubtedly have realized this early—probably before the *Persians*. But we cannot be sure what he did in this respect in the Danaid trilogy.

and no one ever goes into it or enters from it. The background cannot have represented the royal palace, as some scholars believe, for the queen, at her first entry, arrives at the spot in a chariot (ll. 159–60), and at her second entry (l. 607) makes a point of *not* having come in her chariot, as she had done before. She speaks also of preparing the necessary sacrifices εὖτ' ἂν εἰς οἴκους μόλωμεν (230), and asks the chorus to escort Xerxes, when he arrives, to the palace (530); and this, in the last line of the play, they propose to do. The difficulties sometimes raised, that the tomb would be unlikely to be at the door of the Council Chamber,[1] and that though the Council Chamber would naturally be supposed to be at Susa, Darius was actually buried at Persepolis, are not likely to have troubled Aeschylus or his audience.

In the lost *Niobe* the action took place at the tomb of Niobe's children, and there is no reason to suppose that there was any other scenery. The play was evidently one of Aeschylus' earliest.[2]

4. In the *Seven against Thebes* the whole scene represents the Acropolis of Thebes (l. 240), and on the side of the orchestra farthest from the audience was (as in the *Suppliants*) a row or semicircle of ἀρχαῖα βρέτη—ancient images of gods; eight or more are mentioned in the entrance song of the chorus, in the course of which they take refuge by the images. No mention is made of altars; it is quite likely that (as in the *Suppliants*) there was a common altar for the whole θεῶν πανήγυρις. Before the first choral ode the chorus is persuaded to leave the altars and chant its prayers ἐκτὸς ἀγαλμάτων, i.e. in the orchestra. We cannot suppose, as some scholars do, that the ἀγάλματα are raised on a platform representing the Acropolis, while the orchestra represents the city below; it would be hard to explain, in that case, how Eteocles on the Acropolis could converse with the chorus supposed to be far below him. If there was any background— the text does not help to decide this—it might, however simple, represent the palace of Eteocles, provided that it had a door. The opening of the play is not unlike that of Sophocles' *Oedipus Tyrannus*. Eteocles addresses a little crowd of citizens, and the palace steps would be the natural place. (In the *O.T.* also it is clear that there were images of gods and altars before the palace.) It would, in addition, be the natural place for the scout to find

---

[1] In the *Choëphoroe* the tomb of Agamemnon appears to be close to the palace door.　　[2] See *Greek Poetry and Life*, pp. 106 ff.

him, and when he calls for his armour (l. 675), it is to be supposed that it had not to be fetched from a distance. When Antigone and Ismene appear, they probably come out of the palace, meeting the military procession which bears the bodies of the two brothers. There may possibly have been a raised look-out post, but it would not have been necessary. Thus in the first three extant plays we find very simple and very similar arrangements —an erection representing an altar or a tomb at the edge of the orchestra, with (in two plays) a row of images of gods, and probably, in the two later of the three plays, a simple background representing a public building or palace.[1] In each play one or more broad steps may have led to the building or altar.

The buildings may have been of wood or canvas. A canvas or wooden background, representing a tent or military hut, was almost certainly the background of the lost plays, the *Myrmidones*[2] and the *Phryges* (or *Ransoming of Hector*), which formed a trilogy with the *Nereïdes*, and also of the *Threïssai* and the *Memnon*. So soon as such an erection was provided, it may also have served as a dressing-room for actors and chorus, unless it happened to be convenient for actors entering in a chariot, supposedly from a distance, to put on their costume elsewhere. Up to this point there is no evidence of any use by Aeschylus of any mechanical devices, except that in the *Seven against Thebes* the din of battle and clanging armour, which the chorus hear, may have been simulated by noises made out of sight of the audience in the obvious ways.

5. The *Prometheus Vinctus* raises problems of which no solution satisfactory to all scholars is likely to be found. There is no need to discuss the theory put forward by Bethe,[3] that the play as it stands is a revised version dating from the last third of the fifth century; such revision is not likely to have affected essential elements in the structure of the play, and all that is substantial

[1] The conjecture of J. Six (*J.H.S.* xl, pp. 186 ff.) that Agatharchus painted the towers of Thebes (which are pointed out in the play at ll. 549 and 882 ff.) in perspective as a background goes beyond the evidence. It may be doubted whether Agatharchus was active as early as this. See below, pp. 124–5.

[2] See fr. 131.

[3] *Proleg. zur Gesch. des Griech. Theaters*, pp. 158 ff., and *Hermes*, lix (1924), pp. 111 ff. Other revisionists are F. Weise (*Die Frage der Bühnenaufführung des Aeschyleischen Prometheus* (1908), and W. Schmid, *Unters. zum Gefesselten Prometheus* (1929). A sufficient reply is given by Thomson in his edition (1932).

in the arguments put forward for the theory is much better met
by Thomson's dating of the Prometheus trilogy as one of the
poet's latest compositions.[1] The reason why some of the difficulties are insoluble is that we cannot tell how much the poet was
content to suggest by language without presenting it visibly to
the audience. But if we follow the indications in the text, it is
clear in the first place that the rock to which Prometheus is
fastened is supposed to be high up in the air (ll. 4, 5 πρὸς πέτραις
ὑψηλοκρήμνοις, l. 113 ὑπαιθρίοις δεσμοῖς πεπασσαλευμένος, l. 158
αἰθέριον κίνυγμα, l. 269 πρὸς πέτραις πεδαρσίοις). It is also described in l. 15 as a φάραγξ and in ll. 20 and 117 as a πάγος. Evidently there was some high central erection on the far side of
the orchestra from the audience, and to this Prometheus was
fastened. At l. 1016 Hermes threatens that Zeus will split this
rock or cliff (ὀκρίδα | φάραγγα ... σπαράξει) with lightning and thun-
der, and that Prometheus will be carried down to Tartarus. All
editors assume that this must have happened visibly at the end
of the play, and some suggest mechanisms for effecting it. But,
in fact, while the play ends with an utterance of Prometheus
describing the growing storm of thunder, hail, lightning, and
wind, and crying that it is evidently aimed at him, there is *no*
indication that he and the rock are *visibly* swept down into the
abyss after he has spoken the last line of the play, and it seems
very doubtful whether it happened at all. Further, it is commonly assumed that the chorus of Okeanids were swept down
with him. As before, there is no indication of this in the text;
they declare (1067) their resolve to stay with him—μετὰ τοῦδ᾽
ὅ τι χρὴ πάσχειν ἐθέλω: and probably the play ended with the
chorus clustering round him and preparing for the worst, with
noises of thunder and wind from behind the scenes. Thomson
conjectures that Prometheus was finally withdrawn on the ἐκκύκλημα: this, even if there was such a machine at this time, is not
necessary, and he has to suppose that the Okeanids are scattered
to the wings by the thunder and lightning—a treatment which
seems less effective, after their declaration of determination to
stay with Prometheus, than the one which I have suggested. If
the view here taken is right, there is no need of elaborate machinery in the background. The central rock stands, and is ready for
the next play of the trilogy, when Prometheus has been brought

[1] See also Yorke, *Class. Quart.*, 1936, pp. 117, 153–4.

up from Hades and is again fastened to the rock. It would be very odd if the rock were carried down and had to be brought back again.

What was there to be seen besides this central rock? The answer depends upon the view taken of the movements of the Okeanides. In ll. 124–6 Prometheus hears the sound of their wings before he sees them, and at l. 128 they bid him not to fear, φιλία γὰρ ἥδε τάξις | πτερύγων θοαῖς ἁμίλλαις | προσέβα τόνδε πάγον ... | ... κραιπνοφόροι δέ μ' ἔπεμψαν αὖραι, and (l. 135) σύθην δ' ἀπέδιλος ὄχῳ πτερωτῷ. After long conversation, Prometheus bids them descend, l. 272 πέδοι δὲ βᾶσαι τὰς προσερπούσας τύχας | ἀκούσαθ', to which they respond (l. 278) καὶ νῦν ἐλαφρῷ | ποδὶ κραιπνόσυτον θᾶκον προλιποῦσ', | αἰθέρα θ' ἁγνὸν πόρον οἰωνῶν, | ὀκριοέσσῃ χθονὶ τῇδε πελῶ. There follows the scene between Prometheus and Okeanos, and when at 397 the chorus begin the first stasimon, they are presumably in the orchestra.

The natural inference from these passages is that from 123 to 283, or at least at the beginning of this passage, the Okeanids are out of sight of Prometheus, i.e. are above and behind him; in other words on an upper story or flat roof of the stage buildings, like that which the poet employed in the *Oresteia* and the *Psychostasia*. If so, at their arrival, a winged car, capable of holding some or all of them, could have been rolled forward to the front of this roof or upper story. This would not have been so difficult, not to say so impossible, a proceeding, as the alternative which editors frequently prefer—that of a car, with twelve Okeanids on board, and therefore weighing probably not less than a ton and a half, swung forward on a crane, and kept swinging for 160 lines.[1] (Whether Greek engineering skill could have managed this does not seem certain, but the plan seems unlikely in itself, and the absurdity of it would grow in the course of the 160 lines.) When Prometheus bids the Okeanids descend, they presumably come down from the upper story, whether by concealed steps or from behind the scenes, into the orchestra, while Prometheus is

[1] I find it difficult to accept Professor Murray's idea (*Aeschylus*, p. 41), already suggested by Page, *Actors' Interpolations*, pp. 82–3, that the chorus and their father may have been balanced 'at opposite ends of a double crane, and that as Okeanos was swung on ... his daughters by mechanical necessity were swung off'. Unless the winged steed of Okeanos was very huge, the two weights would hardly have balanced. Pollux iv. 126 indicates that the weight which the μηχανή could take was limited.

talking to Okeanos. (To allow this may have been one of the motives of this scene, as the scholiast suggests.) Of course, if there were παρασκήνια or projecting side-wings at this date, equal in height to the upper story, these, or one of them, might have been used for the Okeanids and their car; this would avoid the slight improbability of a long conversation during which he could not see them; and though there is not enough evidence to determine certainly whether such παρασκήνια were in use about 460 B.C. or not, it will be argued below that it is not unlikely.

Thomson[1] has a different suggestion—that there was no car at all, but that in their parodos (the metre of which was lyric, not anapaestic, i.e. a dancing, not a marching tune) the chorus performed a dance conventionally associated with sea-nymphs on their winged sea-horses, but that the sea-horses themselves were left to the imagination. Θοαῖς ἁμίλλαις (l. 129) would certainly suggest a number of persons on separate steeds, each trying to get there first,[2] and passages which he quotes show that there would be no difficulty in the use of ὄχῳ πτερωτῷ of such steeds (as ὄχημα is used of Arion's dolphin[3]), or in the similar use of κραιπνόσυτον θᾶκον. This interpretation is by no means impossible; it depends partly on the evidence of vase-paintings, which is not altogether clear. But there is a real difficulty in the conception of a sea-horse as winged; and further, if this were got over, we could indeed suppose that the chorus, though out of sight of Prometheus as they come up the πάροδοι, very soon come out into the orchestra, where he could see them and, after their dance, cluster round the central θυμέλη (or on its steps, so far as there was room); but this would leave Prometheus' request to them to descend to earth (at l. 272) much more pointless than it would be if they were in a real vehicle and on a height. On the whole, therefore, I am inclined to think Professor Thomson's theory less probable than that given above. There is no reason to depart from the generally received view that Okeanos on his τετρασκελὴς οἰωνός was swung in on the γέρανος, and probably did not leave the car during the short scene in which he appears, as the four-legged bird would hardly be flapping its wings

---

[1] n. on l. 130 in his edition of the play.
[2] But passages quoted by Liddell and Scott show that ἅμιλλα may be applied to any kind of eager motion, without necessarily implying competition.
[3] *App. Anthol.* i. 3.

(ll. 394–5) on the ground. He would be similarly swung off at the end.

The only remaining problem concerns Io. The natural supposition is that her wild dances take place in the orchestra, and that in the dialogue she stands in the part of the orchestra nearest to the rock of Prometheus, or on a slope or steps leading up from the orchestra to the rock. The only reason which leads some editors to reject this view is found in ll. 747 ff., where she cries τί δῆτ' ἐμοὶ ζῆν κέρδος, ἀλλ' οὐκ ἐν τάχει | ἔρριψ' ἐμαυτὸν τῆσδ' ἀπὸ στύφλου πέτρας, | ὅπως πέδοι σκήψασα τῶν πάντων πόνων | ἀπηλλάγην; This is thought by them to imply that she was *already* standing on a high rock: but τῆσδε does not necessarily imply this. It could apply equally well to a cliff facing her—even the rock of Prometheus itself.

Thus the scenery will have consisted of a background, perhaps higher in the middle, representing cliffs with a central rock to which Prometheus is attached; a slope or steps led up to this from the edge of the orchestra, and above this background was an upper story or floor, serving to carry the chorus in their winged chariot, until they descend to the orchestra. This upper floor need not be much, if at all, higher than the raised centre of the background.[1] (Alternatively, though this seems less likely, the chorus may have appeared on the upper part of the παρασκήνια, assuming that there were any.) The only special apparatus required would be the machinery for making noises and the γέρανος for Okeanos. It is very improbable that such apparatus was used to bring in the chorus, or that there was any machinery for carrying Prometheus, his rock, and the twelve Okeanids down to Hades at the end of the play, though he must have been given a rest in some way before the beginning of the next play. Greek audiences must have been thoroughly accustomed to see the scene set or reset between plays, and would feel no incongruity. Whether or not a temporary screen may have been brought in to hide the departure of Prometheus and his return for the next play there is no evidence to show; but it seems unlikely.

---

[1] I cannot accept H. G. Mullen's suggestion (*Greece and Rome*, May 1939) that 'only a representative number of choreutae appeared in the flying chariot', while others entered as unobtrusively as they could from the wings; nor that of P. Orsini (*Mélanges Navarre*, pp. 495 ff.) that the whole play was performed on a λογεῖον above the σκηνή.

The fact that the same Prometheus who is bound in the extant play is released and presumably walks about in the next, and that he was a character in the Πυρφόρος, seems to be sufficient proof that he was not represented by a gigantic puppet with an actor inside as many scholars have supposed. It is argued that an actor cannot have been so long immovable. If this be true (and it is doubtful whether it can be sustained), some very simple supporting devices could easily have been contrived if they were wanted, and the driving of a wedge through his chest could have been effected with as realistic a pretence as on any modern stage. What is certain is that Prometheus cannot have been of different sizes in different parts of the trilogy.[1]

6. As regards the scenery of the *Oresteia* it is obvious that, apart from such slight modifications as could be made between the plays, the structure of the background must have been the same for all three plays. In other words, it must have been such as to serve for either a palace or a temple. In all three plays a wide central door is required, through which (assuming that there was no use of an ἐκκύκλημα) the audience, or a considerable part of them, could see an interior scene, or, at least, a grouping of figures just inside the door. There must have been a place upon the roof of the palace on which the watchman could stand; this same place served perhaps, as we have seen, in the *Prometheus* to receive the chariot of the Ocean nymphs, and (whether with or without further apparatus) in the *Psychostasia* and other plays for the appearance of gods. In front of the palace or temple were probably broad steps, leading up to the door or doors; on the steps there may have been altars (e.g. for Clytemnestra's offerings) and the emblem of Apollo Agyieus, to whom Cassandra appeals. There can have been no high raised stage. Agamemnon enters through the orchestra in a chariot. (Whether Cassandra was in a second chariot with the booty, as the scholiast says, is very doubtful: the king had been shipwrecked and probably had no booty to bring, and he must have had a very small retinue, if any.) He halts at the foot of the palace steps; it is some time before he dismounts to walk on the crimson carpets laid on the

---

[1] Discussions of the scenery are innumerable—among them D.R., pp. 198 ff., 216 ff., 248; Noack, Σκηνὴ τραγική, pp. 14 ff.; Robert, *Hermes*, xxxi, pp. 573 ff.; Frickenhaus, *Die altgr. Bühne*, pp. 11, 12; Wilamowitz, *Interpret.*, pp. 114 ff.; Bulle, *Untersuch.*, pp. 223-4.

steps, and it is difficult to imagine that he and Clytemnestra talked to each other the one below, the other above, a platform of considerable height. It is also practically certain that Aegisthus and his men entered through the orchestra, where they came to grips with the chorus.

The *Choëphoroe* falls into two parts, the first of which is played about the tomb of Agamemnon, the second in front of the same palace as formed the background of the preceding play. Actual change of scene being impossible, there can be no doubt that the structure or mound of earth representing the tomb was in the orchestra or just outside it on the same level; it remained there necessarily throughout the second part of the play, and is in fact mentioned in ll. 722–4. It was probably erected after the conclusion of the *Agamemnon*. It must necessarily have been in front of the palace, however unlikely a burial-place this would have been in real life, especially if we consider the manner of Agamemnon's death; but it is disputed whether it was directly in front or at the side of the orchestra near the parodos as (e.g.) is argued by Dörpfeld and Reisch[1] and by Hampel.[2] The earnest warning given to Orestes (ll. 264–6) to be careful what he says lest he should be overheard suggests proximity to the central door. Both the *Choëphoroe* and the *Eumenides* would act most easily if there were at least two doors, though it might not be absolutely necessary. The γυναικεῖοι πύλαι, *Cho.* 878, *might* conceivably be within the palace, and the guest-chambers to which Orestes and Pylades were conducted *might* have been entered from within, but the probability seems to be in favour of a façade with three doors. (In Euripides' *Alcestis* the guest-chambers have a separate entrance from without.[3]) In the *Eumenides* the Pythia would make her first entrance from a side door. A temple front itself had not ordinarily side doors, but these could represent the houses of officials, &c.

Two of the three doors may have been in paraskenia or side-wings, if such were constructed at this date, and the opening scene of the *Choëphoroe* would certainly be easier to act if Orestes and Pylades, who conceal themselves from Electra and the chorus, while still overhearing what they say, could retreat behind the corner of a projecting side-wing, than it would if Electra and the

[1] pp. 250–1.   [2] *Was lehrt Aischylos' Orestie, usw.*, p. 17.
[3] ll. 546–9 δωμάτων ἐξωπίους ξενῶνας. These may, but need not, have been in a paraskenion. See below, p. 52.

chorus had to pretend for 200 lines not to see them.[1] This type of pretence is common in the drama, both ancient and modern, but is usually kept up for only a very few lines.

Whether either the *Agamemnon* or the *Choëphoroe* requires the use of the ἐκκύκλημα, and whether the *Eumenides* requires either the ἐκκύκλημα or the columned porch or πρόθυρον will be discussed in the next chapter, where a negative answer to both questions will be shown to be probable. In fact, the *Eumenides* seems to require no more than a façade which would serve as a temple, with a wide central door—virtually the same façade as the *Agamemnon*. In the opening scene, ll. 1–234, this represents the Temple of Apollo at Delphi. The priestess who speaks the prologue enters, probably by a side door; she goes into the temple by the central door, opened just wide enough to admit her; she rushes out again, and then the door is opened to its full extent, and reveals Orestes clasping the omphalos, Apollo and Hermes close beside him, and grouped about him, perhaps at first only partly visible, the sleeping Furies on seats. At l. 177 the Furies are driven out of the temple into the orchestra.

In the following scenes the temple represented is that of Athena on the Acropolis at Athens; a very slight change of properties in the interval in which the orchestra was empty would effect this. The essential change would be the substitution of the βρέτας of Athena for the omphalos of Delphi. The ancient βρέτας was of course inside the temple, as every Athenian would naturally assume: to this Orestes clings, and the fancy that in the ὕμνος δέσμιος the Furies dance round him is therefore untenable. Athena herself arrives from Scamander—in other words, through the parodos; probably *not* on a μηχανή or in a chariot, for she speaks of

---

[1] Apart from special scenes, the aesthetic advantage of the paraskenia, as enclosing at each end the space used by the actors and so defining the scene of action, needs no argument to prove it; but this does not help us to decide the date at which they were introduced. It has been suggested that they might also be used, if required, as dressing-rooms, or to support mechanical apparatus; but there is no direct evidence of either use. Paraskenia are found in the earliest remains of the theatre at Eretria, which possibly (though not certainly) date from the latter half of the fifth century. (See below, pp. 199, 200.) Bulle (*Untersuch.*, pp. 223, &c.) thinks that the Athenian theatre had a wooden flooring between the paraskenia, raised above the level of the orchestra by three or four steps. There seems to be no evidence of this; even the analogy of Eretria would only justify one step. (See p. 70.)

having used her aegis as a sail, ἔνθεν διώκουσ᾽ ἦλθον ἄτρυτον πόδα |
πτερῶν ἄτερ ῥοιβδοῦσα κόλπον αἰγίδος, and if the next line (405
πώλοις ἀκμαίοις τόνδ᾽ ἐπιζεύξασ᾽ ὄχον) is genuine (Wilamowitz
thinks it is an actor's addition of later date), it is a metaphorical
description of the speed with which the aegis had brought her.
She speaks from the temple steps, close to the doorway, both to
Orestes and to the chorus. After the arrival of the goddess in
person, Orestes would not need to cling to the βρέτας, but would
come forward to the doorway. At 489, the terms of the trial
having been arranged, the temple doors are closed (probably
leaving Orestes inside), Athena goes off to collect her jury, and
the chorus chant the ode, ll. 490–565, in the orchestra.

At l. 566 Athena returns; during the ode the attendants have
doubtless placed benches for the jury who came with her, and
the temple, the front of which cannot have been changed, is
henceforth neglected. The rest of the play must be supposed to
take place on the Areopagus; at l. 685 Athena uses the words
πάγον δ᾽ Ἄρειον τόνδε and enlarges on the history of the spot,
and the court which she establishes with her present jury as its
first members is the court of the Areopagus. All this is more than
can be explained by a 'deictic' gesture pointing across from the
Acropolis to the Areopagus, and there is no evidence of a second
prehistoric temple of Athena on the Areopagus. (No support for
the idea can be derived from Eur. *El.* 1254 ff.) The placing of the
benches was a sufficient hint of the change of scene, and the
fact that at l. 1021 Athena calls upon the attendants who guard
her βρέτας to join in the procession does not necessarily imply
a consciousness of the presence of the temple on the Acropolis.
When the attendants have left the temple, the temple is forgotten
for the rest of the play. The arguments of Ridgeway,[1] Wilamowitz,[2] and others against the supposition that the trial was intended to be thought of as taking place on the Areopagus are
very inconclusive; most of all perhaps the objection that the
descent of the Areopagus would in fact afford very bad footholds
for the great procession which at the end of the play is marshalled
so as to resemble that of the Panathenaea.

The trial scene appears to be conclusive against the existence
of a high raised stage in the Aeschylean theatre. We cannot
imagine that Apollo and the Furies harangued the jury from

[1] *Cl. Rev.* xxi, pp. 163 ff.   [2] *Interpret.*, p. 182.

very different levels. In the scene, as it may best be pictured, Athena stands or sits in the centre of the broad temple step; Apollo and Orestes are on her right, perhaps on a lower step; the jury in a semicircle before her—the two ends of the semicircle may have overlapped the lower step; the Furies on her left, mostly in the orchestra, but with the spokesman on the lower step, facing Apollo and Orestes. With a high raised stage there could be no tolerable grouping.

7. Thus the plays of Aeschylus required at first, in the three earliest extant plays, only the simplest scenic arrangements, and though later there is rather more elaboration of scenery, particularly in the *Prometheus*, there is no more than could well be provided for each occasion. There may already have been stock sets of wooden and canvas scenery representing a military camp (as in a number of plays that have been mentioned), or the front of a palace or temple, based on one or two broad steps, with a large central door and two side doors, the latter perhaps situated, when convenient, in side-wings (paraskenia). Not only the *Oresteia*, but some lost plays, e.g. the 'Hδωνοί and probably the 'Ιέρειαι, required the palace-front. The possibility that the façade may have been partly painted in perspective will be discussed later. There may also have been stock sets for satyric plays; the *Phorkides*, like a number of later satyric plays, seems to have had a cave in the background. The 'Periclean' reconstruction would afterwards supply a regular framework for such sets of scenery.

Both in the *Oresteia* and in the *Prometheus* the wooden stage buildings must have been sufficiently solid to provide a place for a number of actors—in the *Prometheus* even for the chorus—on the roof, and a support for tolerably heavy machinery either on the roof or on some strong foundation (such as the later T in the Plans) within the main building, or in the paraskenia or upon them. Whether the θεολογεῖον, on which, in the *Psychostasia*, Zeus was seen weighing in the balance the lives of Achilles and Memnon, with Thetis and Eos on either side, each pleading for her son, was simply the roof of the skené or (as Haigh[1] thought) a special erection above it, cannot be certainly decided. The words of Pollux[2] could be interpreted either way. In the lost

[1]   *Attic Theatre*[3], pp. 164, 213.

[2]   iv. 130 ἀπὸ δὲ τοῦ θεολογείου ὄντος ὑπὲρ τὴν σκηνὴν ἐν ὕψει ἐπιφαίνονται θεοί, ὡς ὁ Ζεὺς καὶ οἱ περὶ αὐτὸν ἐν Ψυχοστασίᾳ (cf. Plut. *de aud. poet.* ii. 17 A, and

Φρύγες ἢ ῞Εκτορος Λύτρα Hermes is said[1] to have held a brief dialogue with Achilles early in the play; but here the god was probably on the ground, not on the roof.

To complete this summary, it is only necessary to repeat that it is very doubtful whether the plays of Aeschylus could have been acted on a raised stage.[2] Nearly all involve complete freedom of movement between the orchestra and the space chiefly used by the actors, and in some scenes (such as the first meeting of Agamemnon with Clytemnestra, and the trial scene in the *Eumenides*) a raised stage—as distinct from a broad step or two in front of the façade—would have produced an absurd result.

B. SOPHOCLES

1. There is a gap of sixteen or seventeen years between the *Oresteia* and the *Antigone*, which is usually dated from 443 to 441 B.C. By this time the 'Periclean' reconstruction of the theatre must have begun.

Four of the seven extant plays of Sophocles are acted in front of a palace; only one doorway into the palace is needed. These are the *Antigone*, the *Electra* (probably between 430 and 413 B.C.), the *Oedipus Tyrannus* (possibly soon after 430, but there is really no satisfactory indication of date), and the *Trachiniae* (probably between 420 and 410). In the *Oedipus Tyrannus* there is a group of altars (as ll. 15, 16 suggest) in front of the palace, or at least an altar of Apollo Lykeios (ll. 918 ff.). In the *Electra* also there was an altar of Apollo (ll. 634, 1346). A broad step or sill, such as was required in the *Oresteia*, in front of the palace would make the scene and the acting more effective, but it cannot be said to be necessary. The three other plays require more particular discussion.

2. The *Ajax* is an early play, possibly a little later than the *Antigone*. The play opens in front of the tent, or, more probably, the wooden military hut, of Ajax. (In l. 579 it is called a δῶμα.) It

schol. on *Iliad* viii. 70). In the same passage Pollux mentions that the γέρανος was used in the same play to carry Eos when she descended to bear away the body of Memnon. In Euripides, *Ion*, 1549, *Orest.* 1631, the god is high in air above the house, but this implies the use of the μηχανή rather than of any form of λογεῖον, and cannot be used to interpret Pollux' account of the *Psychostasia*. See below, pp. 55–6.   [1] *Vit. Aeschyli.*

[2] With regard to the ascription of a raised stage to Aeschylus by Horace, see below, p. 72.

must have been moderately roomy inside, and must have had a
wide central opening. The play presents three special problems:
(1) Where did Athena appear at the beginning of the play, or did
she not appear at all? (2) Was the ἐκκύκλημα employed at l. 346
to show the interior of the tent, with Ajax surrounded by
slaughtered animals? (3) How were the death of Ajax and the
change of scene at l. 814 effected? The second of these questions
will be discussed in the following chapter.

In the opening scene Athena was certainly invisible at first
(at least for about 17 lines) to Odysseus, who is in front of the
hut, cf. ll. 14 ff.:

> ὦ φθέγμ' Ἀθάνας, φιλτάτης ἐμοὶ θεῶν,
> ὡς εὐμαθές σου, κἂν ἄποπτος ᾖς ὅμως,
> φώνημ' ἀκούω καὶ συναρπάζω φρενὶ
> χαλκοστόμου κώδωνος ὡς Τυρσηνικῆς.

But, on the evidence of the scholiast on l. 14, she was visible to
the audience (ἔστι μέντοι ἐπὶ τῆς σκηνῆς ἡ Ἀθηνᾶ· δεῖ γὰρ τοῦτο
χαρίζεσθαι τοῖς θεαταῖς),[1] and many scholars suppose that she was
on a θεολογεῖον, i.e. on or raised above the roof, and rather far
back, so as to be invisible to an actor immediately below the
front of the hut. But the dialogue continued for 133 lines, and it
is difficult to suppose either that the pretence of invisibility can
have been kept up so long, or that a long conversation (as distinct, e.g., from the actual or virtual monologues of the θεὸς ἀπὸ
μηχανῆς in Euripides) can have been conducted between an actor
far up on the θεολογεῖον and one on the ground. It is even more
difficult to suppose that the conversation of Athena with Ajax,
who is generally supposed to have remained inside the hut, was
conducted through the roof (ll. 89–117). It seems more likely that
there was no θεολογεῖον (as there is none in any other play of
Sophocles), but that Athena was on the ground, perhaps partly
concealed in the trees of the grove which was required later in the
play, and that she was at first unseen by Odysseus, but came
forward in due course. In fact she was probably not invisible to
Ajax either; he must have come at least to the door of his hut at
l. 90 and returned into it at l. 117. The partial disclosure of the
interior of the hut and its contents, when the chorus were not

---

[1] ἐπὶ τῆς σκηνῆς, here and nearly always, means 'on the scene', visible to the
audience, not 'on the top of the stage building', or 'on the stage'. See pp. 73, 168.

present, would not spoil the full disclosure to the chorus by Tecmessa at l. 346.

The scene was certainly supposed to have changed at l. 814, when the chorus and Tecmessa have left the front of the hut to search for Ajax, and he appears to make his final speech before he runs on his sword, probably entering from one of the wings. The place of his death, where he had just planted the sword, was a grove at the side of the stage, and this was probably represented by some simple symbols or painted panels or canvas at one end of the back wall (possibly round one of the side entrances, if there were any, or in the place occupied in other plays by one of the paraskenia) ; these symbols may either have been present, but ignored, from the beginning of the play, or may have been introduced by attendants at l. 814 during a brief pause ; the hut must have remained,[1] but is henceforth ignored. This seems more likely than that a canvas representing a grove was hurriedly draped over the hut, for it is clear from the use of the word πάραυλος in l. 891 (τίνος βοὴ πάραυλος ἐξέβη νάπους;)[2] that the grove was at the *side* of the main scene, as it is also from the passage in which Tecmessa discovers the body. Ajax makes his great speech before the audience, pointing to the sword hidden in the grove (invisible to the audience, but supposed to be visible to him), and at the end rushes off to fall on it, out of view of the audience, as the normal Greek convention required in cases of sudden death.

The scene in which Tecmessa and the chorus, in two divisions, are looking for Ajax after his death could scarcely be acted without absurdity if she were on a raised stage and they were in the orchestra. The scholiast on l. 866 seems to assume that they are on the same level.[3]

3. The *Philoctetes* (409 B.C.) requires in the background a cave whose mouth (ll. 16 ff.) is higher than the level orchestra which

[1] Reisch in D.R., p. 212, thinks that the background, representing the hut, may have been drawn apart and so removed, revealing a scene of open country behind. This is not impossible, but there seems to be no parallel, and the view given above seems on the whole more likely.

[2] The word only occurs again—in *Oed. Col.* 785 ἀλλ' ὡς πάραυλον οἰκίσῃς— meaning 'near, but outside the city'.

[3] οἱ ἀπὸ χοροῦ προΐασιν ὥσπερ ἐκ διαφόρων τόπων κατ' ἄλλην καὶ ἄλλην εἴσοδον, ζητοῦντες τὸν Αἴαντα, καὶ ἡ Τέκμησσα ἐξ ἄλλων, ἥτις καὶ πρώτη ἐπιτυγχάνει τῷ πτώματι.

represents the beach. The background itself, the front of the temporary wooden skené, would be painted to represent a cliff, and the cave would be the upper part of the central doorway, the lower part being blocked; a rough path led up from the orchestra level to the mouth of the cave. Whether the spring, which was between the beach and the cave, was represented (e.g. by a niche in the rock) we do not know. All this would require only easily contrived adaptations of the conventional façade, aided by appropriate scene-painting. At l. 29 Neoptolemus finds the cave —τόδ᾽ ἐξύπερθε. It was a tunnel with the visible opening facing the audience, and the opposite end leading into the stage building (cf. l. 159 οἶκον γὰρ ὁρᾷς τόνδ᾽ ἀμφίθυρον). It must have been high enough above the beach for Philoctetes to threaten without absurdity to kill himself by throwing himself down from it; perhaps the rock-ledge in front of it had a natural parapet of rock behind which Philoctetes stood.[1] The appearance of Herakles could, but need not, have been made ἀπὸ μηχανῆς.[2] He may have come out of the cave itself and spoken from the rock platform in front of it, where Philoctetes used to sun himself. There can be no question of a simple high raised stage in this play, because the path winding up from the orchestra level (the beach) to the cave is essential, and is many times used in the play by Neoptolemus and Philoctetes. The words used at the end of the play, where chorus and actors go off in one procession (l. 1469 χωρῶμεν δὴ πάντες ἀολλεῖς), would hardly have been used if there were a fixed difference of levels. (Similar departures in united processions occur in several plays of Aristophanes, e.g. *Birds*, *Frogs*, and *Plutus*.)

A similar representation of a cave-mouth in the background in the satyric *Ichneutae* (of which the date is uncertain)[3] may have been contrived in the same way. The background was painted to represent or suggest a wooded hill (l. 215 χλοερὸν ὑλῶδη πάγον). That the cave was on a higher level than the orchestra is indicated by ll. 321–2 (ὀρθοψάλακτός τις ὀμφὴ κατοιχνεῖ τόπου). This disposes of the view of some scholars that there was an elevated mound in or just outside the orchestra (as in Aeschylus' *Suppliants*), with

---

[1] See Woodhouse, *J.H.S.*, 1912, pp. 239–49.

[2] It is doubtful whether Sophocles ever used the μηχανή. In the lost *Peleus* the final settlement was made by Thetis, but not necessarily ἀπὸ μηχανῆς. See Pearson, *Soph. Fr.* ii, p. 142.

[3] See *New Chapters in Greek Literature*, iii, pp. 87–95.

an underground tunnel and Χαρώνιοι κλίμακες by means of which Cyllene rose out of the earth. There is no evidence of Χαρώνιοι κλίμακες in Athens or indeed anywhere except in the ruins at Eretria, Sikyon, Segesta, and Philippi.[1]

4. In the *Oedipus Coloneus*, brought out in 402, the background must have represented a grove of trees (by means, perhaps, of painted panels attached to the façade), with a way in and out among the trees—in other words through the background—and corresponding to the ordinary door. In front of the background there was marked off a sacred precinct, apparently bounded by a ledge of natural rock (l. 192 αὐτόπετρον βῆμα), and occupying part of the space available for the actors. There is a seat of rock within the precinct (ll. 16–19), and another on or in front of the ledge, where Oedipus afterwards sits ἐπ᾽ ἄκρου λάου (195–6). At ll. 113–14 Oedipus hides in the grove (i.e., probably, leaves by the door in the background), and perhaps he and Theseus leave by the same way at l. 1555. The early scenes, in which the chorus rush threateningly upon Oedipus, and the scene in which they defend Oedipus and Antigone against Creon (ll. 826, &c.) could hardly have been possible with a raised stage.

5. It appears, therefore, that the plays of Sophocles demand nothing essentially but a plain background with a single central opening, the necessary effects being produced by scene-painting and quite simple structural adaptations. It is very doubtful whether he ever made use of the roof for the appearance of gods or of any such machinery as was employed by both Aeschylus and Euripides. He may have been more sensitive than they to the least improbability or absurdity, such as these devices evidently suggested to some spectators, and among others to Aristophanes, and he probably felt that such things interfered with the austere and harmonious perfection of the play as a work of art.[2]

[1] See Flickinger, *Greek Theater*[4], Appendix, p. 362. Pollux iv. 132 says αἱ δὲ Χαρώνιοι κλίμακες κατὰ τὰς ἐκ τῶν ἑδωλίων καθόδους κείμεναι τὰ εἴδωλα ἀπ᾽ αὐτῶν ἀναπέμπουσιν. The words κατὰ τὰς . . . καθόδους are illustrated by the remains at Segesta, but not elsewhere. See below, pp. 65, 146, 210.

[2] The fragments of the lost plays of Sophocles throw little light on the theatre. Evidently a large number of the plays were performed before a palace-front, and a few (e.g. the *Ajax Locrus* and the *Palamedes*) in a military camp. The *Peleus* perhaps had a cave as the central feature of the background, and in the *Polyxena* the tomb of Achilles may have been presented. (See Pearson, op. cit., ii, p. 163.)

C. EURIPIDES

1. The greater number of the extant plays of Euripides, and of the lost plays about which there is sufficient information, require for their background the front of a palace or house, viz. the *Alcestis, Medea, Hippolytus, Andromache, Hercules Furens, Electra, Helena, Phoenissae, Orestes,* and *Bacchae*; the imperfect *Hypsipyle,* and the lost *Melanippe Sophe, Melanippe Desmotis, Stheneboia, Alexandros, Phaethon,* and probably others. The palace may have statues in front of it, as in the *Hippolytus* (where the images of Aphrodite and Artemis stood before the house), or a tomb, such as the tomb of Proteus in the *Helena,* or an altar, as in the *Alexandros.*[1] The house in the *Electra* is a workman's cottage and must have been differentiated from the conventional palace by some device of scene-painting or special 'properties'. In the *Andromache* the scene must have included not only the palace of Neoptolemus (ll. 21, 43, 433), but also the shrine of Thetis, at whose altar (l. 162) Andromache takes sanctuary. The supposition that the shrine occupied one of the paraskenia, assuming that they were there, implies that the action for 410 lines took place on one side of the orchestra, and not centrally; possibly the palace and the shrine stood side by side. The play was not acted at Athens, and the theatre need not have conformed to the conventional Athenian scenic arrangements.

In several plays it is clear that there was not only a central door, but entrances at the sides to the guest-chambers or the women's quarters, e.g. in the *Alcestis* (ll. 543–6) and *Helena* (ll. 1180–4). In the *Bacchae* there were on one side of the palace the remains of Semele's dwelling and her grave (ll. 7–12, 597), from which fire and smoke shot up, and on the other side, probably, the stables in which Dionysus was confined (l. 509).

It seems likely that a palace-front with three entrances was normal in Euripides' plays, and that two of these entrances (or possibly two supplementary entrances) were often in paraskenia projecting forward on either side.[2] This is strongly suggested (e.g.) by the phrase used in *Alcestis* 546, δωμάτων ἐξωπίους

---

[1] See *New Chapters in Gk. Lit.* iii, pp. 140 ff.

[2] For the possible use of paraskenia in Aeschylus, see above, pp. 40–4. See also pp. 24, 169 for the existence of structures called paraskenia in the fourth century, though this proves nothing as to their use (or the use of the name) in the fifth.

ξενῶνας, and it is at least a probable view of the difficult scene in the *Orestes* in which the Phrygian appears, that it is upon, or through, the top of the paraskenion that he shows himself (ll. 1369–72), and that he scrambles down thence to the ground πρὸ δωμάτων, where he clearly is when he is entreating Orestes (l. 1507).[1] More than one passage of Euripides emphasizes the height of the palace and the magnificence of its portal,[2] but it is not certain that these were presented to the eye in the theatre.

2. In four plays—the *Herakleidai*, *Suppliants*, *Ion*, and *Iphigeneia in Tauris*—the scene is laid in front of a temple. In the *Herakleidai* an altar of Zeus Ἀγοραῖος stood before the temple, and its steps must have been wide enough to accommodate a large group of suppliants. In the *Suppliants* there was the altar of Demeter and Koré. The question whether a columned portico formed part of the scenery, whether of palace or temple, in Euripides' plays, must be postponed to the next chapter.

In four other plays—the *Hecuba*, *Troades*, *Iphigeneia in Aulis*, and *Rhesus* (though the last is probably not Euripidean)— the background required consists of one or more military huts or tents, and these could be provided either by a continuous background with several doors or, more conveniently, by a central wall and door and two paraskenia.

The scene of the *Andromeda* and the *Philoctetes* (both lost) was the sea-shore, the background being painted to represent a cliff, with the rock in front of which Andromeda was chained[3] or the

---

[1] The Phrygian cries (ll. 1369 ff.) πέφευγα . . . κεδρωτὰ παστάδων ὑπὲρ τέραμνα | Δωρικάς τε τριγλύφους. The explanation suggested assumes the spuriousness of ll. 1366–9, which the scholiast asserts to have been introduced by actors who shrank from these dangerous acrobatics and preferred to enter by the door (see Page, *Actors' Interpolations*, p. 42). In *Iph. Taur.* 113 the spaces between triglyphs are regarded as a possible way of entrance, so why not of exit for the Phrygian? If ll. 1366–9, implying entrance by the door, are kept, ὑπέρ in l. 1371 will have to mean 'beyond', 'passing out of' the columned chamber of the women, with its Doric triglyphs; but this is a very doubtful possibility.

[2] *Helena* 431, πύλαι σεμναί: *Herc. Fur.* 107 ὑψόροφα μέλαθρα and 1029, ὑψιπύλων δόμων: cf. the description of the temple in *Iph. Taur.* 96 ἀμφίβληστρα γὰρ τοίχων ὁρᾷς | ὑψηλά.

[3] In vase-paintings she is sometimes represented as bound to two posts or pillars, which Engelmann (*Archäol. Stud.*, pp. 8 and 9) thinks are the columns of the proskenion. This is most unlikely, and it is quite uncertain whether the vases in question depend at all directly on the theatre. Robert (*Arch. Ztg.* xxxvi, p. 17) and Bethe (*Proleg.*, p. 193) think that the scene in the *Andromeda*

cave of *Philoctetes*. A cave—the abode of a shepherd—in country scenery was central in the *Antiope*,[1] and in the satyric *Cyclops* the chief feature was the cave of the Cyclops. The scene of the *Peirithous* (though this was probably the work of Critias[2]) was in Hades; the background may have been either the palace of Pluto or a cliff, to one of the rocks of which Peirithous was fastened.

3. What seems to emerge from this survey is the probability that there were available for the poet certain stock sets of wooden and canvas scenery, representing a palace or a temple, with a central door, and, when required, two side doors, and that he also made use of entrances in the paraskenia, the convenience and aesthetic advantages of which would be such that once used they are not likely to have been discarded. A third set, with a cave in the centre of the background, whether by the sea or in a rustic setting, will have been available both for tragedy and for satyric drama, which frequently requires the cave. The art of scene-painting no doubt developed as the fifth century went on, and the stock sets could easily have been adapted for particular plays.

4. It cannot be certainly decided whether the contrivances for the appearances of gods in any way modified the conventional form of palace or temple for stage purposes. The house itself, in tragedy as in comedy,[3] seems to have consisted of a lower story with a flat roof, upon which there was set a slightly smaller upper story (*Phoenissae*, l. 90 μελάθρων διῆρες ἔσχατον),[4] to which, at some time or other, the name διστεγία was attached, though the name seems sometimes to apply simply to the flat roof.[5] (The scene on the roof in the *Orestes* must have required considerable space.) It is clear that where a god speaks the prologue he

may have been laid before the palace of Kepheus; but Perseus was shown flying through the air in the play, and it seems more likely that he flew straight to the rock. The scene from the *Andromeda* is one of those for which the use of a curtain is imagined by some scholars, who think that Andromeda could not have been tied up in full view of the audience before the play opened. It may be doubted whether ancient audiences were so sensitive. See pp. 41, 51, 80, 123, 129–30, 194.

¹ See *New Chapters in Gk. Lit.* iii, pp. 106 ff.   ² Ibid., pp. 148 ff.
³ See below, pp. 60–4.   ⁴ Cf. Plato Com. fr. 112 K τὸ διῆρες ὑπερῷον.
⁵ Pollux iv. 129 ἡ διστεγία ποτὲ μὲν ἐν οἴκῳ βασιλείῳ διῆρες δωμάτιον, οἷον ἀφ᾽ οὗ ἐν Φοινίσσαις ἡ Ἀντιγόνη βλέπει τὸν στρατόν, ποτὲ δὲ καὶ κέραμος, ἀφ᾽ οὗ βάλλουσι τῷ κεράμῳ· ἐν δὲ κωμῳδίᾳ ἀπὸ τῆς διστεγίας πορνοβοσκοί τι κατοπτεύουσιν ἢ γράδια ἢ γύναια καταβλέπει. For the question as it affects Aeschylus see above, p. 46.

normally appears on the same level as ordinary human personages.[1] But for the appearances of gods at the end of the play,
Pollux and the scholiasts mention two devices, the θεολογεῖον
and the μηχανή. The former is described as 'high up, above the
skené',[2] and it may either have been the roof of the second story
or a special platform above this, but probably concealed by a
gable or parapet (or, in a temple scene, by the pediment). It
seems to have been employed in the *Hercules Furens* (ll. 816–17)
for the appearance in a chariot of Iris and Lyssa. In the *Hippolytus* in 428 B.C., the *Helena* in 412 B.C., the *Suppliants*, and the
Iphigeneia in Tauris there is no indication of the place of the
god's appearance, but Bethe may be right in thinking that unless
the μηχανή was employed, appearance above the roof was conventional.[3] The *Suppliants* (987 ff., 1054 ff.) requires an erection
representing a rock, rising above the house, from which Evadne
takes her plunge, but this cannot have been the same thing as
a θεολογεῖον and must have been specially devised. In the
Medea also the heroine probably appeared on a tower rising
above the roof, as the scholiast states, but the question is complicated, and the use of the μηχανή cannot be absolutely ruled
out.[4] Medea's address to those coming out of the palace (ll.
1317 ff.) would be most effective if the tower were above one of
the paraskenia. In the *Orestes* a whole scene was enacted by four
persons on the roof of the palace, and when Apollo appears at
l. 1625, it is at a greater height—riding on a μηχανή more probably

---

[1] See *Alcestis* 22, 23, 29; *Hippolyt.* 51 ff.; *Ion* 76; *Troad.* 57. Bethe's arguments to the contrary (*Proleg.*, pp. 131–3) are very unconvincing, and he does
not even notice the line in the *Troades* (Τροίας οὕνεκ', ἔνθα βαίνομεν) which is
really decisive against his idea that the prologue is in Heaven.

[2] Pollux iv. 130, quoted above, p. 46.

[3] A vase-painting described in the next chapter (p. 82, Fig. 9), depicting the
madness of Lycurgus, shows above the pediment at the right-hand corner the
upper part of a veiled female figure, who is conjectured to be Lyssa. (In other
vases presenting the same subject the personification of madness is a flying
figure aiming a dart at Lycurgus.) But as no direct connexion with the theatre
can be asserted of this vase (such as the theatrical costume on some other
Lycurgus vases), it can hardly be used as it is, e.g. by Frickenhaus, to illustrate
the theologeion.

[4] Bethe's argument that Medea cannot have appeared upon a height because
such arrangements are only found later (*Proleg.*, pp. 147 ff.) is obviously a
petitio principii. There is no serious reason for contradicting the schol. on l. 1317,
ἄνω ἐπὶ τοῦ πύργου ἑστῶσα ταῦτα λέγει, and on l. 1320, ἐπὶ ὕψους γὰρ παραφαίνεται

than standing on a raised θεολογεῖον. If ll. 1631–2 are genuine,[1] there is no doubt about it—ἥδ' ἐστίν, ἣν ὁρᾶτ' ἐν αἰθέρος πτυχαῖς | σεσωσμένη τε κοὐ θανοῦσα πρὸς σέθεν—but even if they are not, and whether or not Helen is with Apollo, the general probability is strong.

The use of the μηχανή in the *Bellerophontes* (before 425 B.C.) is certain from the allusions in Aristophanes' *Peace*, ll. 135, 146. It was also clearly used for the appearance of Thetis in the *Andromache*, and perhaps it landed her on the ground (ll. 1228 ff. δαίμων ὅδε τις λευκὴν αἰθέρα | πορθμευόμενος τῶν ἱπποβότων | Φθίας πεδίων ἐπιβαίνει) instead of keeping her suspended.[2] In the *Ion* (l. 1549 οἴκων θυοδόκων ὑπερτελής) and the *Electra* (ll. 1233–7, especially οὐ γὰρ θνητῶν γ' ἥδε κέλευθος) the language suggests motion through the air on the μηχανή rather than a stationary platform on the roof, and so does that of the *Rhesus* (ll. 886–8 τίς ὑπὲρ κεφαλῆς θεός, ὦ βασιλεῦ, | τὸν νεόκμητον νεκρὸν ἐν χειροῖν | φοράδην πέμπει;).[3]

It appears, therefore, that Euripides employed very freely the devices of the θεολογεῖον (however it was actually constructed) and the μηχανή, which had been experimentally introduced by Aeschylus, but not favoured by Sophocles, and that tolerably substantial supporting structures were required; but the provision of these need have caused no difficulty, and the 'Periclean' reconstruction may have arranged for this.[4]

ἡ Μήδεια, ὀχουμένη δρακοντίνοις ἅρμασι καὶ βαστάζουσα τοὺς παῖδας. Aristotle, *Poet.* xv μὴ ὥσπερ ἐν τῇ Μηδείᾳ διὰ μηχανῆς may not be referring to the play of Euripides. There were many different treatments of the story, as vases show. (See Page's edition, Introdn.)

[1] Some edd. bracket the lines because the words ἐν αἰθέρος πτυχαῖς recur in l. 1636; but cf. the repetitions in ll. 1579 and 1587 (and several in Aeschylus). Murray's objection, that ll. 1683–4 show that Helen is not yet in heaven, fails, if ἐν αἰθέρος πτυχαῖς means 'high in air' in 1631 and 1636 (though not at the same height in each place). The phrase used in l. 1574 of Apollo's appearance is δόμων ἐπ' ἄκρων, and it is not agreed whether this means the same as δόμων ὑπὲρ ἀκροτάτων in *Electra*, 1233. Possibly he descended on the μηχανή till his feet touched the roof.

[2] Whether Okeanos in the *Prometheus* was similarly landed is less certain (see above, p. 40). But Trygaeus in the *Peace* certainly was (see pp. 61–2).

[3] According to Pollux, iv. 128, the μηχανή was placed by the 'left' entrance: ἡ μηχανὴ δὲ θεοὺς δείκνυσι καὶ ἥρως τοὺς ἐν ἀέρι, Βελλεροφόντας ἢ Περσέας, καὶ κεῖται κατὰ τὴν ἀριστερὰν πάροδον, ὑπὲρ τὴν σκηνὴν τὸ ὕψος. It is not easy, however, to extract a very clear picture from his words, and we cannot tell of what theatres he is speaking.　　　[4] See Bulle, *Untersuch.*, p. 215.

5. There are many scenes in Euripides' plays which tell strongly against the old theory that they were performed by actors mounted on a raised stage. For instance, in the *Hecuba* at l. 59, Hecuba comes out of her tent in great physical distress, supported by the chorus. At what point did the chorus run downstairs and leave her planted on the stage? In the *Hercules Furens* the hero finds Amphitryon and Megara surrounded by the chorus at l. 527, and later (l. 1172) Theseus asks τί νεκρῶν τῶνδε πληθύει πέδον;— an expression hardly possible if the corpses were raised on a height, for πέδον is most naturally used of the ground level. In the *Ion* the chorus stand about the temple steps (ἀμφὶ κρηπῖδας δόμων θυοδόκων, l. 510), and in the lost *Phaëthon* they entered the orchestra from the palace, as they must generally have done when the chorus consisted of servants of the royal house. In the *Hippolytus* the supplementary chorus of huntsmen enters the palace (l. 108) with Hippolytus; and similarly in the *Helena* free movement is required between chorus, actors, and palace. The chorus enter the palace with Helen at l. 385 (as had been arranged ll. 327 ff.) and return at l. 515, full of the prophecy of Theonoë which they had heard within, and at l. 1627 the chorus supplicate Theoklymenos, not from a lower level, but by clinging to his robes. There are similar supplications in other plays,[1] and in the *Iphigeneia in Tauris* (1068 ff.) Iphigeneia entreats each member of the chorus individually, and must have been on the same level (ἀλλὰ πρός σε δεξιᾶς | σὲ καὶ σ' ἱκνοῦμαι, σὲ δὲ φίλης παρηίδος | γονάτων τε, κτλ). In the *Rhesus* (at l. 684) Odysseus demands the watchword from the chorus at the spear-point, and if, as is highly probable, this was a fourth-century play, the evidence for the absence of a raised stage is carried down to a later date than that of Euripides.

6. The hypothesis of a raised stage has sometimes been supported by reference to certain passages in Euripides, and one in Aristophanes, in which a chorus of old men, or an aged character in the play, complains of the steepness of the ascent to the temple or the house before which the action takes place. The scenes in which the complaint is made by the chorus are (1) the parodos of the *Hercules Furens*, where the old men are stumbling up with difficulty from the lower town to the palace. Although the words in ll. 120–1, ὥστε πρὸς πετραῖον λέπας, do not compel

---

[1] e.g. *Medea* 583, *Phoenissae* 293, *Supplices* 277.

us to imagine them as actually moving uphill, we are probably intended to do so; but the journey is obviously to be regarded as just completed. (2) Aristophanes' *Lysistrata* 286 ff.,
where the chorus of old men has already sung over 30 lines when
they complain of the last steep bit of the road:

> ἀλλ' αὐτὸ γάρ μοι τῆς ὁδοῦ
> λοιπόν ἐστι χωρίον
> τὸ πρὸς πόλιν, τὸ σιμόν, οἷ σπουδὴν ἔχω·
> χὤπως ποτ' ἐξαμπρεύσομεν
> τοῦτ' ἄνευ κανθηλίου.

Again the chorus are just finishing their climb. In both plays
the illusion would be helped if (as is practically certain) the
πάροδοι sloped slightly upwards into the orchestra.[1] The two
choruses may well have begun singing while ascending these
slopes, as soon as the leaders were in view of the audience. But
in any case they were only coming into the *orchestra*, and the
passages are chiefly important as showing that complaints about
a steep ascent have no necessary reference to a raised *stage*.
Accordingly it is not legitimate to treat the similar passages in
which an actor is the complainant as proof that he was struggling
up to the height of a tall stage. The passages are:

(1) *Ion* 738 ff., where the old servant is being helped along by
Creusa:

> ἕλχ' ἕλκε πρὸς μέλαθρα καὶ κόμιζέ με.
> αἰπεινά τοι μαντεῖα· τοῦ γήρως δέ μοι
> συνεκπονοῦσα κῶλον ἰατρὸς γενοῦ.

But (unless the reference is to the temple steps, which is unlikely,
as probably not more than one or two at most were shown) the
steepness spoken of may be that which the speaker has just got
over.

(2) *Electra* 489 ff., where the old man is making his way up to
Electra's cottage, laden with presents:

> ὡς πρόσβασιν τῶνδ' ὀρθίαν οἴκων ἔχει
> ῥυσῷ γέροντι τῷδε προσβῆναι ποδί.
> ὅμως δὲ πρός γε τοὺς φίλους ἐξελκτέον
> διπλῆν ἄκανθαν καὶ παλίρροπον γόνυ.
> ὦ θύγατερ—ἄρτι γάρ σε πρὸς δόμοις ὁρῶ—
> ἥκω φέρων σοι, κτλ.

---

[1] See the indications of the heights above sea-level of various points in the
theatre in D.R., Taf. I.

But again the old man has almost, if not quite, got over his difficulties when he begins to speak, and the words are intended mainly to emphasize the remote stony situation of Electra's cottage.

(3) *Phoenissae* 834 ff. Teiresias complains of the difficulty of making his way in his blindness, but again it is plain that little, if any, of the path remains to be traversed, and there is nothing in the text which obliges us to think that it was uphill at all.

Accordingly none of these passages gives any support to the theory, which may now be regarded as discredited.

D. ARISTOPHANES

1. The background of the action in comedy normally consisted of one, two, or three houses. A stock set consisting of a building with a central door and two side doors either in the background or in two paraskenia (or both) could obviously be adapted for the purposes of comedy; but comedy may have had its own sets, and, especially while there was no rigid stone framework, adaptations for particular plays would present little difficulty.

Three houses are required in the *Acharnians* and the *Frogs*, as well as in the *Autolycus* of Eupolis (fr. 24 K. οἰκοῦσι δ᾽ ἐνθάδ᾽ ἐν τρισὶν καλιδίοις, | οἴκημ᾽ ἔχων ἕκαστος); two in the *Clouds* and *Ekklesiazousai*; one in the *Knights*, *Wasps*, *Birds*, and *Plutus*. The *Peace*, *Thesmophoriazousai*, and *Lysistrata* require special arrangements, and in some of the other plays certain points require a brief mention. It will be convenient to consider the plays in chronological order.

2. In the *Acharnians* (425 B.C.) the scene opens on the Pnyx, but the background of houses must have been there from the beginning, the benches required as seats on the Pnyx being perhaps removed by the attendants at some time between l. 174 and l. 233—unless they were simply represented by the steps of the houses. There can have been no more elaborate change of scene; the conversation between Dikaiopolis and Amphitheos (ll. 175–203) clearly takes place on the Pnyx, and at l. 202 Dikaiopolis goes into his house through the central doorway in the background. At l. 204 the chorus rush into the orchestra. On either side of the house of Dikaiopolis are those of Euripides (ll. 394 ff.) and Lamachus (ll. 1072, 1174 ff.), whether represented by paraskenia or simply by doors in the background. The attack upon Dikaiopolis

by the chorus at l. 280 shows that he cannot have been on a raised stage, and such a stage is virtually impossible in the whole scene which follows. Some writers suppose that there is an imaginary change of scene (with or without some physical indication of the change) at l. 237, where Dikaiopolis re-enters to celebrate his sham 'Rural Dionysia', and a change back again to Athens at l. 280; but there is no hint in the text of either of these changes, and the continuous presence of the chorus is against the supposition that Aristophanes intended them to be imagined or indicated in any way. At l. 202 Dikaiopolis goes into his house at Athens to prepare for the celebration (ἄξω τὰ κατ' ἀγροὺς εἰσιὼν Διονύσια), and he comes out of *that same* house in procession at l. 237. Lines 266–7 (ἕκτῳ σ' ἔτει προσεῖπον ἐς | τὸν δῆμον ἐλθὼν ἄσμενος) only keep up his game of pretending that he is at home again on his farm, and celebrating the 'Rural Dionysia' as if he were there; the audience are not to suppose that he is really there, but only that he is pretending to be; the celebration is a pretence in which he gives play to his imagination. It takes place in front of his house in Athens, and the procession may have been marching into the orchestra when the chorus make their attack upon it (l. 280).[1]

3. The *Knights* (424 B.C.) is played before the house of Demos in the Agora (l. 147). At l. 751 a move is made to the Pnyx, probably indicated by a number of benches, whether these were at one side or were introduced by the attendants and removed again later, e.g. before l. 1317, after which the scene of the action is left undefined, but may have been supposed to be before the house of Demos again. The significance of the words ἀνάβαινε (l. 149) and ἐπανάβηθι (l. 169) will be discussed later;[2] they do not imply a raised stage.

The *Clouds* (first production 423 B.C.; date of second production uncertain) requires only the houses of Strepsiades and Socrates, one of which may have been in a paraskenion.

The *Wasps* (422 B.C.) was played before the house of Philocleon (or Bdelycleon), but included some play on the roof. The house

---

[1] See Starkie's edition of the play, Appendix IV, for a summary of the views which have been held by scholars on this scene. The dissertation of Fensterbusch, *Die Bühne des Aristophanes* (1912), discusses the staging of all the plays minutely. On the *Acharnians* see also Allen, *Greek Theater*, pp. 71–2; I am unable to agree with his view for the reasons indicated.   [2] p. 69.

had a single doorway and a window above it, and on one side was a lower building containing the kitchen.[1] The scuffle between Bdelycleon's slaves and the chorus (ll. 430–60) seems to imply the absence of any raised stage.

4. The *Peace* (421 B.C.) raises much greater difficulties. There is indeed no difference of opinion as to the imaginary scene of the several actions which the play presents. Down to l. 178 the scene is on earth, before the house of Trygaeus; from 179 to 728 the principal actors are in heaven, in front of the palace of Zeus; at 728 Trygaeus gets to earth again, and the action from 819 onwards (after the parabasis) is once more on earth. The principal difficulties arise out of the participation of the chorus as well as the actors in the middle section of the play.

At the outset we have the house of Trygaeus with its door; at l. 30 the servant opens the door a crack, to see what the monstrous beetle is doing, and at l. 49 he goes inside; at l. 60 the voice of Trygaeus is heard from inside; at l. 78 the other servant peeps in, and immediately Trygaeus is seen rising to heaven on the beetle's back—no doubt from behind the house and on the μηχανή, which had been employed in recent years by Euripides, e.g. in the *Bellerophontes* and the *Andromache*. But where was the house of Zeus, at which Trygaeus is deposited?

The two theories put forward by scholars are (1) that the house of Zeus was represented, and the action from l. 179 onwards took place, on the roof of the stage building, with an upper story or ἐπισκήνιον (or θεολογεῖον, or διστεγία), rising above it to represent the house, and the flat roof serving for the performance of the actors; (2) that the house of Zeus was on the same level as that of Trygaeus, either in a line with it, or (if each house was represented by a paraskenion) on the opposite side of the scene. The problem is complicated by doubts as to the position of the cave into which Peace has been thrown. This is described in ll. 223–4:

> ΕΡΜ. ὁ Πόλεμος αὐτὴν ἐνέβαλ' εἰς ἄντρον βαθύ.
> ΤΡ. ἐς ποῖον; ΕΡΜ. ἐς τουτὶ τὸ κάτω.

Now in hauling Peace out of the cave, the greater part of the work is done by the chorus, who are certainly on earth, while Hermes and Trygaeus direct operations. It would be possible that in l. 225 Hermes should be pointing down from far above to

---

[1] See Wilamowitz, *Kl. Schriften*, i, pp. 299 ff.

a cave on the earth; but in that case it would be difficult to see how Hermes and Trygaeus can themselves take a share in the operations as they certainly do; for at l. 361 Trygaeus says, φέρε δὴ κατίδω ποῖ τοὺς λίθους ἀφέλξομεν (not ἀφέλξετε), and Hermes evidently regards him as about to do something himself. (The clearing away of piles of stones *on the roof* would also be difficult.) Again, at l. 469 the chorus say to Trygaeus ἀλλ᾽ ἄγετε ξυνανέλκετε καὶ σφώ (or whatever the reading is), and Trygaeus replies οὔκουν ἕλκω κἀξαρτῶμαι | κἀπεμπίπτω καὶ σπουδάζω; (There is no hint of the chorus throwing a rope up to Trygaeus, and to suppose that when he says these words he is merely going through the gestures of hauling at a rope in dumb show seems rather extravagant.) Again, if the house of Zeus in front of which Trygaeus stands were really far above, on a higher stage, it is difficult to explain Trygaeus' summons in l. 298, δεῦρ᾽ ἴτ᾽, ὦ πάντες λεώ, for even if the chorus could get there from the orchestra, and even if they could be accommodated on the roof themselves, it is doubtful if there would be room also for all the 'supers' who represented the Greek cities.[1]

The conclusion seems to be irresistible that the house of Zeus is really on the same level as the house of Trygaeus,[2] and that Trygaeus after a tremendous ride on the μηχανή, which may have swung him over a great section of the orchestra, is ultimately dumped down on the opposite side of the scene on the same level as his own house. There is no more difficulty in this than there is in the *Frogs*, in which the house of Heracles on earth and the house of Pluto in Hades are represented on the same level,

---

[1] It is true that scholars are divided on the question whether the chorus, who consisted of γεωργοί from all Greece (Πανέλληνες, l. 302), were assisted by a number of supers representing different states, but it seems most likely that they were. At l. 466 the Boeotians are addressed, at l. 475 the Argives, at l. 478 the Spartans are spoken of as pulling badly, and at l. 481 the Megarians; and at last at l. 508 the γεωργοί, i.e. the chorus proper, resolve to do the work alone. Probably the supers came into the orchestra at l. 302, and apparently they did not clear off at once at l. 508—at least if it is these same representatives of πόλεις to whom Hermes refers at l. 539 as delighted to have Peace at last. They may have disappeared after l. 581. If there were no supers, the γεωργοί must have been one division of the chorus and the πόλεις another division; but at l. 603 and always afterwards the whole chorus are evidently regarded as γεωργοί.

[2] I am not convinced by the arguments of Flickinger to the contrary (*Mélanges Navarre*, pp. 191–205), nor by his treatment of the first half of the play in other respects.

with the communication between them by boat instead of by air, and the absurdity would add to the fun.

If so, there is not much difficulty. We have a house on either side of the skené (or in each paraskenion), and in the intervening space is a heap of stones in front of what on other occasions might be a central door through the background, but is now the mouth of a cave, out of which Peace emerges with Opora and Theoria. How was the *depth* of the cave managed? Either it was not managed, i.e. the illusion was partly sacrificed and Peace simply came out of the background, or advantage may have been taken of the fact that there was a considerable drop in the ground behind the banked-up orchestra terrace, especially on the east side, and the statue was really hauled up from below this bank.[1] At l. 427, εἰσιόντες ὡς τάχιστα τοὺς λίθους ἀφέλκετε, the chorus having already (or having first) pulled away the stones which conceal the mouth of the cave, enter the mouth (i.e. the opening in the background) to clear away the stones which have been piled on the top of the goddess (l. 225 ὅσους ἄνωθεν ἐπεφόρησε τῶν λίθων). (If so, there is no need for the many emendations[2] of εἰσιόντες which have been suggested, and the citation by commentators of the undoubted use of the word to describe actors coming on the scene in many places is irrelevant here; εἰσιέναι is commonly used without any such reference; e.g. in l. 49, of an actor leaving the scene and entering his house through one of the doors provided.) At l. 550 the γεωργοί forming the chorus are bidden to go off εἰς ἀγρόν. They have been close up to the background while hauling up the statue, and ll. 564–5 show that they now draw up in proper formation again (ὡς καλὸν τὸ στῖφος αὐτῶν φαίνεται), and they doubtless go back into the open orchestra, where they dance at l. 582. (Of course they do not actually go off to the country until the end of the play. At l. 819, after the parabasis, they are in front of the house of Trygaeus.)

From l. 658 onwards the statue of Peace has a confidential talk with Hermes, who whispers into her ear, or at least catches her

---

[1] Such phrases as εἰς τὸ φῶς ἀνελκύσαι (307), εἰς φῶς ἀνελθεῖν (444) confirm this, as they are phrases used of rising from the dead (Soph. *Phil.* 621, &c.). (If the hall was already built, there was a considerable drop from the orchestra level to the floor of the hall; see p. 24.)

[2] See Fensterbusch, p. 43, for these—e.g. εἴ ἰόντες (Herwerden and Bachmann), εἶα πάντες (Kock), εἶ ἄπαντες (Sharpley).

whispers with his ear. This presents no difficulty on the view of the staging here offered. But on the other view, if the cave, and therefore the statue, are on earth, and Hermes is far above, there would be great difficulty; so that some scholars are driven to assume a statue so colossal that its head reached up to the higher story, representing heaven, and so could be whispered to by Hermes. This is almost too grotesque, and there is not the faintest hint of it in the text. The idea that the statue was a colossal one comes not from the text, but from the scholiast on Plato, *Apol.* 19 c κωμῳδεῖται δὲ (sc. Aristophanes) ὅτι καὶ τὸ τῆς Εἰρήνης κολοσσικὸν ἐξῆρεν ἄγαλμα. Εὔπολις Αὐτολύκῳ. Πλάτων Νίκαις. The authority of the scholiast is very weak compared with the evidence of the play, and we do not even know that this play is referred to, as Aristophanes composed a number of plays turning on the subject of peace, including an earlier Εἰρήνη.

Ultimately, at l. 720, Trygaeus wants to return to earth (where he has really been all the time). The beetle has disappeared (no doubt it had been drawn into the door of the house of Zeus). He asks Hermes (725) πῶς δῆτ' ἐγὼ καταβήσομαι; and Hermes says 'that's easy enough, τῃδὶ παρ' αὐτὴν τὴν θεόν—just step here, *past the goddess*'—in other words, 'walk across the scene and out by the parodos', and so he goes out, taking Opora and Theoria with him.

When the action reopens (819) we are once more on earth; the statue of Peace has remained where it was—opposite the central opening, but is now made the subject of an inaugural ceremony and feast (l. 923) τί δ' ἄλλο γ' ἢ ταύτην χύτραις ἱδρυτέον; for which an altar is brought out (l. 938), and Peace with the altar are now the central spot for the rest of the play.

This account of the scenic arrangements seems to meet all the requirements of the text. Two rival theories, which have had some vogue in England, must be rejected. Merry, in the introduction to his edition, gives a scheme based on the assumption, now almost universally discarded, that the theatre of Dionysus in the fifth century B.C. had a raised stage. He quite rightly rejects the notion that Trygaeus and Hermes are mounted on a theologeion or distegia during the middle section of the play, and in a good many points his account tallies with that just given; all that is needed is the elimination of the idea that the two houses stand on a raised stage. This idea misleads him into thinking that εἰσιόντες in l. 427 can mean ἀναβαίνοντες, 'mounting the stage'. He thinks that the statue was drawn up out of a trap-door in the stage, and if there *was* a stage this would be the obvious thing; but it is not necessary, as we have seen. His difficulty in finding room on the stage for the chorus and supers of course disappears if there was no stage. It may be added that Merry can hardly be right in supposing that the statue was hauled up with the help of the μηχανή. The indications in the text are perfectly clear—that it was done by human labour, and there is no difficulty about this.

The other theory is that of Sharpley, who thinks that the cave was in the orchestra. He connects this with the existence in the theatre at Eretria of an underground chamber in the orchestra, with a passage leading back under the stage building. Something of the kind appears to have been found in one or two other theatres, and some brief remarks on these chambers will be found elsewhere in this book.[1] Here it need only be repeated that there is no trace of any such arrangement in the theatre at Athens, with which alone we are here concerned, and that it is probable that even at Eretria the arrangement does not go back to the fifth century. Sharpley combines this with the theory of a colossal statue. But there would be no room for such a statue in the subterranean passage at Eretria, and it would certainly require powerful machinery to extract it from a passage or chamber of the Eretrian type.

5. In the *Birds* (414 B.C.) the background is a rock, in the centre of which is the door of the house of Epops, entered by Peithetaerus at l. 675, and in front of the rock (or of some part of it) is a thicket (λόχμη), which must have been represented by scene-painting or some simple symbols; possibly the greater part of the background may have been provided by screens or canvas so painted as to represent wild country, as in a satyric play.

6. The scene of the *Lysistrata* (411 B.C.) is laid in front of the propylaea of the Acropolis, the columns of which, with the central entrance and the flanking rock-walls, doubtless formed the background. The entrance is open until l. 245, when Lysistrata goes in to assist in barring it. Afterwards it is opened when required for the passage of the actors, and in the last scenes probably remains open. The only question in dispute is whether there was also a representation of the houses of Lysistrata and Kalonike.

[1] See pp. 51, 146, and 210.

At l. 5 Lysistrata, impatiently waiting for her supporters, sees Kalonike 'coming out' (ἐξέρχεται). She might indeed be coming out of the propylaea, but it would be equally possible for her to come out of, e.g., one of the paraskenia. At l. 199 Lysistrata says φερέτω κύλικά τις ἔνδοθεν καὶ σταμνίον. These are not objects which one would naturally fetch out of the Acropolis, and it is easy to suppose that the other paraskenion represented the house of Lysistrata. (She and Kalonike are neighbours—l. 5 ἡ ἐμὴ κωμῆτις.) The question must probably be left open. In a later scene (at ll. 916, 921, 926, 933, 938) Myrrhine fetches out various articles—a couch, mat, cushion, blanket, and flask; but there is less difficulty in the idea of fetching such things from inside the Acropolis when a large body of women were already encamped there (as they were from l. 241 onwards). Some[1] may prefer the simple solution that the incongruity of bringing all the articles mentioned out of the citadel did not worry either Aristophanes or his audience, and that the Acropolis alone, without any houses, formed the background; but if there were paraskenia, Aristophanes may well have made use of them in his early scenes. In the early part of the scene which begins at l. 829, Lysistrata and Myrrhine speak from the roof, i.e. the top of the rock.

7. The *Thesmophoriazousai* requires the Thesmophorion as its background, together with the house of Agathon in the opening scene—possibly represented by one of the paraskenia. The walled precinct of the Thesmophorion had probably a central entrance, through which, at about l. 278, an altar was brought forward, but it will be more convenient to discuss this in the next chapter, in connexion with the problem of the ἐκκύκλημα. The Thesmophorion no doubt stood on a basis of steps, and this may explain ἀνῆλθεν in l. 893, and ἀναπέμψαι in ll. 585, 1045, though these expressions may merely refer to the position of the Thesmophorion on the slopes of the Pnyx (cf. l. 657 καὶ περιθρέξαι τὴν πύκνα πᾶσαν): cf. Hesychius s.v. 'ἄνοδος'· ἀνάβασις · ἡ ἑνδεκάτη τοῦ Πυανεψιῶνος, ὅτε αἱ γυναῖκες ἀνέρχονται εἰς Θεσμοφόρια. The Herald doubtless came out of the Thesmophorion at about l. 280, while the chorus and other women streamed up from the parodoi and took their places for the Assembly in front of the sacred precinct.

8. In the *Frogs* (405 B.C.) the centre of the background is

---

[1] With Fensterbusch, op. cit., pp. 29 ff.

occupied by the house of Pluto, before which most of the action
is played—from l. 460 onwards. (At what point Pluto himself
appeared is uncertain. He first speaks at l. 1414; perhaps the
doors of his palace are rolled back at l. 1378 and reveal him
enthroned, or he may have been present throughout the trial
scene.) Some scholars[1] think that in the opening scene of the
play this same part of the background served as the house of
Herakles, which Dionysus and Xanthias approach through the
orchestra; but it seems more likely that Herakles was lodged in
one of the paraskenia, and that this was matched on the other
side of the orchestra by the house of the Innkeeper. Charon's
boat enters by one parodos, picks up Dionysus, rows (or is rolled)
across the orchestra and out by the other parodos.

9. The *Ekklesiazousai* (about 392 B.C.) requires two houses,
though their occupants are not the same throughout the play.
From l. 1 to l. 729 they are the houses of Blepyrus and a neighbour, who perhaps speaks out of the window, drops out of the
conversation at l. 357, and breaks in again, also speaking from the
window, at 568. From ll. 730 to 876 the dialogue is that of two
men in the street in front of the houses. From ll. 877 to 1111 the
houses are those of an Old Woman and a Young Courtesan, of
whom the former certainly, and the latter probably, display
themselves on the flat roof surrounding the upper story, which
(as in other plays) is slightly smaller than the lower. (So in the
Acharnians the wife of Dikaiopolis watches the 'Rural Dionysia'
from the roof, and Pollux iv. 129 notices that in comedy ἀπὸ τῆς
διστεγίας πορνοβοσκοί τι κατοπτεύουσιν ἢ γρᾴδια ἢ γύναια καταβλέπει. Cf. also the dialogue of Antigone and the Old Servant
on the roof in the *Phoenissae*.[2]) The change in the ownership of
the two houses at l. 876 is made easier[3] by the choral dance which
occurred at that point. The words, if there were any, were not
preserved. From l. 1111 onwards the action is in the street, and
it makes no difference who are the occupants of the houses in the
background. The words of the invitation in l. 1114, ὑμεῖς θ' ὅσαι

---

[1] e.g. Reisch in D.R., p. 213.

[2] See especially E. Fraenkel, in *Greek Poetry and Life*, pp. 257 ff., and Radermacher, *Beiträge*, pp. 3, 4. The same scenic structure is implied in Plato fr. 112 K,
ὁρᾶτε τὸ διῆρες ὑπερῷον. See above, p. 54.

[3] It is in any case no more difficult than the change in the ownership of the
temple in the *Eumenides*.

παρέστατ' ἐπὶ ταῖσιν θύραις would be unnatural if there were a raised stage.

In the *Plutus* (388 B.C.) the action begins in the orchestra, and before l. 323 the travellers reach the house of Chremylus, before which the rest of the play is acted.

SUMMARY

1. The evidence of the extant plays, taken as a whole, points to the use, except in the very earliest plays, of a wooden stage building, which, during the greater part of the fifth century, might, and perhaps usually did, have an upper story, upon which speeches could be made and some restricted dramatic action carried through, as for instance in the *Prometheus*, *Agamemnon*, and *Psychostasia* of Aeschylus, and the *Hercules Furens*, *Orestes*, and *Phoenissae* of Euripides. (It is doubtful whether any speaker in Sophocles' plays appeared in this position.) Action on the roof was common in comedy, and it is probable that both in tragedy and comedy the upper story did not occupy the whole of the roof of the lower, but left room for a certain amount of action. It seems most likely that, while the main entrance to the stage building was naturally in the centre, the two side entrances, which are required in a number of plays, were or might be included in projecting side-wings or paraskenia, though, in default of any remains, it can only be conjectured what was the structure and size of these wings. The background most often represented a palace or a temple, or one, two, or three houses, and admitted of a good deal of adaptation; it might sometimes represent a cliff with a central cave, and when scene-painting was introduced it could be applied to suggest a grove or wooded country. In some plays at least, broad steps in front of the building seem to be required, carrying one or more altars, and such steps may have been regular where a palace or a temple was presented. During a considerable part of the century, mechanical devices—μηχανή or γέρανος—were used for the appearances of divine beings and for flights through the air, such as those of Bellerophon, Perseus (in the *Andromeda* of Euripides), and Trygaeus.[1] That many of the requirements of the plays may have been met by stock sets has

---

[1] Pollux iv. 128 says that the κράδη in comedy corresponded to the μηχανή in tragedy, but we do not know how they differed or of what period he is speaking. See below, p. 127.

already been suggested, and that the Periclean reconstruction had such stock sets in view when it provided sockets for posts in the terrace wall (and probably also in front of it) is more than probable. Obviously the wooden scenic buildings thus provided would serve as green-rooms for the actors, and also for the chorus in plays in which the chorus entered the orchestra from the house or temple, as they often did; but when the chorus entered from outside (e.g. by the parodoi), they would probably require dressing-rooms at convenient spots in the line of the parodoi; and in fact Aristophanes refers in the *Peace*[1] to these σκηναί, in which the chorus left their things and often returned to find them stolen by thieves who habitually hung about them.

2. It has become clear in our consideration of individual plays that the old theory, maintained in different forms by nearly all scholars till towards the end of the nineteenth century and by some even later, that the dramatic actors of the fifth century performed on a raised stage, is untenable. There are no scenes in extant plays which require a raised stage and could not be acted without it; there are many in which the action would have been ruined or impossible with such a stage. Had there been one, the poets would not have composed so many scenes requiring free access between actors and chorus. The use of expressions such as ἀναβαίνειν and καταβαίνειν[2] of the entrance and exit of actors is sufficiently accounted for in every case by the fact that the parodoi sloped upwards to the orchestra level, so that the words came to be used as technical terms for coming on to the scene or going off. (If there were one or more broad steps in front of the background, it would reinforce this explanation, but they are not required for the purpose.) The passages in which speakers complain of a steep ascent have already been shown[3] to lend no support to the old theory.

3. It should be added that while there is no archaeological

---

[1] l. 731.

[2] In *Acharn.* 732 and *Knights* 149 the persons who are bidden ἀναβαίνειν have not yet reached the orchestra level but are coming up the parodoi. For ἀνάβαινε in *Wasps* 1342, see Starkie's note ad loc.: but the gestures and pose of the actors at the moment probably afforded the explanation. In *Wasps* 1514 καταβαίνειν, as Starkie says, means *in certamen descendere* as it does in Herodotus v. 22, and in *Ekkl.* 1152 it refers to exit by the parodos.

[3] See pp. 57–9. The whole case against a raised stage, so far as it is based on the plays, is very thoroughly argued by Reisch in D.R., pp. 180–93.

evidence in the Athenian theatre itself which can be used in regard to the question of a raised stage in the fifth century, there is one small, but perhaps significant, piece of evidence from a theatre which may well have been strongly influenced by the Athenian—that of Eretria. This, in its first state, included a *scaenae frons* with the doors opening on to the orchestra level, and paraskenia projecting from it on either side, also with openings on to the orchestra. Between the front corners of the two paraskenia are traces of a layer of clay and stones (connecting the two corners); this, it is considered, must have been a foundation for wooden beams, and probably the whole space enclosed by the paraskenia and the *scaenae frons* was covered with boards laid upon beams which raised it by one low step (and no more) above the orchestra level. This was not of course a 'raised stage' in the sense under discussion, but merely afforded the actors a standing ground, acoustically and otherwise more convenient than the beaten earth of the orchestra a few inches below it. This arrangement would be very like that which some plays have suggested to us as probable in Athens itself, and could in no way interrupt the free intercommunication of actors and chorus. The three doors in the *scaenae frons* at Eretria are also evidence that the action was on the ground level (or practically so); they would have been redundant as entrances to a hyposkenion or chamber below a raised stage.[1]

4. The argument which seems to have appealed most strongly to the advocates of the raised stage, both in England and in Germany, is the belief that without a raised stage the actors would have been confused in the spectators' view with the chorus. Now, apart from the very striking differences in costume between actors and chorus, this is largely a matter of practice in stage management and efficient rehearsal; and in a performance of the *Rhesus* many years ago in the gardens of New College, Oxford, in which the spectators had not even the advantage of raised seats,

---

[1] See Bulle's account of the theatre at Eretria in his *Untersuchungen*, pp. 81 ff., and Fiechter's monograph on that theatre; and below, pp. 198–200. For the date see pp. 23, 198–9. Bulle and Fiechter place it in the last third of the fifth century, but it may well be half a century or more later. The south Italian vases described in the Appendix to Ch. IV show that tragedy in south Italy in the fourth century did not employ a raised stage, but inferences from Magna Graecia to Athens are not always safe.

they had not the least difficulty from start to finish in keeping the actors quite distinct from the chorus; and for those who saw the performance this little piece of experience is not cancelled by all the elaborate mathematical diagrams of *Sehverhältnisse* which are presented to prove the impossibility of seeing what in fact we did see perfectly well.

5. When and why the use of a raised stage became regular is a matter for later discussion, but one or two considerations may make it easier to understand why there should have been no such stage in the fifth century. Tragedy in Athens began as the ritual dance of a chorus in the level orchestra, nor would it be natural to erect a stage simply because either a member of the chorus detached himself from the rest and entered into conversation with them, or else an outsider, a single actor, appeared, answered their questions, and held dialogue with them. If for any reason any such need was felt on a particular occasion, there was the altar on its base or step, or the sacrificial table which stood near it, though the statement of Pollux that such an ἐλεός was used for this purpose in the days before Thespis is open to objections.[1] Further, even the introduction of a second and a third actor would not make the introduction of a stage natural, so long as tragedy remained essentially a ritual, and so long as, for the due performance of the ritual, the essential element was the chorus which originally executed it. A separate and elevated stage for the actors would not naturally come in until the performance became more entertainment than ritual. A stage implies that it is no longer the chorus, with its ritual solemnity and its prophetic function, as embodying the spirit and soul of the poets' teaching, that is the main interest of the audience, but the actors and their histrionic skill. This transference of interest from religion to technique happened in Athens, or began to happen, as Aristotle tells us,[2] in the fourth century, and there is ample confirmation. Then the chorus lost ground; it had indeed begun to do so with Euripides and Agathon, but now, for dramatic purposes, it largely disappeared or only sang *intermezzi* unconnected with the action,

[1] Cf. *Dith. Trag. Com.*, pp. 118 ff.
[2] *Rhet.* III. i. There was a similar decline from an original purpose—a passage from religion to technique or entertainment—when Christian congregations began to go to church, not to receive religious inspiration or teaching, but to listen to a 'fine' sermon and sing popular tunes.

and did not need to come into contact with the actors (as it constantly did in the fifth century), so that the physical separation from them did not matter. Even so it may have been (and probably was) a considerable time before the Athenians took the significant step of erecting a permanent stage on stone supports; this may have been the more readily done when the theatre came to be frequently used for meetings of the Assembly, instead of the Pnyx, or for competitions of soloists, instead of the Odeum.[1]

6. Two passages in ancient authors are still sometimes quoted in defence of the view that there was a raised stage in the Athenian theatre in the fifth century B.C.

(1) Horace, *Ars Poet.* 278–80.

> post hunc personae pallaeque repertor honestae
> Aeschylus et modicis instravit pulpita tignis
> et docuit magnumque loqui nitique cothurno.

On the common assumption that the reference in the second of these lines is to a raised stage, the historical value of the passage is indicated by the fact that the mask and the high-soled cothurnus are also ascribed to Aeschylus, who certainly was *not* the first to use either of these. The lines with regard to Thespis which precede these are also of doubtful accuracy. Dörpfeld can hardly be right (D.R., pp. 32, 348) in treating *pulpita* as = σκηνή or stage buildings; it must mean 'stage'; but it is far from certain that *tignis* means 'uprights', though it does so in Caesar, *B.G.* IV. xvii. 3; and it is probable that Horace is saying that Aeschylus 'laid a stage over beams of moderate *length*' and has nothing more in mind than the contrast between the much larger stages of Roman theatres, and the more modest beginnings which he assumes Aeschylus to have made. But the Greek theatres of his own day had a raised stage, and he may have assumed that those of the fifth century also had—a conclusion which the extant plays do not support.

(2) Plato, *Sympos.* 192 b. ἐπιλήσμων μεντἂν εἴην, ὦ Ἀγάθων . . . εἰ ἰδὼν τὴν σὴν ἀνδρείαν καὶ μεγαλοφροσύνην ἀναβαίνοντος ἐπὶ τὸν ὀκρίβαντα μετὰ τῶν ὑποκριτῶν, καὶ βλέψαντος ἐναντία τοσούτῳ θεάτρῳ, μέλλοντος ἐπιδείξεσθαι σαυτοῦ λόγους, καὶ οὐδ' ὁπωστιοῦν ἐκπλαγέντος, νῦν οἰηθείην σε θορυβηθήσεσθαι ἕνεκα ἡμῶν ὀλίγων ἀνθρώπων.

This is now interpreted by practically all scholars to refer to

---

[1] The date of the introduction of a high stage at Athens and elsewhere will be discussed in Ch. V.

the proagon or preliminary display in the Odeum (on the 8th Elaphebolion), not to any performance in the theatre itself, in which, so far as any evidence goes, the poet did not parade with his actors. θέατρον = 'audience' as in some other passages (e.g. Herod. vi. 21 εἰς δάκρυα ἔπεσε τὸ θέητρον; Aristoph. *Knights* 243 τὸ θέατρον δεξιόν; Aristot. *Poet.* xiii τὴν τῶν θεάτρων ἀσθένειαν). There is some reason to think that ὀκρίβας refers only to temporary structures;[1] but this would not necessarily exclude a wooden stage, if there was one, in a fifth-century theatre, any more than in the Odeum. This passage of Plato is the only evidence for a proagon before the Lenaea, as well as before the Dionysia; but it appears to be good enough.

7. It is sometimes argued from the use of expressions such as οἱ ἀπὸ τῆς σκηνῆς for actors (Dem. *de Cor.* § 180), τὰ ἀπὸ τῆς σκηνῆς for lyrics sung by actors (Aristot. *Poet.* xii; cf. *Probl.* xix. 918 b, 920 a, 922 b), and ἐπὶ τῆς σκηνῆς (Dem. *F.L.* § 337, Aristot. *Poet.* xvii and xxiv, cf. ἐπὶ τῶν σκηνῶν ibid. xiii) for performances in the theatre imply a raised stage in the pre-Lycurgean period (if Demosthenes and Aristotle can be treated as pre-Lycurgean); but Dörpfeld and Reisch[2] by a very full enumeration of passages have shown that the phrases cannot be made to bear this interpretation.[3]

The other passages which are commonly used to prove the existence of a raised stage all belong to and refer to later periods. As regards the pre-Lycurgean period, there is point in Dörpfeld's question, why, if there was a stage, no name for it has ever come down to us; only the names θέατρον, ὀρχήστρα, σκηνή, and, for the

---

[1] Rohde, *Rh. Mus.* xxxviii, p. 255; cf. D.R., p. 303.

[2] D.R., pp. 283 ff.

[3] See also Flickinger, *The Meaning of* ἐπὶ τῆς σκηνῆς *in Writers of the Fourth Century* (Chicago, 1902), *Plutarch on the Greek Theater* (1904), and *Scaenica* (*Trans. Am. Phil. Ass.*, 1910, pp. 109 ff.). It is clear that in the great majority of instances ἐπὶ τῆς σκηνῆς simply means 'in front of the skené' in the sense of 'in a theatrical performance', or 'on the scene'. In Dem. *F.L.* § 337 it means no more than 'in a play', 'in the theatre'; and in the *Poetics* xviii and xxiv what is performed ἐπὶ τῆς σκηνῆς is opposed to what is merely read (in an epic); in ch. xiii it means 'in an actual performance', and so on. That the conventional meaning in writings on the drama had no reference to the *stage* (λογεῖον) is illustrated by the schol. on Aristoph. *Clouds* 344, δῆλον οὖν ὅτι ὁπόσα ἐν τοῖς ἄνω λέλεκται χορικὰ οὐκ ἐπὶ σκηνῆς (on the scene) ὄντος τοῦ χοροῦ εἴρηται, ἀλλ' ἔξω ἑστῶτος καὶ κρυπτομένου ἡ φωνὴ μόνη τοῖς ἔνδον ἐξηκούετο. οὐ γὰρ ἠδύναντο ἐντὸς εἶναι τῆς σκηνῆς αἱ μὴ καταπτᾶσαι μηδέπω.

usual place of the actors, the designation 'near' or 'in front of' or 'on the side of' the σκηνή as opposed to the auditorium, σκηνή being, of course, the building (originally, in all probability, a tent) which formed the background of the performance.

8. A remarkable painting on a vase found in Attica, published by G. Caputo[1] and discussed further by Bulle,[2] depicts a low wooden stage on posts, on which an actor who is a caricature of Perseus is dancing in the presence of two spectators, who according to Caputo are a priest of Dionysus and a choregus, but according to Bulle a patron of drama and his young lover, the performance, on this view, being a private one. They are seated on chairs like the one which is well known from the stelé of Hegeso. Across one side of the painting a curtain is draped, which is thought by Caputo to represent a kind of *siparium* capable of being drawn across the front of the stage, according to Bulle a linen background of the action. The actor is very like those on the Italian vases depicting performances of phlyakes, though the vase is stated (not quite convincingly) to be of Attic manufacture and of the latter part of the fifth century—much earlier than any extant phlyakes vases. But the use of such a raised stage in an improvised show of this kind obviously proves nothing as to the arrangements for serious drama in the theatre of Dionysus.

Note

It has not been thought worth while to discuss the hypothesis of a *low* raised stage (e.g. three or four feet high) which contented many scholars in the nineteenth century. There is no evidence whatever of this, either in architectural remains or in the plays. Such a stage would have the disadvantage of impeding the free intercourse between actors and chorus which many scenes in the plays demand, and on the other hand its height would not be sufficient to give the full advantages undoubtedly obtained by a raised stage when such free intercourse was no longer necessary. (See Ch. V.) All that seems to have been required in the fifth century is the provision (in certain plays) of one or two broad steps supporting (e.g.) an altar, or of the steps which would naturally form the basis of a temple or palace—in other words, the basis of the *scaenae frons*.

[1] *Dioniso*, iv (1935), No. 6.   [2] *Das Theater zu Sparta*, pp. 51 ff.

SPECIAL PROBLEMS OF THE THEATRE BEFORE LYCURGUS

THE present chapter will be devoted to the discussion of a number of problems in regard to the Athenian theatre in the Classical period, which have been reserved in order not to interrupt the treatment of the theatre buildings as a whole.

A. THE PROTHYRON

Some scholars are convinced that in many or even in all plays in which the background is a palace or a temple there was in front of the central entrance a columned porch or portico, to which they appropriate the name prothyron. They support their opinion partly by indications in the plays themselves, partly by their interpretation of a number of vase-paintings depicting subjects taken or supposed to be taken from drama.

i. It should be made clear at the outset that the use of the word πρόθυρον (or the plural πρόθυρα) in the text of a passage does not necessarily imply either a columned porch or a portico extending along some part of the façade. In Homer the word (singular or plural) means sometimes 'entrance' generally, or the space in front of an entrance door, whether of the door from the outer world into the αὐλή or forecourt, or of the door from the αὐλή itself into the μέγαρον. In Odyssey iv. 20 and vii. 3 the πρόθυρον is large enough for several persons and one or two chariots, but in other passages it may indicate the break in the wall in front of a set-back door, or the recess itself.[1] There is not in any passage any suggestion of a columned porch, though in some passages the πρόθυρον is connected with the αἴθουσα or colonnade surrounding the interior of the αὐλή. The word is probably used of a recessed entrance in Herodotus iii. 140, and in Plato, Protagoras 314 c, Symposium 175 a, where one or two persons stand in the πρόθυρον before entering the house. The vaguer meaning 'space before the door' is more probable in Pindar, Pyth. iii. 78, Herodotus iii. 35, and Thucydides vi. 27.

[1] A door set back in a recess is sometimes found in architectural remains, e.g. at Priene (Wiegand and Schrader, Priene, p. 285).

(The Hermae, whose position is described in the last passage, probably did not stand in a porch.)

2. But in the extant plays and fragments of the fifth century the passages to be considered are few:

(1) As regards houses or palaces:

(a) Aeschylus, *Choeph.* 966 τάχα δὲ παντελὴς χρόνος ἀμείψεται
πρόθυρα δωμάτων.

This passage, in which the meaning is quite indefinite, does not help us.

(b) Euripides, *Alcestis* 98–102 πυλῶν πάροιθε δ' οὐχ ὁρῶ
πηγαῖον ὡς νομίζεται
χέρνιβ' ἐπὶ φθιτῶν πύλαις.
χαίτα τ' οὔτις ἐπὶ προθύροις
τομαῖος.

The words here seem to mean 'at the doorway', with no implication of a porch.

(c) Eur. *Troades*, 194 τὰν παρὰ προθύροις φυλακὰν·κατέχουσα.

This again is quite vague.

(d) Eur. *Hypsipyle*, 30–4 (Page) τί σὺ παρὰ προθύροις, φίλα;
πότερα δώματος εἰσόδους
σαίρεις ἢ δρόσον ἐπὶ πέδῳ
βάλλεις οἷά τε δοῦλα;

The phrase need mean no more than 'by the front door'. The space in front of this would naturally be kept clean, no less than a porch.

(e) Eur. *Kresphontes* (Hyginus, *Fab.* 137) says that Merope, intending to kill Cresphontes in his sleep, *in chalcidicum cum securi venit*, and Vitruvius v. i. 4 treats *chalcidicum* as a columned structure. But we do not know what Greek word Hyginus is translating. If it was πρόθυρον, he merely chose one out of its many possible meanings— perhaps influenced by the Roman stage or by vase-paintings.

(f) Aristoph. *Wasps* 800–4 ἠκηκόη γὰρ ὡς Ἀθηναῖοί ποτε
δικάσοιεν ἐπὶ ταῖς οἰκίαισι τὰς δίκας,
κἂν τοῖς προθύροις ἐνοικοδομήσοι πᾶς ἀνὴρ
αὑτῷ δικαστηρίδιον μικρὸν πάνυ,
ὥσπερ Ἑκάταιον, πανταχοῦ πρὸ τῶν θυρῶν.

This proves nothing as regards stage arrangements. The words ἐν τοῖς προθύροις probably = πρὸ τῶν θυρῶν and no more. There is no reason to think that the Ἑκαταῖα (= τὰ πρὸ τῶν θυρῶν Ἑκάτης ἀγάλματα, Hesych.) were built into porches, any more than were the Agyieus stones.

(The expression used in *Wasps* 875, ὦ δέσποτ' ἄναξ γεῖτον Ἀγυιεῦ τοὐμοῦ προθύρου προπύλαιε obviously does not prove that the πρόθυρον was a porch.)

(2) As regards temples, which of course in reality had usually some kind of columned entrance or portico:

(a) Eur. *Iph. Taur.* 1159 ἄναξ, ἔχ' αὐτοῦ πόδα σὸν ἐν παραστάσιν.
   This is commonly quoted as implying a porch. But παραστάδες are regularly 'door-posts' or pillars in a line with the threshold, not part of a structure projecting from it: cf. Pollux i. 76 εἶτα οὐδὸς καὶ τὰ περὶ τὰς θύρας μέρη, θαιρὸς μὲν ὁ στροφεὺς ὀνομαζόμενος, σταθμοὶ δὲ τὰ ἑκατέρωθεν ξύλα κατὰ πλευρὰν τῶν θυρῶν, ἃ καὶ παραστάδας φασίν. Cratinus, fr. 42, παραστάδας καὶ πρόθυρα βούλει ποικίλα, probably implies a distinction between the two; and cf. Eur. *Andromache* 1121 παραστάδος κρεμαστὰ τεύχη πασσάλων καθαρπάσας. Pegs for armour would probably not be hammered into a columned porch.

(b) Euripides' *Ion* is generally held to require a columned portico—at least, columns between the *antae* of the temple entrance—and this is probably right, as the opening words of the parodos-chant,

   οὐκ ἐν ταῖς ζαθέαις Ἀθάναις
   εὐκίονες ἦσαν αὐλαὶ θεῶν μόνον,

   would be pointless unless there were columns visible, and it is likely that the temple with its columned façade was raised on steps (κρηπῖδες, ll. 38 and 510: lit. 'foundations' but probably, at least in l. 38, projecting as steps); but there is no need to imagine a projecting porch.

Accordingly, it seems quite likely that the regular 'set' representing a temple should, when required, have provided columns as part of the façade, but not a porch or colonnade standing out in front of it. The treatment of the sides of the façade may have varied. In the *Ion* there was evidently the representation, on one side, of a grove—the δαφνώδη γύαλα into which Hermes retires; and this was perhaps matched on the other side by the dwelling of the temple servants whom Ion summons to work.

But as regards houses or palaces, although the occasional erection of a porch is not impossible, there is no sufficient evidence of it in extant remains either of tragedy or comedy. Rees, indeed, argues[1] that because (as he believes) in Roman comedy phrases

[1] In *Class. Philol.* (1915), pp. 117 ff. Similarly Lundström (*Eranos*, i, pp. 95 ff.) concludes (1) that in Plautus *via* (the street) is a place distinct from *ante aedes* or *ante ostium*; (2) that generally nothing happens *in via* which would not happen

like *ante aedes, ante ostium, ante ianuam* appear to be identical
with *in vestibulo*, a πρόθυρον in the sense of a porch is implied
whenever in Greek comedy the words πρόσθε τῶν θυρῶν or πρὸς
ταῖς θύραις occur. This is obviously fallacious. A *vestibulum*, and
a porch, when they are there, are necessarily *ante aedes*, πρὸ τῶν
θυρῶν, but everything that happens *ante aedes* or πρὸ τῶν θυρῶν
need not happen in a *vestibulum* or porch. Nor does the phrase
ἐν τῷ προθύρῳ in Alexis fr. 266 (K) necessarily imply a porch, nor
the word πρόθυρον in Theopompus fr. 63 (K). (*Vestibulum* itself is
not necessarily a roofed structure. It is defined in Gellius xvi. 53
as *locum ante ianuam domus vacuum*.)

3. But Rees goes farther, and imagines that in many plays there
was a projecting porch in which scenes were presented which in
real life would have taken place indoors, or which in the play
were spoken of as having happened indoors; and he argues that
such a porch—which is not a real porch, but an interior which
has somehow got outside—was the conventional place for the
theatrical representation of interior scenes. The utmost that he
proves is that such scenes were represented outside the door of
the house, not that they were represented in a porch; but it will
be as well to consider them briefly.

The *Clouds* of Aristophanes opens with a scene in which Strepsiades and Pheidippides are seen in bed; but it is clear that they
are thought of, not as in an 'interior', but as outside the house.
This is the only possible conclusion from l. 19, ἔκφερε τὸ γραμ-
ματεῖον and l. 125 ἀλλ' εἴσειμι, σοῦ δ' οὐ φροντιῶ. At ll. 183–4 the
Μαθηταί are revealed inside the house by the opening of the door,
and are seen in the attitudes described; but as just afterwards
they are clearly regarded as outside (being ordered to go back
into the house at l. 195, because, as explained in ll. 198–9, the
open air is bad for them) it is probable that when the door was
opened at l. 183 some of them rushed out and assumed their
various characteristic attitudes. When at ll. 195–9 they go indoors

in the street in real life; (3) that *ante aedes* or *ante ostium* is the place of all
that in real life would generally happen indoors; (4) that *ante aedes*, &c. imply
a *vestibulum*, which is a translation of πρόθυρον, πρόσθε τῶν θυρῶν, &c., and is a
place in front of the house, but within its precincts and not in the street. Unfortunately he identifies this place with structures of the *aedicula* type depicted
on vases. In any case we cannot tell how far the Roman poets in imitating
Greek plays adapted the setting to Roman theatres with a deep stage. (See
Legrand, *Daos*, pp. 437 ff.)

again, they leave behind them maps, &c., which Strepsiades
examines, until at l. 217 he catches sight of Socrates himself,
swinging in his basket, and then the Μαθητής who has been con-
versing with Strepsiades also goes indoors. None of the difficulties in the scene are solved by the assumption of a porch, which
would only obstruct the vision of the audience when the door is
thrown open at l. 183. (The scene was very successfully acted
without one in an Oxford performance of the play many years
ago.)

In the *Hercules Furens* of Euripides Rees imagines a porch with
a curtain in front of it concealing Herakles tied to a broken
pillar of the porch with his victims lying about him, the curtain
being drawn aside at the right moment (about l. 1029). It is very
doubtful if this is consistent with the text. From ll. 887 to 907
the chorus in the orchestra hear the cries of Amphitryon and the
noise of the slaughter of the children by Herakles within, and at
l. 905 they see the convulsion of the house when Athena (as they
afterwards learn (ll. 1001 ff.) dashes him to the ground, so that
he falls senseless against a pillar broken in two by the fall of the
roof (l. 1008 ὃς πεσήμασι στέγης | διχορραγὴς ἔκειτο κρηπίδων ἔπι).
All this, as the Messenger's narrative makes clear, takes place in
the interior of the house, unseen by the spectators, and there the
servants lash Herakles to this same pillar, which is described as
lying or standing κρηπίδων ἔπι, on the floor of the palace, with no
hint of a porch; and there is also no hint in the text that any
pillar of a porch was broken. (If it had been, the chorus must
have been aware of it.) And at ll. 1029 ff. it is quite clear that the
revelation of Herakles and his victims was made by the throwing
open of doors, not by drawing aside a curtain—ἴδεσθε, διάνδιχα
κλῆθρα | κλίνεται ὑψιπύλων δόμων. Whether the ἐκκύκλημα was
then instantly employed will be discussed later. If it was, it
would give an easy explanation of l. 1422, ἀλλ᾽ ἐσκόμιζε τέκνα, but
this is quite intelligible if the children were lying just inside the
house, or if (as is quite possible) they had been borne out into
full view by attendants.

In the *Hippolytus* there is no suggestion of a porch, and the
stress which is laid on the open air and sky (ll. 178, &c.) is against
it. At l. 179 the Nurse has brought Phaedra out, probably on a
wheeled couch, ἔξω δὲ δόμων ἤδη νοσερᾶς | δέμνια κοίτης. Nor is
there any suggestion of a porch at l. 575: Phaedra bids the chorus

listen at the door—ταῖσδ' ἐπιστᾶσαι πύλαις | ἀκούσαθ' οἷος κέλαδος ἐν δόμοις πίτνει. A porch would be badly in the way at 806 ff., when the doors are flung open and the dead Phaedra is seen.

A porch is also assumed by Rees in the *Orestes*, at the opening of which (ll. 35–6) Orestes is lying on a couch πρὸ δωμάτων. Rees argues that the keeping of the chorus at a distance from him (ll. 170 ff.) for fear of disturbing him suggests a porch; this is obviously inconclusive; and so is the same inference from the fact that when Menelaus arrives (l. 375) he does not at first see Orestes. There are countless instances in drama, ancient and modern, of characters entering without seeing immediately someone who is in full view, and in this scene Orestes may well have been closely covered up at the moment. Rees lays stress on the point that Orestes, who has been ill·for six days, ought to be found on the couch at the beginning of the play, instead of having to enter and lie down on it in full view of the assembling audience, and he thinks that the difficulty was solved by the scene being set in a porch, with a curtain drawn across it and drawn back at the opening of the play. But since Orestes' illness sometimes took the form of rushing wildly about (ll. 44–5), he may well have rushed in and flung himself on the couch before Electra entered and found him there. Rees suggests that the scene was set in the same way—in a porch with a curtain over it—in Aristophanes' *Clouds* and *Wasps*; but it may be doubted whether Greek audiences were really sensitive enough in such matters to object to the preparatory setting of the scene before their eyes (if they were already in their seats) before the play began.[1]

4. The theory that a projecting porch was a frequent and even normal feature of the scenic background in the fifth century was strongly maintained by Dörpfeld and Reisch,[2] as well as later by Rees and, perhaps with less confidence, by others; and the evidence adduced consists partly of certain vase-paintings, in which some of the figures are represented as standing or acting inside a structure resembling a small temple—a ναΐσκος or *aedicula*—which, it is supposed, was suggested to the painter by the porch of the tragic scene. Dörpfeld is uncertain whether the scenes represented are supposed to be taking place in the porch itself or

---

[1] See pp. 41, 54, 66, 123, 129–30, 194.

[2] D.R., pp. 208, 309, &c.; Rees, *Class. Philol.* l.c. I am indebted for some points, here and elsewhere, to Allen, *Greek Theater*, esp. ch. vii.

in the interior of the house, which may be imagined as visible through the porch. Rees, as we have seen, thinks that the prothyron was itself the place where interior scenes were presented to the audience. Frickenhaus[1] offers a strange variant of the latter theory, and suggests that the porch-like structure is not a structural porch at all, but is the ἐκκύκλημα, and that the whole structure was rolled forward through the central opening when interior scenes had to be represented. This seems to be really impossible. We can understand the rolling out of two, three, or even four persons on a low platform, such as the ἐκκύκλημα is commonly supposed to have been (the mechanism being made as inconspicuous as possible and involving only the slightest conflict with probability), but not the emergence from the front door of a large columned and roofed portico, carrying, if necessary (as, e.g., in the opening scene of the *Eumenides*), more than a dozen persons, and representing indifferently, as required, the interiors of temples, palaces, tents, or caverns.

5. Now there is no doubt that most of the vases cited represent subjects which had also been the subject of dramatic performances at Athens in the fifth century, and that the treatment of the subject by the painters is strongly influenced by the work of the poets from whom, in all probability, the painters derived them, whether directly or through the intermediate stage of some great painting. This is proved not only by the behaviour of the persons as portrayed in the paintings, but by the fact that many of them wear the characteristic costume of tragic actors. But it by no means follows that the paintings represent the scenes exactly as they were presented in the theatre. Indeed, some of them cannot possibly do so, as the events represented are often events which in the theatre were only narrated as having taken place behind the scenes or at a distance, and were not presented to the audience at all. Moreover, some of the vases represent several events taking place simultaneously, and introduce characters unknown at any rate from extant plays,[2] and more in

---

[1] *Die altgr. Bühne*, pp. 7 ff. This view is not sufficiently decisively ruled out by Séchan, *Études sur la Tragédie grecque*, p. 559; cf. von Gerkan, *Das Theater von Priene*, p. 109.

[2] Dörpfeld and Reisch of course recognize that the vases cannot represent the actions exactly as they must have been performed on the stage (see esp. pp. 309–10); but they nevertheless think that they support the normal use of the prothyron in the fifth-century Attic theatre.

number than the Greek drama ever presented at once. The truth seems to be that, while the vases present scenes derived from, or strongly influenced by, tragedy, they do so in accordance with the conventions of the quite different art of vase-painting, and of vase-painting in Italy in the fourth century; for it is from that country and period that the vases practically all come. It is

FIG. 9. The Madness of Lycurgus (Column krater from Ruvo in Jatta Collection)

noteworthy that on Attic vases of the fifth century structures of the *aedicula* pattern do not occur, and it is a mere assumption on the part of Dörpfeld and others that what is presented on Apulian vases of the fourth century must have its origin in the Athenian theatre of the fifth. Italy in the fourth century had a vigorous theatrical and artistic life of its own.

6. Of the vases cited in this connexion we shall consider first those in which there appears the commonest form of *aedicula*— that which has four light columns to support its roof, which may or may not have a gabled pediment.

(1) *Column krater from Ruvo: the Madness of Lycurgus* (Fig. 9). Lycurgus, King of the Edoni in Thrace, opposed the introduction of the worship of Dionysus and persecuted the Bacchanals who worshipped the god. This was the subject of a lost trilogy of Aeschylus (Ἠδωνοί, Βασσαρίδες, Νεανίσκοι, and satyric Λυκοῦρ-γος). In the madness sent on him by Dionysus he killed his son

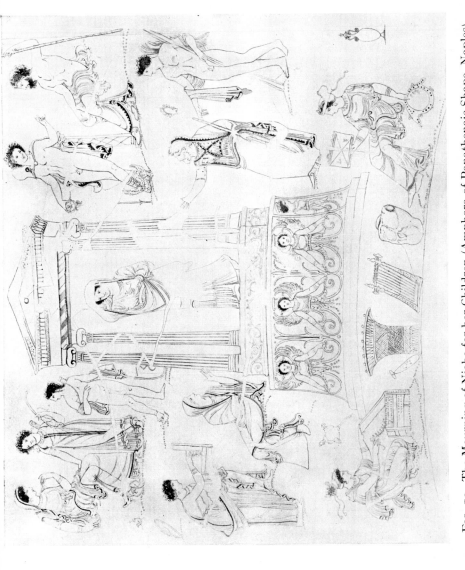

FIG. 10. The Mourning of Niobe for her Children (Amphora of Panathenaic Shape, Naples)

Fig. 11. Orestes and the Furies (Calyx krater, Leningrad)

Dryas and his own wife. In this painting he is attacking his son with the double axe, which is his weapon in nearly all of several vase-paintings which depict the scene; its special significance is unknown. Though two pillars of the house are represented, at least two others are implied. But the murder is probably *not* being committed inside the so-called porch, as it ought to be if we had here an interior scene transferred to a porch, for the figures seem to be half inside and half outside. If it *is* intended to be an interior scene, then either the execution is careless, or the artist is representing the pillars as tottering from the convulsion which in Aeschylus[1] (as in the *Bacchae* of Euripides) shook the palace of the king. But in fact it cannot represent a scene presented to a theatrical audience at all, because it was contrary to the Greek custom to present murders *coram populo*, and what the vases depict was doubtless narrated in the play by a messenger, and the pillars and roof are merely a conventional indication of the palace.

(2) *Amphora in Naples Museum: Niobe mourning for her children* (Fig. 10). Niobe had boasted that her children were as fair as Apollo and Artemis, the children of Leto; whereupon Apollo and Artemis slew all Niobe's children. The subject was treated in the *Niobe* of Aeschylus, of which only fragments survive.[2] In the painting Niobe stands within the pillars of the monument, which closely resembles the funereal monuments depicted on many south-Italian vases, and there can really be no question here of the reproduction of a scenic prothyron. The structure of the monument itself rules this out. The figures on either side of the tomb are almost certainly Antiope, who perhaps spoke the prologue of Aeschylus' play, and Tantalus, the father of Niobe, who tried to persuade her to conquer her grief and come away with him. Each is accompanied by an attendant. In the lower register offerings to the deceased are being produced; in the upper, the gods—Leto with her children—contemplate the result of their activities, and on the other side Hermes, who may have had a part in the play, and Zeus do likewise. The painting, while strongly reminiscent of the play of Aeschylus, lends no support to the theatrical prothyron.

(3) *Calyx krater from Ruvo: Orestes surrounded by Furies* (Fig.

[1] ἐνθουσιᾷ δὴ δῶμα, βακχεύει στέγη (fr. 58).
[2] See *Greek Poetry and Life*, pp. 106 ff.

11). The painting obviously recalls the opening of the *Eumenides* of Aeschylus; there are Orestes taking sanctuary inside the temple of Delphi, and clasping the omphalos, five of the Furies lying on the ground, and the terrified priestess of Apollo. The Furies are black-skinned and wingless, as in the *Eumenides*. (On other vase-paintings they are winged.) But there is no attempt to reproduce

FIG. 12. The Theft of the Palladium (Pelike, Naples)

the scene in the *Eumenides* exactly; the Furies are not sleeping on chairs inside the temple, as in the play, but lying on the ground, partly inside and partly outside the *aedicula*, which is clearly not a porch, but a conventional indication of the temple. The structure has a back wall, as is indicated by an object hung on it.

(4) *Pelike in Naples Museum: The Theft of the Palladium at Troy* (Fig. 12). The vase represents the theft of the statuette of Athena, the Palladium, by Odysseus and Diomedes: the priestess Theano, carrying the key of the temple, is fleeing in terror. On the left stands Helen, who was perhaps an accomplice; she always had a certain liking for Odysseus, and it is probable that in the Λάκαιναι, a lost play of Sophocles, which dealt with this adventure, she was given this role. Above sits Athena, the patroness of Odysseus and his helper in many perils, and on the other side

FIG. 13. Antigone and Herakles (Amphora of
Panathenaic shape from Ruvo, Jatta Collection)

Hermes and a diminutive winged Victory. It is impossible to imagine that what is represented was acted in a prothyron on the stage; the *aedicula* is just a conventional symbol of a temple—this time that of Athena.

(5) *Amphora from Ruvo, Jatta Collection: Antigone and Herakles* (Fig. 13). The scene is based on a version of the story of Antigone different from that of Sophocles, but followed also on other vases —notably on an amphora in Berlin.[1] The details of the story are keenly disputed, but this much seems fairly clear, that when Antigone had disobeyed Kreon, the ruler of Thebes, by burying her brother Polyneikes, Kreon condemned her to death and charged his son Haimon to execute the sentence; but Haimon, being in love with Antigone, carried her off into safety: she bore him a son, who, when he became a youth, went to Thebes; he was detected by Kreon, who, having obtained possession of Antigone, was about to send her to execution, when Herakles intervened—with what result is unknown. On the present vase (though not on the Berlin amphora) Herakles is the central figure, and his name is inscribed over his head on the *aedicula*. This does not necessarily mean (as, e.g., Miss Harrison thought)[2] that the *aedicula* was his temple or ἡρῷον, as all the other characters also have their names above their heads, and it is difficult to see where else the name of Herakles could be written. Moreover, the name is not central, as it would be if it belonged to the building. The *aedicula* is probably a conventional symbol for the palace of Kreon—certainly not a porch; and as all the three central persons at least are concerned in one and the same scene, though one is inside and two outside, Herakles was probably placed inside simply for artistic convenience, and he is in the centre because as an intercessor he must stand between the two parties. It is not indeed certain that he *is* intended to be inside, and not really in front of the building. The other figures are, on the right, Kreon, wearing the royal robe of the tragic stage, with a small attendant, and his queen Eurydike, the mother of Haimon, and Ismene, the sister of Antigone, carrying a kind of work-box; on the left, Antigone with her hands bound, in charge of a guard, and Haimon on higher ground in an attitude of grief. Robert thinks that the painter may have followed the *Antigone* of Euripides; others as strenuously deny the possibility of this and suggest the

[1] See Séchan, *Études sur la Tragédie grecque*, p. 275, Fig. 86.   [2] *Themis*[2], pp. 376–7.

Antigone of Astydamas, of which nothing at all is known—not even which Astydamas wrote it.

(6) *Volute krater once in Buckingham Collection: Iphigeneia gives Pylades a letter* (Fig. 14). It has been settled that Orestes is to die as a sacrifice to the Artemis of the Tauric Chersonese, whose priestess is Iphigeneia, and that Pylades is to take a letter

FIG. 14. Iphigeneia in Tauris (Volute krater, Buckingham Collection)

from her to her friends in Argos. On the vase, Iphigeneia wears a rich costume of the tragic pattern, Pylades a travelling cap; Orestes, leaning on the περιρραντήριον or lustral basin, wears a laurel wreath in token of his dedication as a victim; Artemis wears a foreign head-dress, as befits the goddess of that wild region; the satyr in the top left-hand corner is unexplained, unless he is put in just to fill space. The *aedicula*, as on some other vases, has doors in the back; the action takes place entirely outside it, so that it is not the place of an 'interior scene' at all, but simply indicates the temple in the conventional manner.

(7) *Volute krater in Hermitage Museum, Leningrad: Iphigeneia*

in the Temple of Artemis (Fig. 15). Iphigeneia stands inside an *aedicula* in which is the image of Artemis. The structure obviously represents a temple and not a porch; cult-images are not known to have been kept in porches, and it was only at a later point in the story that the image was brought out to be purified in the sea. No back wall or doors are indicated, but the building has obviously some depth. Iphigeneia seems to be giving instructions to Pylades, though no letter is visible, and Orestes, as on the previous vase, is leaning on the lustral basin. It is clear that there is no distinction, for conversational purposes, between the inside and the outside of the *aedicula*; possibly Iphigeneia is to be regarded as standing on the temple step. In the upper register are Nike, Athena, Artemis, and Hermes. The painting, like many others of the same period and style, includes a number of groups not directly connected with the main theme—especially two conversations, each between a Thracian and a young woman. The young deer may be an allusion to the transformation of Iphigeneia when she was sacrificed at Aulis.

(8) *Calyx krater in Moscow: Iphigeneia gives Pylades a letter* (Fig. 16). Iphigeneia with the image of Artemis is inside the *aedicula*, Pylades outside; on the right are Apollo and Artemis; Orestes is absent. As on the last vase, the robe of Iphigeneia is probably reminiscent of Tragedy. It is thought by some scholars that all three Iphigeneia vases go back to some one well-known painting, which they reproduce with different degrees of fullness and exactness. This painting must obviously have been inspired by Euripides' play, with which the vases correspond closely,[1] but there seems no reason for supposing that the conventional representation of a temple should have been derived from a porch in a Euripidean theatre.

(9) *Volute krater in Boston: Achilles Thersitoktonos* (Fig. 17). Achilles slew Thersites in anger at his gibes, and ordered Automedon to prevent anyone from taking the body away for burial. The story was told in the *Aethiopis*, a poem of the late epic period,

---

[1] On the relation of the many vases and wall-paintings, as well as sarcophagi, depicting the story of Iphigeneia, to one another and to a possible original (whether by Timomachus or some other) vide Robert, *Arch. Zeit.* xxiii (1875), p. 137 f., and *Archäologische Hermeneutik*, pp. 193 ff., and especially Löwy, *Jahrb. Arch.* xliv (1929), pp. 86 ff., where full refs. to other discussions are given. See also H. Philippart, *Iconographie de l'Iphigénie en Tauride*, pp. 21 ff., &c.

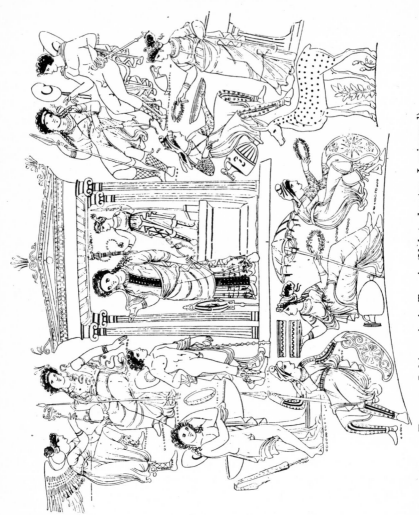

FIG. 15. Iphigeneia in Tauris (Volute krater, Leningrad)

and was dramatized in the fourth century by Chairemon. On the vase we see Achilles in his tent at Troy, with his old and prosaic friend Phoinix, who is properly distressed. Below the tent are Thersites and his head, Automedon on the watch, and all the signs of a recent scrimmage. On the right of the tent is Diomedes, eager to avenge his cousin (since both he and Thersites

FIG. 16. Iphigeneia in Tauris (Calyx krater, Moscow)

were grandsons of Oineus), but held back by Menelaus; on the left Agamemnon comes to read the Riot Act. In the upper register are Pan, Poina (the personification of revenge), Athena, and Hermes; the other figures need not detain us. What is remarkable is the use of the conventional *aedicula* to represent not a palace or temple (nor anything which is likely to have had a porch), but a tent or military hut. (The heroes' dwellings outside Troy were doubtless more solid than tents in the strict sense.) At the back of the tent hang Achilles' shield, greaves, and helmet, and the spare wheels of his chariot. Clearly no one scene in the play as performed is reproduced here, and the *aedicula* represents a building in the manner conventional in these vase-paintings. In the same way English stained glass, at more than one period, used the same conventional forms to represent more than one kind of building—house, church, or tomb.

(10) *Volute krater from Ruvo: Death of Neoptolemus* (Fig. 18). The painting is inspired, not by any acted scene in a play, but by the Messenger's narrative in Euripides' *Andromache*, describing how Orestes conspired against Neoptolemus at Delphi and slew him. Neoptolemus, already wounded, takes refuge at the altar, still prepared to defend himself, while Orestes dodges round the omphalos to inflict a second blow. Apollo looks on with interest, his priestess with horror. On this vase the *aedicula* (once more furnished with doors) with omphalos, altar, and tripods, indicates the sanctuary of Apollo at Delphi, but no action takes place in the *aedicula*. The painter's indifference to exactness of position is shown by his placing the omphalos and tripods outside the temple, whereas in fact they were inside. (The young man with a spear must be one of Orestes' Delphian fellow-conspirators.)

(11) *Volute krater from Ruvo: Iphigeneia and Orestes* (Fig. 19). Orestes has taken refuge at an altar beside a bay-tree, and Pylades stands by; Iphigeneia is addressing them, accompanied by an elderly attendant; Apollo and Artemis are above. The usual *aedicula*, denoting the temple, is at a little distance, its columns truncated because of rising ground which intervenes. Here is no reproduction of a stage scene, and no conclusions as to theatrical properties can be drawn from it, though the subject is evidently taken from Euripides, *Iph. Taur.* 625 ff.

7. The eleven vases which have been considered all present or imply a four-columned structure; but others depict a six-columned, and it may well be asked why the four-columned should be selected, as it usually is, as representing a theatrical prothyron, any more than the six-columned, which fulfils on the vases precisely the same function, as a conventional representation of a building of any kind. The following are the vases in question, which are very well known:

(12) *Volute krater from Ruvo: The Mourning for Archemoros* (Fig. 20). Hypsipyle, Princess of Lemnos, having been abandoned by Jason, had become the slave of Lycurgus and Eurydike,

Fig. 17. Achilles Thersitoktonos (Volute krater, Boston)

FIG. 18. The Death of Neoptolemus (Volute krater from Ruvo, Rome, De Luca Resta)

king and queen of Nemea, where the king was also priest of the
Nemean Zeus. Hypsipyle was charged with the care of their
infant son Archemoros. Now the Seven Heroes, who were on
their way from Argos to attack Thebes, chanced to call at the
palace and asked Hypsipyle for water. She laid down the infant
by the spring while she drew the water; the infant was bitten by
a serpent and died. Hypsipyle was condemned to death by the
infant's mother Eurydike, but was spared on the intercession of
Amphiaraos, one of the Seven. The vase shows Eurydike in an
aedicula supported by six columns (two being at the back), with
Hypsipyle and Amphiaraus on either side. In the lower register
the infant is laid out for burial and offerings are being brought;
in the upper are Dionysus, and the special deities of the place,
Zeus and Nemea. On the left are Euneos and traces of Thoas;
they were the two sons of Hypsipyle by Jason, and played some
part in the *Hypsipyle* of Euripides, by which the painting is
obviously inspired. On the right are two more of the Seven
Heroes—Parthenopaios and Kapaneus. Clearly the painting
does not depict any one scene as performed on the stage, but
gives reminiscences of several parts of the story.

(13) *Volute krater from Canosa: the Revenge of Medea* (Fig. 21).
The scenes depicted are based on the dramatic treatment of the
story, but not by Euripides only, as characters are included who
have no place in Euripides—among them Merope (probably wife
of Kreon), Hippotes (brother of Kreousa), the ghost of Aeëtes
(Medea's father), and Oistros, the charioteer; and the name of
Medea's victim on the vase is Kreonteia, not, as in Euripides,
Kreousa. The central scene, the death of Kreonteia in the arms
of her father Kreon, evidently takes place inside the *aedicula*,
but it is not a scene which ever was or could be acted in a Greek
theatre, in a prothyron or anywhere else; it could only be
narrated, as in Euripides, by a messenger; and the *aedicula*
itself, with the suspended shield, is simply the conventionalized
palace. In the upper register are Herakles, Athena, and the
Dioskouroi.

(14) *Volute krater from Armentum: Death of Meleagros* (Fig. 22).
The painting is probably based on the *Meleagros* of Euripides.
In the six-columned *aedicula* (one column being invisible) is
the dying Meleagros, supported by Tydeus and Deianeira, and
(probably) Althaia, his mother, the cause of his death. Oineus, his

FIG. 19. Iphigeneia in Tauris (Volute krater from Ruvo, Naples)

FIG. 21. The Revenge of Medea (Volute krater from Canosa, Munich)

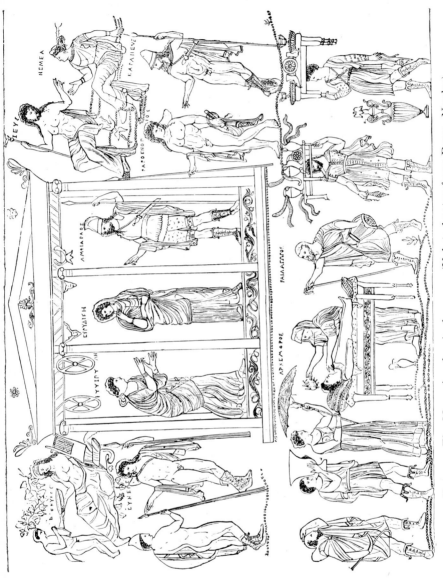

FIG. 20. The Mourning for Archemoros (Volute krater from Ruvo, Naples)

father, is outside. Below are Peleus and Theseus, two of Meleagros' companions in the Calydonian boar-hunt, and above are Aphrodite and a diminutive figure labelled Φθόνος. This painting also presents a scene which was probably never acted, but was narrated by a messenger. Engelmann indeed conjectures[1] that the

FIG. ·22. The Death of Meleagros (Volute krater from Armentum, Naples)

scenic background was drawn apart and the dying hero revealed to the audience, Aphrodite appearing aloft ἀπὸ μηχανῆς; but though this would give an ending not unlike that of the *Hippolytus*, there is really no evidence for it.

(15) *Situla in Villa Giulia: Arrival of Pelops at the palace of Oinomaos* (Fig. 23). Oinomaos had offered his daughter Hippodameia in marriage to anyone who could defeat him in a chariot-race, he himself having the horses of Ares, which were supposed to be invincible; the unsuccessful suitor was always slain. Pelops came to try his luck and bribed Myrtilos to tamper with Oinomaos' chariot-wheels; he consequently won. The vase shows the three front columns of what may be a six-columned *aedicula*, or possibly the façade of the palace. The figures from right to left

[1] *Archäolog. Stud. zu den Tragikern*, p. 83.

are Hippodameia, Oinomaos, Myrtilos (significantly holding a wheel), Pelops, and an Asiatic attendant, who for some reason carries an umbrella. Above are Πόθος (Desire) and Aphrodite, and the heads of four chariot-horses seen through an opening at the back. These horses indicate that we have no reproduction of an actual stage-scene, though the *Oinomaos* of Sophocles or Euripides or some other poet may have inspired it.

8. But if the theory that the central *aedicula* on the Italian vases representing dramatic subjects reproduces an actual porch in the theatrical background is rendered less easy by the facts that the *aedicula* may have a varying number of columns, and that on some vases it is not central, a further difficulty arises from the fact that the scheme of a central *aedicula* with some figures inside and others outside it is not peculiar to vases presenting dramatic subjects, but occurs also when the subjects are not dramatic, and particularly on a number of vases in which the scene is laid in Hades and has no direct connexion with the drama. Among the most striking are the following:

(16) *Volute krater from Canosa: Scenes in Hades* (Fig. 24). The central figures in the six-columned *aedicula*, which is obviously the palace of Pluto, are Pluto enthroned and Persephone. The other figures are, in the upper register, on the left, the two sons of Herakles and their mother Megara, and on the right Dike (though some say Medea), Peirithous, and Theseus; in the middle row, a family group (perhaps on their way to the Elysian Fields) and Orpheus, and on the right, an uncertain Oriental figure, with Aiakos and Rhadamanthys: below are Sisyphus, a Fury, Hermes, Herakles and Kerberos, a Fury, Tantalus. The other side of the vase shows (Fig. 25) the heroon of a dead man; a son is bidding farewell to his father. The special interest of this will appear later.

(17) *Volute krater from Altamura: Scenes in Hades* (Fig. 26).[1] Pluto and Persephone are sitting and feasting; the front supports of the *aedicula* which represents their palace are caryatids, standing on short columns decorated with acanthus leaves. In the upper row of figures are once more the sons of Herakles and Megara, and, on the right, Pelops, Myrtilos, and Hippodameia:

---

[1] Only the building and its occupants are here reproduced; Professor Beazley informs me that the figure given in *Mon. Inst.* viii, pl. 9, from which the description is taken, includes a good deal of uncertain restoration.

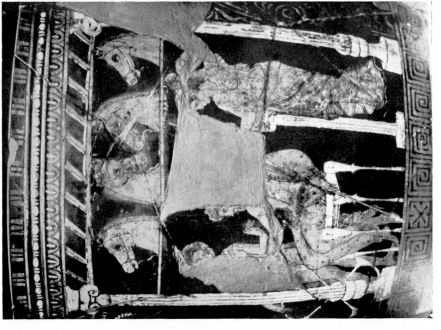

Fig. 23. Pelops and Oinomaos (Situla in Villa Giulia)

FIG. 24. Scenes in Hades (Volute krater from Canosa, Munich)

FIG. 25. Other side of same krater as in Fig. 24

in the middle, two Poinai (Avenging Spirits) and Orpheus—the Poinai perhaps charmed by Orpheus' song; on the right, Tripto- lemos, Aiakos, and Rhadamanthys; and below Ananke (with a

FIG. 26. Scene in Hades (Volute krater from Altamura, Naples)

whip), Sisyphus, Hermes, Herakles, and Kerberos, a female figure riding a hippocamp, and three Danaids.

(18) *Volute krater from Ruvo: Scene in Hades* (Fig. 27). Pluto is standing, Persephone enthroned, with a Fury on her right. Before the palace is Orpheus, with two Furies apparently listen- ing to his song; opposite to him an ivy-crowned man and two women, one carrying a water-pot like a Danaid. Above these

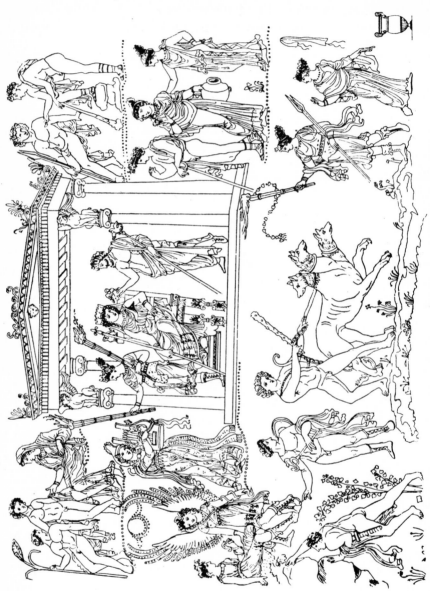

FIG. 27. Scene in Hades (Volute krater from Ruvo, Karlsruhe)

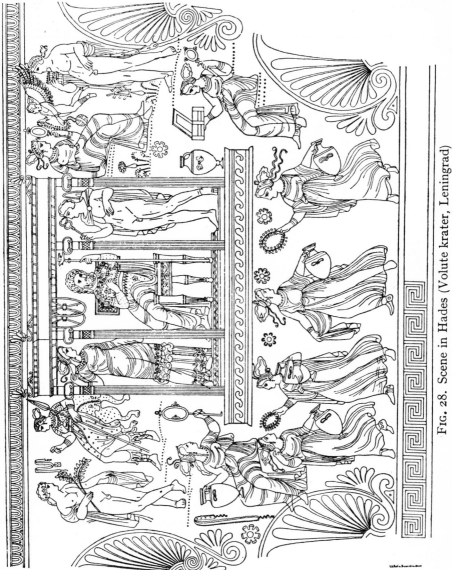

FIG. 28. Scene in Hades (Volute krater, Leningrad)

are again Megara and her sons, and on the right Theseus and Peirithous.

(19) *Volute krater in Leningrad: Scene in Hades* (Fig. 28). Again the palace of Pluto is in the middle; there are Pluto and

FIG. 29. Scene in Hades (Fragments of Volute krater from Ruvo, Fenicia)

Persephone, with Hermes, and round about are various deities of the upper world—Apollo and Artemis on the left; Aphrodite, Eros, and Pan on the right. At the bottom are six women, of whom five carry water-pots, approaching the entrance to the palace. Some connexion with the Mysteries may be suspected. On the neck of the vase are Ixion, Zeus, Hephaistos, and Iris.

(20) *Fragments of Volute krater from Ruvo: Scene in Hades* (Fig. 29). A scene similar to those preceding. The highly decorative robe worn by Orpheus seems to be modelled on that of tragic actors.

9. These Hades-vases have no more connexion with Tragedy than the fact that some of the persons depicted as enjoying the hospitality of Hades had been heroes of Tragedy in virtue of

earlier events in their career. The scene of a few tragedies was laid in Hades; to these there is a reference in Aristotle's *Poetics*, ch. 18; the *Sisyphus* of Aeschylus and the *Peirithous* of Critias or Euripides are fifth-century instances. The scheme of the arrangement of the pictures, with a central *aedicula*, is the same in the Hades-vases as in those representing subjects from Tragedy, and it is remarkable that some vases in both series have on the other side the heroon or shrine of a deceased person in the form of an *aedicula*. We have seen one instance of this, in which a son in the heroon offers a libation to his father; and this recalls a number of scenes on the sculptured tombs, with which all scholars are familiar. There are similar funereal scenes on the reverse side of the Niobe vase, the Medea vase, and the vase representing Achilles Thersitoktonos, which is thought to be the earliest of this series of south-Italian amphorae. These facts have not unnaturally led some scholars to suggest that the use of the *aedicula* form in dramatic and other scenes on vases is derived from its regular use as a heroon. However this may be, the occurrence of the *aedicula* on so many vases (for the instances might be greatly multiplied) which have nothing to do with the drama is strongly against the special connexion of it with a supposed prothyron in the theatre; and there is no ground for supposing that the scheme of arrangement found on the Italian vases which have been cited goes back to an Attic original of the fifth century. Nothing is known of any such original,[1] and the Italian vase-paintings cannot be used to support the idea that the Attic theatre regularly (or at any time) employed a prothyron in the form of the *aedicula*. This form was conventionally used on fourth-century Italian vases whenever it was desired to suggest in a small space an occupied building of any kind—palace, temple, tent, or tomb. Tragedy had no need of it for this purpose, as it represented most of these things by means of the skené and paraskenia; and since Tragedy was not in the habit of representing interior scenes at all, it had no need of a prothyron constantly there and pretending to be something else (the interior of a house). If in any play a porch was required for actions actually taking place in a porch, it could doubtless have been easily provided, but this seems to have happened seldom, if at all, in the Greek theatre.

[1] See Séchan, op. cit., p. 562 n. for refs. on this suggestion, and on the equally unproved 'derivation' of the scheme of the vase-paintings from votive tablets.

Additional Notes

(1) Dr. Margarete Bieber figures[1] the two sides of an Apulian vase in the
Metropolitan Museum of New York, one of which shows the body of
Sarpedon being borne through the air by Sleep and Death, the other the
visit of Thetis to Hephaistos. In the former Europa, mother of Sarpedon,
in the latter Hephaistos is seated in or outside an *aedicula* (unless the
pillars and cross-beam in the latter merely indicate a door). The two
pillars and pediment enclosing the figure of Europa are merely a conventional indication of her palace. The one scene may, as Dr. Bieber conjectures, be reminiscent of Aeschylus' *Kares* or *Europa* (Europa wears
the tragic robe), the other of his *Nereids*; but it is very doubtful if, as
she suggests, the painter had the flying-machine in mind. At least the
group of three persons—two carrying the other—would not have been
easy to transport by any such machine.

(2) An illustration is given (Fig. 32) of an interesting Apulian amphora
giving a funeral scene including an *aedicula* (Leroux, *Vases grecs de
Madrid*, pl. XLII).

B. THE 'Εκκύκλημα

Introduction. The question whether or not a device of the kind
termed ἐκκύκλημα was employed in the theatre in the fifth
century is one upon which little agreement exists. The word
ἐκκύκλημα is not found before the second century A.D., but it is
possible that the lexicographers and scholiasts who use it or
describe the device which it denotes may have found it in the
writings of Alexandrian scholars; it may have been used by
Aristophanes of Byzantium in a criticism of the language of
Euripides, *Hippolytus*, l. 172 (see below), and he may have
ascribed the use of the device to Euripides. But he was writing
more than 200 years after Euripides, and may have been influenced
by the practice of later theatres at Alexandria and elsewhere;
and the only evidence from the fifth century itself consists of the
use of the verbs ἐκκυκλεῖν and εἰσκυκλεῖν in two comedies of
Aristophanes of Athens; this will be considered immediately.
Apart from this the only first-hand evidence for the employment
of such a device, whatever it was, is found in the mention of the
ἐξώστρα (which the lexicographers, rightly or wrongly, identify
with the ἐκκύκλημα) in an inscription of the year 274 B.C. at

---

[1] *History of the Greek and Roman Theater*, p. 147. I am indebted to Professor
Beazley for photographs of these two vases, from which Figs. 30 and 31 are
taken.

Delos. Otherwise our information comes entirely from lexicographers and from the comments of scholiasts on passages in
which the verb ἐκκυκλεῖν is used or on scenes in which they suppose the ἐκκύκλημα to have been employed. In these writers
(whose notices will be found collected later in this chapter) there
are clearly two conceptions of the device, some thinking of it
as a kind of platform wheeled or pushed forward, others as a
revolving structure, the turning of which disclosed an interior
scene. Modern scholars are equally divided, some holding that
the one, some that the other, was the device actually employed.
The former (as, for instance, Haigh) think that the words implying a revolving structure (στρεφομένου, περιστρεφόμενον, στραφέντα, &c.) are not to be taken too strictly, and this can only mean
that they are false (for the fact that the wheels on which the
structure ran 'turned round' would not justify a description of
the whole structure as 'turning round'); the latter think that a
revolving platform was the means by which an interior scene was
rolled forward, and that this is not excluded by words which seem
to imply 'pushing' (ὠθεῖται, ἐξώστρα, &c.), since even for it to
revolve it might have to be pushed. These alternatives will be
discussed later. It will be convenient to consider first the passages from the comedies of Aristophanes which have been brought
into the argument.

I

1. In the *Acharnians* Dikaiopolis is anxious to see Euripides
and to borrow from him the rags, &c., which made his heroes so
pitiable. Kephisophon (Euripides' attendant) explains that it is
impossible, because the Master is composing—l. 399, αὐτὸς δ'
ἀναβάδην ποιεῖ | τραγῳδίαν. Dikaiopolis insists, and Euripides
replies (ll. 407 ff.):

> EY.   ἀλλ' οὐ σχολή.
> ΔΙ. ἀλλ' ἐκκυκλήθητ'. EY. ἀλλ' ἀδύνατον. ΔΙ. ἀλλ' ὅμως.
> EY. ἀλλ' ἐκκυκλήσομαι, καταβαίνειν δ' οὐ σχολή.
> ΔΙ. Εὐριπίδη, EY. τί λέλακας; ΔΙ. ἀναβάδην ποιεῖς,
> ἐξὸν καταβάδην; οὐκ ἐτὸς χωλοὺς ποιεῖς.

Euripides then offers to lend him the rags of several heroes, but
they are not lamentable enough; at last he asks for those of
Telephos, and Euripides tells the attendant where to find them.
Dikaiopolis adds further requests—it is not stated whether the

attendant fetched and handed each of the articles, or whether the poet is supposed to have them with him—and at last Euripides sends him away: l. 479 ἀνὴρ ὑβρίζει· κλῇε πηκτὰ δωμάτων.

In the *Thesmophoriazousai* it is Agathon who is wheeled out— also in the throes of composition, ll. 95–6:

EY. Ἀγάθων ἐξέρχεται.
MN. καὶ ποῖός ἐστιν; EY. οὗτος οὑκκυκλούμενος.

On which the scholiast says, ἐπὶ ἐκκυκλήματος γὰρ φαίνεται.

Euripides borrows from him a number of articles, which apparently Agathon has with him, and Agathon concludes the interview (264):

ἀλλ' ἔχεις γὰρ ὧν δέῃ,
εἴσω τις ὡς τάχιστά μ' εἰσκυκλησάτω.

There is nothing in the language of either play which need imply more than that the poet is wheeled out and in on a couch; certainly no platform, revolving or other, is required. The fact that in each passage it is a tragic poet that is wheeled out may, but need not, imply a travesty of some theatrical device, or there may be some topical point, no longer clear to us, about 'highbrow' poets composing with their feet up.

In the *Thesmophoriazousai* it is clear that the poet is wheeled out in front of the house, and what is presented is not an interior scene, but a scene outside in the sunshine, concluded by the poet being wheeled back into the house. On the other hand, the scholiast on the *Acharnians*, prompted doubtless by the occurrence of the verb ἐκκυκλεῖν, quotes a definition of ἐκκύκλημα which suggests that the scene presented is an interior one: ἐκκύκλημα δὲ λέγεται μηχάνημα ξύλινον τροχοὺς ἔχον, ὅπερ περιστρεφόμενον τὰ δοκοῦντα ἔνδον ὡς ἐν οἰκίᾳ πράττεσθαι καὶ τοῖς ἔξω ἐδείκνυε, λέγω δὴ τοῖς θεαταῖς. If this definition really applies to this scene and is not merely (as parallel passages in lexicographers and scholiasts suggest) a stock definition, without special reference to the particular scene, it means that Euripides, rolled out on the ἐκκύκλημα, is thought of as in his room all the time. There is actually nothing in this scene itself (as there is in the *Thesmophoriazousai*) that is inconsistent with this, and Fensterbusch argues further that the poet would not be likely to have the properties of so many plays on his couch, though they would naturally be in his room. (It is true that Agathon in the *Thesmo-*

phoriazousai has a number of feminine 'properties' with him, but a special reason is given for this.) Further, whereas Agathon is expressly wheeled back into his house (l. 264), Euripides simply orders the doors to be shut, as if he were theoretically inside all the time. This, however, is not quite conclusive; he may have been wheeled in without the use of the word, and the 'properties' may each have been fetched out of the house by Kephisophon as required. The upshot is that though the presentation of an interior scene on an ἐκκύκλημα is not impossible in the *Acharnians*, it is not proved. In the *Thesmophoriazousai* it is ruled out by the text. (The scholiast obviously cannot imagine the action described by ἐκκυκλεῖν without an ἐκκύκλημα: but it is clearly possible to roll out a couch or wheel-chair without a special platform.)

2. A further difficulty, however, is introduced by the use of the words ἀναβάδην and καταβάδην in the *Acharnians*. For the former the scholiasts offer two interpretations: (1) on l. 399 τὸ δὲ ἀναβάδην ἀντὶ τοῦ ἄνω τοὺς πόδας ἔχων ἐπὶ ὑψηλοῦ τόπου καθήμενος. ἄνω τοὺς πόδας ἔχων must mean 'with his feet up', and this is the meaning of ἀναβάδην wherever else it is used (it refers to persons reclining on a sofa or divan[1]); (2) on l. 410 ἀναβάδην ποιεῖς· φαίνεται γὰρ ἐπὶ τῆς σκηνῆς μετέωρος, and it is natural to equate this μετέωρος with the ἐπὶ ὑψηλοῦ τόπου καθήμενος of the previous note, and to suppose that both expressions imply elevation in some way above the ground-level, e.g. on an upper story, such as the houses which formed the background in Comedy certainly had in a number of plays. In the *Ekklesiazousai* at least, this upper story is slightly set back, and persons could walk in front and at the sides of it on the roof of the lower story,[2] and if that were so in the *Acharnians* Euripides might be wheeled out of the front of the upper story to the edge of the roof of the lower. (This is consistent with the fact that at Delos in 274 B.C. the ἐξώστρα seems to be a contrivance on the upper story.) This interpretation would give to καταβάδην (a word which does not occur elsewhere) the meaning 'downstairs', and this does not necessarily imply that ἀναβάδην must mean 'upstairs'—which it never does elsewhere—but only that Aristophanes is playing with his words

---

[1] Cf. Aristoph. *Plut.* 1123 νυνὶ δὲ πεινῶν ἀναβάδην ἀναπαύομαι, and Schol. ἄνω ἔχων τοὺς πόδας, ἀναπαυόμενος: Athenaeus xii. 528 f. (of Sardanapallus); Plut. *de Alex. fortuna*, § 30; Dio Chrys. *Or.* lxii, p. 323; Pollux iii, § 90, vi, § 175, &c.

[2] See above, pp. 54, 67.

and possibly inventing καταβάδην. οὐκ ἐτὸς χωλοὺς ποιεῖς is best
explained if ἀναβάδην means here, as elsewhere, 'with your feet
up'. If Euripides was really wheeled out on the upper story as
is suggested, the various 'properties' must have been thrown down
to Dikaiopolis—or handed down if the lower story was not too
high for Dikaiopolis to reach up. But no more machinery would
be needed than a couch on wheels as in the *Thesmophoriazousai*,
and it is quite likely that in both plays the supposed use of a
special platform called ἐκκύκλημα is a false inference by the
scholiast from the use of the verbs ἐκκυκλεῖν and εἰσκυκλεῖν.

3. The scholiast also asserts the use of an ἐκκύκλημα of the
revolving kind in the *Clouds*. At ll. 181 ff. the Μαθητής opens the
door of the φροντιστήριον:

> 181. ἄνοιγ' ἄνοιγ' ἀνύσας τὸ φροντιστήριον,
> καὶ δεῖξον ὡς τάχιστά μοι τὸν Σωκράτη·
> μαθητιῶ γάρ· ἀλλ' ἄνοιγε τὴν θύραν.
> ὦ 'Ηράκλεις, ταυτὶ ποδαπὰ τὰ θηρία;

on which the scholiast says: ὁρᾷ δὲ ὡς φιλοσόφους κομῶντας,
στραφέντος τοῦ μηχανήματος. This is in accordance with the third
Argument to the play: ἐκκυκληθείσης δὲ τῆς διατριβῆς οἵ τε μαθηταὶ
κύκλῳ καθήμενοι πιναροὶ συνορῶνται (unless ἐκκυκλεῖν is simply
used here, as often, for 'reveal'). But a number of expressions
in the lines that follow show that the poet is *not* here presenting
an interior, but a scene in the open air—in which the μαθηταί
must not stay too long.

> 195. ΜΑ. ἀλλ' εἴσιθ' (= εἴσιτε), ἵνα μὴ 'κεῖνος ὑμῖν ἐπιτύχῃ.
> ΣΤ. μήπω γε, μήπω γ'· ἀλλ' ἐπιμεινάντων, ἵνα
> αὐτοῖσι κοινώσω τι πραγμάτιον ἐμόν.
> ΜΑ. ἀλλ' οὐχ οἷόν τ' αὐτοῖσι πρὸς τὸν ἀέρα
> ἔξω διατρίβειν πολὺν ἄγαν ἐστὶν χρόνον.

It is probable that the scholiast is wrong in seeing the use of any
machinery here.

4. There is another difficult passage in the *Thesmophoriazousai*,
276 ff. Euripides is leaving Mnesilochos in female attire to play
his part, and Mnesilochos approaches the Thesmophorion to
make his offering. At this point the Ravenna MS. has the *parepigraphe* (or stage-direction) ὀλολύζουσί τε ἱερὸν ὠθεῖται, for which
Fritzsche's emendation is commonly accepted: ὀλολύζουσι· τὸ
ἱερὸν ὠθεῖται, 'the women raise a sacred cry' (i.e. the women

FIG. 30. Europa and Sarpedon (Bell krater, New York)

FIG. 31. Thetis, Hephaistos, and Aphrodite (Bell krater, New York)

assembled or assembling for the Thesmophoria), 'the shrine is pushed forward'—presumably, it is argued, on an ἐκκύκλημα. The text gives the information that the signal for the assembly is hoisted in the Thesmophorion, and that a great smoke is being raised by the lighting of the gathering women's torches. Mnesilochos makes his offering and finds a seat where he can hear the speakers. The women's herald makes a proclamation and the chorus sing a chant to Zeus, Apollo, Poseidon, and the Nymphs. The natural explanation of the text is that the Thesmophorion— the building—forms part of the background, and that the Assembly takes place in front of it, the crowd of worshippers gathering gradually from 276 to 295 and sitting on seats (as the men do in the Assembly in the *Acharnians*), the chorus, who form part of the worshipping crowd, being in the orchestra. Mnesilochos makes his offering either on an altar already in position in front of the building, or, if the stage direction is correct, at a shrine pushed forward through the central door. The latter view is taken by the scholiast on 277 παρεπιγραφή· ἐκκυκλεῖται ἐπὶ τὸ ἔξω τὸ Θεσμοφόριον. The opening scene of the play (down to 276) takes place before the house of Agathon, which was probably on one side of the background—quite possibly represented by one of the παρασκήνια. From l. 276 onwards the action is entirely within the sacred precinct and in front of the shrine of the Thesmophorion, which was doubtless central, and it is possible that at this point its doors were opened and an altar pushed forward. (The altar is in front of the building when Mnesilochos takes refuge at it, about l. 695, and the whole action from that point is certainly outside the Thesmophorion building. Euripides is evidently at the door of the building at ll. 871 ff.) But it is not certain, since it is disputable[1] whether the words τὸ ἱερὸν ὠθεῖται were originally part of the παρεπιγραφή, such 'stage directions' being only inserted by poets to indicate something which a reader could not otherwise know and which is necessary for the understanding of the passage. Thus ὀλολύζουσι is required to explain the hurried breaking-off of the conversation between Euripides and Mnesilochos, but the text itself makes plain at once that the Thesmophorion was visible. It had probably been visible all the time, though the doors may not have been open at first, and the scholiasts may well be wrong here, as we shall find reason

---

[1] See Bethe, *Rh. Mus.* lxxxiii (1934), pp. 27 ff.

to think they were in other places. Bethe put forward in his *Prolegomena* the view that an ἐκκύκλημα was rolled out bearing not only an altar, but the herald and a chorus of twenty-four, representing the worshippers gathered for an assembly in the Thesmophorion. But there is no reason to suppose that the Thesmophorion was an assembly-hall, and not rather a simple temple or shrine standing in the sacred precinct in which the women assembled and encamped. The mechanical difficulties connected with such an ἐκκύκλημα would be considerable; the total weight would be something like two tons, and the opening in the background would have to be very wide. Bethe wisely renounced this view in his later years.

II

1. Nearly all modern writers are agreed in ascribing to Aeschylus the use of the ἐκκύκλημα in the *Agamemnon* and *Choëphoroe*, and many believe that it was also used in the opening scene of the *Eumenides*. As regards the first two plays, it can only be said that, though it may have been so, there is no ancient authority for it, and nothing in the text that requires it. In the *Agamemnon*, at l. 1372, the bodies of Agamemnon and Cassandra are revealed to the chorus and spectators, with the net in which Agamemnon was entangled, and Clytemnestra standing in triumph over them. They remain visible until the end of the play, and Clytemnestra is on the scene, though not necessarily or probably in the same position, all the time. Those who think that the ἐκκύκλημα revealed interior scenes lay stress on Clytemnestra's words in l. 1379, ἔστηκα δ' ἔνθ' ἔπαισ' ἐπ' ἐξειργασμένοις, and suppose that what is on the ἐκκύκλημα is the bath-room where Agamemnon was slain, or at least the bath. Apart from obvious objections to the display of Agamemnon in the bath, it is unlikely that Cassandra was also in the bath-room when she was slain, and the text nowhere gives a hint of the display of the bath, but only of the blood-stained net, in which the chorus see him still enveloped (l. 1492). Clytemnestra's words are sufficiently true if she is shown standing over the bodies now exposed side by side in the doorway, where it was the early Greek custom to lay the dead.[1] Some kind of ἐκκύκλημα

[1] Cf. *Iliad* xix. 212 ἀνὰ πρόθυρον τετραμμένος: Schol. on Aristoph. *Lysistrata* 611 τοὺς νεκροὺς γὰρ οἱ ἀρχαῖοι προετίθεσαν πρὸ τῶν θυρῶν καὶ ἐκόπτοντο; Hesych.

(in a wide sense) *may* have been used; certainly some sort of bier would be necessary, and this may have been on wheels; but the conditions of the text would be satisfied by the display of the bodies in a moderately wide doorway, on a very simple and unobtrusive vehicle.

The same is true of the scene at *Choëph*. l. 892, when Orestes is seen standing over the body of the slain Aegisthus, except that here it seems very unlikely that an ἐκκύκλημα was rolled out in front of the palace with the body of Aegisthus and then rolled back again so that Orestes might carry out his purpose (l. 904) of slaying Clytemnestra alongside of Aegisthus—for which end he drives her indoors at l. 930. Probably the slain Aegisthus is simply displayed in the doorway, and the doors are afterwards closed, leaving the body inside. At l. 973 both bodies are revealed, together with the net in which Agamemnon had been entangled. Once more the ἐκκύκλημα *may* have been used as the scholiast on 973 asserts (ἀνοίγεται ἡ σκηνὴ καὶ ἐπὶ ἐκκυκλήματος ὁρᾶται τὰ σώματα), but the text does not actually require it, and we do not know how much the scholiast knew about the fifth-century theatre.

2. The problem of the opening scene of the *Eumenides* is more complicated, and close attention to the text is necessary. At l. 33 the Pythia enters the temple (probably through the central door in the background, only partly opened), but rushes out again on hands and feet, unable for the moment to stand, and describes the horrible sight which she had seen—the hideous band of Furies surrounding a suppliant with hands and sword dripping with blood. She describes the scene so fully that it is clear that the spectators do *not* see it for themselves. But at l. 64 the doors are opened; Apollo is seen addressing Orestes, and obviously the Furies must have been partly, though perhaps not fully, visible. At l. 90 Orestes, in the care of Hermes, leaves the temple. Then the Ghost of Clytemnestra appears—probably in, or close to, the doorway—and rouses the Furies, who, when thoroughly awake, sing their first chant, voicing their anger against Apollo. This still takes place within the temple, because at l. 179 Apollo bids them go out of it—ἔξω, κελεύω, τῶνδε δωμάτων τάχος. They no doubt do so, and the rest of the conversation is conducted in front of the temple (down to l. 234).

διὲκ θυρῶν· τοὺς νεκροὺς οὕτω φασὶν ἑδράζεσθαι, ἔξω τοὺς πόδας ἔχοντας πρὸς τὰς αὐλείους θύρας.

Those who think it impossible that the whole scene from l. 64 to l. 179 should be conducted within the temple doors—however widely opened—suppose that this interior scene is rolled out on the ἐκκύκλημα, and rolled back at 234 when the scene changes to Athens. The ἐκκύκλημα would have to carry Apollo, Orestes, and the ὀμφαλός, Hermes, and twelve Furies—a heavy load and a very awkward method of displaying them.[1] The scholiast on l. 64 says καὶ δευτέρα δὲ γίνεται φαντασία· στραφέντα γὰρ μηχανήματα ἔνδηλα ποιεῖ τὰ κατὰ τὸ μαντεῖον ὡς ἔχει, implying some kind of revolving apparatus; but it is quite uncertain whether this and similar phrases imply a circular or semicircular platform swung on a pivot, and carried on wheels, or simply a means of throwing open the front wall of the building sufficiently to show the interior. It seems at least possible that the lexicographers and scholiasts are transferring back to classical times devices with which they had become familiar in theatres at Alexandria or in theatres of the Roman pattern,[2] and there is certainly room for the possibility that such things were not used in the Trilogy at all, and that the sole device used was a wide opening in the wooden screen which represented the front wall of the temple. (The theory of Rees that the whole scene was conducted in a πρόθυρον is inconsistent with the text.)

A remark in the *Vita Aeschyli* records a tradition that the Eumenides came into view of the audience σποράδην 'one by one'. τινὲς δέ φασιν ἐν τῇ ἐπιδείξει τῶν Εὐμενίδων σποράδην εἰσαγαγόντα τὸν χορὸν τοσοῦτον ἐκπλῆξαι τὸν δῆμον, ὡς τὰ μὲν νήπια ἐκψῦξαι, τὰ δὲ ἔμβρυα ἐξαμβλωθῆναι. If there is anything in the tradition, it entirely excludes the idea of an ἐκκύκλημα as a platform rolled out in front of the temple, on which the Furies were all seen sleeping around Orestes from l. 64 onwards. It is, however, possible that they rushed out one by one while singing the choral ode ll. 143–77, and that Apollo at l. 179, ἔξω, κελεύω, τῶνδε δωμάτων τάχος, is only chasing out the last of them. (The fact that the ode seems to be distributed among a number of voices is consistent with this.)

---

[1] Reisch (D.R., p. 244) notes other technical difficulties, and asks pointedly how, if Apollo and the interior of the temple are on the ἐκκύκλημα in front of the temple, Apollo can retire *into* the temple at 93, to emerge again at 179?

[2] See Virg. *Georg.* iii. 24 and comm.; Plut. *de glor. Ath.* 6, *de esu carn.* i. 7; Val. Max. ii. 4. 6 (refs. given by Reisch).

III

It is usual to assume the use of the ἐκκύκλημα in the *Ajax* of Sophocles to display to the audience the interior of the hero's tent, where he sits surrounded by slain animals—this scene being, it is supposed, rolled forward out of the central door in the background, representing the door of his tent or wooden hut. When the scene which serves as a prologue and the parodos are ended, Tecmessa enters (at l. 201)[1] and tells the chorus what is to be seen in the tent (τοιαῦτ' ἂν ἴδοις σκηνῆς ἔνδον); and how Ajax has learned from her the real nature of his acts.[2] His groans are heard from within, and at l. 346, in response to the request of the chorus she opens wide the tent door, so that Ajax may be seen by the chorus (who had not been present during the prologue) in the midst of the slaughtered animals. It is at this point that the ἐκκύκλημα is commonly supposed to have been rolled forward bearing the hero and his victims. The scholiast writes: ἐνταῦθα ἐκκύκλημά τι γίνεται, ἵνα φανῇ ἐν μέσοις ὁ Αἴας ποιμνίοις· εἰς ἔκπληξιν γὰρ φέρει καὶ ταῦτα τὸν θεατήν, τὰ ἐν τῇ ὄψει περιπαθέστερα. δείκνυται δὲ ξιφήρης, ᾑματωμένος, μεταξὺ τῶν ποιμνίων καθήμενος. But, apart from the possibility that the scholiast is ascribing to Sophocles the devices of a much later age, it is very doubtful whether in the scholium ἐκκύκλημα signifies any kind of machinery, and not simply 'a disclosure' or 'revelation' in accordance with a well-attested late usage of the verb ἐκκυκλεῖν. That the latter is the meaning is strongly suggested by the verb γίνεται, which cannot mean 'the ἐκκύκλημα is *employed*'; it must mean 'a sudden disclosure is made' (cf. schol. on Aesch. *Eum.* 64 καὶ δευτέρα δὲ γίνεται φαντασία). The *chorus* is clearly *supposed* to see the slaughtered animals through the tent door, but it is not certain that they were seen by the spectators at all, still less that a platform bearing a number of bleeding carcasses was thrust forward under their eyes. It seems much more likely that Ajax from l. 349 onwards speaks from just inside the tent, probably

[1] She possibly enters from a side entrance; if she enters by the central door, it cannot have been opened wide. Of course, like captive women in the *Iliad*, she shares the tent or hut with her lord, but there may have been a separate women's apartment.

[2] He must have learned this while the parodos of the chorus was in progress. In the introductory scene in which he takes part from ll. 91 to 117 he had not yet been undeceived.

close to the entrance. (That there would be no difficulty in hearing him is clear, if in ll. 91–117 he was speaking from within, as is
commonly supposed, though this is far from certain.) He is certainly supposed to be still inside the tent for some time, since at
l. 369 he answers Tecmessa's supplication with οὐκ ἐκτός ; οὐκ
ἄψορρον ἐκνεμῇ πόδα ; Probably at l. 430 he comes outside for his
long speech, and from l. 578 onwards gradually withdraws back
into the tent,[1] the door of which is closed at l. 595, Tecmessa
going in with him. (At ll. 651–2 he ascribes his change of mind
to her influence, and she doubtless came out again with him at
ll. 646.) The lines 545–6, which some quote as proving that the
slaughtered beasts must be in sight of the audience,

αἶρ᾽ αὐτόν, αἶρε δεῦρο· ταρβήσει γὰρ οὔ,
νεοσφαγῆ που τόνδε προσλεύσσων φόνον,

do not do so; they would be sufficiently explained if the door
were wide open, even if the words refer to the slain beasts at all,
and not, as is far more likely, to the blood-stains on Ajax himself.
(The infant would not see the *beasts* any better from Ajax' arms
than from Tecmessa's, and in any case he could be supposed to
see them without their being visible to the audience.) Accordingly
it seems very unlikely that an ἐκκύκλημα was used in this scene
at all. Nor is there any room for it at l. 992, where the puppet
representing the body of Ajax is plainly carried in by Teucer's
men.[2]

At l. 1293 of the *Antigone*, where the body of Eurydike is
revealed (ὁρᾶν πάρεστιν· οὐ γὰρ ἐν μυχοῖς ἔτι), the scholiast says
ἐγκέκλεισται ἡ γυνή—probably a corruption of ἐκκυκλεῖται—and
editors (including Jebb) think that the ἐκκύκλημα here brought
forward the body and, perhaps, the altar by which she had slain
herself. But there is nothing in the text to suggest this; the body
may simply have been borne out to the entrance or wheeled on
a bier.

In the *Electra* of Sophocles, at l. 1458, Aegisthus orders the
doors to be thrown open, expecting to see the corpse of Orestes.
A covered corpse is shown to him, which at l. 1475 he discovers to
be that of Clytemnestra. Here again a simple bier is all that is

[1] It seems impossible to suppose that a platform covered with dead animals
was rolled back with him without some absurdity.
[2] Bethe's suggestions (*Prolegomena*, pp. 125–9), involving several rollings of
the ἐκκύκλημα backwards and forwards, seem quite impossible.

required, not any elaborate machinery—perhaps the kind of bier seen on vases depicting the πρόθεσις of the dead, who were customarily laid and lamented at the door of the house.[1]

The view of Frickenhaus[2] that an ἐκκύκλημα is used in the *Philoctetes* and *Oedipus Coloneus* is entirely unconvincing. It seems improbable that it was used at all by Sophocles, any more than the μηχανή, which he was also led to avoid by his extreme sensitiveness in regard to improbability and incongruity.

IV

1. The use of an ἐκκύκλημα is spoken of in connexion with several plays of Euripides. The scholia on the *Hippolytus* 170–1,

ἀλλ᾽ ἥδε τροφὸς γεραιὰ πρὸ θυρῶν
τήνδε κομίζουσ᾽ ἔξω μελάθρων,

though partly unintelligible, appear at least to show that Aristophanes of Byzantium (2nd cent. B.C.) believed that the ἐκκύκλημα was used to bring Phaedra out of the house. The first runs : τοῦτο σεσημείωται τῷ Ἀριστοφάνει, ὅτι καίτοι τῷ ἐγκυκλήματι[3] χρώμενος τὸ ἐκκομίζουσα προσέθηκε περισσῶς. On the surface this seems to mean that the ἔξω (κομίζουσ᾽ ἔξω being treated as = ἐκκομίζουσα) is superfluous, because it was, anyhow, the proper business of the ἐκκύκλημα to bring things out, and this is consistent with the first sentence of the second scholium : τοῦτο σεσημείωκεν Ἀριστοφάνης, ὅτι κατὰ τὸ ἀκριβὲς τὸ ἔγκλημα (*leg.* ἐγκύκλημα) τοιοῦτόν ἐστι τῇ ὑποθέσει. (The criticism is a very puerile one, but Alexandrian criticisms sometimes were.) But the second scholium goes on : ἐπὶ γὰρ τῆς σκηνῆς δείκνυται τὰ ἔνδον πραττόμενα, ὁ δὲ ἔξω προϊοῦσαν αὐτὴν ὑποτίθεται. This is probably not part of Aristophanes' own criticism, but a bad attempt on the part of the scholiast to explain it, and the text of the sentence is very probably corrupt ; it

---

[1] The suggestion of Tycho von Wilamowitz-Moellendorff (*Die dramatische Technik des Sophokles*, p. 226) that the body is rolled out on a platform, that Orestes, Pylades, and Aegisthus then mount this platform, and that from 1491 onwards the scene is supposed to be inside the house, seems both needless and absurd. [2] *Die altgr. Bühne*, p. 13.

[3] In many passages ἐγκύκλημα and ἐγκυκλεῖν appear in place of ἐκκ-, which has the balance of authority. It seems much more likely that ἐγκ- is a euphonic modification of ἐκκ-, than that it was a real alternative name for the thing (as Exon supposes) with the connotation 'rotating' (cf. ἐγκύκλιος φορά, κτλ.). (Cf. ἔκγονος and ἔγγονος.)

seems to attribute to Aristophanes a quite different criticism, viz. that Euripides is using the ἐκκύκλημα to bring Phaedra *really* out of doors, whereas it should only be used to show the audience something which is supposed to be really going on *in*doors. But it is difficult to suppose that Aristophanes of Byzantium was right in thinking that an ἐκκύκλημα was employed here. Phaedra is clearly wheeled out on a couch by her attendants, and no machinery is needed; and she is of course, *really* out of doors (ll. 179–80 ἔξω δὲ δόμων ἤδη νοσερᾶς | δέμνια κοίτης) until she goes inside or is wheeled in at l. 731. Nor need there be any use of such machinery later in the play. At l. 786 the dead Phaedra is laid out within the house, close to the entrance, as custom was; there Theseus sees her when he has the doors opened at 809, and there Hippolytus suddenly catches sight of her at 905, immediately after his arrival: but again nothing is needed but a wheeled bier or couch.

2. No solution of the scene in the *Hercules Furens* from 1029 onwards is entirely free from difficulties. The doors are thrown open at 1029: ἴδεσθε, διάνδιχα κλῇθρα | κλίνεται ὑψιπύλων δόμων, and the chorus see the dead children (and their mother) lying in front of Herakles, who (ll. 1038, 1096) is tied to a broken pillar— l. 1032: ἴδεσθε δὲ τέκνα πρὸ πατρὸς | ἄθλια κείμενα δυστάνου | εὕδοντος ὕπνον δεινὸν ἐκ παίδων φόνου. (The relative positions are confirmed by the fact that, when Theseus arrives, he sees the children's bodies before he perceives Herakles.) Is this collection of corpses and their slayer still inside the open doors, or was it rolled or swung out on the ἐκκύκλημα? In favour of the former view are these considerations: (1) If they were all in the open air outside the door, Theseus could hardly help seeing all at once, whereas if Herakles was farther back inside the door, he might not see him till he was quite close, and this is more in accordance with the text. (2) Even if the rolling out of Herakles and the bodies would be easily accepted, the rolling out of *one* of the broken pillars of a shattered mansion is much more difficult, and emphasizes too strongly the contrast between the supposed interior scene and the actual fact that the scene is *out*side (on the ἐκκύκλημα).[1]

[1] Rees thinks that the scene is laid in the supposed πρόθυρον, which he regards as the conventional place for the presentation of interior scenes, that Heracles is tied to one of the pillars of the πρόθυρον, and that a curtain was drawn over the front of the πρόθυρον until l. 1029. But if any of the columns of the πρόθυρον

Fig. 32. Funeral Scene (Apulian Amphora, Madrid)

(3) There is no difficulty in supposing that Herakles' speeches from l. 1088 to l. 1124 would be audible even if he were within the door, and, given a reasonably high doorway, he would probably be also visible to practically all the audience, especially if the interior were lighted from above (as it might well be after the convulsion that had shattered the house). At l. 1125 he doubtless came forward, when freed from his bonds, but retired again when the approach of Theseus was announced. Some have argued that the exclamation of Theseus at l. 1172, ἔα· τί νεκρῶν τῶνδε πληθύει πέδον; points to the bodies being *outside* the house, πέδον being more commonly used of the natural earth than of the floor of a house; but there are a few possible exceptions, e.g. the fragment of the *Hypsipyle*,[1] where it may be either the floor of the entrance to the palace or the ground just in front; and even if the bodies were on an ἐκκύκλημα representing the interior of the house, πέδον would still be (*ex hypothesi*) the floor of the interior, and not the natural earth. Others have thought that when, at l. 1070, the sleeping Herakles begins to stir and Amphitryon says ἀπόκρυφον δέμας ὑπὸ μέλαθρον κρύψω, it would be easier to suppose that Herakles was definitely outside the house. But if he were outside on an ἐκκύκλημα, the spectators would be expected to regard him as *inside* (if the ἐκκύκλημα displayed interiors); and the line is quite intelligible if Herakles were just inside the open door, but visible.[2]

3. In the *Hecuba* at l. 1049, when Hecuba and the Trojan women have blinded Polymestor and killed his sons inside the tent, Hecuba says:

ὄψῃ νιν αὐτίκ' ὄντα δωμάτων πάρος
τυφλὸν τυφλῷ στείχοντα παραφόρῳ ποδί,

was shattered (of which there is no hint) it must have happened during the play, when the πρόθυρον, curtained or not, was facing the audience, and if so, how did it happen without their perceiving it? or why should it have to be narrated by a messenger? And if the πρόθυρον was curtained, what of the exits and entrances by the central door down to 1029?

[1] See Ch. III, p. 76; cf. also *Orestes* 1433, 1438, though the adverbial πέδῳ or πέδοι seems to be less restricted in its meaning than πέδον.

[2] This play and the *Ajax* are the only plays in which any question could arise as to the visibility or audibility of the speaker just within the doorway. Generally speaking it may be assumed that in scenes in which corpses are revealed the slayer or speaker stood well forward, and probably advanced beyond the doorway to speak.

παίδων τε δισσῶν σώμαθ', οὓς ἔκτειν' ἐγὼ
σὺν ταῖς ἀρίσταις Τρῳάσιν.

Polymestor staggers out, and the children's bodies were probably
brought out by the women at the end of Hecuba's speech (1055)
or simply revealed by the opening of the tent doors. (Agamemnon sees them at l. 1118.) The ἐκκύκλημα is at least unnecessary.

4. The same is the case in the *Electra*. At l. 959 the body of
Aegisthus (which Orestes had brought with him at 895) is carried
into the house, and at 1172, after killing Clytemnestra, Orestes
and Electra rush out on foot and point to both bodies obviously
lying on the ground where Clytemnestra had fallen, i.e. just
within the doorway:

ἰὼ Γᾶ καὶ Ζεῦ πανδερκέτα,
βροτῶν ἴδετε τάδ' ἔργα φόνι-
α μυσαρά, δίγονα σώματ'
ἐν χθονὶ κείμενα πλαγᾷ
χερὸς ὑπ' ἐμᾶς.

They were certainly visible to the chorus and may have been
carried out after Orestes had spoken thus. The words of the
Dioskouroi, speaking δόμων ὑπὲρ ἀκροτάτων (ll. 1242–3), ὡς ἐσεί-
δομεν | σφαγὰς ἀδελφῆς τῆσδε, do not necessarily imply this, nor
does (l. 1294) οὐ μυσαραῖς τοῖσδε σφαγίοις, as ὅδε does not invariably
imply visibility to the speaker, but they lend a certain probability
to the supposition; and at l. 1227 Orestes orders them to be
covered up, but there is no trace of an ἐκκύκλημα, and no need
of one.

5. Bethe, who in his *Prolegomena* had argued for the use of the
ἐκκύκλημα in the *Medea*, afterwards (and rightly) changed his
mind.[1] Medea had slain her children inside the house, and the
chorus at l. 1313 expect that Jason will find their bodies there;
but Medea has carried them off with her in the snake-drawn
chariot, in which she appears, whether on the μηχανή or on a
tower above the roof of the palace, at l. 1316 (schol. on l. 1320
ἐπὶ ὕψους παραφαίνεται ἡ Μήδεια, ὀχουμένη δρακοντίνοις ἅρμασι καὶ
βαστάζουσα τοὺς παῖδας):

[1] But his view in *Rh. Mus.* lxxxiii (1934), p. 24, that Medea appears in her
magic chariot in the open doorway is also improbable. The chariot would have
to back into the doorway again—probably not an easier manœuvre for snakes
than for horses.

1313 *XO.* πύλας ἀνοίξας σῶν τέκνων ὄψῃ φόνον.

    IA. χαλᾶτε κλῇδας ὡς τάχιστα, πρόσπολοι,
        ἐκλύεθ᾽ ἁρμούς, ὡς ἴδω διπλοῦν κακόν,
        τοὺς μὲν θανόντας, τὴν δὲ τείσωμαι δίκην.

    MH. τί τάσδε κινεῖς κἀναμοχλεύεις πύλας,
        νεκροὺς ἐρευνῶν κἀμὲ τὴν εἰργασμένην;
        παῦσαι πόνου τοῦδ᾽· εἰ δ᾽ ἐμοῦ χρείαν ἔχεις,
1320   λέγ᾽, εἴ τι βούλῃ, χειρὶ δ᾽ οὐ ψαύσεις ποτέ.
        τοιόνδ᾽ ὄχημα πατρὸς Ἥλιος πατὴρ
        δίδωσιν ἡμῖν, ἔρυμα πολεμίας χερός,

and at 1377

    IA. θάψαι νεκροὺς μοι τούσδε καὶ κλαῦσαι πάρες.
    MH. οὐ δῆτ᾽, ἐπεί σφας τῇδ᾽ ἐγὼ θάψω χερί,
        φέρουσ᾽ ἐς Ἥρας τέμενος Ἀκραίας θεοῦ.

6. The result of this survey of the passages in extant Tragedy and Comedy in which the use of a machine called by the name ἐκκύκλημα is asserted by ancient or modern commentators is an unsatisfactory one. It amounts to this—that there is no play in which its use can be considered necessary, and some in which it is definitely improbable (such as the *Eumenides*, the *Ajax*, the *Hippolytus*, and the *Clouds*); that in several plays it *could* have been used (though there is no sufficient evidence to prove the use) but that the scenes could quite well have been acted without it. In the *Acharnians* and *Thesmophoriazousai* there was evidently some absurd effect connected with the words ἐκκυκλεῖν and ἐσκυκλεῖν, but it may have been simply the travesty of scenes of a type of which Euripides affords more than one instance, such as that of Phaedra on her couch or Alcestis wheeled in front of the door.

V

We have still, however, to survey the passages in lexicographers and commentators which bear on the subject. (For the sake of completeness, the scholia, &c., already quoted are repeated.)

(1) Pollux iv. 128: καὶ τὸ μὲν ἐκκύκλημα ἐπὶ ξύλων ὑψηλὸν βάθρον, ᾧ ἐπίκειται θρόνος· δείκνυσι δὲ τὰ ὑπὸ σκηνὴν ἐν ταῖς οἰκίαις ἀπόρρητα πραχθέντα, καὶ τὸ ῥῆμα τοῦ ἔργου καλεῖται ἐκκυκλεῖν. ἐφ᾽ οὗ δὲ εἰσάγεται τὸ ἐκκύκλημα, εἰσκύκλημα ὀνομάζεται, καὶ χρὴ τοῦτο νοεῖσθαι καθ᾽ ἑκάστην θύραν, οἱονεὶ καθ᾽ ἑκάστην οἰκίαν.

Pollux (2nd cent. ᾿A.D.) was interested in cataloguing the meanings of words from the standpoint of philology, not of history or archaeology, and for ἐκκύκλημα he gives 'a high platform on wooden supports, with a chair on it'. This must be a reference to some particular play —probably not the *Acharnians* as some have supposed, as θρόνος would be inaccurate ; nor the *Thesmophoriazousai*, in regard to which ὑψηλὸν (or ὑψηλῶν as the Clementine scholiast quotes it) would have no point. The next sentence (δείκνυσι δὲ . . . πραχθέντα) must refer to the display of murdered bodies, but may also regard the machine as displaying an interior scene.

There is no certain interpretation of the words about εἰσκύκλημα— there can hardly have been separate machinery for rolling the ὑψηλὸν βάθρον out and for rolling it in, though both names may have been used. The last words indicate that at some unspecified period the machinery might be employed at any of the three doors in the theatrical skené. (Thus it is alleged by scholiasts to be used at two different parts of the background in the *Thesmophoriazousai*.)

(On the value of Pollux as an authority for the theatre of the Classical period see von Gerkan, *Das Theater von Priene*, pp. 119–20. He points out that his authorities are largely scholiasts, and that he cannot be taken as reliable for any particular period. His material is of all dates, and is classified and set down irrespective of date.)

(2) Clem. Alex. *Protrept.*, ch. ii, § 12 (vol. i, p. 11 Stählin) : τὴν γοητείαν τὴν κεκρυμμένην αὐτοῖς . . . οἷον ἐπὶ σκηνῆς τοῦ βίου τοῖς τῆς ἀληθείας ἐκκυκλήσω θεαταῖς.

Schol. ad loc. (vol. i, p. 301 Stählin) : ἐκκυκλήσω· ἐγκύκλημα ἐκάλουν σκεῦός τι ὑπότροχον ἐκτὸς τῆς σκηνῆς, οὗ στρεφομένου ἐδόκει τὰ ἔσω τοῖς ἔξω φανερὰ γίνεσθαι. ἐγκυκλήσω οὖν ἀντὶ τοῦ φανερώσω, γυμνώσω.

διεξοδικώτερον δὲ περὶ τοῦ αὐτοῦ εἰπεῖν, ἐγκύκλημα ἐλέγετο βάθρον ἐπὶ ξύλων ὑψηλῶν, ᾧ ἐπίκειται θρόνος· δείκνυσι δὲ τὰ ὑπὸ τῇ σκηνῇ ἐν ταῖς οἰκίαις πραχθέντα ἀπόρρητα· ὑφ᾽ οὗ δὲ εἰσάγεται τὸ ἐγκύκλημα, ἐσκύκλημα ὀνομάζεται, καὶ χρὴ τοῦτο νοεῖν καθ᾽ ἑκάστην θύραν, ἵν᾽ ᾖ καθ᾽ ἑκάστην οἰκίαν. (Cf. Pollux.)

(3) Clem. Alex. *Protrept.*, ch. vii, § 76 (vol. i, p. 58 Stählin) : (Εὐριπίδης) γυμνῇ τῇ κεφαλῇ ἐκκυκλεῖ τῷ θεάτρῳ τοὺς θεούς (i.e. 'displays'). The gods certainly did not appear on an ἐκκύκλημα as ordinarily understood. The theory of Bulle (*Das Theater zu Sparta*, pp. 81 ff.), that they appeared on an ἐξώστρα, will be discussed below.

(4) Clem. Alex. *Stromata*, iii, ch. iv, § 26 (vol. ii, p. 208 Stählin) : ὧν οὕτως ἐχόντων ἀποβολὴ πάθους ἦν ⟨ἡ⟩ εἰς μέσον τῶν ἀποστόλων [ἡ] τῆς ζηλοτυπουμένης ἐκκύκλησις γυναικός.

(5) Clem. Alex. *Stromata*, vii, ch. xiv, § 88 (vol. iii, p. 63 Stählin) : οὐ γὰρ ἐκκυκλεῖν χρὴ τὸ μυστήριον, ἐμφαίνειν δὲ ὅσον εἰς ἀνάμνησιν τοῖς μετεσχηκόσι τῆς γνώσεως.

(6) Schol. on Aristoph. *Ach.* 408 ἐκκύκλημα δὲ λέγεται μηχάνημα ξύλινον

τροχοὺς ἔχον, ὅπερ περιστρεφόμενον τὰ δοκοῦντα ὡς ἐν οἰκίᾳ πράττεσθαι καὶ τοῖς ἔξω ἐδείκνυε, λέγω δὴ τοῖς θεαταῖς. (See above, p. 102.)

(7) Schol. on Aristoph. *Clouds* 184: ὁρᾷ δὲ (sc. τοὺς μαθητὰς) ὡς φιλοσόφους κομῶντας, στραφέντος τοῦ ἐγκυκλήματος. (See above, p. 104.)

(7a) Argum. iii to Aristoph. *Clouds*: ἐκκυκληθείσης δὲ τῆς διατριβῆς οἵ τε μαθηταὶ κύκλῳ καθήμενοι πιναροὶ συνορῶνται . . . . (See above, p. 104.)

(8) Schol. on Aristoph. *Thesm.* 96: ἐπὶ ἐκκυκλήματος γὰρ φαίνεται (sc. ὁ Ἀγάθων).

(9) *Parepigraphe* at Aristoph. *Thesm.* 276: ὀλολύζουσι· τὸ ἱερὸν ὠθεῖται (Fritzsche for ὀλολύζουσί τε ἱερὸν ὠθεῖται). (See above, p. 104.)

(10) Schol. on Aristoph. *Thesm.* 277: παρεπιγραφή· ἐκκυκλεῖται ἐπὶ τὸ ἔξω τὸ Θεσμοφόριον. (See above, p. 105.)

(11) Schol. on Aesch. *Choeph.* 973: ἀνοίγεται ἡ σκηνὴ καὶ ἐπὶ ἐκκυκλήματος ὁρᾶται τὰ σώματα.

(12) Schol. on Aesch. *Eum.* 64: καὶ δευτέρα δὲ γίνεται φαντασία· στραφέντα γὰρ μηχανήματα ἔνδηλα ποιεῖ τὰ κατὰ τὸ μαντεῖον ὡς ἔχει.

(13) Schol. on Soph. *Ajax* 346: ἐνταῦθα ἐκκύκλημά τι γίνεται, ἵνα φανῇ ἐν μέσοις ὁ Αἴας ποιμνίοις· εἰς ἔκπληξιν γὰρ φέρει καὶ ταῦτα τὸν θεατήν, τὰ ἐν ὄψει περιπᾰθέστερα· δείκνυται δὲ ξιφήρης, ἡματωμένος, μεταξὺ τῶν ποιμνίων καθήμενος. (See above, p. 109.)

(14) Schol. on Eur. *Med.* 96: τάδε λέγει ἡ Μήδεια ἔσω οὖσα οὐδέπω ἐκκεκυκλημένη.

(Here there is no possible reference to any machine.)

(15) Schol. on Eur. *Hippolyt.* 172. (1) τοῦτο σεσημείωται τῷ Ἀριστοφάνει, ὅτι καὶ τῷ ἐγκυκλήματι χρώμενος τὸ ἐκκομίζουσα προσέθηκε περισσῶς.

(2) τοῦτο σεσημείωκεν Ἀριστοφάνης, ὅτι κατὰ τὸ ἀκριβὲς τὸ ἔγκλημα (*leg.* ἐγκύκλημα) τοιοῦτόν ἐστι τῇ ὑποθέσει, ἐπὶ γὰρ τῆς σκηνῆς δείκνυται τὰ ἔνδον πραττόμενα, ὁ δὲ ἔξω προϊοῦσαν αὐτὴν ὑποτίθεται.

(These scholia are discussed above, p. 111.)

(16) Bekker, *Anecd.* i. 208–9: μηχανή ἐστι παρὰ τοῖς κωμικοῖς ἐκκυκλήματός τι εἶδος ἀπὸ συνθήκης πρὸς ὃ φέρεται ὁ ⟨ὑποκριτὴς, Crusius⟩ ἐπὶ τὴν σκηνὴν δείξεως χάριν θεοῦ ἢ ἄλλου τινὸς ἥρωος.

(17) Lucian, *Philops.* 29: καὶ τὸ τοῦ λόγου, θεὸν ἀπὸ μηχανῆς ἐπεισκυκληθῆναί μοι τοῦτον ᾤμην ὑπὸ τῆς τύχης.

Here, as in No. 16, the business of the ἐκκύκλημα seems to be the revelation of a god or hero, but Lucian seems to think of the revelation as made by the μηχανή, and if so, the verb is used in a quite untechnical sense; but the same confusion seems to occur in

(18) Philostratus, *Vit. Apoll.* VI. xi. 11 (2nd–3rd cent. A.D.): φιλοσοφίας ἡττηθεὶς εὖ κεκοσμημένης, ἣν εἰς τὸ πρόσφορον Ἰνδοὶ στείλαντες ἐφ᾽ ὑψηλῆς καὶ θείας μηχανῆς ἐκκυκλοῦσιν. (Here simply 'display'.)

(19) Schol. on *Iliad*, xviii. 477: δαιμονίως τὸν πλάστην αὐτὸς διέπλασεν, ὥσπερ ἐπὶ σκηνῆς ἐκκυκλήσας, καὶ δείξας ἡμῖν ἐν τῷ φανερῷ τὸ ἐργαστήριον.

This seems to imply the revelation of an interior scene which would not otherwise be visible.

Other related compounds are used in both early and late Greek in a quite untechnical sense, e.g.:

(20) Aristoph. *Wasps*, 1474–5: νὴ τὸν Διόνυσον ἀπορά γ' ἡμῖν πράγματα | δαίμων τις ἐσκεκύκληκεν ἐς τὴν οἰκίαν.

(21) Heliod. *Aithiop.* vii. 7 (? 3rd cent. A.D.): παρεκκύκλημα is an interlude 'thrown in' in a drama. Cf. schol. on Aristoph. *Clouds* 18 ταῦτα πάντα παρεγκυκλήματά εἰσι καὶ παρεπιγραφαί, and schol. on Aristoph. *Clouds* 20 καὶ τοῦτο παρεγκύκλημα ἐφίστησιν.

(22) Pollux ix. 158 (a list of equivalent expressions): προσόμοια καὶ ταῦτα, εἰσῆλθεν ἐπῆλθεν ἐπεισῆλθεν . . . εἰσεκυκλήθη ἐπεισεκυκλήθη.

(23) Philostr. *Vit. Apoll.* VI. x. 6: τρίποδας δὲ ἐσκυκλήσει πίνοντι καὶ χρυσοῦς θρόνους.

(24) Athen. vi. 270 e: θεασάμενος πλῆθος ἰχθύων καὶ ἄλλων παντοδαπῶν ὄψων παρασκευὴν εἰσκυκλουμένην.

There are also a few passages in which the ἐξώστρα is mentioned:

(25) Pollux. iv. 127: εἴη δ' ἂν καὶ τῶν ἐκ θεάτρου καὶ ἐκκύκλημα καὶ μηχανὴ καὶ ἐξώστρα καὶ σκοπὴ καὶ τεῖχος, κτλ.

(26) Pollux iv. 129: τὴν δὲ ἐξώστραν ταὐτὸν τῷ ἐκκυκλήματι νομίζουσιν.

(27) Hesych. s.v. ' ἐξώστρα ': ἐπὶ τῆς σκηνῆς τὸ ἐκκύκλημα.

(28) *C.I.G.* xi. 2, No. 199 (Delos: 274 B.C.), ll. 94–5: Ἐπικράτῃ τῷ ἐγλαβόντι τὰς σκηνὰς τὰς παλαιὰς ξῦσαι καὶ ἐπισκευάσαι καὶ τὰς ἐπάνω σκηνὰς καινὰς ποιῆσαι δύο καὶ τὰ παρασκήνια τὰ ἄνω καινὰ ποιῆσαι δύο καὶ τοῖς παλαιοῖς πίναξι τῶν παρασκηνίων κύκλῳ περιφράξαι καὶ τὰ ἔξωστρα καὶ τὴν κλίμακα καὶ τοὺς βωμοὺς ἐπισκευάσαι ⳋΔΔΔΓΙΙ (i.e. 537 dr.). From the position of the words it seems probable that τὰ ἔξωστρα were connected with the upper story of the stage building. The use of the plural (here alone neuter) may be connected with the statement of Pollux iv. 128 that there might be an ἐκκύκλημα at each of the doors. Bulle (*Das Theater zu Sparta*, pp. 84 ff.) thinks that the exostra issued out of the doors of the skené on to the logeion and ran to the edge of the proskenion, whether for use as a theologeion or for other undiscoverable purposes, as (he thinks) the supposed exostra at Eretria did (see below). Alternatively he suggests that they may have been fixed balconies in a wooden *scaenae frons*, erected experimentally at this period at Delos, like the *maeniana* in the Roman forum (see below).

(29) Polyb. XI. vi. 8: τῆς τύχης ὥσπερ ἐπίτηδες ἐπὶ τὴν ἐξώστραν ἀναβιβαζούσης τὴν ὑμετέραν ἄγνοιαν.

(30) Cicero, *de prov. cons.* § 14: iam in exostra helluatur, ante post siparium solebat.

The Glossographers (quoted in Pauly–W. s.v. *maenianum*) interpret ἐξώστρα and ἐξώστης by *maenianum*, of which Festus (134 b. 22) says 'Maeniana appellata sunt a Maenio censore (348 B.C.), qui primus in foro ultra columnas tigna proiecit, quo ampliarentur superiora spectacula', so as to give a better view to spectators of shows, and Vitruvius (v. vi. 9) uses the word of the balconies of private houses, such as were reproduced in *comicae scaenae* and on Pompeian wall-paintings. But a movable type of *maenianum* known as *exostra* was used by military engineers. Veget. IV. xi 'exostra dicitur pons, quem superius exposuimus, quia de turri in murum protruditur'—a bridge which could be let fall into position. Unfortunately these passages have little value as evidence for the classical or Hellenistic theatre.

VI

According to these various notices, the ἐκκύκλημα was:

(a) A high platform (Pollux), supported on wooden timbers (id.) and made of wood (schol. Aristoph. *Ach.*).

(b) On wheels (Eustathius, schol. Clem. Alex., schol. Aristoph. *Ach.*).

(c) Rolled out from an opening in the background (schol. Aesch. *Choëph.*) or at any of the openings (Pollux).

(d) Operated by pushing (*Parepigr.* ad Aristoph. *Thesm.* 276). This is implied also by the identification with ἐξώστρα (Pollux).

(e) Operated by turning (schol. Clem. Alex., schol. Aristoph. *Clouds*, schol. Aesch. *Eumen.*).

(f) Used to reveal interior scenes, or to bring objects and persons out from the interior (Pollux, Eustathius, schol. Clem. Alex., schol. Aristoph. *Ach.*, Argt. Aristoph. *Clouds*, schol. Aesch. *Eumen.*, schol. Eur. *Hippol.*, and probably schol. *Il.* xviii. 477).

(g) Used to display or reveal gods (Clem. Alex., Bekker *Anecd.*, and perhaps Philostratus).

(h) Identified (or confused) with the μηχανή (Bekker *Anecd.*, Lucian, Philostratus).

Evidently the ἐκκύκλημα was commonly thought of as a platform on wheels, which appeared out of an opening in the *scaenae frons* (ordinarily on the ground-level, but perhaps occasionally on the first story (see above on the *Acharnians* and the Delian inscription), propelled by being pushed forward or else revolving in some way, and normally revealing either an interior scene or the results of actions done in the interior of the building (τὰ ἐν ταῖς οἰκίαις ἀπόρρητα πραχθέντα, Pollux).

Possibly, as suggested in the Introduction to this chapter, there were two varieties of ἐκκύκλημα, one pushed straight forward (? the ἐξώστρα proper), the other revolved into position and turning on a pivot or on wheels in a circular or semicircular track. Even the revolving variety would have to be operated by pushing. As to its form, the simplest conjecture is perhaps that of Exon[1] (Fig. 33). Flickinger (with insufficient evidence) sup-

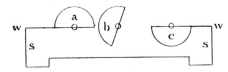

FIG. 33. The Ekkyklema according to Exon

poses that this was the earlier type of ἐκκύκλημα, and was succeeded, later in the fifth century, by the square platform pushed out through the doorway (the ἐξώστρα). But whether any such devices were employed at all in the fifth century seems very doubtful. The ἐξώστρα type may have been used in the late Hellenistic theatres which had wide thyromata, but there are no plays of this period to enlighten us as to the possible uses of either type.

The notices which ascribe, or imply the ascription, to the ἐκκύκλημα of the special function of revealing gods are very unsatisfactory. Clement probably uses ἐκκυκλεῖ in the general sense of 'display', 'reveal', though the scholiast's comment gives what was probably a stock definition of the ἐκκύκλημα, which certainly does not apply to this passage. The notice in Bekker's *Anecdota* seems to be explaining a conventional use of the μηχανή in Comedy to display gods and heroes (possibly when they appeared as 'prologues' in the New Comedy), and calls it a species of ἐκκύκλημα, and here again the word can only be general, 'a means of revealing', since, whatever else it may have been, the μηχανή as used to

[1] *Hermathena*, 1900, pp. 132 ff.; cf. Navarre, *Rev. Ét. anc.* 1901, p. 102; Flickinger, *Gk. Theater*[4], p. 286. Exon calculates that his semicircular platform might be (e.g. at Epidaurus) 16 feet wide and 8 feet deep in the middle, but the calculation seems very hazardous (and still more the general application of it).

display gods was not an ἐκκύκλημα in the technical or special sense. (The text of the notice is partly corrupt and has not been restored.) Lucian also probably speaks simply of the θεὸς ἀπὸ μηχανῆς as being 'revealed', when he uses the word ἐπεισκυκλη-θῆναι, just as in the schol. on Eur. *Med.* 96 ἐκκεκυκλημένη means 'brought on the scene' without any reference to machinery. The explanation of ἐφ' ὑψηλῆς καὶ θείας μηχανῆς ἐκκυκλοῦσι in Philostratus is similar. It appears therefore that this group of passages gives no reason to suppose that any machine called ἐκκύκλημα was used especially for the display of gods.

Such a use in Hellenistic or later times has indeed been imagined by archaeologists in connexion with the remains of theatres at Eretria and Ephesus. When the theatre at Eretria was excavated there were found traces of marble tracks for wheels running out of the scene building on the level of the stage or λογεῖον above the proscenium of the later theatre.[1] These traces have long disappeared, but it has been conjectured that they marked the track on which an ἐκκύκλημα or ἐξώστρα was pushed forward Bulle[2] is of opinion that, owing to the level on which the track ran, it could not have belonged to the first theatre (commonly dated in the last third of the fifth century), and that from its structure it must have been intended for something very heavy —not for a mere group of actors or a light chariot. This heavy object he conjectures to have been the exostra, which he conceives (as has already been mentioned) as a balcony or platform pushed forward and used as the speaking-place of gods in Hellenistic times—projecting well beyond the upper edge of the proskenion (the front supporting wall of the stage in the later theatre), so that the god appeared to be really in the air; and he further conjectures that the *scaenae frons* was painted blue, to represent the sky. This machinery was used, he supposes, in the Hellenistic age, when fifth-century plays and satyric plays, which also required a chorus, were (as he believes) acted wholly in the orchestra, as in the fifth century. It is obvious that he is asking us to take a good deal upon trust, and the idea that a god, poised on such a platform, run out·from the first floor, would seem to a post-classical Greek audience to be in the air, is not very convincing.

---

[1] Fossum, *Am. J. Arch.* ii (1898), pp. 287 ff. and pl. IV. See below, pp. 199, 200.
[2] *Untersuch.*, p. 90 and *Das Theater zu Sparta*, pp. 81 ff.

R

Similarly Dörpfeld[1] thinks that the large θυρώματα in the upper story of the theatre at Ephesus (probably belonging to the reconstruction of the theatre in the first century B.C.) were intended to allow gods to come out on to the stage above the proskenion in winged chariots—these being hauled in and out by a crane—and that the use of the words ἐκκυκλεῖν and εἰσκυκλεῖν of the appearance of gods in Comedy is explained by this practice. But this is pure guess-work, and nothing is known of such appearances. Dörpfeld may have had in mind such passages as Nos. 16 to 18 of the quotations collected earlier in this chapter, but his interpretation of the relevant words has no justification.

C. SCENERY AND STAGE PROPERTIES

1. In the preceding chapter it has been shown to be probable that while the earliest plays of Aeschylus required only the simplest setting, greater elaboration had become necessary by 458 B.C., when the *Oresteia* demanded a palace- or temple-front as a façade, with the provision of (probably) three doors and the enclosure of the actors' territory by paraskenia. Not many years after this the 'Periclean' theatre doubtless provided the necessary framework for the erection of backgrounds of this and of the other types which seem to have been recurrent throughout the rest of the fifth century. These all had in common a central opening, serving for the entrance to a palace or temple, or the door of a house, or the mouth of a cave. It would be easy to adapt it for any of these purposes and to close or cover up or disguise any of the other entrances which were not required for a particular play. As about two-thirds of the extant tragedies were played before a palace or a temple, it may be that this, if any, was the permanent or semi-permanent background. That it was taken down between one festival and another is very likely; a wooden structure would hardly have been left in position all the year. But it may have remained through each Dionysiac festival, and been subjected between the plays to such modifications as would be necessary (e.g.) to differentiate palace from temple, or to transform the façade (perhaps by the use of painted canvas or screens or panels, which could be easily moved into position)[2]

---

[1] *Jahrb. Arch.* xxviii (1913), *Anz.*, col. 41.

[2] It is probably a mistake to ascribe the invention of movable decorated walls or screens to Phormos of Syracuse, the contemporary of Epicharmus. The

into a representation of one, two, or three tents, or a country district (indicated in the simplest possible way), with or without a central cave, or of the sea-shore and cliffs, or, in Comedy, of private houses. Probably there were, as has been suggested, 'sets' for each type of scene, easily transferable, so that when (e.g.) in 431 B.C. Euripides presented the *Medea*, the *Philoctetes*, the *Dictys*, and the satyric *Theristai*, the changes of background from palace to sea-shore and from sea-shore to country could be quickly effected. Slight special adaptations would be made for particular scenes—for Sophocles' *Philoctetes* and *Oedipus Coloneus*, Euripides' *Electra* or Aristophanes' *Thesmophoriazousai*—and we need imagine no alterations which would take much time, though possibly a longer interval was left before the comedy which probably finished each day's performance. We may be sure that the theatre servants had reduced all these changes to routine, and that the changes could be made openly in the presence of the spectators without offending their sensibilities. It has been calculated that in a twelve-hour day of the festival not more than two hours at most can have been available for intervals between plays; so that both a fixed structure as a framework and great rapidity in making the necessary changes would be necessary.

2. How simple the indications of particular kinds of scenery might be is illustrated by the analogy of vase-painting, in which both interiors and landscape were suggested by the slightest indications—a military tent by a shield hanging on the wall, a wood by a single tree, the sea-shore by a rock and a few shells, and so on: and the same was the case in more elaborate works such as those which Polygnotus painted at Delphi.[1] Probably equally simple devices were employed in the Athenian theatre.

---

passage relied on in Suidas, s.v. *Φόρμος*, is doubtful as regards both reading and sense: ἐχρήσατο δὲ πρῶτος ἐνδύματι ποδήρει καὶ σκηνῇ δερμάτων φοινικῶν, with which is compared Aristotle, *Eth. Nic.* IV. vi οἷον . . . κωμῳδοῖς χορηγῶν ἐν τῇ παρόδῳ πορφύραν εἰσφέρων, ὥσπερ οἱ Μεγαρεῖς, with the schol. σύνηθες ἐν κωμῳδίᾳ παραπετάσματα δέρρεις ποιεῖν, οὐ πορφυρίδας. There is no reason to suppose that, whatever Phormos did, it had any influence on Athenian performances, which, as Aristotle's language suggests, did not follow such 'Megarian' practices; nor to connect (as some do) his innovations at Syracuse with the καταβλήματα which Pollux iv. 131 describes as draped over περίακτοι to produce particular effects (see pp. 126, 235). In any case, nothing suggests that Phormos' invention was used to effect changes of scenery.

[1] See P. Gardner, in *J.H.S.* 1899, esp. p. 254.

Whether in the scenes laid in Hades (some of which were certainly presented in the Classical period[1]) any hints were taken from Polygnotus' famous painting we cannot tell; but the artists are not likely to have indulged in much detail.[2]

3. Of the way in which the palace- or temple-front may have been represented on the wooden background, we get some indication in the scanty notices which remain to us of scene-painting in the fifth century B.C. Aristotle[3] says that scene-painting was introduced by Sophocles (τρεῖς δὲ καὶ σκηνογραφίαν Σοφοκλῆς). Vitruvius[4] writes that 'primum Agatharchus Aeschylo docente scaenam fecit et de eo commentarium reliquit', adding that from the work of Agatharchus Democritus and Anaxagoras learned the principles of perspective, about which they also wrote, showing how the painted representations of houses on the stage could be so made that 'quae in directis planisque frontibus sint figurata, alia abscedentia, alia prominentia esse videantur'. In other words, he painted an architectural design in perspective on the flat background. Whether he was first employed by Sophocles (who began to exhibit in 468 B.C.) or by Aeschylus (whose last plays were produced in 458), it is not possible to be certain; Vitruvius may only mean that he first displayed his art while Aeschylus was still alive and exhibiting, and, if so, he may quite well have received his first commission from Sophocles.[5] In any case, the description of the work of Agatharchus would well suit the backgrounds required in the *Oresteia*. At a later date Apollodorus went further and began the use of colour and shading to increase the illusion. (He was known both as σκηνογράφος and as σκιαγράφος.) Agatharchus is also said[6] to have painted the interior of the house of Alcibiades,

---

[1] e.g. the *Sisyphus* of Aeschylus and the *Peirithous* of Euripides (or of Critias; see *New Chapters in Greek Lit.* iii, p. 148), the *Frogs* of Aristophanes (on which see above, pp. 62, 67), and a number of lost plays of the Old Comedy.

[2] In the vases depicted in the first section of this chapter there is no essential difference between the background of scenes in Hades, with the palace of Pluto, and that of scenes in the upper world, and there was probably none between the comedies in which the scene was laid in Hades and the rest.

[3] *Poet.*, ch. iv.   [4] VII, *praef.* § 11.

[5] J. Six (*J.H.S.* xl, p. 185) conjectures that it was Apollodorus who painted scenery for Sophocles, while Agatharchus painted e.g. the towers of Thebes in the *Septem* for Aeschylus, but his reasons are not convincing.

[6] Andok. iv, § 17; Demosth. *in Meid.*, § 147, Plut. *Alcib.* 16. Cf. P. Gardner, *J.H.S.* 1899, pp. 252 ff. Attempts by Frickenhaus and others to discredit

and, if so, he may by decorating walls with architectural designs have begun a tradition which was in vogue for centuries and ultimately developed into the rich styles of the painted walls of Pompeii and Rome. Whether he painted any other types of background or decoration for the theatre there is nothing to show. We may be sure that at this period there was no elaboration of scenery.

4. We cannot be certain how much of the architectural detail referred to in the plays was represented in the backgrounds painted in perspective by Agatharchus and others; some details may of course have been included in the actual structure. What is certain is that such details are far more frequently mentioned in Euripides than in Aeschylus and Sophocles, and although these may often have been presented only to the imagination and not to the eyes of the audience, there may have been actually greater elaboration in the latter part of the fifth century. In the *Orestes*, l. 1569 f. there may have been something solid, and not merely painted, to represent the coping-stone which Orestes threatens to hurl down:

$$ἢ τῷδε θριγκῷ κρᾶτα συνθραύσω σέθεν$$
$$ῥήξας παλαιὰ γεῖσα, τεκτόνων πόνον$$

(cf. 1620 *Πυλάδη, κάταιθε γεῖσα τειχέων τάδε*). There are other references to coping-stones and triglyphs which may merely have been painted on the background; e.g. to *θριγκοί* in *Helena* 70 (*βασίλειά τ’ ἀμφιβλήματ’ εὔθριγκοί θ’ ἕδραι*), and *Iph. T.* 128 (*εὐστύλων ναῶν χρυσήρεις θριγκούς*), and to triglyphs in *Iph. T.* 113, and *Orestes* 1372 (*Δωρικάς τε τριγλύφους*). But the columned entrance to the temple in the *Ion* and the door-posts in *Iph. T.* 1159 (*ἄναξ, ἔχ’ αὐτοῦ πόδα σὸν ἐν παραστάσιν*) must have been structurally presented. In the *Hypsipyle* there is a mention of paintings in the pediment of the palace (*γραπτούς ‹τ’ ἐν αἰετοῖσι πρόσβλεψον τύπους*), and the chorus in the parodos of the *Ion* admire a series of mythological scenes on the temple-front,

Vitruvius' statement about Agatharchus are sufficiently met by Bulle, *Untersuch.*, pp. 215 ff. The importance of Agatharchus' work is significantly indicated by the fact that perspective became technically known by the name *σκηνογραφία*. It is useless, on the evidence now available, to try to determine how much of the 'effects' required in a background was secured by perspective drawing and how much was structural.

though there are wide differences of opinion as to the way in which these scenes were presented, whether as metopes in the frieze or as akroteria or as sculptures in the pediment.[1]

5. Many scholars also suppose that features in the landscape which are pointed out by speakers in the text must have been presented to the eye; and the periaktoi, of which more will be said in connexion with the later theatre, are often called in to supply the vehicle for the representation. It may be doubted whether the supposition is necessary. For instance, when Helen begins the play (Eur. *Helena* 1) with the words Νείλου μὲν αἵδε καλλιπάρθενοι ῥοαί, must we suppose that the river was shown on periaktoi or in some other way? or when in the *Hecuba* 823 (καπνὸν δὲ πόλεως τόνδ' ὑπερθρῴσκονθ' ὁρῶ) the smoke and in *Troad.* 1295 the flames of burning Troy are discerned by the speaker, is it certain that they must have been shown on some erection behind the tents which formed the background? or even that some real smoke—a poor substitute for the fires of Troy— was raised behind them?

The periaktoi as described by Pollux and Vitruvius[2] were triangular prisms of wood, placed in openings in the scenic background farther from the centre than the two regular side-doors; each face of the prism could carry a decoration suitable to the scene in which it was to be used, and by the revolving of the prisms changes of scene could be indicated. Their use seems to be fully attested in the later Hellenistic period; Vitruvius is evidently thinking of his own day, and Pollux of a theatre with a high stage,[3] but there is no evidence at all that they were used in the Classical period, and the writers, such as P. Gardner and Navarre, who believe that they were, do no more than infer from the simplicity or crudity of the device that it must belong to the earliest period, and point to a few scenes where it could have been used, had it existed. It might, they suggest, have been used to change the statue of Apollo for that of Athena in the *Eumenides*. But is it really likely that the statue of the god would have been placed away at the side of the façade of his temple? Again, it is suggested that the change of scene in the *Ajax* might have been effected by revolving one of the periaktoi. It might, but was it? Navarre thinks that the distant view of Argos at the beginning

---

[1] See Homolle in *B.C.H.* 1901 and 1902; Allen, *Gk. Theater*, pp. 44–5.
[2] Pollux iv. 126 ff.; Vitruv. v. vi, § 8.   [3] Pollux iv. 127. See pp. 234–5.

of Sophocles' *Electra*, the laurel grove in the *Ion*, and the river Nile in Euripides' *Helena*, may have been presented or indicated on the periaktoi. But no revolving machine would be required for this, and in these plays no change of scenery was involved. It is also to be noted that no ancient commentator explains anything in the Classical drama by the periaktoi,[1] though there are many such explanations, right or wrong, by reference (e.g.) to the ἐκκύκλημα. It is practically certain that the device belongs to the later history of the stage, and therefore the discussion of the difficulties connected with it may be postponed.

6. In our survey of the extant plays we have found frequent instances of the use of the μηχανή, a kind of crane for swinging personages, human or divine, through the air, so as to give the illusion of flying.[2] It was employed both in Tragedy and (with ludicrous effect) in Comedy. So Socrates swings in his basket in the *Clouds* and Iris makes her descent in the *Birds*. What may have been a quotation from some lost comedy called it by the name of κράδη, the 'Fig-branch'.[3] It was furnished with ropes (αἰῶραι) and a hook (ἅρπαξ or ἀγκυρίς), for the suspension of the actor.[4] The absurdity of the intended illusion is sometimes rubbed in by Aristophanes, when (e.g.) he makes Trygaeus in the *Peace*[5] entreat the man who is working the μηχανή to be careful, or in fr. 188 (K) of the *Daedalus*, where a speaker cries

ὁ μηχανοποιός, ὁπότε βούλει τὸν τροχὸν
ἐλᾶν ἀνεκάς, λέγε, Χαῖρε, φέγγος ἡλίου.

It is impossible to say for certain whether the γέρανος, which Pollux[6] describes as μηχάνημα ἐκ μετεώρου καταφερόμενον ἐφ' ἁρπαγῇ σώματος, and by means of which Eos in the *Psychostasia* of Aeschylus carried off the body of Memnon, was the same as the μηχανή, but it cannot have been very different.

It is not surprising that the facile introduction of gods by the μηχανή to solve difficulties apparently insoluble was sometimes the subject of sarcasm, as in Plato, *Cratylus* 425 d, οἱ τραγῳδοί,

[1] Cramer's *Anecd. Paris.* i. 19 refers to persons who ascribed to Aeschylus every device used at any time in tragedy, and mentions the periaktoi among others.   [2] See pp. 41, 55–6, 61–2, 68.
[3] Pollux v. 128; cf. Plut. *Prov.* 116 Paroemiogr. Götting. i, p. 338) κράδης ῥαγείσης· νῦν οὐχ ὁ σύκινος κλάδος, ἀλλ' ἡ ἀγκυρίς, ἀφ' ἧς οἱ ὑποκριταὶ ἐν ταῖς τραγικαῖς σκηναῖς ἐξαρτῶνται θεοῦ μιμούμενοι ἐπιφάνειαν. Hesych. s.v. κράδη· συκῆ· κλάδος· καὶ ἀγκυρίς, ἐξ ἧς ἀνήπτοντο οἱ ἐν ταῖς τραγικαῖς μηχαναῖς ἐπιφαινόμενοι: cf. D.R., p. 231.   [4] Pollux iv. 131; Bekk. *Anecd.* i. 132.   [5] l. 174.   [6] iv. 130.

ὅταν τι ἀπορῶσιν, ἐπὶ τὰς μηχανὰς καταφεύγουσι θεοὺς αἴροντες, and Antiphanes, fr. 191 (K),

> ἔπειθ' ὅταν μηδὲν δύνωντ' εἰπεῖν ἔτι,
> κομιδῇ δ' ἀπειρήκωσιν ἐν τοῖς δράμασιν,
> αἴρουσιν ὥσπερ δάκτυλον τὴν μηχανήν,
> καὶ τοῖς θεωμένοισιν ἀποχρώντως ἔχει.

Aristotle in the *Poetics* (ch. xv) plainly regards the θεὸς ἀπὸ μηχανῆς as an inferior means of achieving a solution.

The use made by Aeschylus, also in the *Psychostasia*, of the θεολογεῖον has already been mentioned.[1] It was probably an extra stage, raised above the roof of the σκηνή, and may have been concealed behind the pediment. In the *Psychostasia* it must have been fairly substantial, to carry not only Zeus and the scales, but Eos and Thetis on either side. It may have served for the appearance of gods at the end of other plays, where they are not distinctly described as sailing through the air—in other words, as using the μηχανή. The attempt to prove that one device belongs to an earlier, the other to a later, period in the fifth century is not supported by evidence, and the critics are not agreed as to which device was the earlier;[2] but neither could be used till there were sufficiently substantial stage buildings, since even the μηχανή needed a strong foundation, and this would probably have been of a permanent character. (Pollux places this by the 'left' parodos, but we do not know of what period he is speaking, nor which side he means by 'left'.) It should be noted that while references to the μηχανή are frequent, the θεολογεῖον is in fact only mentioned in connexion with the *Psychostasia*.

7. It has been argued in an earlier section[3] that there is no need to imagine that in the *Hercules Furens* and the *Orestes* there was a projecting porch which was at first veiled by a curtain. But the question of the use of a curtain in the theatre of the fifth century affects more than these two instances, and some scholars suppose that a curtain must have been used to conceal the setting of the scene before the opening of the play in the *Prometheus Unbound*

---

[1] pp. 39, 42, 46, 68.

[2] Wilamowitz, *Herakles*, i, p. 148, makes the theologeion a substitute for the awkward and ungainly μηχανή; Reisch in D.R., pp. 227 ff., and Bodensteiner, *Szenische Fragen*, pp. 665 ff., make the μηχανή a picturesque substitute for the primitive theologeion.

[3] pp. 79, 80, 112–13.

of Aeschylus,[1] in the *Hercules Furens, Herakleidai, Suppliants,*
and perhaps other plays of Euripides, and in the *Clouds* and the
Wasps, on the ground that the setting of the scene and the placing
in position of persons who are supposed to have been in that position for a long time would have been intolerable if it had taken
place before the eyes of the audience, and that the language of
the first speakers would have been contradicted by the evidence
of the spectators' eyes. Others think it unlikely that it would
have attracted the attention of an audience gathering for a play
or moving about between plays, and that even if they had noticed
it, the inconsistency would not have worried them any more than
it worried either the spectators of some of Shakespeare's plays
when first produced or modern spectators of open-air plays, who
are quite accustomed to see the necessary changes of places,
properties, and persons made before their eyes. We do not know
enough about the *Prometheus Unbound* to discuss the matter
profitably. In each of the three plays of Euripides the play opens
with a group of suppliants gathered round an altar. In the
Hercules Furens, 44 ff., Amphitryon says:

> ἐγὼ δέ . . .
> 47 σὺν μητρί, τέκνα μὴ θάνωσ' Ἡρακλέους,
> βωμὸν καθίζω τόνδε σωτῆρος Διός . . . .
> 51 πάντων δὲ χρεῖοι τάσδ' ἔδρας φυλάσσομεν,
> σίτων·ποτῶν ἐσθῆτος, ἀστρώτῳ πέδῳ
> πλευρὰς τιθέντες· ἐκ γὰρ ἐσφραγισμένοι
> δόμων καθήμεθ' ἀπορίᾳ σωτηρίας.

In the *Herakleidai,* Iolaus says (ll. 31 ff.) :

> πάσης δὲ χώρας Ἑλλάδος τητώμενοι,
> Μαραθῶνα καὶ σύγκληρον ἐλθόντες χθόνα
> ἱκέται καθεζόμεσθα βώμιοι θεῶν

and adds that Alcmena with the female suppliants is already
inside the temple.

In the *Suppliants* Aethra sits by the altars of Demeter and
Kore with the chorus of suppliants, while Adrastus lies prostrate ;
the language of ll. 28 ff. suggests that she has not been there long ;
and in the *Herakleidai* καθεζόμεσθα does not imply this either,

---

[1] One or two scholars have also mentioned the *Oedipus Tyrannus* of Sophocles
as an instance ; but here there could be no incongruity if Oedipus did not come
out of his palace door until the suppliants had taken their places.

nor does καθίζω in the *Hercules Furens*, nor do the words which add that the suppliants are on the bare ground and have nothing to eat or drink. It seems almost incredible that anyone should be so hypercritical as to take offence at the slight incongruity (if there is one) arising out of the fact that he had seen the suppliants come in. After all, the play did not begin till they were there, and there was therefore no incongruity within the play.

Bethe adds the *Andromache* to the plays in which the person speaking is supposed to be already there before the play opens; but the words of *Andromache* 42 ff.

δειματουμένη δ᾽ ἐγὼ
δόμων πάροικον Θέτιδος εἰς ἀνάκτορον
θάσσω τόδ᾽ ἐλθοῦσ᾽ . . .

could quite well have been spoken if she had come out and taken up her position forty lines before. The more difficult case of the opening of the *Troades*, where Poseidon points to Hecuba lying prostrate on the ground (l. 37) is not one which could rouse much criticism if, at the beginning of the play, and before the appearance of Poseidon and Athena, Hecuba came out of the tent and flung herself down.

As regards the opening scene in the *Clouds*, where Strepsiades and Pheidippides are in bed, and are supposed to have been there for a long time, there is of course an absurdity when the spectators (if they are looking) see them settle themselves there, but if it were accompanied by sufficient comic 'business' it would offend no one—in Comedy, and might add to the fun; and the same is true of the *Wasps*.

Where there is no proof, judgement on the question must be subjective; and if a curtain *was* necessary, it could easily have been run across from one paraskenion to the other, or across any part of the background, and drawn back again; but it seems very doubtful whether the necessity need be accepted.[1]

---

[1] The curtain is advocated by Bethe, *Prolegomena*, pp. 186 ff., and by D.R., pp. 252–5; Müller, *Lehrbuch der gr. Bühnenalt.*, p. 169, takes the other view. Bethe thinks that the curtain came into use (along with other innovations) about 427 B.C.; but Robert (*G.G.A.* 1897, p. 31) points out that the *Myrmidons* and *Niobe* of Aeschylus also opened with a veiled figure already in position, and asks why the audience should not have endured this after 427 as well as in the time of Aeschylus. That there was a substantial curtain in late Hellenistic and Roman theatres, and special provision made for it in the stage buildings,

8. In the scenes just discussed, in which a large group of suppliants is gathered round an altar, a difficulty has been felt[1] as
regards the position of the altar relatively to the temple or palace
represented by the stage building, and it has been suggested that
the altar and its steps would have been so large as to bar the way
into the central door, if it were placed centrally, and that therefore it may have been placed on one side—though not so as to
obstruct the orchestra, the space between the paraskenia being
sufficient without this. This is not impossible; the altars of Zeus
Soter and Zeus Agoraios (in the *Hercules* and *Herakleidai*) were
obviously not tied to the particular building, and could be at any
convenient spot, and in the precinct of Demeter and Kore at
Eleusis (in the *Suppliants*) the altar of the goddesses would not
necessarily be central; but there is a certain difficulty in supposing that a substantial part of the plays was acted on one side
of the scene, and traditional practice may have accepted a central
altar or tomb—perhaps as an inheritance from the early Aeschylean plays, in which there may have been no background of any
significance. In the *Choëphoroe* also the tomb of Agamemnon
was probably central, as we have seen,[2] though it may have been
in gentle criticism of this that Sophocles in the *Electra* removed
it out of sight altogether, and that Euripides, *Helena* 1165 ff.,
makes Theoklymenos give a special explanation of his having
buried his father Proteus close to the entrance of his palace. In
the *Hercules Furens* it would certainly be convenient, in view of
later scenes, to leave the central doorway unobstructed, and in
regard to this play at least, the suggestion of a less central (if not
too remote) position for the altar may be right.

It is hardly necessary to repeat that the altar at which suppliants
in various plays made their entreaties is totally distinct from the
ritual altar of Dionysus which belonged to the festival, not to the
play, and was in the centre of the orchestra;[3] though, naturally,

admits of no doubt. Rizzo, *Teatro di Siracusa*, pp. 77–81, thinks that a curtain
in the theatre at Syracuse goes back to Classical times. This is not proved, and
in any case proves nothing about Athens, where provision for a curtain is not
found before Imperial times (see p. 260).

[1] e.g. D.R., pp. 250 ff.   [2] Above, p. 43.

[3] Cf. Pollux iv. 123 ἡ δὲ ὀρχήστρα τοῦ χοροῦ, ἐν ᾗ καὶ ἡ θυμέλη, εἴτε βῆμά τι οὖσα
εἴτε βωμός. (On this expression see *Dith. Trag. Com.*, pp. 175 ff.) Holes for the
reception of altars are found in the centre of the orchestra in Athens and in
Epidaurus. See pp. 34, 147. The altar at Priene just in front of the first row of

this may have formed a central point round which the chorus stood or moved in its dances. There is perhaps an indication of this in a fragment of Aeschylus in the scholia on *Iliad* xiv. 200 ὅμως δὲ Αἰσχύλος τὰς ἐν κύκλῳ ἑστώσας ἐν ἀπείρονι σχήματί φησιν ἵστασθαι·

> ὑμεῖς δὲ βωμὸν τόνδε καὶ πυρὸς σέλας
> κύκλῳ περίστητ' ἐν λόχῳ τ' ἀπείρονι
> εὔξασθε.

Probably the flute-player who accompanied the chorus stood on the step of this central altar.

9. For the rest, it is plain from the texts that, when the play required it, altars, statues, and cult emblems of gods[1] and heroes could be introduced in front of the stage building, though the rich adornment of this building described by Vitruvius[2] belongs to a later period.

There is no trace either in the fifth century, or probably before the time of Lycurgus, of the custom of erecting statues of famous persons, both poets and others, of which we hear later, or of the use of the walls of theatre buildings to receive important inscriptions, though it is probable that this also had begun by the middle of the fourth century. These matters will be referred to in their place.

10. It is difficult to know how much weight, if any, is to be attached to a statement about scenery by an anonymous writer on Comedy, whom Kaibel identifies with Ioannes Tzetzes. (Kaibel thinks that some of the statements in this and parallel treatises may go back to an unknown work on the subject, contemporary with the early period of the New Comedy, and that an intermediate source may have been the *Chrestomatheia* of Proclus, who wrote in the fifth century A.D. However this may be, this and the parallel treatises are full of confusions.) The passage occurs in an account of the Old Comedy, and is as follows: ἐν ἐαρινῷ καιρῷ πολυτελέσι

---

seats belongs to a later period. Some scholars (e.g. Bieber, *Denkm.*, pp. 10 ff.) think that the vase of Brygos (*c.* 480–460 B.C.) representing satyrs around an altar and Dionysus is based on the theatre. There is no ground for this, and nothing in the costumes—or absence of costumes—to suggest it, and the Dionysus represented is not like a statue, as is suggested.

[1] e.g. *Agam.* 524, Soph. *El.* 1375; cf. palace of Nestor in *Od.* iii. 406.

[2] v. vi. 9. Throughout these sections Vitruvius is evidently thinking mainly of his own day.

δαπάναις κατεσκευάζετο ἡ σκηνὴ τριωρόφοις οἰκοδομήμασι, πεποι-
κιλμένη παραπετάσμασι καὶ ὀθόναις λευκαῖς καὶ μελαίναις, βύρσαις τε
παταγούσαις καὶ χειροτινάκτῳ πυρί, ὀρύγμασί τε καταγαίοις καὶ
ὑπογαίοις καὶ ὑδάτων δεξαμεναῖς, εἰς τύπον θαλάσσης Ταρτάρου
Ἅιδου, κεραυνῶν καὶ βροντῶν, γῆς καὶ νυκτός, οὐρανοῦ ἡμέρας,
καὶ ἀνακτόρων καὶ πάντων ἁπλῶς. αὐλάς τε οὐ μικρὰς εἶχεν ἐξειρ-
γασμένας καὶ ἁψῖδας εἰς τύπον ὁδῶν. διὰ μὲν οὖν ἀριστερᾶς
ἁψῖδος ἐχώρουν, εἰ ὡς ἐκ πόλεως ἦσαν ὁδεύοντες ὡς πρὸς ἀγροὺς ἢ καὶ
θέατρα· ἂν δὲ πρὸς πόλιν ὡς ἐκ θεάτρων ἢ ἀπ' ἀγροῦ, διὰ δεξιᾶς.
τοιαύτη μὲν ἡ τῆς σκηνῆς ἐργασία.[1] The composer of this jumble
seems to assume that all the circumstances which are mentioned
or assumed in the plays which he had read, such as the differences
of day and night,[2] were represented in the scenery; and other
expressions seem to refer to the βροντεῖον and similar devices, and
to scenes such as those in the *Frogs* and the *Peace* of Aristophanes.
But it may be doubted whether there was ever in the fifth century B.C. a three-storied building erected as a skené, and some
of the stage effects referred to, such as βύρσαις παταγούσαις, are
not easily intelligible.

[1] Anon. de Com. Dübner, p. xx; Kaibel, *Fragm. Com. Gr.* i, p. 22. See Kaibel,
Die Prolegomena περὶ κωμῳδίας, p. 3 and passim.

[2] A number of plays open before dawn, and some (such as the *Rhesus*) in
the night, but there can have been no representation of darkness.

IV

THE LYCURGEAN THEATRE

WE have now to trace, so far as the evidence permits, the history of the theatre in the fourth century B.C. The name of Lycurgus is especially associated with theatrical history in this period, and particularly with the third quarter of the century. He died in

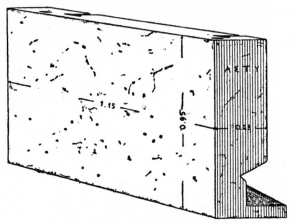

FIG. 34. The Astydamas basis

324 B.C., a year or two before the birth of Menander, and the period with which we are now concerned is, roughly speaking, that of the Middle Comedy and of that later Tragedy which, though not comparable to the Tragedy of the fifth century, seems to have been in part composed by poets of considerable distinction. The buildings as reconstructed in the strictly Lycurgean period are not likely to have been substantially altered for some time after his death, and it will therefore be convenient to consider in this chapter the evidence to be derived from Menander (who died in 292–291 B.C.) and the Early New Comedy.

I

The reconstruction of the theatre which, if not literally 'Periclean', is conveniently so named because of its close connexion with the building of the Odeum by Pericles, was probably not completed by the end of the fifth century. By that time there was certainly an auditorium made of regular earthen embankments and upheld on the east, south, and west by strong supporting walls. The western wall as we know it is a double one and was probably so planned, but the outer of its two walls may not have been finished until the early years of the fourth century. It will be remembered that there was built into it a stone bearing an inscription which had once indicated the place allotted in the auditorium to the servants of the Council, and that the lettering of the inscriptions suggests a date not long before (possibly even some years after) the archonship of Eucleides in 404 B.C., so that the wall into which it was built after its rejection from the auditorium must have been later still.[1] It is also possible that the building of the long Hall or Stoa overlapped the fourth century, or even fell wholly within it, though it must have been part of the 'Periclean' plan.[2]

It will also be remembered[3] that in the 'Periclean' theatre the western division (a A in the plan) of the southern supporting wall was not quite symmetrical with the eastern, oA, but formed a slightly more acute angle with the axis of the orchestra and auditorium. At some time in the fourth century this defect was corrected. The offending wall a A was levelled to the ground (though its foundations remain), and the existing wall wA was built in its place in symmetry with oA. It is natural to connect this with the construction of the stone auditorium, and this construction was probably the work which Lycurgus completed.

An attempt has been made to date the wall wA more exactly with the help of a portion of the basis of the statue of Astydamas the younger, a tragic poet, the success of whose *Parthenopaios* in 341 B.C. caused the Athenians to erect his statue in the theatre,[4]

---

[1] See above, p. 20.   [2] pp. 16, 21.   [3] See p. 18.

[4] Suidas, s.v. *σαυτὴν ἐπαινεῖς*. Suidas refers his story to the older Astydamas, but the date of the *Parthenopaios* is fixed at 341 B.C. by *IG*. ii–iii². 2320, and the reference must be to the younger. (The older was exhibiting tragedies in 398 B.C.) Suidas and Photius (502. 21) say that the stone originally bore four elegiac lines of self-praise by Astydamas, which the Athenians caused to be erased. It is not clear on what part of the basis they were inscribed; the lettering must have been fairly small. (The stone is about 22 inches wide on the side which is inscribed ΑΣΤΥ, and that side when complete must therefore have been 3 ft. 8 in. wide. The basis is about 3 ft. 1 in. high, and the long side, which ran back into the wall, is about 3 ft. 9 in. long.)

probably by the following year. The stone in question stands in the corner formed by the eastern (or lower) end of the wall wA; on it are inscribed the letters ΑΣΤΥ, and it is generally assumed that the missing fellow of this stone bore the letters ΔΑΜΑΣ. The stone is so cut as to fit into the coping of the wall,[1] in a line with the front row of seats, and the whole basis of which it formed a part is supposed by Dörpfeld to have served also as a buttress to support the end of the wall. It is implied that if the basis was thus specially adapted for this particular place, the wall must have been built before 340 B.C. But a doubt has been raised by Fiechter[2] whether, in fact, the stone was originally placed in 340 on the spot indicated, and was not rather adapted to it later. He points out that the cutting made in the stone, to fit it upon the coping of wA, could well have been made at a later date, and that in the absence of the upper stone of the basis, and of the plinth, it is unsafe to state positively where the statue originally stood, so that we are not compelled to assign to wA a date before 340 B.C.

II

Lycurgus had the supreme control of public finance at Athens[3] from about 338 to 326 B.C., and it was probably during those years that he played his special part in the building of the theatre. But our authorities make it clear that he only completed what others had begun. Some have thought that a decree of 343–342 B.C.[4] in honour of the Council may refer to some constructive activity of the Council in regard to the theatre: Κηφισοφῶν Καλλιβίου Παιανιεὺς εἶπεν· ἐπειδὴ ἡ βουλὴ ἡ ἐπὶ Πυθοδότου ἄρχοντος καλῶς καὶ δικαίως ἐπεμελήθη τῆς εὐκοσμίας τοῦ θεάτρου, ἐπαινέσαι αὐτήν, κτλ. Here, however, the reference is much more probably to orderly conduct than to ornamentation; and similarly οἱ λαχόντες ἐπιμεληταὶ τῆς εὐκοσμίας τῆς περὶ τὸ θέατρον in a decree of 328–327 B.C.[5] are not likely to have been concerned with building so much as with the discharge of routine functions such as minor officials elected by lot might perform.

As regards the activities of Lycurgus himself, the evidence is partly contemporary and partly later, but satisfactory:

[1] Fig. 34, after D.R., pp. 38 and 71.   [2] i, p. 87.
[3] It is not necessary here to discuss his precise constitutional position.
[4] *I.G.* ii–iii². 223 B; cf. Müller, *Bühnenalt.*, p. 87. 4; D.R., p. 39.
[5] *I.G.* ii–iii². 354.

(1) Hypereides, fr. 118 (Kenyon) : οὗτος (sc. ὁ Λυκοῦργος) ἐβίω μὲν σωφρόνως, ταχθεὶς δ' ἐπὶ τῇ διοικήσει τῶν χρημάτων εὗρε πόρους, ᾠκοδόμησε δὲ τὸ θέατρον, τὸ ᾠδεῖον, τὰ νεώρια, κτλ.

[The reference to the building of the Odeum is not clear. Some scholars suppose that ᾠδεῖον is a textual error for στάδιον (see below) ; others that he may in some way have repaired or improved the Odeum of Pericles.]

(2) *I.G.* ii–iii². 351, an inscription of 330–329 B.C.: [ἐπὶ Ἀριστ]οφῶντος ἄρχοντ[ος . . .] ἔδοξεν τῷ δήμῳ. Λυκοῦργος Λυκόφρονος Βουτάδης εἶπεν· ἐπειδὴ Εὔδημος πρότερον ἐπηγγείλατο τῷ δήμῳ ἐπιδώσειν εἰς τὸν πόλεμον εἴ τις δέοιτο [XXXX δ]ραχμὰς καὶ νῦν ἐπιδέδωκεν εἰς τὴν ποίησιν τοῦ σταδίου καὶ τοῦ θεάτρου τοῦ Παναθηναϊκοῦ χίλια ζεύγη καὶ ταῦτα πέπομφεν ἅπαντα πρὸ Παναθηναίων καθὰ ὑπέσχετο, δεδόχθαι τῷ δήμῳ ἐπαινέσαι Εὔδημον, κτλ.

[This is only quoted here because some scholars, by an 'emendation', which places the words τοῦ Παναθηναϊκοῦ after τοῦ σταδίου, try to make τοῦ θεάτρου refer to the Dionysiac theatre. But this is wrong ; the whole expression refers to the Stadium, στάδιον being the flat race-course and θέατρον the raised seats all round it for spectators.]

* (3) *I.G.*ii–iii². 457 : A decree of Stratokles in 307–306 B.C. enumerating the merits of Lycurgus, in a proposal for the benefit of his children . . . τὴν δὲ σ[κευοθήκην καὶ τὸ θέατρον τὸ] Διονυσιακὸν ἐξηργάσα[το τό τε στάδιον τὸ Παναθην]αϊκὸν καὶ τὸ γυμνάσιον τ[ὸ κατὰ τὸ Λύκειον κατεσκεύ]ασεν, κτλ.

[This is practically identical with words of the decree of Stratokles slightly and not always quite accurately abbreviated in Plut. *Vit. X Orat.*, p. 852, see below.]

(4) Plut. *Vit. X Orat.*, 852 c: τούς τε νεωσοίκους καὶ τὴν σκευοθήκην καὶ τὸ θέατρον τὸ Διονυσιακὸν ἐξειργάσατο, καὶ ἐπετέλεσε τό τε στάδιον τὸ Παναθηναϊκὸν καὶ τὸ γυμνάσιον τὸ κατὰ Λύκειον κατεσκεύασε, κτλ.

(5) Id. 841 c, d: καὶ τὸ ἐν Λυκείῳ γυμνάσιον ἐποίησε καὶ ἐφύτευσε καὶ τὴν παλαίστραν ᾠκοδόμησε καὶ τὸ ἐν Διονύσου θέατρον ἐπιστατῶν ἐπετέλεσε.

(6) Pausan. I. xxix. 16: οἰκοδομήματα δὲ ἐπετέλεσε μὲν τὸ θέατρον ἑτέρων ὑπαρξαμένων, κτλ.

It cannot be determined with absolute certainty whether the θέατρον which others had begun and Lycurgus finished refers to the whole group of buildings connected with the theatre or only to the stone auditorium which undoubtedly dates from this time ; but the precise share which the orator himself took in the large works carried out in the latter half, or, as we may probably say, in the third quarter of the fourth century is not a matter of great importance. It was certainly his enlightened financial administration which made the work possible. He is also said[1] to have passed a decree for the erection of bronze statues of Aeschylus, Sophocles, and Euripides, but it is not known where they stood.

III

1. The stone auditorium built in the fourth century, in place of the old auditorium of earthen embankments and wooden seats, is substantially that of which the remains are visible to-day, though minor alterations were made afterwards, affecting chiefly the front rows of seats. As the work progressed the double wall on the western side must have been carried northwards, but it is uncertain how far northwards the Lycurgean auditorium went. Some think that it was carried right up to the perpendicular cutting in the Acropolis rock (the κατατομή)[2] which ultimately finished it off; others that it only reached the public road which ran above the Odeum and across the auditorium from side to side. The choregic monument of Thrasyllus, which was embedded in the κατατομή, belongs to the year 319 B.C.[3] and it is hardly likely that such monuments would have been placed there until the theatre had been brought up to, or very close to, the cutting and the rock had been prepared as a suitable background to them.

2. On the east side the auditorium, the eastern boundary of which had been planned so as to conform with the wall of the Odeum, was broadened when it had passed beyond and above that building; and either now or later the public road, just referred to, which originally crossed the theatre about 48 ft. 6 in. above the level of the Lycurgean orchestra, was pushed upwards about 26 ft. 6 in.,

---

[1] Plut. *Vit. X. Orat.*, p. 841 f. At the same time he had a correct copy of the works of the three poets deposited in the public archives, and forbade actors to depart from this official text in their performances.

[2] Philochorus fr. *ap.* Harpokr. s.v. κατατομή. Αἰσχραῖος Ἀναγυράσιος ἀνέθηκε τὸν ὑπὲρ θεάτρου τρίποδα . . . καὶ ἐπέγραψεν ἐπὶ τὴν κατατομὴν τῆς πέτρας. The reference in Hypereides' speech against Demosthenes (also quoted by Philochorus, l.c.), καὶ καθήμενος κάτω ὑπὸ τῇ κατατομῇ, οὗπερ εἴωθε καθῆσθαι, must refer to a cutting in the Pnyx, where the Assembly usually met. When it met in the theatre, Demosthenes is not likely to have chosen for his usual seat a place at the very back of the audience. A note on the κατατομή above the theatre is appended to this chapter (Appendix I, p. 169).

[3] See Appendix I and D.R., p. 39. Dörpfeld detects some resemblances in technical finish between the stones of this monument and certain stones in the auditorium; but these afford no safe ground for inference as to date, since Puchstein (p. 37) finds the same technical features in fifth-century buildings.

FIG. 35. View of Auditorium

and utilized as a passage (about 15 feet wide) from side to side of the auditorium at about three-quarters of the way between its foot and the cutting in the rock. This is the only such passage (διάζωμα)[1] of which the existence is actually proved; but it would make a very uneven division of the theatre into upper and lower sections, and most archaeologists assume that there must also have been a lower passage half-way between this road and the orchestra. Dörpfeld calculates that while the upper section (above the road) contained fourteen rows of seats, each of the two lower (divided by the hypothetical passage) contained thirty-two rows. It is at first sight disconcerting to find that a coin in the British Museum[2] (of the Imperial period) which gives a rough representation of the Athenian theatre shows only one διάζωμα (Fig. 36); but the coin is inaccurate as regards the number of seats and staircases, and may have suppressed the lower passage; this was possibly much narrower

FIG. 36. Coin showing
Auditorium

and less conspicuous than the upper, which served also as a road. Dörpfeld conjectures[3] that there was an ascent from outside to this lower diazoma near the south-east corner of the auditorium, but it is difficult to accept this, as access to it must have been obstructed by the Odeum.

3. The auditorium, in the portion of which the seats are still preserved, was divided by twelve narrow stairways, each 27 inches wide, into thirteen wedge-shaped blocks (κερκίδες,[4] so named from their resemblance in shape to the κερκίς used in weaving); two other staircases, making fourteen in all, ran just inside the two southern supporting walls. The staircases differed in one respect from those found in most Greek theatres.[5] Instead of giving two steps to each row of seats, they gave only one, which was sloping,

---

[1] The name διάζωμα is Hellenistic: *C.I.G.* (Boeckh) ii. add. 2755, iii. 4283 (A.D. 147); Vitruv. v. vi. 7.

[2] B.M. *Cat. of Gk. Coins*, Attica, No. 806 (pl. XIX, fig. 8).

[3] D.R., p. 41.   [4] Pollux iv. 123.

[5] The theatre at the Peiraeus, which was closely modelled on the Athenian, presents the same peculiarity.

so as to reduce the height of each step above the one below it. The front edge of each step is almost 4 inches lower than the back, and the perpendicular height of each step in front is thus reduced to about 8½ inches. The surface of each step was roughened (with parallel grooves) to save the spectators from slipping.

4. The formation of the rows of seats can best be seen in a sectional diagram (Fig. 38). The front part of the surface of the

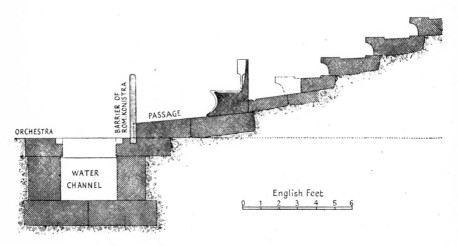

Fig. 37. Section of lower part of Auditorium

seat, 13 inches from back to front and 13 inches high, was for sitting on and it was the custom for each spectator to bring his cushion. The middle part, 2 inches lower than the rest, was for the feet of the spectators in the row behind. The effective height of the seat was thus 15 inches, and this, with a cushion, would be tolerable, though still somewhat cramping for a long day's sitting. The overhanging edges made it possible to fit more rows of seats into the available space than could have been placed there if each seat had had a perpendicular front. (Dörpfeld calculates that the whole theatre was thus made to hold seventy-eight rows instead of sixty-nine only.) The rows of seats were bedded on the natural rock, or, when necessary, on made-up earth laid upon the rock-surface. The front of each row was marked with vertical lines about 13 inches (one Greek foot) apart, perhaps simply for the purpose of convenient calculation. A second series of lines, less strongly cut, about 16 inches apart appears on some of the rows, and these may mark the limits of individual seats.[1] If these limits were strictly observed, the theatre, when complete, would have held about 17,000 persons, but it is generally thought that a total of 14,000 is nearer the truth.[2]

5. In place of the front two rows of seats we see to-day a row of chairs or 'thrones' of Pentelic marble, originally sixty-seven in number, standing on a foundation of poros. Of these, sixty

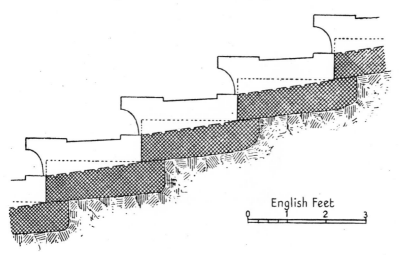

English Feet

Fig. 38. Sectional view of Auditorium seats

are still extant, fourteen having been found in their original positions by the excavators, and the rest restored, for the most part with virtual certainty, to their proper places. Each bears the name of the priest or other official to whom it was assigned. These inscriptions, in their present form, are all later than the fourth century, and most belong to the Hellenistic and Roman periods; but there are signs of the erasure of earlier inscriptions, and some of the spellings—such as AΘΕΝΑΣ and ΣΩΤΕΡΟΣ—point to the fourth century, and suggest that the thrones may be exact copies of fourth-century originals, the imitation extending even

[1] Schultz (*Excavations at Megalopolis*, p. 42) ascertained (in 1912) that London theatre managers regarded 16 inches as an adequate allowance for each person in seats without arms, and that the regulations of the London County Council were said to allow 18 inches.

[2] Plato's estimate (*Symp.* 175 e) of an audience of 30,000 persons must be a great exaggeration, though he is speaking of the time before Lycurgus, when many may have stood. On an allowance of 16 inches the theatre at Epidaurus would have held about 17,000, that of Megalopolis about 19,000.

to the forms of the letters. Other evidence is consistent with this view. The excellence of the carving of the reliefs on the central throne—that of the priest of Dionysus—has led Dörpfeld and others to assign it to the fourth century; but there are details which are said to indicate a later period, though the original sculpture may have been in the main closely copied. The existing

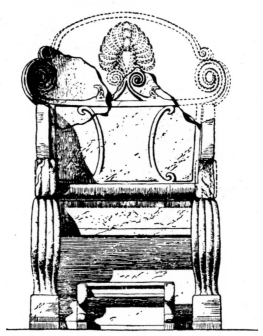

Fig. 42. Throne in Delos, front view

thrones may provisionally be regarded as dating from the first century B.C.[1] (some of the inscriptions being still later), but also as reproducing in their general appearance and, for the most part, in detail, the work of the Lycurgean period. The row of thrones seems to be approximately in its original position, and at first there was an ordinary row of seats immediately behind it; but the front part of this was at some time cut back, so as to leave a wider passage behind the thrones. (See Fig. 37.)

Of the sixty-seven seats, six are placed at the lower termina-

[1] Fiechter, i. 72, who thinks that the existing thrones date from a restoration of the theatre after its supposed destruction by Sulla; but there is no evidence of this destruction, though the date may be right.

FIG. 39. Front view of Central Throne

FIG. 40. Side view of Central Throne

FIG. 41. General view of Central Thrones

tion of each of the outermost kerkides (or blocks of seats), and five at the foot of each of the other eleven blocks. In front of them provision was made for footstools, and traces of this remain before many of them. The central throne had also at some time a canopy, and the holes for the uprights of this may still be seen.

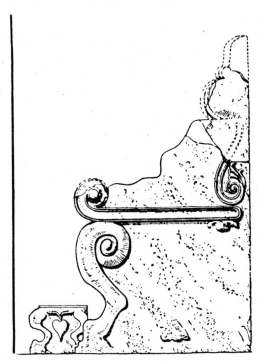

FIG. 43. Throne in Delos, side view

The accompanying illustrations will give some idea of the thrones. That of the Priest of Dionysus is distinguished by its more elaborate shape and its fine sculpture. The upper part of the back is unfortunately lost. On what remains are two satyrs supporting a grape-vine. On the front are griffins in combat with two human figures, and on the outside of each of the arms a winged boy with a fighting cock—perhaps an allusion to the theatrical contest.[1]

---

[1] Möbius (*Ath. Mitt.* li, 1926, p. 121) gives strong reasons for thinking the throne a late Attic reproduction of a fourth-century original. Risom (*Mélanges Holleaux*, 1913, pp. 257 ff.), on a comparison of this with the very similar thrones

6. In front of the thrones the pavement on which they stood sloped gently downwards, ending in a short step down to the drainage channel which carried off the water from the auditorium after rain. (There would be a larger volume of water from a stone auditorium than from an earthen one.) This pavement formed a passage giving access to the staircases, and the curve of the rows of seats was so drawn as to make this passage grow gradually broader from the central throne (where the breadth is about 4 feet) to the two corners of the auditorium (where it is over 8 feet wide). More space was thus given where it was most needed when the audience crowded down the staircases to leave the theatre.

IV

1. The water channel is about 3 feet wide; it is about 2 ft. 11 in. deep opposite the south-west corner of the auditorium, and 3 ft. 7 in. deep at the south-east corner,[1] after which there is an abrupt drop in preparation for the passage of the watercourse under the skené. It was crossed by twelve bridges of poros, each in line with one of the staircases of the auditorium, and since they accordingly conform to the auditorium circle and not to the orchestral circle (the centre of which is different) they appear to enter the orchestra at a slightly awkward angle. (In the theatre in the Peiraeus, which was probably modelled on the Athenian, this particular problem was more elegantly solved.) Between the bridges the channel was ordinarily open—probably until Roman times, when a marble covering was provided throughout; but it is difficult to suppose that it was left open, to the common danger and with great loss of valuable space, when the adjoining pavement was crowded with spectators pressing to or from their seats, or that the risk to members of choruses of falling in when they approached the edge of the orchestra, would long have been

found in Delos and in the garden of the Zappeion at Athens, gives a conjectural restoration of the throne when it was intact. Some details remain uncertain, but the restoration is very probable. He thinks that the holes in the pavement, supposed to be for the supports of the canopy, are too small for this, and were probably meant to receive thyrsi and other emblems. This seems doubtful.

[1] These are the measurements of Dörpfeld (D.R., p. 52); there is some confusion in the figures given by Fiechter, i, p. 55. See Broneer in *Classical Studies presented to Edward Capps*, p. 30.

tolerated; and Broneer is probably right in supposing that on occasions which required it wooden covers were laid over the spaces between the bridges. He may also be right in thinking that the letters of the alphabet which appear on the inner edge of the upper stones of the wall of the channel on the orchestral side

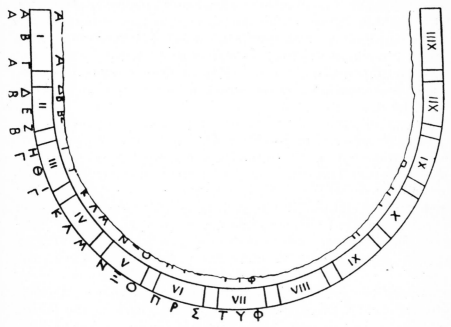

FIG. 44. Letters in Water Channel

marked the places for each wooden slab so that the whole cover could be quickly put in position. These letters have long been a problem;[1] Broneer's Figure 2, which is here reproduced, shows their original arrangement; there were (where they can be clearly traced) three to each space between bridges, and this implies the use of three wooden slabs in each space; but there are also the remains of another series of letters, in which each space was marked AA, BB, &c., and these seem to show that at some time

---

[1] The solutions previously offered—that the letters helped to enable spectators to find the right κερκίς, or that they are masons' marks—are rightly rejected by Broneer and by Dörpfeld himself. It is a strong confirmation of Broneer's theory that the letters remained intact until they were partly cut away in making the rabbet into which the permanent marble covering was fitted.

a single larger wooden slab was fitted to each space. Dörpfeld and Fiechter assign the letters, from their form, to the fourth century, and if this is right, the plan suggested by Broneer would go back to the Lycurgean period, as the channel itself must;[1] but Broneer himself thinks that they are later, though of course earlier than the Roman period. The channel, planned in harmony with the Lycurgean auditorium, no doubt replaced an earlier channel of some kind surrounding the pre-Lycurgean orchestra, which was almost certainly a few feet south of the Lycurgean.[2]

2. The dimensions of the orchestra can be determined by drawing a circle coinciding in the northern half of its circumference with the inner edge of the water channel. This gives a circular orchestra of 19·61 metres or 60 Greek feet in diameter, the equivalent of 66 ft. 1 in. English.[3] This circle may have originally been marked out, as it is in the theatre of Epidaurus (also of the fourth century) and some others, by a stone edging level with the ground; and other lines may have been drawn to assist the movements of the chorus. But there is no actual evidence of this, or of the manner in which the orchestra was surfaced. It may have been only of beaten earth, top-dressed as required.[4] But none of the visible remains of the orchestra go back to the Lycurgean period. At various times there were excavations under the orchestra, subsequently filled up, the dates and purposes of which are quite unknown; some of them may go back to the fourth century, and there are traces of a prehistoric spring, but nothing which gives any ground for supposing that there was any underground passage or 'Charon's steps' as at Eretria.[5]

[1] See Fiechter, iii, p. 55 note.

[2] See above, pp. 15, 25–6, and Fiechter (iii, p. 74), who thinks that the centre of the Lycurgean orchestra was about 3 ft. 6 in. north of that of its predecessor. But certainty only begins with the Lycurgean orchestra itself and the water channel surrounding it.

[3] On the precise equivalent of the Greek foot in metres and in English feet and inches, see Flickinger, *Philol. Quart.* 1926, pp. 103–5. He agrees that the orchestra of Lycurgus was probably 'at least intended to have a diameter of sixty feet, a round number'.

[4] An inscription from Delos (*I.G.* xi. 2, 203 A, ll. 79–80) records the dressing of the orchestra in the theatre, probably with clay or chalk (*B.C.H.* 1894, p. 162).

[5] See D.R., pp. 56–8, fig. 18; Bulle, *Untersuch.*, pp. 22–3; Fiechter, i, pp. 52–3. The idea put forward by Frickenhaus, *Die Altgr. Bühne*, p. 61, that there was a large hollow space excavated under the Lycurgean orchestra, and boarded over to serve as a stage, the boards resting on the unoccupied front half of the wall

It may be assumed that there was an altar in the middle of the orchestra in this, as in the 'Periclean' theatre,[1] to serve both for offerings and as a centre for the movements of the chorus.

3. The *Parodoi*, or passages giving entrance to the theatre and

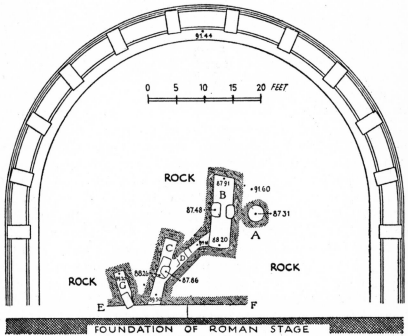

FIG. 45. Excavations in Orchestra

running along the southern walls of the auditorium, were about 8 ft. 6 in. wide at their narrowest points, i.e. at the corners of the projecting paraskenia. Statues and votive dedications were sooner or later ranged along their sides, but (apart from the basis of the statue of Astydamas already described) none of these remains in its place, except a part of the monument dedicated

of the *scaenae frons* (see p. 149), is rightly rejected by Fiechter. It seems impossible to base any sound arguments on the potsherds and other materials found in the rubbish underneath the surface of the orchestra, which evidently underwent many disturbances at different periods for unknown purposes.

[1] See above, pp. 9, 71, 131-2. In *Hermes*, xxxvi (1902), Dörpfeld mentions a small sunk circle in the middle of the orchestra, which can hardly have been anything but the place of an altar. The round stone in the centre of the orchestra at Epidaurus must also have been set for an altar.

by Xenokles, who was agonothetes or master of the ceremonies in or soon after the year 307–306 B.C., and some bases of dedications of Roman date. It is not known whether the parodoi were closed by gates at their outer end.

V

1. Of the *Stage Buildings* or *Skené* of this period the foundations are largely preserved. The central structure clearly consisted of a large building erected to the north of, and back to back with, the long hall or stoa, which was probably the latest constructed of the buildings of the 'Periclean' plan. The back of this new skené was provided by the wall in which we found a row of sockets for posts[1] and from which projected northwards the foundation called T in the Plan. How far this wall was altered for its new purpose—whether, for instance, having risen little, if at all, above ground before, it was now raised to a greater height—there is no direct evidence to show, but it may be assumed that it was so. But of the front wall of the new skené (V–V in Plan III and Fig. 52) the breccia foundations remain. They are composed of four layers of breccia blocks, regularly laid, the lowest being on the natural rock, cut and levelled where necessary to receive it; and it is clear that the new building consisted of a long chamber, from which there projected northwards at either end of V–V two rectangular paraskenia, of which similar breccia foundations have been partly exposed. It is uncertain whether the main chamber extended unbroken to east and west, or whether part of it at each end was separated off as a distinct room. It is thought by several archaeologists that on the outer side of each of the paraskenia there was a narrow room (running east and west) containing (as is conjectured) a staircase to the roof or to an upper story of the skené.

2. The details of the Lycurgean skené and paraskenia, and of the buildings which flanked each of the latter on the outside, are

---

[1] See above, p. 21. It was shown in Ch. I to be probable that the stage buildings (and their paraskenia) in the 'Periclean' theatre were of wood and continued to be so for many years. But the construction of the 'Lycurgean' theatre had begun before Lycurgus himself took a hand in it, and the replacement of the wooden skené and paraskenia by stone structures may have been a long and gradual process. The evidence does not admit of any precise dating. All that is certain is that the 'Lycurgean' theatre did in fact include the buildings here described.

keenly disputed, because they underwent great alterations, in which the materials of which they were composed were re-used in different positions. The chief of these alterations were (1) in the Hellenistic period, when a proskenion (serving as the front supporting wall of a stage) was erected at some distance in front of V–V, and the paraskenia were shortened down, and (2) in the Roman period, when a general reconstruction probably suppressed at least part of the paraskenia, and made great changes in the skené. There may have been many other alterations no longer traceable, and it is a very hazardous proceeding to conjecture from the marks, &c., on each stone and the condition of its surface, what exactly was done with it at various periods some two thousand years ago. There are keen differences of view on many points between Dörpfeld, Puchstein, Bulle, Fiechter, and von Gerkan—to mention only a few of the countless contributors to the discussion.[1] It is not proposed to enter into this discussion minutely here; to do so would contribute little that is of human interest, and could lead to no conclusive result, but certain points may be mentioned.

3. It is thought by some archaeologists that the row of pillars, J 1 to J 4 in the Plan, which appears to divide the main chamber into two aisles, belongs to this period, but there is no agreement about this, and the existing remains do not really suffice to determine their date or dates or their precise purpose. Some possibilities will be noted later.

4. What stood upon the breccia foundations of the wall V–V is also keenly debated. They are about 4 ft. 4 in. wide from front to back, and in the continuation of V–V behind each of the paraskenia there is at one point a longitudinal layer of poros, about 2 ft. $3\frac{1}{2}$ in. wide, along the back half of the wall.[2] From this Dörpfeld argues that the back half of V–V supported a closed wall—closed, that is, except for three doorways—and that against this, on the front half of V–V, stood a row of columns. The argument involves a good deal of hypothesis,[3] and others

---

[1] For instance, the two walls Z1 and Z2 in Plan III are assigned dates differing by several centuries by Fiechter and von Gerkan respectively.

[2] There is also at one point only, at the back of the west paraskenion, a little bit of a marble layer, 1 ft. 11 in. wide, but it is very doubtful if this is in its original place. It may be only one of many fragments from various places which have been 'dumped' on the foundations of the paraskenia.

[3] Dörpfeld tries to construct a row of columns, with the necessary *inter-*

have pointed out that such a structure of full columns against a closed wall is both late and very rare in its occurrence, and is most improbable at this period; they suppose that V–V supported simply a wall with three doors, the front half of the foundations having perhaps carried originally a layer of poros blocks parallel to those on the back half.[1]

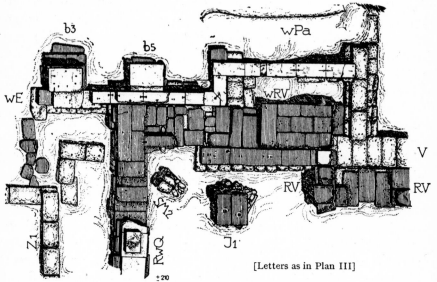

[Letters as in Plan III]

FIG. 46. Remains of W. Paraskenion and structures to W. (after Fiechter)
(For explanation of symbols, see p. 287)

5. The history of the paraskenia, the remains of which are in some confusion, is a matter of great difficulty. Their foundations project about 16 ft. 6 in. in front of the northern edge of V–V; the distance between them—in other words, the length of V–V visible from the auditorium—was about 66 ft. 1 in. (60 Greek feet). The foundations of the paraskenia consist, as was stated above, of breccia blocks, similar to those of V–V, to which they

columnia for three doors, on the assumption of intervals between the columns equal in width to the intervals between the columns of the paraskenia, and he thinks that the indications given by fragments of architrave and triglyphs lying about can be made to fit this scheme. But the possibility of such reconstruction does not prove that it was ever a fact, and the improbability of it at this date is great. Allen, *Gk. Theater*, p. 12, says that Dörpfeld himself, *Jahrb. Arch.* xxviii (1913), *Anz.*, col. 38, gave up the columned *scaenae frons*, but I cannot find that he gave up anything but the stone proskenion in the Lycurgean theatre.

[1] See Puchstein, pp. 103, 132, and von Gerkan, *Gnomon*, 1938, p. 240.

are structurally tied.[1] The outside breadth of each paraskenion on the level of the foundations is approximately 23 ft. 4 in. On the foundations and on a level with the floor of the orchestra was a layer of poros,[2] and some stones of this remain;[3] but there is a difference of opinion whether this layer was contemporary with the breccia foundations or (as Fiechter thinks) with the marble stylobate of the Hellenistic proskenion,[4] with which it agrees as regards the sizes of the stones composing it. This agreement, however, on which Fiechter relies, is obviously not conclusive, and von Gerkan questions this view.

About 5 ft. 3 in. behind the northern edge of the west paraskenion as it was in the Lycurgean building, the stylobate of the front of the abbreviated Hellenistic paraskenion is still in position.[5] On it stand the broken shafts of two of the columns of this front (not quite in their original places). These columns (and perhaps others of which fragments are found in different parts of the theatre) previously belonged to the Lycurgean front; but the stylobate on which they stand (and which also belonged to the Lycurgean front) bears marks (brought out in Dörpfeld's figure) which show that they were spaced at different intervals on the Lycurgean front from those which separated them on the Hellen-

---

[1] According to Fiechter (i, Abb. 14, 15) the southern foundations of the paraskenia are very slightly out of line with V–V, and the northern edge of the foundations was also not quite parallel to V–V. But von Gerkan (l.c., p. 239) argues that the appearance of irregularity is largely the work of Fiechter's own attempt at a reconstructed plan. Fiechter himself (i, p. 25 and iii, p. 73) admits that the superstructure showed no such irregularity, and even if it *were* shown in foundations which are below ground and invisible, it would prove nothing but slight carelessness. It is difficult to imagine what could possibly be its object, if it were deliberate.

[2] Dörpfeld and Bulle call the material poros and this it is in the generally accepted sense. Fiechter says *Kalkstein*, 'limestone', using the word to cover a whole group of closely related kinds of stone.

[3] Chiefly on the outer sides of each paraskenion and on the breccia foundations of the wings which were built out (doubtless as part of the same plan) beyond the paraskenia.

[4] See below, pp. 176 ff.

[5] See Fiechter, i, pp. 29 ff. and below, pp. 177 ff. and Fig. 60. That several of the stones (viz. Nos. 28–30 in Fig. 60) remain in their original connexion is proved by the marks of the clamps and the sequence of the masons' marks *ΒΓΔ*. Whether Rousopoulos in 1862 found the two columns standing where they now are or re-erected them (not quite correctly) himself appears to be uncertain. See 'Εφημ. 'Αρχ. 1862, col. 135, and Fiechter, i, p. 30.

istic, and Dörpfeld reconstructs the earlier or Lycurgean front as
follows:

0·29 m.   ○   1·12 m.   ○   1·27 m.   ○   1·27 m.   ○   1·27 m.   ○   1·12 m.   ○   0·29 m.
= 8¼ in.   = 3 ft. 7½ in.   = 3 ft. 11½ in.

The four central columns seem each to have been placed exactly
over the junctions of the stones of the stylobate, as indicated by

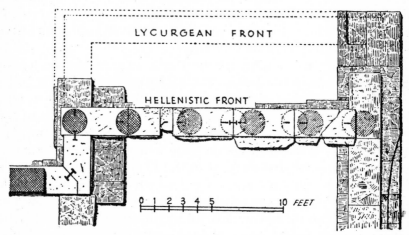

FIG. 47. Part of W. Paraskenion showing positions of columns (after Dörpfeld)

finely dotted outlines in Fig. 47, and this part of Dörpfeld's
reconstruction seems certain. Fragments of the blocks originally
supported by the columns and forming the architrave and the
row of triglyphs[1] above it give corresponding measurements.
But doubts have been raised

(1) Whether each end of the stylobate originally carried a
column or whether the front was terminated by *antae*.
Dörpfeld favours the first alternative, on the ground that
what must have been the corner block of the architrave is
polished underneath and was therefore intended to be
visible and not to be merely the top stone of a pillar
(Fig. 50), and though this and other arguments are not

---

[1] In these blocks Dörpfeld (D.R., p. 63) finds some technical resemblances to
the monument of Thrasyllus (late fourth century; see p. 138), and this may be
thought to confirm his ascription of them to the Lycurgean theatre; but the
same peculiarities are in fact found in buildings of both earlier and later dates
(see Puchstein, p. 137).

FIG. 48. View of W. Paraskenion from N.

FIG. 49. Wall of W. Parodos

absolutely conclusive, he is probably right as to the fact. (Puchstein takes the opposite view.)

(2) Whether the stylobate and row of columns as reconstructed did in fact form part of the *north front* of the Lycurgean paraskenion, as Dörpfeld maintains, or a part of the east or inner side, as is believed by Fiechter,[1] who

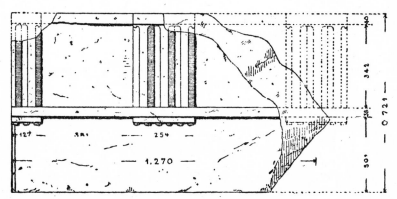

FIG. 50. Fragment of Architrave, W. Paraskenion

thinks that the north front was closed, and the inner side partly columned, just as, in the first theatre at Eretria, which he believes to date from the latter half of the fifth century, the openings from the paraskenia on to the scene of action were on the inner side and the fronts were closed. But the comparison with Eretria is certainly no decisive proof, and the probability, in the light of the remains, seems to rest with Dörpfeld's view that the paraskenia had an open row of columns both on the north and on the inner sides.[2]

The existing columns, which we may now assume to have stood originally on the Lycurgean front of the west paraskenion, are calculated to have been, when entire, about 10 ft. 4 in. high, and the total height of the paraskenia to have been about 13 ft. 6 in.; but the nature of the roof is unknown. No fragments of cornices remain,[3] though there must almost certainly have been

---

[1] iii, p. 17.

[2] Puchstein (p. 133) denies columns on the inner sides, on the ground that the breccia foundations can only have been meant to take stout walls. (See p. 155.)

[3] Fiechter, iii, p. 15, argues that the *Hellenistic* paraskenia had no cornices

such cornices; and the roof may have been either gabled or flat (as some think,[1] to enable actors to appear on it). The style of the front was Doric.

6. It is right to mention that Bulle[2] argues at length that the

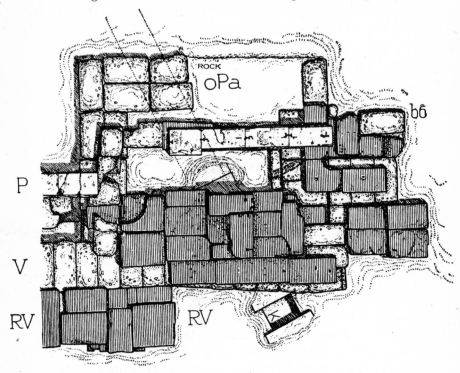

FIG. 51. Ground-plan of E. Paraskenion
(For explanation of symbols, see p. 287)

stylobate and architraves found in the paraskenia as they are. were not originally part of the Lycurgean theatre at all, but were brought soon after 86 B.C. from some other building, which was not a theatre but some kind of 'hall', of the same type as the monument of Thrasyllus, the Lesche in Thasos, and (possibly) the choregic monument of Nikias. The argument depends upon

(γεῖσα); but even if this was so, it proves nothing as to the Lycurgean, which, it is natural to assume, were in normal Doric style.

[1] e.g. Fiechter, iii, p. 18. See below, p. 177.

[2] *Untersuch.*, pp. 27 ff. A minuter examination of Bulle's hypothesis would take up a disproportionate space in the present work.

the possibility of determining the exact character and history of individual stones, and appears to be very hazardous; Fiechter[1] gives a brief but sufficient reply.

7. Bulle's argument does, however, incidentally emphasize a difficulty to which Puchstein[2] had already called attention, viz.

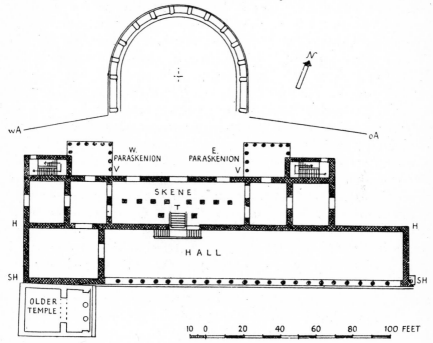

FIG. 52. Sketch-plan of stage buildings of Lycurgean Theatre
(For explanation of symbols, see p. 287)

that the Lycurgean front as reconstructed by Dörpfeld is only about 21 ft. 8 in. in width, whereas the breccia foundations on which it stands are about 23 ft. 4 in. wide, and therefore cannot (it is argued) have been intended for such a front. Moreover, such solid foundations, it is said, must have been intended for solid, closed walls, not for a colonnade. But it must be remembered that the breccia foundations were underground and invisible, so that a precise fit was not necessary, and the explanation may quite possibly be that breccia blocks of a regular or standard size were ready to hand and that it was not worth while

[1] iii, p. 16, and Broneer (*Am. J. Arch.* xxxix, 1935, p. 417) notes that Bulle's description of this imaginary monument is really unlike any known choregic monument. [2] pp. 131 ff.

to trim them down, or that the precise measurements of the superstructure were finally settled later; and after all, the discrepancy is not a very serious one.[1]

8. In the preceding exposition, reference has been made only to the west paraskenion, on the remains of which Dörpfeld's argument was mainly based. But the remains of the east paraskenion (Fig. 51) also include those of a Hellenistic stylobate,[2] of which the stones had been used previously (see Fig. 60), and though there are inevitable difficulties in reconstructing the history of this part of the building, there is nothing that is inconsistent with the account of the Lycurgean paraskenia given above.

9. On the outer sides of each paraskenion the building was extended in the form of a wing, the northern front of which was slightly set back from the line of the front of the paraskenion. The character of these wings in the Lycurgean period is quite uncertain. It has already been stated that some archaeologists think that each contained among other things a staircase leading to the roof (shown in Fig. 52). In the Hellenistic period the stylobate which has already been described was continued westwards in the western wing, but continued as the base of a wall, of which some layers of stone still remain. But the earlier history of this wing, and still more that of the eastern wing, is practically undiscoverable on account of alterations at several periods, and the rough outline given in Fig. 52 of the probable shape of the Lycurgean building, according to the views here provisionally adopted, must suffice.

VI

1. We have still to deal with the question, which has been the subject of much controversy, whether there was in the fourth-century theatre any separate προσκήνιον, distinct from the front wall of the σκηνή which has already been discussed. This is bound up with the question where the actors and chorus at this period performed, and as the plays of Menander must have been acted in the theatre as Lycurgus left it, it is from these and from the plays of his contemporaries that our evidence must mainly be drawn. Dörpfeld's own view[3] was that in the fourth-century

[1] Cf. Versakis in *Jahrb. Arch.* 1909, pp. 200 ff.; Schleif, ibid. 1937, *Anz.*, col. 39 f.
[2] Fiechter, i, pp. 26, 27.
[3] D.R., pp. 69, 70. In *Jahrb. Arch.* xxviii (1913) Anz., cols. 38, 39 he denies the

theatre plays were acted, not immediately in front of the *scaenae frons* V–V, which formed merely a background for non-dramatic occasions, but before a temporary screen or proskenion erected some way in front of V–V and decorated, as occasion demanded, to represent a house, a temple, a cave, or whatever might be required. The space between this proskenion and the *scaenae frons* was, he thinks, covered with a wooden roof, and this roof served as a θεολογεῖον or for the erection of a temporary second story or any other kind of ἐπισκήνιον. But he is bound to admit that this is only conjecture. No trace remains of any stone foundations for such a proskenion, and if any such foundations had existed, they would naturally have been very slight and would have long disappeared;[1] so that we are still thrown back on the literary evidence.

2. That there was something or other called προσκήνιον in the Lycurgean theatre seems certain from the fact that a courtesan named Nannion, who was notorious in the latter half of the fourth century,[2] was nicknamed προσκήνιον, so Athenaeus[3] informs us: Ἀντιφάνης δὲ ἐν τῷ περὶ Ἑταιρῶν ' Προσκήνιον ' φησίν ' ἐπεκαλεῖτο ἡ Νάννιον, ὅτι πρόσωπόν τε ἀστεῖον εἶχε καὶ ἐχρῆτο χρυσίοις καὶ ἱματίοις πολυτελέσι, ἐκδῦσα δὲ ἦν αἰσχροτάτη.' But this does not enable us to determine what the theatrical proskenion was, except that it was something decorative concealing something plain, and the name might quite well be given to a screen

existence of a *stone* proskenion in the Lycurgean theatre and dates the first one in the first century B.C. in the theatre at Ephesus.

[1] See Puchstein, p. 137, who agrees with Dörpfeld's idea of a movable proskenion at this period (though not of one variable in character) and thinks it may have stood where Ziller's plan (reproduced in Plate II) marks a wall (*T–Y*) which has now disappeared, just in front of a line joining the north fronts of the paraskenia. But surely this would be too far forward, and would sacrifice all advantage for dramatic purposes from projecting paraskenia. Even the Hellenistic reconstruction did not do this. In *Ath. Mitt.* xlix (1924), p. 89, Dörpfeld says that recent excavations have proved the existence of a wooden proskenion in the Lycurgean period; but he gives no details, and his *ipse dixit* is not sufficient.

[2] She is mentioned by Hypereides Κατὰ Πατροκλέους (fr. 139 K), and by Anaxilas (fr. 22), Amphis (fr. 23), Timocles (fr. 25), and Alexis (fr. 223), as well as in Menander's Ψευδηρακλῆς (fr. 524 K) and Κόλαξ (fr. 295 K), which may have been fourth-century plays. Whether or not there were two courtesans of the name does not matter, as both would fall within the period of the Lycurgean theatre (vide Breitenbach, *De genere quodam titulorum Comoediae Atticae*, pp. 131–3).

[3] xiii. 587 b 2; cf. Phot. and Suid. s.v. Νάννιον.

with variable decorations, whether using curtains, canvas, wooden panels, or what not, erected against the *scaenae frons* (V–V). This interpretation perhaps gets some support from Suidas' gloss on προσκήνιον as τὸ πρὸ τῆς σκηνῆς παραπέτασμα, though we do not know to what age or to what theatre he refers.[1] It is suggested by von Gerkan[2] that the special scenery for each play was erected on the front portion of the foundations of the *scaenae frons*—the part not covered with a longitudinal layer of poros.[3]

3. Three other passages have to be considered in this connexion, referring to events of the Lycurgean period or immediately after it; but two of them are from Plutarch, who is so much in the habit of using theatrical terms in the sense which they bore in his own time, and as if the theatre of earlier days had been like that which he knew, that no certain inference can be based upon them.

(1) Plut. *Non posse suav. viv.*, p. 1096 b (the context refers to the treatment of the floor on which actors performed): καὶ τί δήποτε τῶν θεάτρων ἂν ἄχυρα τῆς ὀρχήστρας κατασκεδάσῃς ἢ χοῦν, ὁ λαὸς τυφλοῦται, καὶ χαλκοῦν Ἀλέξανδρον ἐν Πέλλῃ βουλόμενον ποιῆσαι τὸ προσκήνιον οὐκ εἴασεν ὁ τεχνίτης, ὡς διαφθεροῦντα τῶν ὑποκριτῶν τὴν φωνήν. Here προσκήνιον may quite possibly bear its later sense of 'stage', but it may conceivably refer to some kind of background, and the uncertainty permits no conclusion from the passage.[4]

(2) Douris *ap.* Athen. xii. 536 a: γινομένων δὲ τῶν Δημητρίων Ἀθήνησιν ἐγράφετο ἐπὶ τοῦ προσκηνίου ἐπὶ τῆς οἰκουμένης ὀχούμενος. Douris was a contemporary of Demetrius Poliorketes, who is the subject of the sentence, and of Menander. Reisch[5] thinks that the reference is to the movable wooden proskenion which he and Dörpfeld place some way in front of the

---

[1] The quotation by which he illustrates his gloss has (since Casaubon) been generally ascribed to Polybius, but the reading is uncertain at the crucial point— ἡ δὲ τύχη παρελκομένη τὴν πρόφασιν καθάπερ ἐπὶ προσκήνιον παρεγύμνωσε τὰς ἀληθινὰς διανοίας. (To illustrate his gloss, ἐπὶ should be bracketed, or Schubart's καθάπερ τι προσκήνιον accepted.)

[2] *Das Theater von Priene*, p. 126. He finds the same arrangement in the theatre at Magnesia.

[3] See above, p. 149.

[4] Reisch (D.R., p. 293) is so afraid that the passage may be used to prove that there was a stage in the Lycurgean theatre that he interprets προσκήνιον as meaning the whole façade facing the spectators. But even if the word does mean 'stage' here, it is of no value as evidence for a stage at the time in question, in view of Plutarch's habits: cf. Puchstein, p. 42; Flickinger, *Plut. on Gk. Theat.*, pp. 52, 53.   [5] D.R., p. 291.

skené, others that it is to the *scaenae frons* itself. But it may equally well refer to a screen erected against the *scaenae frons*.

(3) Plut.*Demetr.* ch. 24 (referring to the conduct of the same Demetrius in Athens in 292 B.C.) : οὕτως οὖν τῆς πόλεως ἐχούσης εἰσελθὼν ὁ Δημήτριος καὶ κελεύσας ἐπὶ τὸ θέατρον ἀθροισθῆναι πάντας, ὅπλοις μὲν συνέφραξε τὴν σκηνὴν καὶ δορυφόροις τὸ λογεῖον περιέλαβεν, αὐτὸς δὲ καταβάς, ὥσπερ οἱ τραγῳδοί, διὰ τῶν ἄνω παρόδων, ἔτι μᾶλλον ἐκπεπληγμένων τῶν Ἀθηναίων, τὴν ἀρχὴν τοῦ λόγου πέρας ἐποιήσατο τοῦ δέους αὐτῶν. The passage has been used to prove the existence in Demetrius' day of a raised stage or λογεῖον, with a προσκήνιον supporting it in front. But Plutarch is probably translating the account given by his authority into language appropriate to the theatres of his own day, which had a stage and ἄνω πάροδοι (probably passages on a level with the stage at the side of the skené, as distinct from the parodoi leading into the orchestra).[1] He imagines that Demetrius spoke from the raised stage,[2] or, if the force of the preposition in καταβάς is to be pressed, that after entering on the stage like an actor, he descended to the orchestra to speak ;[3] but it is uncertain whether the preposition need mean as much as this.[4] In any case, the passage is valueless as evidence for our purpose.

The greater probability seems to rest with the view that the word προσκήνιον, as used of the late fourth-century theatre, applies to a decorative screen (or curtains) attached to, or erected just in front of, the front wall of the skené itself when required, and that this, when in use, formed the background of the action, an upper story being erected above and behind it on the skené as required. (The word προσκήνιον itself is first found in inscriptions at Delos about 300 B.C. ; see pp. 206–8.)

[1] Dörpfeld, *Ath. Mitt.* xxviii (1903), pp. 422–3, thinks that ἄνω πάροδοι means the ordinary entrances used by choruses and audience, as distinct from the entrances into the orchestra from the side wings. But when are the latter ever called πάροδοι? and could the main entrances be distinguished from them as ἄνω?

[2] By a similar anachronism Plutarch, *Thes.* 16, speaks of οἱ τραγικοὶ in old days denouncing Minos ἀπὸ τοῦ λογείου.

[3] There is the same doubt in Plut. *Arat.* 23 (ἐπιστήσας δὲ ταῖς παρόδοις τοὺς Ἀχαιοὺς αὐτὸς ἀπὸ τῆς σκηνῆς εἰς τὸ μέσον προῆλθεν), whether the speech was supposed to be made from the stage or from the orchestra.

[4] καταβαίνειν is regularly used of the orator descending from his tribune, and may therefore mean that Demetrius descended into the orchestra to speak. But what was it that 'increased the alarm' of the Athenians? Was it that he thus confronted them at close quarters, or was it simply the appearance of Demetrius himself, as well as of his soldiers? The passage is hazy even for Plutarch.

4. A very unconvincing attempt has been made by Petersen[1] to claim for the Lycurgean theatre the Hellenistic proskenion which has been mentioned above, and which will be described in the next chapter; the question of the date of the proskenion will be considered there. In the meantime it may be assumed that the evidence of such a proskenion at some distance in front of the skené in the Lycurgean period is non-existent. It will be argued later that a proskenion in such a position would not be *necessary*, until there was a raised stage for actors, requiring it as a supporting wall, and such a stage would not be tolerable so long as the plays produced still required free communication between chorus and actors, and therefore required that they should be on approximately the same level. We have therefore to consider the literary evidence[2] so far as concerns the fourth century and the early decades of the third—the period of Menander, who died c. 292 B.C.—since it is not likely that the work completed by Lycurgus was drastically altered so soon as this.

VII

1. It is sometimes supposed that the chorus virtually disappeared as an integral part of the drama comparatively early in the fourth century. It will be well to examine carefully certain passages of Aristotle which bear on the point. (Aristotle died in or about the year of Menander's first appearance.)

(1) *Poet.* xviii, 1456 a 25–30: καὶ τὸν χορὸν δὲ ἕνα δεῖ ὑπολαβεῖν τῶν ὑποκριτῶν, καὶ μόριον εἶναι τοῦ ὅλου καὶ συναγωνίζεσθαι μὴ ὥσπερ Εὐριπίδῃ ἀλλ' ὥσπερ Σοφοκλεῖ. τοῖς δὲ λοιποῖς τὰ ᾀδόμενα ⟨οὐδὲν⟩ μᾶλλον τοῦ μύθου ἢ ἄλλης τραγῳδίας ἐστίν· διὸ ἐμβόλιμα ᾄδουσιν πρῶτον ἄρξαντος Ἀγάθωνος τοῦ τοιούτου. This shows on the one hand that choral odes continued to be a part of tragedy, but that there was a tendency to write odes unconnected with the plot (as Euripides sometimes did[3]), so that they would do as well for one play as for another. If all the odes in a play were of this character, there would be little need for physical communication between chorus and actors and little objection to a raised stage. But it is to be observed that Aristotle deprecates this practice, and demands a chorus intimately asso-

---

[1] *Jahrb. Arch.* xxiii (1908), pp. 35 ff.

[2] See E. Capps, 'The Chorus in the Later Greek Drama' (*Am. J. Arch.* 1895), A. Körte, 'Das Fortleben des Chors im gr. Drama (*Neue Jahrb.* 1900, pp. 81–9), and K. J. Maidment, 'The Later Comic Chorus' (*Class. Quart.* 1935).

[3] Euripides never writes such detached odes throughout a play, but single stasima are sometimes of this character, e.g. in the *Helena* and *Andromache*.

ciated with the plot, and he would hardly have done this, if a sharp physical separation of chorus from actors had already been made.

(2) *Probl.* xix. 48:[1] διὰ τί οἱ ἐν τραγῳδίᾳ χοροὶ οὔθ' ὑποδωριστὶ οὔθ' ὑποφρυγιστὶ ᾄδουσιν; . . . ἔστι γὰρ ὁ χορὸς κηδευτὴς ἄπρακτος· εὔνοιαν γὰρ μόνον παρέχεται οἷς πάρεστιν. This also shows that the tragic chorus did sing and not merely dance, as some have supposed; but that its connexion with the plot was not very active.

(3) *Politics* iii. 1276 b (published probably about 335 B.C.) : εἴπερ γάρ ἐστι κοινωνία τις ἡ πόλις, ἔστι δὲ κοινωνία πολιτῶν, πολιτείας γινομένης ἑτέρας τῷ εἴδει καὶ διαφερούσης τῆς πολιτείας ἀναγκαῖον εἶναι δόξειεν ἂν καὶ τὴν πόλιν εἶναι μὴ τὴν αὐτήν, ὥσπερ γε καὶ χορὸν ὁτὲ μὲν κωμικὸν ὁτὲ δὲ τραγικὸν εἶναί φαμεν, τῶν αὐτῶν πολλάκις ἀνθρώπων ὄντων. This at least proves the continued existence of both tragic and comic choruses down to this date, though it tells us nothing of the character of their performance in tragedy and comedy respectively.

2. Further, it is certain that satyric plays continued to be regularly composed by tragic poets at Athens. It is true that by 340 B.C. their popularity had so far diminished that one satyric play was acted at the beginning of each Dionysiac festival, instead of one as an appendage to each tragic trilogy : but a satyric play without a satyr-chorus having free access to the actors seems unlikely so early as this. We know of satyric plays composed by Astydamas and Chairemon, and Python (if it was not Alexander himself) composed a satyric play called *Agen*, which was performed in Alexander's camp in the East, though it must be admitted that, as it was full of topical allusions, it was different in character from the satyric plays of Athens in the fifth century,[2] and later references to satyric drama imply that such allusions continued to occur. One at least of these references—the epigram of Dioskorides[3] on Sositheos, probably in the third century— seems to imply a satyric chorus, though it is not absolutely necessary. A satyric play without a chorus of satyrs does not seem a very probable conception, and it is certain that Lyco-

---

[1] I agree with Professor E. S. Forster (*Class. Quart.* 1928, p. 164) that Book XIX is probably Aristotelian in substance.   [2] Athen. xiii, p. 595 f.

[3] *Anth. Pal.* vii. 707. It is uncertain whether Sositheos, who was one of the Alexandrian 'Pleiad', composed at Athens as well as at Alexandria. He is said to have ridiculed Cleanthes in the theatre in his presence (Diog. L. vii. 173), and some of Diogenes' anecdotes about Cleanthes have their scene in Athens. There was an actor named Sositheus, but whether he was the same as the poet is uncertain.

phron's *Menedemus* had a chorus which was addressed by Silenus,[1] who can hardly have been separated from his satyrs by a high stage. (Menedemus of Eretria lived approximately 351–277 B.C.; Lycophron, also a native of Euboea, must have been well known by 283 B.C., when Ptolemy Philadelphus invited him to Alexandria.) But the history of satyric drama after the fifth century is so uncertain that too much stress must not be laid upon it.

3. It is of greater significance that plays of Sophocles and Euripides continued to be revived in the fourth century, as is proved by references in Demosthenes, Lycurgus, and others, and there is no reason to suppose that the manner of the performance differed substantially from that which was in vogue earlier. Lycurgus passed a law to prevent actors from tampering with the text of the great tragedians, and it seems unlikely that the choruses were tampered with so long as his influence lasted.[2] An anecdote recorded of Aeschines also seems to imply that in the fourth century chorus and actors continued to perform on the same level. Aeschines, while acting the part of Oinomaos and pursuing Pelops, fell down and had to be picked up by Sannio the chorus-trainer. Sannio is not likely to have been on a different level from his chorus.[3]

Fragments of a play dealing with the story of Oineus,[4] and probably of the fourth century, include portions of two scenes, which are separated by *XOPOY M . . . .*, which is probably restored as χοροῦ μέλος. If the restoration is correct, it confirms what Aristotle says about ἐμβόλιμα, and helps to prove that these were odes and not merely dances.[5] If, on the other hand, the *Rhesus* is really a fourth-century play, we have an instance of a

---

[1] Athen. x, p. 420 b μαρτυρεῖ δὲ καὶ περὶ τούτων Λυκόφρων ὁ Χαλκιδεὺς γράψας σατύρους Μενέδημον, ἐν οἷς φησιν ὁ Σιληνὸς πρὸς τοὺς σατύρους, κτλ.

[2] See also D.R., pp. 258 ff.

[3] The authority is no better than Demochares, the nephew of Demosthenes (*Vit. Aesch.* ii), though Demosthenes probably alludes to the incident (*de Cor.* § 180); but whether the story is true or invented, it is not likely to be misleading as to the theatrical conditions. There is no need to conjecture with Reisch (D.R., p. 259) that the χοροδιδάσκαλος was also κορυφαῖος on this occasion.

[4] Brit. Mus. Pap. 688 and 2822 = Pap. Grenf. ii. 1 and Hibeh Pap. i. 4. See *New Ch. in Gk. Lit.* iii, p. 154.   [5] The fragment of Plato's (?) Σκευαί (130 K), which appears to refer to tragedy, is of uncertain date and may not fall within the period under discussion, but if it does, it proves that a chorus might sing (and that badly) without dancing: ὥστ' εἴ τις ὀρχοῖτ' εὖ, θέαμ' ἦν· νῦν δὲ δρῶσιν οὐδέν, | ἀλλ' ὥσπερ ἀπόπληκτοι στάδην ἑστῶτες ὠρύονται.

tragedy in which the chorus are still closely connected with the action, and there are no mere ἐμβόλιμα.

The conclusion is that, so far as tragedy and satyric drama are concerned, there is no reason to suppose that a raised stage for actors was introduced during the period which we are considering, and that such indications as there are point the other way. The evidence with regard to comedy, though it needs careful scrutiny, seems to lead to the same conclusion.[1]

4. As regards the latest plays of Aristophanes himself, there is no reason why *XOPOY*, which in the text takes the place of written choral odes, should not refer to such ἐμβόλιμα as Aristotle mentions as occurring in tragedy, and the direction κομμάτιον χοροῦ, at *Plutus* 771, can hardly refer to a mere dance. It is usual to refer in connexion with our problem to the *Orestauto-kleides* of Timokles, a play variously dated by different scholars from 345 to 330 B.C. In fr. 25 (K) Autokleides is spoken of as beset by eleven named ἑταῖραι—obviously like Orestes surrounded by the Furies,[2] and if the analogy was exact, these women must have formed a chorus, and cannot have been separated from their victim by a raised stage. Meineke ingeniously conjectures, from the fact that the word παράβυστον occurred somewhere in the play, that the eleven ἑταῖραι took the place of the eleven magistrates at Athens who tried criminals in the court called παράβυστον. But this goes far beyond the evidence, and the passage in fragment 25 reads as if it came in a descriptive prologue, and does not prove that the eleven formed a chorus. We know of no chorus the members of which were individually named, and the number is an unusual one for a chorus, though it is probable that comic choruses were reduced in size late in the century. It is quite possible that the women, or some of them, may have appeared singly or in succession in the play, and on the whole it is safer not to use the passage as evidence of a chorus.

The reference by Aeschines[3] to a jest made in speaking to the

---

[1] Maidment's discussion (l.c.) is particularly valuable, though on one or two points it is possible to differ from him.

[2] περὶ δὲ τὸν πανάθλιον | εὕδουσι γρᾶες Νάννιον Πλαγγὼν Λύκα | Γνάθαινα Φρύνη Πυθιονίκη Μυρρίνη | Χρυσὶς Κοναλλὶς Ἱερόκλεια Λοπάδιον.

[3] *In Tim.* § 157 ὥστε πρώην ἐν τοῖς κατ᾽ ἀγροὺς Διονυσίοις κωμῳδῶν ὄντων ἐν Κολλυτῷ Παρμένοντος τοῦ κωμικοῦ ὑποκριτοῦ εἰπόντος τι πρὸς τὸν χορὸν ἀνάπαιστον, κτλ.

chorus by the actor Parmenon in a comedy performed at the Rural Dionysia at Collytus (close to Athens) shows no more than that there was still a chorus which took part in dialogue, but is not sufficient to prove anything as regards stage arrangements. Exactly the same is the case with a fragment (237 K) of the *Trophonius* of Alexis, in which a speaker requests a chorus of Boeotians to dance.[1]

5. In a number of fragments a speaker sees a κῶμος approaching, which (in most of these fragments) he regards with some apprehension. These are:

(1) Antiphanes' *Δωδωνίς*, fr. 91 K; date unknown (the fragments ascribed to Antiphanes range over a great number of years):

> πόθεν οἰκήτωρ ἤ τις ὅμιλος
> τρυφεραμπεχόνων ἁβρὸς ἡδυπαθὴς
> ὄχλος ὥρμηται;

(2) Alexis, *Κουρίς*, fr. 107:

> καὶ γὰρ ἐπὶ κῶμον ἀνθρώπων ὁρῶ
> πλῆθος προσιόν, ὡς τῶν καλῶν τε κἀγαθῶν
> ἐνθάδε συνόντων· μὴ γένοιτό μοι μόνῳ
> νύκτωρ ἀπαντῆσαι καλῶς πεπραγόσιν
> ὑμῖν περὶ τὸν βαλλισμόν· οὐ γὰρ ἄν ποτε
> θοἰμάτιον ἀπενέγκαιμι μὴ φύσας πτερά.

(3) Menander, *Epitrepontes*, fr. incerti loci:[2]

> ῎Ιωμεν· ὡς καὶ μειρακυλλίων ὄχλος
> εἰς τὸν τόπον τις ἔρχεθ᾽ ὑποβεβρεγμένων,
> οἷς μὴ ᾽νοχλεῖν εὔκαιρον εἶναί μοι δοκεῖ.
> ΧΟΡΟΥ.

[1] See Maidment, l.c., p. 14 for other points of interest in regard to this fragment. We do not know whether the play belonged to Alexis' earlier or later life—to the fourth century or the third. The fact that the fragment is in Eupolideans possibly points to his earlier period. Körte, l.c., refers to Plautus' *Rudens* 290 ff., and *Poenulus* 504 ff., in which *Piscatores* and *Advocati* appear, as confirming the survival of an active chorus in the Greek originals of these plays. (The original of the *Rudens* was by Diphilus.) The Fishermen at first address the audience and then converse with Trachalio. (The metre of the address is the *comicus quadratus* associated commonly with Atellanae.) But it is evident that only one speaks, and that they do not perform the functions of a chorus. Still less do the *Advocati*, whose representative speaks only in dialogue with the actors, and whose part is simply that of any actor in a plot of intrigue.

[2] Capps places it at the end of Act IV, Allinson and Wilamowitz (more probably) at the end of Act. I; Körte doubts whether it belongs to this play.

(4) Menander, *Perikeiromene*, fr. :[1]

$\Delta AO\Sigma$. παῖδες, μεθύοντα μειράκια προσέρχεται
πάμπολλ'. ἐπαινῶ διαφόρως κεκτημένην·
εἴσω πρὸς ὑμᾶς εἰσάγει τὴν μείρακα·
τοῦτ' ἔστι μήτηρ· ὁ τρόφιμος ζητητέος·
ἥκειν γὰρ αὐτὸν τὴν ταχίστην ἐνθάδε
εὔκαιρον εἶναι φαίνεθ', ὡς ἐμοὶ δοκεῖ.
ΧΟΡΟΥ.

The fact that in the last two passages the revellers clearly form the chorus of the play makes it practically certain that they do so in the two other (closely parallel) passages, and that we have in all a stock scene in which the actors make themselves scarce at the approach of a riotous band, and their alarm would scarcely seem so natural if they were already elevated above the revellers on a high stage.[2] The argument is not indeed conclusive. If, as is probable, a regular division into Acts was already observed in Menander's time and the only function of the chorus was to bring an Act to an end by its appearance, the actor might well sight the chorus at a distance from a high stage without rousing any strong sense of improbability. But so far as it goes, it supports the conclusion already reached, that nothing in the literary remains suggests that there was a high raised stage, and that the slight evidence which they afford favours the opposite view.

6. There is, however, a scene, imperfectly preserved, from the Θεοφορουμένη, *The Possessed Maiden*, of Menander, which seems almost to prove that the action of the play took place in the orchestra.[3] Two men, Lysias and Kraton, at least one of whom strongly suspects that the alleged 'possession' is a fraud, are secretly watching the inspired maiden, who is soliloquizing just in front of the door of the house. Lysias suggests that if she is genuine, the sound of a flute will throw her into an ecstatic dance, in which she will leap with inspiration. They call to the flute player and hide themselves, probably behind the columns of the paraskenion. The passage runs:

[1] ll. 141–6 in Allinson's edition (end of Act II).
[2] So also Maidment, l.c., p. 17, n. A fragment of an unknown play in a papyrus from Ghorân (Demianczuk, *Suppl. Com.*, p. 100) is probably a relic of a similar scene in which *ΧΟΡΟΥ* again appears.
[3] The fragment was found at Oxyrhynchus by Evaresto Breccia and the scene fully explained by Körte in *Hermes*, lxx (1935), pp. 431 ff. Its significance as regards the theatre was first made clear by Lesky, ibid. lxxii (1937), pp. 123–7.

εἰ θεοφορεῖται ταῖς ἀληθείαισι γάρ,
νῦν εἰς τὸ πρόσθεν ἐνθάδ' ἐκπηδήσεται
μητρὸς θεῶν, μᾶλλον δὲ κορυβάντων, πλέα.
αὔλει· παράστα δ' ἐνθαδὶ πρὸς τὰς θύ[ρας
τοῦ πανδοκείου. [ΚΡΑ.] νὴ Δί', εὖ γε, Λυσία·
ὑπέρευ γε· τοῦτο βούλομαι· καλὴ θέα.

The second line shows clearly that the two men are on the same level as the maiden, and this must be the orchestra, because the narrow logeion would not give room for the kind of dance which is evidently expected of her. Like Io in the *Prometheus*, she would need more space.

7. Reference is sometimes made, in connexion with this subject, to the fragment (165 K) of Menander's Ἐπίκληρος, in which he speaks of choruses in which only a few of the members actually sang, while the rest merely filled places in the files. This might show that these choruses were regarded as comparatively unimportant, and so forecast the reduction in the number of choreutae in the succeeding period. But we do not know to what choruses Menander refers. They may have been dithyrambic. If there *is* a reference to tragedy, it would at least attest the continuance of sung choral odes.

8. The view here taken is also supported by a fragment (5 K) of Heniochus, apparently from a prologue, in which the speaker says that the orchestra represents Olympia, with the skené as the σκηνὴ θεωρητική there and all the πόλεις gathered together —there was probably a chorus of Πόλεις: the cities were being thrown into disorder by two women, Demokratia and Aristokratia. The fact that the χωρίον, i.e. the orchestra, is Olympia and the skené a tent at Olympia almost proves that the skené must have been on the same level as the orchestra, and that there was no high stage. Meineke would date the play as late as the end of the Chremonidean War (266 B.C.), but Breitenbach[1] is probably right in assigning to it an earlier date on the ground of Suidas' ascription of the poet to the Middle Comedy, and the resemblance of some of the fragments to those of the Middle Comedy rather than the New, with other indications.

9. It is impossible to connect any changes as regards theatrical presentation or stage buildings with the two important adminis-

[1] Op. cit., p. 40.

trative changes of this period—the transference of the choregia
for comedy from individuals appointed by the archon to the
tribes, before the date of Aristotle's *Constitution of Athens*,[1] and
the replacement of choregi altogether by an *agonothetes* acting for
the state, in or before the year 307–306 B.C.[2] Nor can anything to
the point be inferred from the reduction in the size of comic
choruses, which is attested by inscriptions relating to performers
in the third century at Delphi, Delos, and other places, when the
touring companies of Διονύσου τεχνῖται took only a few choreutae
of either kind with them. We do not even know how many
choreutae composed the choruses at Athens itself. All that can
be said is that the more detached from the action of the play the
chorus became, the less difficulty there would be in introducing
the raised stage, and that whenever there *was* a raised stage,
there may have been room on it for the attenuated choruses,
numbering from four to seven, which the 'Artists of Dionysus'
took with them on tour. But as the evidence in regard to these
small choruses belongs to the last two-thirds of the century, the
consideration of it may be postponed to the next chapter.

10. An inscription from Tegea[3] records the victories of an actor
who specialized in the performance of old tragedies, and includes
the mention of several victories gained with plays of Euripides:
Διονύσια ἐν ταῖς Ἀθήναις Ὀρέστῃ Εὐριπίδου, Σωτήρια ἐν Δελφοῖς
Ἡρακλεῖ Εὐριπίδου . . . ταίῳ Ἀρχεστράτου, Ἡραῖα Ἡρακλεῖ
Εὐριπίδου, Ἠλέκτρᾳ (?) Εὐριπίδου, Νάια ἐν Δωδώνῃ Ἀχελώῳ
Εὐριπίδου, Ἀχιλλεῖ Χαιρήμονος. The inscription is undated, except in so far as it must be later than 276 B.C., at about which time
the Soteria were instituted. If the plays were performed as in the
fifth century, there is a strong presumption against a high stage,
but it is impossible to exclude entirely the possibility of adaptation and selection to suit altered theatrical conditions. We know
nothing of the part which the chorus may have taken in the new
tragedies produced at Athens in the third and later centuries.

[1] ch. 56.

[2] There was an agonothetes in 307–306 B.C. (*I.G.* ii. 1289 = *I.G.* ii–iii². 3073).
Plutarch, *Phoc.* xxxi, speaks of Nikanor as agonothetes after the death of
Antipater (who died in 319 B.C.), but does not say how soon after. The inscrip-
tions which mention choregi at Aixone in 317–316 B.C. (*I.G.* ii². 1200) and Rhamnus
(*I.G.* ii². 1198) at about the same date seem to refer to local festivals, not to the
City Dionysia.

[3] *I.G.* v. ii. 118.

11. The attempt has been made to date the introduction of the raised stage by tracing the history of the words θυμελικοί and σκηνικοί as applied to different kinds of contest and actor. Frei[1] dates the distinction as far back as the fourth century, and infers that it imports a distinction between orchestral and stage performances. But in fact the records which he so diligently collected show that θυμελικοὶ ἀγῶνες, including contests of instrumental musicians, reciters of epic poems, and others, are first mentioned in inscriptions of the *third* century relating to the Μουσεῖα at Thespiae and other Boeotian festivals. An anecdote about the citharist Stratonikus of Athens, quoted by Athenaeus[2] from Charikles Περὶ τοῦ ἀστικοῦ ἀγῶνος, possibly carries the distinction of θυμελικοὶ and σκηνικοὶ ἀγῶνες a little further back: ἐν Ῥόδῳ δ᾽ ἐπίδειξιν ποιούμενος, ὡς οὐδεὶς ἐπεσημήνατο, καταλιπὼν τὸ θέατρον ἐξῆλθεν εἰπών ᾽ ὅπου τὸ ἀδάπανον οὐ ποιεῖτε, πῶς ἐγὼ ἐλπίζω παρ᾽ ὑμῶν ἔρανον λήψεσθαι; γυμνικοὺς δὲ ἀγῶνας᾽ ἔφη ᾽ διατιθέτωσαν Ἠλεῖοι, Κορίνθιοι δὲ θυμελικούς, Ἀθηναῖοι δὲ σκηνικούς.᾽ But there is nothing to show that the term θυμελικοί was ever used of any contests or performances at Athens, and even if Frei were justified in dating the beginning of the distinction in the fourth century (and this goes far beyond the evidence), we should not be justified in concluding that the raised stage, as distinct from θυμέλη in the sense of 'orchestra', came in then. Σκηνικοί need not (and probably could not) mean 'acting (or acted) on a raised stage' any more than ἐπὶ σκηνῆς does in Aristotle and other writers. It is at least equally possible that σκηνικοί denotes performers who did their part close to the σκηνή, as distinct from those who played in the centre of the orchestra, where the θυμέλη was,[3] and it is even more likely that the two terms are not strictly local at all, but merely distinguish the contests of dramatic performers who required a σκηνή or decorative background from those of musicians and reciters, who required only the θυμέλη on the step of which they stood.[4]

---

[1] *De certaminibus thymelicis* (1900).   [2] viii. 350 c.

[3] That θυμέλη was used as a name for the orchestra itself as early as this is extremely doubtful. (In the fragment of Pratinas it almost certainly signifies the altar.) For the history of the word, vide Müller, *Unters. zu den Bühnenalt.*, pp. 93 ff. It was commonly used for the orchestra in late Hellenistic and Roman times, and sometimes for the stage or for the theatre as a whole.

[4] So also von Gerkan, *Das Theater von Priene*, pp. 122–3.

FIG. 53. The Monument of Thrasyllus in 1761

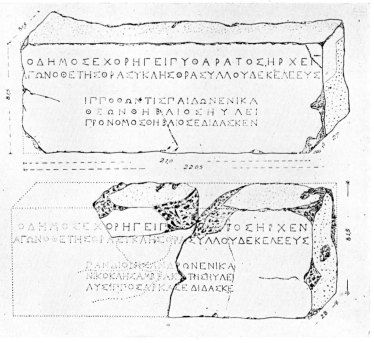

FIG. 54. Details of Monument of Thrasyllus

APPENDIX I

Note on the κατατομή *and the monument of Thrasyllus*

The best account is that of G. Welter in *Jahrb. Arch.* 1938, *Anz.*, cols. 33 ff. But the original description by Stuart and Revett (*Antiq. of Athens*, 1787, vol. ii, ch. iv, pp. 29 ff., pls. 1–6) is still indispensable. This was drawn up in 1761, before the church of Panagia Spiliotissa, into which the monument of Thrasyllus was converted, was destroyed by the Turks (in 1827) (Fig. 53). The rock was cut down perpendicularly in the time of Lycurgus; certain chambers or grottoes were left or newly cut in the face, and in 319 B.C. the monument of Thrasyllus—a marble sanctuary with a Doric façade—was inserted in one of these. Inside this sanctuary, which was 19 ft. 8 in. high, 20 ft. 6 in. broad, and 4 ft. 7 in. deep, were (according to Pausan. I. xxi, § 3) 'Apollo and Artemis destroying the children of Niobe '— probably (as Welter thinks) a painting on the back wall. Figure 54 includes a representation of the architrave, with its inscription as restored by Oikonomos, and fragments of the frieze.

In 270 B.C. Thrasykles, son of Thrasyllus, celebrated his dithyrambic victories with choruses both of men and boys by erecting two bases, fitted into the top of his father's monument, and setting upon them his own two tripods. These bases were renewed in less good workmanship about A.D. 200. Between the two bases, on what was originally the base of a tripod, there was placed in Roman times a sitting female figure, which was there when Stuart and Revett described the monument, but was afterwards taken by Lord Elgin for the British Museum. Statues were also placed on the two bases of Thrasykles, but these had been lost before the time of Stuart and Revett.

The tall columns, which are still very conspicuous on the rock above the monument of Thrasyllus, were erected in Roman times to carry tripods.

APPENDIX II

Note on the term παρασκήνιον

The term παρασκήνιον has been used in this work, in accordance with custom and for the sake of convenience, to designate the (usually) projecting side-chambers at each end of the skené or proskenion. But there is no certain ancient authority for this use. It has already been noted (p. 24) that its meaning in Demosthenes' *Meidias*, § 17, where it first appears, is uncertain, but that it probably designates store-rooms for theatrical properties. It is next found in inscriptions from Delos, where (in 274 B.C.) τὰ παρασκήνια, fitted with pinakes, and apparently of wood on a stone foundation, are contrasted in one item with the μέση σκηνή,[1] in

---

[1] Cf. Suidas, s.v. σκηνή. σκηνή ἐστιν ἡ μέση θύρα τοῦ θεάτρου, παρασκήνια δὲ

another with the' σκηναί on each story; the reference is evidently to structures at either end of the façade as distinct from the central portion, but whether projecting or not is quite uncertain. In another item a contractor is spoken of as undertaking ποιῆσαι τὸ παρασκήνιον τὸ ἐν τῷ θεάτρῳ. The meaning of the singular is disputed, both here and in an inscription of 269 B.C. in the same series; but the explanation may be that the particular contractor was only concerned with one of the two paraskenia. Some archaeologists believe that the word refers in both passages to the side wall of the stage building, as contrasted with the front, but this seems very unlikely. Much later, Aristeides, ii, p. 397 d (2nd cent. A.D.) uses the word for some parts of the structure which were evidently insignificant as compared with the main stage building: καὶ σὺ τὴν σκηνὴν θαυμάζων τὰ παρασκήνια ᾐτιάσω καὶ τοὺς λόγους ἀφεὶς ἐτήρεις τὰ παραφθέγματα. Finally, Pollux iv. 109 records a quite eccentric use of the word: ὁπότε μὲν ἀντὶ τετάρτου ὑποκριτοῦ δέοι τινὰ τῶν χορευτῶν εἰπεῖν ἐν ᾠδῇ, παρασκήνιον καλεῖται τὸ πρᾶγμα, ὡς ἐν Ἀγαμέμνονι Αἰσχύλου· εἰ δὲ τέταρτος ὑποκριτής τι παραφθέγξαιτο, τοῦτο παραχορήγημα ὀνομάζεται, καὶ πεπρᾶχθαί φασιν αὐτὸ ἐν Μέμνονι Αἰσχύλου. Here παρασκήνιον seems to be a song delivered 'off-stage' by one of the choreutai in place of an actor (? an actor who had no 'singing voice'). But why τετάρτου? Pollux may have in mind, as he sometimes has, some special incident unknown to us; but the reference to the *Agamemnon* remains obscure.

APPENDIX III
Two Italian Vases

Some light is thrown on the possible forms of paraskenia (using the word in its conventional sense) in theatres of the fourth century, by two Italian vases,[1] though, as they plainly reproduce the appearance of Italian wooden theatres of the time, they cannot be used to prove anything as regards the theatre of Dionysus at Athens. The first is a krater of Tarentine manufacture, now at Würzburg, depicting the first meeting of Pelias and Jason, who appear in front of a background flanked by square projecting para-

τὰ ἔνθεν καὶ ἔνθεν τῆς μέσης θύρας. In the Delian inscription the μέση σκηνή and the παρασκήνια on each side of it seem to be collectively termed αἱ σκηναί, and if so, the παρασκήνια will be the parts of the façade which include the side doors to right and left of the μέση σκηνή (with its μέση θύρα). Photius and the *Etym. Magnum* gloss on παρασκήνια as αἱ εἴσοδοι αἱ εἰς τὴν σκηνήν, doubtless following Didymus, who (on Dem. *Meid.*) described them as τὰς ἑκατέρωθεν τῆς ὀρχήστρας εἰσόδους.

[1] They are admirably described and figured by Bulle, *Eine Skenographie* (1934), from which figs. 55–7 are taken. The second was originally published by Lehmann-Hartleben, *Jahrb. Arch.* 1927, pp. 27 ff.; cf. also Bulle, *Untersuch.*, pp. 230–2.

Fig. 55. Fragment of Tarentine Calyx krater (Würzburg)

FIG. 56. Fragment of Tarentine Calyx krater (Würzberg)

skenia, each entered by a door in the back wall.[1] One of the Peliades looks out anxiously from each of these doors. The Ionic half-columns depicted in the back wall and the full columns in the front of the paraskenia, which are open, are all wooden, as is the Doric architrave. On the akroteria are figures (which must represent bronze figures in the real or supposed original) of an unusual type. It is noteworthy that there is no central door on to the scene of action, which is entered only through the para-skenia. Bulle conjectures that if the picture were complete, the building

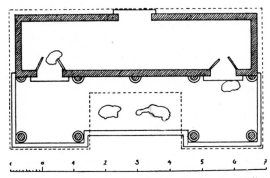

Fig. 57. Ground-plan implied in Tarentine Krater

would be seen to stand on two steps, and that Jason (as in the well-known legend) would have one sandal missing.

The second vase is a Campanian krater in the Louvre, representing Artemis, Iphigeneia, Orestes, and Pylades, but implying a version of the story somewhat different from that of Euripides' *Iphigeneia in Tauris*, and probably based on some lost play.[2] The left paraskenion, representing a temple, is more richly decorated than the right, which is a house. Both paraskenia have closed walls, and their doors are in the ends (or fronts) which face the audience; and again there is no central entrance. The structures which the painter has in mind are again obviously wooden.[3]

The vases depict the personages without masks, and this might be supposed to exclude any connexion between them and the theatre, par-

---

[1] For doors in the back wall of paraskenia Bulle compares the Hellenistic theatre at Segesta; cf. his *Untersuch.*, Taf. 25.

[2] In Euripides the two young men are brought before Iphigeneia already bound, and when, later in the play, they appear unbound, it is not Artemis but Athena who comes to settle the issue. The Artemis depicted on the vase is clearly the goddess herself, taking part in the action, and not merely her statue in the temple.

[3] Bulle argues this from the rich painting of steps, door-posts, cornice, &c., and the evidently small dimensions of the theatre depicted. He regards this as a special adaptation of the 'paraskenia-type' for a miniature theatre.

ticularly as contemporary vases representing comic scenes depict the actors as masked. But, as Bulle points out, in the representations of such comic figures the masks are required for the expression of grotesqueness, whereas masks generally, and particularly tragic masks, were intended to compensate for the disadvantages of a distant view—not to make the actors look unlike life, as comic actors did, but to make them look like life in spite of the distance; it would be absurd to use them for a close-up view, such as that given on a vase.

The vases are interesting as showing that the Greeks could freely vary the type of scene-building as they desired, though they have otherwise little to contribute to our knowledge of the Athenian theatre, in which structures of a heavier type are implied by the massive foundations and other remains,[1] and in which Ionic and Doric styles were not mixed as they obviously were in the Graeco-Italian style of the fourth century. (The date of the first vase falls probably in the second quarter of the fourth century or thereabouts, that of the second somewhat later—not earlier than 350 B.C. The theatres depicted should be compared with those of the phlyakes, whose temporary wooden stages are represented on many vases, though they differ in many respects from them.[2])

APPENDIX IV

On the staging of New Comedy plays (Menander, &c.)

Attention has been called above[3] to the absence of evidence for Dörpfeld's view that during the period with which this chapter deals (roughly 380–280 B.C.) plays were acted in front of a temporary proskenion erected at some distance in front of the *scaenae frons*, the top of this erection being connected with the *scaenae frons* by a roof or floor, which might serve as a θεολογεῖον or (apart from drama) as a platform for orators. Neither of these purposes would seem to require a platform projecting for a considerable distance—10 feet or so, according to Dörpfeld—forward across the whole breadth of the skené between the paraskenia. We know,

[1] Vide Fiechter, iii, p. 70.

[2] Bulle mentions also the south Italian vase of Assteas in Madrid, representing the mad Herakles murdering his children, as giving another variant of the south-Italian tragic stage; but it is improbable that this really represents an actual theatrical performance. So far as is known, the murder was never presented on the stage, but took place indoors, and the buildings depicted cannot be assumed to be a stage background. (Cf. von Gerkan, *Das Th. von Priene*, p. 109.) Further, the murder of the children by *burning* which the vase depicts, was not, so far as we know, the subject of any tragedy; but the suggestion of Bieber (*Denkm.*, pp. 107–9) that the subject of the vase may be taken from the hilarotragodia of Rhinthon, &c., seems very improbable (vide Körte, *Neue Jahrb.* 1921, p. 311). (See also below, pp. 221–3.)   [3] pp. 157 ff.

FIG. 58. Campanian Bell krater

indeed, nothing about the appearances of gods in later tragedy; but we do know that plays of Euripides were often reproduced, and it is very doubtful whether such a platform would satisfy the conditions implied in the text of Euripides, e.g. when the god is spoken of as appearing ὑπὲρ δόμων. On Dörpfeld's view, the god would have to appear in front of the second story or out of a door in the upper part of the skené. The allegorical personages who sometimes figure in the New Comedy (such as Agnoia in the *Perikeiro-mene* of Menander, and Air in a fragment of Philemon[1]) may either have appeared on the same level as ordinary actors, or on the θεολογεῖον as used in tragedy.[2]

It is much easier to suppose that plays were acted in front of the skené, and that the front of this included the three entrances which were normal, but any of which could be covered if not required, while further adapta-tions could be made for particular plays in any of the obvious ways.[3] The setting of Menander's plays seems commonly to require two houses, or a house and a temple or shrine (as in Menander's Ἱέρεια and Δύσκολος).[4] These may have been on either side, or close together (as in plays in which a common wall is required, such as Menander's Φάσμα and Plautus' *Miles Gloriosus*). For the two houses it would be possible to use the two side entrances in the skené, or, if more convenient, the paraskenia. The space between the houses might be treated as a street or a garden with very little scenic adaptation. Sometimes there may have been three houses, but this is not certain;[5] a few plays of Plautus and Terence require three houses, but it is not certain that their originals had three.[6] In some plays an upper story is required, e.g. in the house of Demeas in Menander's *Samia* (ll. 16 ff.), and although in some comedies[7] there was certainly a space in which actors could move in front of this upper story and on the roof of the lower, there would be no need of nearly so large a space as the

---

[1] fr. 91 (K). [2] See above, pp. 42, 46, 55.

[3] Such as screens, παραπετάσματα, the use of stock sets of 'properties' for the several kinds of drama, and so on.

[4] Also in Plautus' *Rudens* and *Curculio* and in a fr. of Alexis (publ. in *Sitz. Berlin*, 1918). See Wilamowitz, Menander, *Das Schiedsgericht*, p. 8.

[5] e.g. possibly in the Περικειρομένη: but there is only clear evidence of the houses of Polemo and Myrrhina. That Pataecus' house also was shown is certainly unproved; there is nothing in the text to show that after the recogni-tion he takes Glycera and Moschion into a house on the spot. The Κόλαξ need have presented only the houses of Bias and the Πορνοβοσκός, not that of Pheidias as well.

[6] Frickenhaus, *Die altgr. Bühne*, pp. 25 ff., makes a strong case for supposing the third house in Plautus' *Stichus* and Terence's *Phormio* and *Hecyra* to be due to *contaminatio*. Plautus' *Aulularia* requires the door of a *Fanum Fidei* as well as the two houses.

[7] See above, pp. 67, 103.

advanced proskenion imagined by Dörpfeld requires. In the few plays[1] in which scenes were certainly acted in a portico in front of the main house, such a portico could obviously be erected *ad hoc* in front of any of the doors of the skené, just as well as in front of Dörpfeld's imaginary proskenion. (There is in fact no indication of a portico in any of the extant remains of the New Comedy itself, but only in its Roman imitations; but this may be an accident.)

Whether or not the Hellenistic proskenion, which really did exist, whatever its date, was ever the background of plays will be discussed in the next chapter. But there seems to be no reason for accepting the temporary and movable proskenion imagined by Dörpfeld in the theatre of the fourth century and the early New Comedy. All that the plays of this period require could be better secured by adaptations made as required in and immediately in front of the skené itself.

[1] e.g. Plautus' *Mostellaria* and *Stichus*.

V

THE HELLENISTIC THEATRE

FROM the completion of the 'Lycurgean' reconstruction of the theatre until the time of the Roman Empire no changes that can be traced were made in the orchestra or the auditorium;[1] but to the stage buildings a striking and significant addition was made at a date which different scholars respectively place in the third or second or first centuries B.C. This was the erection of a permanent proskenion in stone at about 4 ft. 5 in. to the north of the skené. At the same time the north façade of each of the paraskenia was rebuilt with its front line about 6 ft. 3 in. nearer the skené, so that the paraskenia now projected only about 3 ft. 7 in. in front of the new proskenion, while the width of the parodoi at the corners of the paraskenia was increased from 8 ft. 6 in. to 14 ft. 9 in.

As regards the date of this change, the opinions of scholars have been influenced by their theories of the date at which the action of the drama was transferred from the orchestra to a raised stage, and by analogies drawn from some of the theatres which were springing up in many parts of the Greek world from the latter half of the fourth century onwards, at least as much as by the character of the extant remains at Athens itself. The opinion which will be maintained in this chapter is that the erection of the proskenion and the transference of the action to a raised stage were probably parts of one and the same change, whenever it took place, and that the view of Dörpfeld and others, that there was a period when there was a raised stage, of which the proskenion was the support in front, but when the action nevertheless continued to take place regularly in the orchestra (in front of the proskenion), is very improbable.

It will be best to begin with an examination of the 'Hellenistic' proskenion and paraskenia which are so variously dated. (What has to be said about the paraskenia has been partly anticipated in the previous chapter.)

---

[1] This must not be taken to exclude the possibility of alterations in the front row of 'thrones', some of which bear inscriptions dating probably from the first century B.C. See above, pp. 141–2, and Fiechter, i, p. 72. But the detailed history of these changes is not traceable with certainty.

I

1. The new proskenion is represented in the ruins by a stylo-bate (P–P in Plan III and Fig. 59) of bluish Hymettian marble, about 2 ft. 3 in. wide, of which (as the workmanship shows) only

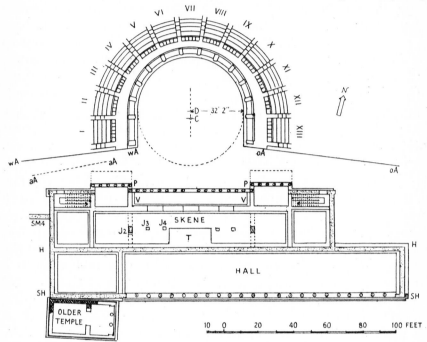

Fig. 59. Sketch-plan of Hellenistic Theatre
(For explanation of symbols, see p. 287)

the upper surface and the upper edge of the northern face were intended to be visible, so that this stylobate scarcely rose above the level of the orchestra. The slabs of which it was composed were of unequal length, and there were slight inequalities in width, some of the slabs projecting an inch or two beyond the rest at the back. They rested upon a foundation of very mixed materials (mainly small stones) roughly heaped together. The surface of the slabs bears marks which show where round columns stood, each about 20 inches in diameter.[1] There were originally

[1] Dörpfeld conjectures that the columns were those which (according to him) originally stood on the Lycurgean *scaenae frons* (V–V), but which would now be partly hidden (if they remained there) by the new proskenion. As, however, the existence of such columns on the Lycurgean *scaenae frons* is most unlikely (see above, pp. 149–50) there is no need to discuss this conjecture.

fourteen of these, standing from 4 ft. 4½ in. to 4 ft. 6 in. apart (from centre to centre), except that the middle intercolumnial interval was about 8 feet. The position of each of the columns was defined for the guidance of the builders by two small curved marks or *lunulae,* of which many can still be seen. These marks and the average diameter of the columns are the same as are found in the stylobate of the abbreviated Hellenistic paraskenia, and this is an indication that the proskenion and the shortened paraskenia formed part of the same plan.[1] It is a not unnatural conjecture that the columns in both places were of about the same height, which in the paraskenia has been calculated[2] to be about 10 ft. 4 in. On the top of the columns in the paraskenia lay an architrave with a row of triglyphs above it. Whether or not there was above this a projecting *geison* or cornice is disputed.[3] The columns of the proskenion were about 6 inches farther apart than those of the paraskenia (which stood at intervals of about 3 ft. 11 in. from centre to centre), and no inference can safely be drawn from the paraskenia as regards what lay above the columns of the proskenion, nor, therefore, as regards the height of the whole proskenion, which may have been anything from (roughly) 11 feet to 13 ft. 6 in. But an architrave with a row of triglyphs and a projecting cornice would be a natural finish, and would give, it is calculated, a total height of 13 ft. 3 in.[4] There are no

[1] Fiechter, iii, p. 76, notes that in the proskenion the stylobate slabs are a little broader and thinner than in the paraskenia, and that the *lunulae* are used not only on the edge of the stylobate, but also in the middle, and he infers from these differences a slight difference in date; but this is surely very insufficient evidence where the general resemblances are so clear.

[2] See above, p. 153. Fiechter, iii, p. 15, says it was not less than about 9 ft. 9 in. (2.96 m.).

[3] Fiechter, ibid., argues that there were no *geisa* in the Hellenistic paraskenia, because they would be kept as low as possible, to conform with the new proskenion; but corniced and even gabled paraskenia might be quite artistic, even if the top of the proskenion (supporting the logeion or stage) were flat. He objects (p. 18) to gabled ends in the paraskenia, because the elevated roof would not be one on which actors could walk. But there is no evidence of actors walking on the roofs of the paraskenia.

[4] D.R., p. 76, Fig. 25: cf. Fiechter, iii, p. 77, who suggests about 11 ft. 3 in., on the strength of a conjecture that when the Lycurgean paraskenia were reduced in depth, they were also reduced in height, and that, at least after Sulla's supposed attack on the theatre (of which we know nothing), they had no cornice (see previous note). But this is no more than guess-work.

certain remains of the columns of the proskenion; it is fortunate
that parts of two of those of the western paraskenion should have
been preserved almost in their original position.[1]

Figure 60 shows the position and present arrangement of the
marble slabs composing the proskenion and its apparent exten-
sions on either side into the paraskenia and beyond them into the
outlying wings.[2] But these stones are not all in their original
position, and Fiechter shows reasons for thinking that in the
east paraskenion Nos. 6–8 (though originally connected with one
another) were brought there from elsewhere; that No. 9 also was
not one of the series of stylobate slabs at all, that the fragment of
a Doric pillar, which stands on it, is also not *in situ*, and that all
this part of the east paraskenion had undergone reconstruction,
in which a number of stones from elsewhere were re-used in a
new connexion. In the west paraskenion (as already noticed[3]),
the stones numbered 28–30 (originally part of the Lycurgean
north front) are in their original sequence, as shown by the traces
of the clamps and the masons' marks, *ΒΓΔ*. Nos. 31 and 32 are
obvious patchwork, and none of Nos. 28–33 are in their original
position, though most of them formed part of the Lycurgean
stylobate. Nos. 34–8 appear to occupy their original place, but
Nos. 36–8 (in the wing beyond the west paraskenion) cannot be
examined because of the upright marble blocks standing upon
them (as part of a rising wall). Nos. 1 and 39, at either end, are
very like one another, but their history cannot be traced. The
nature and history of the buildings which at different periods
stood on the outer sides[4] of the paraskenia cannot be certainly
determined, owing to the many alterations which they underwent; nor, from the point of view of the history of the drama, is
the matter of any great importance.

2. The bearing of the archaeological evidence on the date of
the 'Hellenistic' reconstruction is differently estimated by different scholars. Dörpfeld, while regarding any date between that of
Lycurgus and that of Nero as not impossible, inclines strongly to

[1] See above, ch. iv, p. 151, and Fig. 48.
[2] The numbering is taken for the sake of convenience from Fiechter, who
follows Bulle, though disagreeing with some of his conclusions. It would be
unprofitable here to follow these and other matters of controversy stone by
stone, and it could lead to no certain conclusions.
[3] p. 151.   [4] i.e. the sides remote from the orchestra.

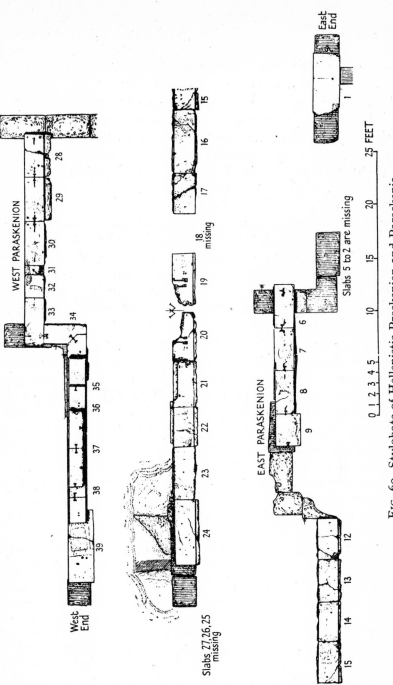

WEST PARASKENION

West End

Slabs 27, 26, 25 missing

Slabs 27, 26, 25
missing

18
missing

EAST PARASKENION

East End

Slabs 5 to 2 are missing

0 1 2 3 4 5   10   15   20   25 FEET

FIG. 60. Stylobate of Hellenistic Proskenion and Paraskenia

the early part of the first century B.C. He thinks that the irregular workmanship of the slabs of the stylobate and the construction of its foundations are too bad for the early third century, but that the mortar used in the foundations is of a different composition from that of the Neronian reconstruction of the theatre and belongs to an earlier date.[1] He thinks it likely that the proskenion may have been erected soon after 86 B.C. when the Odeum of Pericles was partly destroyed by Sulla[2] or by the tyrant Aristion;[3] the theatre, he conjectures, may have suffered also (though there is no evidence of this), and may have correspondingly benefited when Ariobarzanes of Cappadocia rebuilt the Odeum.[4]

Petersen[5] is anxious to claim the stone proskenion as part of the Lycurgean reconstruction. He thinks that the roughness of the surface of the stylobate (which Dörpfeld had treated as evidence of late and careless work) was really due to weathering and wear and tear, that the badly fitting connexions between the slabs were due to disturbance by accidental damage, and that the unevenness of the backline of the stylobate was to be explained by the edges being covered with earth, so that they need not be trimmed to an exact line. The unequal lengths of the stylobate slabs (as compared with the equality of those of the paraskenia) he explains by their not being (like the stylobate of the paraskenia) close to the parodos but at a distance from the spectators, who would not notice the inequality. He thinks that even the smooth front edge of the slabs was hidden with earth or other flooring materials of the orchestra. It is obvious that we are here in a region of facile conjectures, and Dörpfeld seems to be justified[6] in describing Petersen's view as the result of over-rapid and inaccurate observations.

---

[1] D.R., p. 81.

[2] Paus. I. xx, § 4. Bulle also (*Untersuch.*, p. 33) would date the proskenion immediately after the siege of Athens by Sulla, but thinks that the columns, like those of the paraskenia, were hurriedly brought from some other building. See above, p. 154. The attempt of M. Thompson (*Hesperia*, x, pp. 217–24) to connect a series of coins found in the agora and bearing the figure of Dionysus with an (unrecorded) Dionysiac festival of special magnificence in honour of the restoration of the theatre after its supposed destruction in the first century B.C. rests entirely on a series of hypotheses of which there is no proof.

[3] Appian, *Mithrid.* 38.   [4] Vitruv. v. ix, § 1; *I.G.* iii. 541. See p. 1.

[5] *Jahrb. Arch.* xxiii (1908), pp. 36 ff. See above, p. 160.

[6] *Jahrb. Arch.* xxiv (1909), pp. 225–6.

In contrast to Petersen, Versakis[1] proposes to make the abbreviation of the paraskenia and the erection of the proskenion part of the Neronian reconstruction. To this Dörpfeld replies[2] convincingly that no known Roman reconstruction in any theatre has a row of full columns in this position, and that the foundations of this proskenion are of quite different materials from those known to have been used in the Neronian period. He adds that the forms of the letters on the stylobate slabs of the paraskenia, which neither Petersen nor Versakis notices, confirm the Hellenistic reconstruction which Versakis denies.

3. A more probable date is suggested by Frickenhaus[3] and Fiechter,[4] who think that the change must have been made before the building of the theatre in the Peiraeus, which is generally assigned to the middle or the second quarter of the second century B.C.,[5] and also presents a proskenion with full columns—seven on each side of the central opening, with open intervals; the central opening here also was twice as wide as the other intervals, and each of the paraskenia had five columns on its façade. The agreement between these two neighbouring theatres in these and other respects is so close that it can hardly have come about by accident, and it is natural to suppose (though obviously the converse supposition is not impossible and is adopted by Bulle) that the Dionysiac theatre served as the model for its less important neighbour. Fiechter[6] agrees with Dörpfeld that the placing of the proskenion columns elsewhere than upon the junctions of the stones of the stylobate does not accord with the technique of the best period, but this does not disprove a second-century date. He notes signs of even greater carelessness in parts of the paraskenia as he reconstructs them,[7] and suggests that these, and perhaps the alterations in the central door of the proskenion (to be discussed later), may have been due to hasty reconstruction after the supposed damage done to the theatre at the time of the destruction of the Odeum in 86 B.C. But the case for a date not long before that of the theatre in the Peiraeus for the Hellenistic reconstruction as a whole is a strong one. That it may have been assisted by the benefactions of the Pergamene Kings

---

[1] Ibid., pp. 194 ff. [2] Ibid., pp. 224–6. [3] *Die altgr. Bühne*, p. 43.
[4] iii, pp. 76, 77.
[5] D.R., pp. 97 ff.; Bulle, *Untersuch.*, pp. 203–4.
[6] i, pp. 29, 30. [7] iii, p. 14.

Eumenes II (197–159 B.C.) or Attalus II (154–138 B.C.), who showed much generosity to Athens,[1] is not more than an interesting possibility. The result of the discussion is that while no exact dating is possible, and while poor technique and careless work are possible at any time, and a great theatre may quite conceivably copy a smaller one, there is at least some reason, so far as the archaeological evidence is concerned, for dating the erection of the proskenion about or shortly before the middle of the second century B.C., and it will be found that this is consistent with the conclusions rendered probable by the history of the drama and the structure of other theatres, which will be considered shortly.

II

1. Before we inquire, as we must, into the function of the Hellenistic proskenion, it will be well to notice certain points in its structure. We have seen that it presented a row of columns with a wider interval between the middle pair. In this central interval there are clear traces of sockets for the fitting, at different times, of a wider and of a narrower double door.[2] (The former gave a clear opening of about 5 ft. 7 in., the latter, one of 4 ft. 3 in.) It is impossible to say which was the earlier, i.e. whether at some time the wider door was narrowed or the narrower one widened; nor can it be affirmed that either dates from the first erection of the proskenion. Bullé also finds slight traces of a third door in this central interval, but thinks that this may have been a light temporary erection for some special occasion; it may be neglected for the purposes of this discussion. Nor is it necessary to discuss Bulle's theory[3] that the central doors, of which the above-mentioned traces exist, did not strictly belong to the proskenion at all, but were inserted in a wall which he believes to have been substituted for the row of columns in some Byzantine adaptation of the theatrical buildings for use as a residential

---

[1] Eumenes gave the Great Stoa, of which the remains exist, to the west of the theatre of Dionysus. See Judeich, *Topogr. Ath.*, p. 325.

[2] Shown in Fig. 60 on the slabs marked 19 and 20 (in accordance with Fiechter's numeration), which are the central slabs of the proskenion. (No. 19 is no longer *in situ*, but its original place is not doubtful.) Some traces on No. 21 are almost certainly not, as Dörpfeld supposed, those of a door, but of the frame of some kind of panel or screen.

[3] *Untersuch.*, p. 26.

mansion. Fiechter rightly points out[1] that there is no evidence whatever of any such adaptation.[2]

2. Dörpfeld is of opinion that between the round fluted columns erected to form the proskenion there were movable pinakes or panels of wood, which carried the scenic decorations required, and could, if necessary, be taken out to provide doors in addition to the main doorway in the central interval. But whereas in a number of theatres there is special provision in the structure of the supports of the proskenion for the fixing of such panels,[3] there is no trace of any such provision in Athens, either in the theatre of Dionysus or in the theatre at the Peiraeus, which (as has been argued above) was probably almost contemporary with the Hellenistic proskenion now under discussion. The mere fluting of the columns, on which Dörpfeld relies for the purpose,[4] would be quite inadequate,[5] and his suggestion that the side doors might have been fitted on to a special wooden base inserted for the purpose would be more convincing if it were not that practically all such doors known to us were fitted into the stone stylobate. The evidence points to an entirely open colonnade of full columns,[6] though of course it would have been possible to erect a temporary wooden screen behind the columns along the whole or part of the structure, if for any reason it were desired to do so.[7]

[1] i, p. 20; iii, p. 15.

[2] Broneer (*Am. J. Arch.* xxxix, 1935, p. 416) replies further to Bulle's theory, and makes some further suggestions as to possible uses of the two doorways, which, he thinks, may have existed together, but it is obvious that this is a matter upon which no certainty is possible.

[3] See Appendix I.   [4] *Ath. Mitt.* xlix (1924), p. 90.

[5] If the panels were fitted into the fluting of these full columns, they would be broader at the top than at the bottom, and it is doubtful whether this would be aesthetically acceptable. It appears that at Megalopolis special care was taken to avoid this (see Puchstein, p. 13).

[6] If Bulle is right in ascribing the wear and tear, of which the surface of the stylobate slabs shows signs, to constant treading, this might be thought to confirm the belief that the colonnade was open throughout, but if, as he very reasonably suggested, the supposed pinakes would have been removed between performances, this would give plenty of opportunity for wear and tear, so that it is better not to use this argument against the supposed employment of pinakes.

[7] e.g. for acoustic reasons, when cyclic or similar choruses sang in the orchestra, or when for any purpose a background was required or it was desired to close the hyposkenion (the chamber enclosed by the proskenion and the *scaenae frons*).

It is no answer to this to say that, if there were an open colonnade, a doorway in the central interval would be an absurdity, and that there could be no point in making this interval wider than the rest. For we know very little about the doors, for the sockets of which there are traces in this interval: it is quite possible that they did not belong to the original plan at all, but to some now undiscoverable adaptations of the proskenion at later periods in its history. Moreover, if, for some of the many purposes for which the theatre was used, the colonnade was temporarily closed by a screen behind the columns, a central doorway would probably be a necessity, and the provision of sockets, &c., for its reception might even be made from the first. The width of the central interval might be determined by the requirements of this doorway, or simply by aesthetic reasons. It is also conceivable that behind the central interval an enclosed passage may have led through the hyposkenion to a central doorway in the skené; it is easy to imagine the reasons why this might be desirable, and the traces of such a passage might well have been obliterated in the drastic reconstructions which this part of the theatre underwent later. It if existed, it would of course have required a doorway in the central intercolumnium of the proskenion.

III

1. Dörpfeld's theory of the function of the proskenion is that it was the background against which plays were acted down to the Roman period, the floor or λογεῖον supported by the proskenion and connecting it with the skené being used for the appearances of gods (i.e. as a θεολογεῖον), and the part of the skené above this λογεῖον serving, when required, as an upper story, some 9 or 10 feet (as he calculates) behind the front edge of the logeion, which probably projected slightly beyond the actual columns of the proskenion. The intervals between the columns were filled, he supposes, with painted pinakes or panels of wood, the central interval only being fitted with a permanent doorway.[1] But since

---

[1] In most Hellenistic theatres in which the intervals were closed with pinakes, for the securing of which special modifications were made in the columns, there is only one door. At Megalopolis there was possibly none, in Delos probably only a narrow one, though opinions differ about these two instances. Dörpfeld's statement that in many plays only one house was represented is contrary to the evidence of the remains of the New Comedy.

the plays of the New Comedy require at least two houses (or a house and a shrine or some other building), he supposes that the central door was supplemented by one or two other doors,[1] necessarily narrower than the central one, and supplied by the removal of the pinakes in one or more of the intercolumnia. If some special setting were required, e.g. by a satyric play, or a play set in the country, with a cave or a wood, this would be provided by special screens drawn in front of the proskenion. These arrangements, as he believes, merely continued with a stone proskenion those which he thinks were customary in the Lycurgean theatre with a wooden one.

But it has already been shown that no evidence exists for the use of such a proskenion in the fourth century. The natural place for the action would be in front of the skené itself, in which three doors and an upper story (whether in stone or wood) could easily be provided. To suppose that the Athenian playwrights were content with such a makeshift arrangement as the improvised doors which Dörpfeld imagines for a hundred or two hundred years is very difficult. It is much more likely that so long as the whole action of the play lay on the level of the orchestra, it took place before the skené,[2] and that the proskenion at a distance was only built when it was required to support a stage for actors. It may be added (1) that the removal of a pinax would not provide a proper doorway, but only a hole in the wall, (2) that a background in the form of a screen drawn across the proskenion would hardly be possible in theatres in which statues were placed in front of the proskenion.

2. Further difficulties arise when we ask whether the proskenion would afford a satisfactory background. Whether a structure from 11 to 13 feet high, as at Athens, would be adequate for the representation of a row of houses or other buildings, is a matter on which two opinions are possible. It is not safe to place too narrow limits upon the influence of convention in such matters, and in modern theatres also houses are not represented

---

[1] He suggests (D.R., p. 274) that there may have been a pediment on the proskenion over every door, or over any temple represented. The effect of this, with a skené in the background beyond the logeion, would be very odd.

[2] The *scaenae frons* may of course have been altered as required by the use of screens or curtains, such as appear to have been called προσκήνιον before a fixed structure bearing the name was erected. See above, pp. 157–8.

to scale. But the houses were often intended to be those of wealthy citizens, which would naturally be of larger dimensions,[1] and in most other theatres (probably in all) the proskenion was much lower. At Oropos it was only 8 feet or so, and the effect of a tall actor emerging from a door only about 6 ft. 6 in. high might easily be absurd.

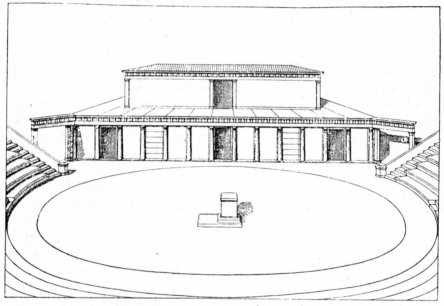

FIG. 61. Dörpfeld's restoration of Hellenistic Theatre

3. Again, it is not easy to see why a stage some 9 feet or more in depth should be needed for the appearances of gods; nor why, if (as Dörpfeld supposes) there was an upper story, they should not have appeared above it, as they had done in earlier times. Nor is there much plausibility about an upper story so far in rear of the lower. It is true that in certain plays of the Old Comedy[2] the actors must have room to move in front of and by the side of the upper rooms, from the windows of which other actors look out, and the same thing may have happened in the New Comedy. But a stage 9 feet in depth is not required for

[1] In better-class houses at Delos the ground-floor rooms rose to 12 feet or more (Chamonard in *B.C.H.*, 1896, p. 294). The evidence as to the height of contemporary houses in Athens is very slight.

[2] See above, pp. 67, 103.

this. (In the figure by which Dörpfeld illustrates his conception a wide space is also left on each side of the upper story.)

4. It is part of Dörpfeld's theory that the scenery was changed as required by the removal of pinakes and substitution of others; and it is sometimes asked[1] what was the use of devices for changing the pinakes, such as some theatres appear to present, if they were not required for the purpose of varying the background. But the devices shown[2] are primarily devices for holding the pinakes in position; no doubt the pinakes could be taken out, but it does not necessarily follow that they were often changed. If they were removed from time to time, it may have been from the very natural desire to preserve them from the weather by storing them when the theatre was not in use, particularly if they were painted with some artistic (though not necessarily scenic) design, as the cost of painting them at Delos[3] (100 drachmae per panel, as compared with 30 drachmae for making each) seems to imply. The words on the proskenion at Oropos recording the dedication of 'the proskenia and the pinakes' do not suggest a number of sets of variable pinakes, and the same impression is made by the inscriptions at Delos[4] which record the repair or replacement of 'the old panels'. Dörpfeld[5] lays stress on the fact that in a number of theatres in Asia Minor,[6] where the action admittedly took place on a raised stage, there are no columns and no panels in the supporting walls of this stage, but only a closed wall. This, he thinks, implies that the purpose of the columns and panels in the Hellenistic theatres which had them must have been to serve as a background of the action. This does not seem to follow, unless it is assumed that the only conceivable use of decorative designs was to make backgrounds for dramatic performers. The difference between the two types of proskenion may well have been one of those differences of style which, like many architectural changes, are not dependent upon function, but upon fashion, or cost, or convenience.[7]

---

[1] e.g. by Noack, *Philol.* xii, 1899, pp. 1 ff.   [2] See Appendix I to this chapter.

[3] *I.G.* xi. 2, No. 158, ll. 67–9. The reading '100 drachmae' seems certain. Statements giving 3 dr. 1 obol as the figure, by Puchstein (p. 34) and others, rest on a misreading.   [4] *I.G.* xi. 2, 199A, ll. 94–5 (274 B.C.).

[5] *Ath. Mitt.* xxiii (1898), p. 342; xxviii (1903), p. 403.

[6] Though not in all—not, e.g., in Priene.

[7] With a closed wall, the trouble of the periodical removal and reinsertion of pinakes would be avoided.

It should be noted that the passage in Pollux[1] which is some-times quoted in support of the theory of a proskenion on which scenery was depicted by means of painted pinakes expressly attributes such pinakes, not to the proskenion, but to the periak-toi, of which something has already been said,[2] and, as usual, Pollux, who is interested, not in the history of antiquities, but in the meaning of words, gives no date.

5. There is a further difficulty in the supposition that the pinakes which Dörpfeld believes to have been in use represented scenery. Most of them would presumably, on his theory, have had to depict parts of two or three houses—whether with or without windows that could be opened he does not say; but he also mentions gardens and human figures among the subjects painted on them,[3] and it is not clear how he supposes them to have been treated, or how they fitted in with the row of houses—particularly the representations of human figures. A panel with a tree or two painted on it might symbolically represent a garden separating two houses, but the comparison, by his colleague Reisch, of the scenery which he imagines with the wall-paintings at Pompeii seems to indicate that they are thinking of something much more elaborate.[4] Even if panels of the size assumed in this proskenion might be used to depict such perspective views in a modern indoor theatre, it is difficult not to feel that in the open air, in the magnificent real scenery of Greece, the effect would be almost contemptible.[5] In theatres in which there were actually intercolumnar pinakes in the proskenion (whether it was the background of action or not) it is probable that (as has already

---

[1] iv. 131 καταβλήματα δὲ ὑφάσματα ἢ πίνακες ἦσαν ἔχοντες γραφὰς τῇ χρείᾳ τῶν δραμάτων προσφόρους· κατεβάλλετο δ' ἐπὶ τὰς περιάκτους ὄρος δεικνύντα ἢ θάλατταν ἢ ποταμὸν ἢ ἄλλο τι τοιοῦτον.

[2] See pp. 123, 126, and below, pp. 234 ff.

[3] D.R., p. 381. Reisch (ibid., p. 274) thinks that the proskenion was especially devised to serve the purpose of the New Comedy with its typical street scenes.

[4] D.R., pp. 336 ff. The value of these paintings as evidence for the character of Hellenistic theatrical scenery is discussed in Appendix III to this chapter. It should be added that Reisch is much more cautious in his estimate of the relation between the Pompeian paintings and the theatre than Puchstein, Bulle, and others. But Reisch definitely thinks of the pinakes of the proskenion as carrying landscapes, while later writers think mainly of the thyromata of late Hellenistic theatres, particularly in Asia Minor, as fulfilling this purpose.

[5] So also Fiechter, *Baugesch.*, p. 30.

been suggested) they carried a simple quasi-architectural or geo-metrical design.[1]

6. For satyric drama, Dörpfeld and Reisch give up the pro-skenion, pure and simple, as a background, and even for many tragedies, and postulate a painted screen drawn in front of the proskenion, showing a temple or the gateway of a city or a cave in the country.[2] They affirm, indeed,[3] that the fixed proskenion was rendered possible because all Hellenistic plays required the same background; but this is, on their own admission, not the case, and there is no justification for treating tragedy and satyric drama, which continued to be regularly performed as an im-portant part of the festivals for centuries, as though they were a kind of extra for which only *ad hoc* provision need be made. (In the large thyromata which in some theatres formed the back-ground of the action on a raised stage there would be more opportunity to provide the varieties of scenery required for all forms of drama.)

It must also be repeated that in fact the theatre at Athens, like that in the Peiraeus, shows no trace of any arrangement for pinakes at all, and that in consequence the discussion of their uses there has a certain unreality.

7. In one of his many writings on the subject[4] Dörpfeld argues that if the proskenion was a good enough background for such 'dramatic' dithyrambs as the *Cyclops* and similar compositions,[5] it would be good enough for the drama proper. It must be replied (1) that though these dithyrambs of Timotheus and Philoxenus introduced soloists, there is no reason to suppose that they employed scenery, or that the soloists acted or presented a plot; (2) that we know of such (loosely termed) 'dramatic' dithyrambs only in the late fifth and early fourth centuries B.C., when it is certain that there was no proskenion in Dörpfeld's sense.

[1] The fact that a doorway is painted in one division of the proskenion at Priene is supposed by Frickenhaus to show that all intercolumnia were filled with such sham doors. But Dörpfeld rightly notes that this painted doorway occurs in a proskenion which has the three regular doors already, and may merely represent the way into the yard of one of the houses. (It is in one of the end intercolumnia.) (*Woch. Klass. Phil.* 1918, col. 364.)

[2] D.R., pp. 274–5, 382.

[3] Ibid., pp. 253, 377, &c. [4] *Jahrb. Arch.* xvi (1901), p. 23.

[5] See *Dith. Trag. Com.*, pp. 63, 73, &c.

8. The conclusion of the discussion must be that it is highly improbable that for a great number of years—two hundred, perhaps—plays should have been acted before a proskenion some way in front of the *scaenae frons* (the front of the main building), with an upper story set far back behind the lower (i.e. behind the proskenion according to this theory). It seems much more probable that throughout the Lycurgean and the early Hellenistic periods, the action took place (still, of course, on the level of the orchestra) before the *scaenae frons* itself, which, by reason of the greater height possible, would afford a far more dignified background, and would allow of the introduction of great variety into the setting, by means which have already been discussed.[1] This arrangement would come to an end only when, for reasons mainly internal to the drama (and particularly owing to the dropping out of the chorus) it became desirable to transfer the action to a raised stage, with all the advantages that such a stage would possess, as soon as the necessity of intercommunication between actors and chorus was removed.[2] Then and then only a proskenion was introduced as the supporting wall of such a stage.

IV

What were the advantages of a raised stage, and what more can be said as to the date at which the change was made?

1. It was argued in an earlier chapter,[3] against the advocates of a raised stage in the fifth century, that such a stage was not necessary in order to enable the audience to distinguish actors from chorus, since experiment showed that they could quite well be distinguished when all were playing on the same level, and Dörpfeld and others succeeded in showing that the position in which the action of a play would be most completely within the view of a great number of spectators, without serious effort by

---

[1] See above, pp. 122 ff. It should be added that this *scaenae frons* would often include an upper story only slightly, if at all, set back from the front (see above, esp. on the evidence afforded by Aristophanes, pp. 67, 103).

[2] In some theatres, e.g. those of Epidaurus, Oropos, and Sikyon, the action was probably on a raised stage from the first (see below, pp. 197, 204). In others, such as that of Athens, the raised stage was not introduced until, perhaps, towards the middle of the second century (see above, p. 182).

[3] p. 70, etc.

many by way of adjustment of vision, would be between the centre of the orchestral circle and the skené. (This at least is what the many arguments respecting 'lines of vision' seem to amount to.) But after the fourth century the conditions were altered. The auditorium was by this time enlarged up to the foot of the κατατομή, and there was no longer, in all probability, the same need for close physical intercommunication between actors and chorus. A raised stage would in time be demanded in order to give the more remote spectators a better view of the actors, in whom the main interest now centred; and when all allowance is made for the flexibility of the human head and shoulders, there is no doubt that those sitting in the uppermost rows would find their vision often interrupted, or made difficult by distance, unless the actors were raised above the level of the orchestra.

2. Against this, Dörpfeld and others object that a high stage would spoil the view of the action of the play from the *front* seats, which were the seats of honour and must have been placed with a view to performances in the orchestra. But the diagrams by which Dörpfeld demonstrates this[1] place the seats much closer to the stage than they were in reality. In an actual Hellenistic theatre with a stage of the height and size of the Athenian—in all other theatres the height was less—the occupants of the front two or three rows would see all but a small fraction of the actor's person, even if he were some way from the front of the stage,[2] and the disadvantage would be no greater than that which is suffered in many modern theatres by those who occupy the front row of the stalls, and whose appreciation of the play is very little diminished by inability to see the actor's boots. Some rough experiments tried in 1928 at Athens and Epidaurus[3] confirmed this belief in the unimportance of the supposed disadvantage. *Some* disadvantage of course there was, and the removal at a later date of some of the front rows in certain theatres[4] which had a high stage, as well as the erection of supplementary seats of honour higher up in the auditorium, may have been due to this; but no such action seems to have been taken generally, and at Athens itself the front row of thrones would give a good view

---

[1] D.R., pp. 353 ff.
[2] See Müller, *Philol.* Suppl. Bd. vii, p. 108 f., Taf. A, who shows this clearly.
[3] By the author and some other members of the Hellenic Travellers' Club.
[4] e.g. Assos, Pergamon, Delphi, Mantinea, but not (e.g.) Priene or Magnesia.

of the performance. There is no ground whatever for the suggestion made by some scholars that the front rows must have been left unoccupied at dramatic performances; and any slight disadvantage inflicted on the occupants of one or two rows of seats was compensated by the improvement of the view for a much larger proportion of the audience.

3. It is some confirmation of the view here taken that (as has been demonstrated by Maass[1]) the height of the proskenion—and consequently of the stage—in Hellenistic theatres generally varies with the distance of the proskenion from the central point of the circle of the auditorium—obviously to accommodate the height of the stage to the view of the audience. This would be meaningless unless the actors were performing on the stage.[2]

4. A secondary consideration may sometimes have had some influence on the height of the proskenion, viz. the need of providing a suitable background for non-dramatic performances in the orchestra, such as those of dithyrambic choruses,[3] which would need a background both for aesthetic and for acoustic reasons, and of the performers known in some places (at least from the third century B.C.) as *thymelici*.[4]

5. The gain to the actors from a raised stage can hardly be doubted. Whether greater elevation gives improved audibility or not (and it is fairly certain that it does), anyone who has made a speech or sung a song must be aware of the greater command of his audience which is afforded by a platform, and, in view of the great interest which seems to have been taken in the actor's professional skill at this period, this fact may have had some influence.

[1] *Woch. Klass. Phil.* 1899, p. 260—followed in the main by A. Müller, *Philol.* lix, p. 342. Those who wish to follow the controversy about conditions of vision may refer also to A. Müller, *Philol.* Suppl. Bd. vii, pp. 108 ff.; Dörpfeld, *Ath. Mitt.* 1899, pp. 310 ff.; Bulle, *Untersuch.*, p. 299, and Haigh, *Attic Theatre*, pp. 158 ff.

[2] Maass's figures, corrected by Müller, are: Oropos, distance from proskenion to proedria 11 m.; height of stage 2·51 m.; Priene, 13·47 m. and 2·72 m.; Delos, 18 m. and 3 m.; Sikyon, 21 m. and 3·25 m.; Eretria 22 m. and 3·50 m.; Epidaurus, 23·50 m. and 3·50 m.; Athens, 24·70 m. and 4 m.

[3] Whether or not tribal contests in dithyramb ceased early in the third century B.C., as Wilamowitz believed (*Gött. Gel. Anz.* 1906, p. 614), dithyrambs continued to be performed at the Dionysia at Athens down to at least A.D. 100. See *Dith. Trag. Com.*, p. 79. There are good reasons for doubting the opinion of Wilamowitz; see Appendix V.   [4] See above, p. 168.

In view of all these considerations, there is nothing paradoxical in the supposition that, as soon as close communication between actors and chorus ceased to be necessary, Greek architects gave their performers and audiences the advantages of a raised stage. This would naturally be accompanied by the shortening of the projecting paraskenia, which would no longer be required as a framework of action in the orchestra, nor yet to serve as houses or temples, and which, if required on the stage as side-wings, need not project before the front line of the stage itself. That in fact in some theatres they were still built so as to project slightly may have been due to a natural conservatism, or to the desire to give the stage structures a neat and dignified finish on each side. In such an attenuated form they were preserved (e.g.) at Athens, Sikyon, and Epidaurus, but having no essential function they could easily be given up, as at Magnesia and in all later theatres. It would be much more difficult to account for their abbreviation or disappearance if the action were in front of the proskenion.

6. Some other arguments used by Dörpfeld and his followers against action on a raised stage at this, or indeed at any, period, need only a brief consideration. They urge that a stage from 7 to 9 feet deep[1] and from 10 to 13 feet high would be too narrow and too dangerous for satisfactory dramatic action,[2] apart from the appearances and the calm delivery of gods using the proskenion-roof as a theologeion, and Bethe[3] so far shares this misgiving that he suggests that the action on such a stage may have been facilitated by the extension of the stage backwards into the interior of the skené. Such a supposition is quite unnecessary, and the extension might have optical disadvantages from the point of view of the audience. The experience of Greek plays acted at Bradfield for over half a century shows that a stage of this width is ample for the action of a Greek play, and it is difficult to suppose that even a narrow stage of this height would present serious danger to a professional or well-trained actor who had any skill or who had rehearsed his part.

7. The arguments drawn by Dörpfeld and Reisch[4] from certain scenes in Plautus, which are said to require a stage of 13 feet

---

[1] It is not likely to have been less than 9 feet, and may have been 10 feet.
[2] D.R., pp. 360–1.
[3] *Prolegom.*, pp. 260 ff., *Gött. Gel. Anz.* 1897, p. 709, &c.
[4] pp. 269, 275, &c.

or more in depth, are not very conclusive, partly because there is little agreement as to the staging of these scenes, and partly because we do not know how far the Greek originals may have been modified by Plautus for presentation on the ampler Roman stage.[1]

8. Nor can much importance be attached to Dörpfeld's assertion that to present a street scene (such as are many scenes in the New Comedy) on the top of a row of pillars would be an absurdity and would destroy all illusion. Illusion is in any case not entirely or mainly supplied by the decorative setting, and (as countless modern performances witness) can exist with no setting at all. (It would not even be wholly destroyed by Dörpfeld's queer row of three low, columned houses.) Ancient audiences, moreover, are just as likely to have been tolerant of such conventions as modern, by whom the illusion is not required to begin below the level of the stage floor, and the gilded supports of this (as well as the heads of the band) are obligingly disregarded.

9. We may assume then, once more, that so soon as the nature of the plays performed permitted it, there would be every inducement to transfer the action to a raised stage. But when was this? The answer, if any is possible, must be found partly by an examination of our scanty knowledge of the plays and other performances of the period after the death of Menander; partly from considerations derived from the study of Greek theatres outside Athens.

V

1. The conclusion reached in the last chapter was that nothing in the literary remains suggested a high raised stage (with a proskenion at a distance from the *scaenae frons* to support it) down to the time of Menander's death, and that the slight evidence which they afforded favoured the opposite view. Inscriptions[2] take the formal records of contests and victories in tragic contests at Athens beyond the middle of the second

---

[1] On this see above, p. 173.

[2] Esp. *I.G.* ii–iii². 2323, 2325. In some years the contest in comedy was omitted, e.g. three times in the decade 190–180 B.C., and four times in the decade 170–160 B.C. The statement of Reisch (*Zeitschr. Öst. Gymn.* 1907, p. 301) that comic contests at the Lenaea ceased and that tragic producers at the Lenaea brought out only old plays, is disproved by Capps, *Berl. Phil. Woch.* 1908, pp. 637 ff.

century B.C., though they give no information about the character
of the plays. Other inscriptions[1] make it fairly evident that the
performance of new tragedies long continued to be the chief
event of the City Dionysia, but do not tell us whether or not these
new tragedies involved a chorus performing in the orchestra; and
it is equally uncertain how far old tragedies were performed in
their completeness, and in particular whether the chorus danced
or only sang its odes. There is a possible reference to Athens in
words quoted by Philodemus[2] from Diogenes of Babylon, the
Stoic, who was one of the three philosophers sent as ambassadors
to Rome by Athens in 156–155 B.C. to plead the Athenian case in
a dispute with Oropos: καὶ ὅτι περιῃρημένης τῆς ὀρχήσεως ἐκ τῶν
δραμάτων οὐδὲν ἔχομεν ἔλαττον, ἐπειδήπερ οὐδὲν ἦν ἐν οὐδεμιᾷ πρὸς
τὸ καλὸν καὶ γενναῖον συνέργημα. The reference is probably to
tragedy, as it is doubtful whether the word δρᾶμα was applied
to comedy at this time. The natural inference would be that the
choral odes were sung, without dancing—perhaps by a reduced
chorus as in some other places,[3] and so possibly, though not
necessarily, on a raised stage, and that the change was a recent
one when Diogenes spoke of it. (This would harmonize with the
archaeological evidence pointing to this period as that at which
the raised stage was introduced at Athens.[4])

2. The passage, however, which is sometimes quoted[5] as proving that choruses were omitted in the reproduction of old tragedies, is of no use for this purpose. It is in Dio Chrysostom,[6] who
(speaking of the delight given by citharodes and actors as compared with the improvisations of rhetoricians) writes: καὶ τά γε

---

[1] e.g. *I.G.* iii². 682 (275–274 B.C.), ll. 71 ff. δοκεῖ τῇ βουλῇ ἐπαινέσαι Φαῖδρον
Θυμοχάρου Σφήττιον καὶ στεφανῶσαι αὐτὸν . . . καὶ ἀναγορεῦσαι τὸν στέφανον Διονυσίων μεγάλων τραγῳδιῶν τῷ ἀγῶνι τῷ καινῷ κτλ.: and *I.G.* ii–iii². 956, l. 33
(*c.* 161 B.C.) ἀναγορεῦσαι δὲ τὸν στέφανον Διονυσίων τε τῶν ἐν ἄστει καινοῖς τραγῳδοῖς
κτλ. An inscription from Delphi of the first century B.C. (*B.C.H.* xviii (1894),
p. 93) which honours the Athenian Thrasykles for services to Delphi also mentions
his victory at Athens—ἀγωνισάμενός τε ἐν τᾷ ἰδίᾳ πατρίδι καινῇ καὶ νικάσας ἐστε-
φάνωσε τὸν δᾶμον ἁμῶν. (Couve dates this inscription between 94 and 81 or
between 40 and 10 B.C.)

[2] *De Mus.* iv. 7, p. 70 (Kemke). He was a contemporary of Cicero.

[3] In the inscriptions relating to the Soteria at Delphi there is no mention of
tragic choreutae at all. (See below, p. 240.)

[4] See above, p. 182.

[5] See Bethe, *Neue Jahrb.* 1907, p. 84, and Schmid–Stählin, II. i, pp. 171 ff

[6] *Or.* lxix, p. 487 R (= ii. 258. 20 von Arnim). See below, p. 245

πολλὰ αὐτῶν ἀρχαῖά ἐστι καὶ πολὺ σοφωτέρων ἀνδρῶν ἢ τῶν νῦν· τὰ
μὲν τῆς κωμῳδίας ἄπαντα· τῆς δὲ τραγῳδίας τὰ ἰσχυρά, ὡς ἔοικε,
μένει· λέγω δὲ τὰ ἰαμβεῖα· καὶ τούτων μέρη διεξίασιν ἐν τοῖς θεάτροις·
τὰ δὲ μαλακώτερα ἐξερρύηκε τὰ περὶ τὰ μέλη. But this only shows
that 'parts of the iambic portions', i.e. select scenes, were acted,
and does not refer to reproductions of whole tragedies at all. The
date also (*c.* A.D. 100) is too late to allow the use of the passage as
evidence in regard to the date of the raised stage, which on any
theory was in use long before this. Nor is Dio necessarily speaking of Athens.

3. Satyric drama evidently enjoyed much more popularity
away from Athens than in the city itself, where we hear little of
it, except that for a time a single satyric play was acted during
the festival, instead of one appended to each tragic trilogy.
Bulle[1] insists strongly that satyric plays, in which a chorus was
essential, must have been acted in the orchestra, and it must be
admitted that so long as the satyr chorus danced the *sikinnis*, of
which high springing was characteristic, even a chorus reduced
in numbers might have had difficulties on a relatively narrow
stage. But in fact we do not know in what ways satyric drama
had been altered in the course of time, and it may have been so
changed as to be capable of being produced entirely on the stage,
as it certainly must have been on the deeper Roman *pulpitum*.
The possibility cannot be entirely excluded that when the actors
of new plays had been transferred to the logeion, satyric plays
and old plays which required frequent contact between actors
and chorus may have been acted entirely in the orchestra; but
the satisfactory adaptation of the proskenion for the purposes of
a background would have presented difficulties, as has already
been argued, and it is perhaps more likely that only those old
tragedies were selected in which the chorus (in the orchestra) and
the actors (on the stage) could be separated without serious loss.

4. The records of performances in theatres outside Athens are
summarized in an appendix to this chapter. These were for the

[1] *Das Theater zu Sparta*, pp. 91 ff. But his treatment of the scenery on certain
reliefs as reproducing a proskenion used as the background of a satyric play is
very speculative, however ingenious. These reliefs (Figs. 62, 63), on which stage
satyrs appear, may be, as he thinks, based on paintings which were votive
dedications, and naturally include reminiscences of the theatre, but need not
be supposed to reproduce the theatrical scene in particular details. (They
obviously do not do so as regards the costume of the satyrs.)

Fig. 62. Satyr relief in Conservatori Museum

Fig. 63. Relief in Ince-Blundell Collection

most part performances given by the organized guilds of Artists of Dionysus, and the records suggest that these guilds felt free to adapt tragedy to their needs, reducing the chorus to a very few singers or omitting the choral odes altogether, and treating comedy with almost equal freedom. This reduction of the size of choruses, or their omission, would have been necessary in theatres of the Roman pattern, and in Greek theatres in which the whole action was transferred to the logeion; but the records give no hint of the date of this transference, and would be consistent with any date between the death of Menander and the beginning of the Christian era, if it be allowed, as it must, that the Artists enjoyed a reasonable freedom of adaptation. We do not in fact know what the taste of different towns may have preferred; but there is at least a strong probability that the most favoured performances were those of the New Comedy, and that many theatres were built mainly with these in view. (Some scholars believe that at Epidaurus, for instance, tragedy was not acted at all, though one of the reasons given—the depressing effect which tragedy would have had on the patients of Asklepios— is not very convincing.) The records also suggest that the contests turned largely upon the technique of individual actors—as indeed they had begun to do even at Athens as early as Aristotle's day, when μεῖζον δύνανται τῶν ποιητῶν οἱ ὑποκριταί.[1] But the value of all this fragmentary information from remote theatres as evidence in regard to performances at Athens is limited by the possibility that at Athens itself there was a more conservative spirit, especially as regards tragedy, which may still have possessed there some remains of its old religious sanctity and have been performed with its full choral splendour. Even if it was from the Athenian Guild of Artists of Dionysus, which held a leading position in the Greek world,[2] that companies of actors were sent far and wide, they may not have restricted their productions at Athens itself to the attenuated performances required in the provinces, but may have presented tragedies in a more generous way, with choruses which could only have found their place in the orchestra, and the action may thus have remained wholly on the orchestral level longer than elsewhere, so that even if (e.g.) at Epidaurus (built towards the end of the fourth century) and some other theatres the action may have been on the stage from the

[1] *Rhet.* iii. 1, § 4.   [2] Cf. Ferguson, *Hellenistic Athens*, p. 370, &c.

first, there would be nothing paradoxical in the maintenance of
the older custom at Athens for another century and a half.

5. In Attica itself there were at least eleven theatres[1] besides
that of Dionysus in the city—at Rhamnus, Thorikos, Acharnai,
Aixone, Eleusis, Icaria, Collytus, Phlya, Salamis, Myrrhinus, and
in the Peiraeus—and the performances in these may have been
of very different degrees of completeness and magnificence, and
plays may have been freely adapted to suit the local conditions.

VI

1. It is to be feared that the study of the remains of the
theatres outside Athens, which were built in great numbers from
the end of the fourth century onwards, can yield equally little
certainty as to the date at which the action was transferred to
a raised stage at Athens itself. There is very little agreement
among archaeologists as to the history of the various stage
buildings, and the point upon which agreement is most rare is the
date of the erection of a permanent proskenion supporting a
logeion on which the performers acted. Archaeologists have been
largely swayed in their judgement by *a priori* theories. Dörpfeld,
for example, had long made up his mind that a stone proskenion
must everywhere have been preceded by a wooden one (a belief
for which, as we have seen, no evidence exists in the case of
Athens), and that at no time before the Roman epoch was the
action on the logeion, and he interpreted the ruins accordingly.
Others, with other theories, date the stone proskenia, if possible,
in the second or the first century; and so on. The honest truth is
that the evidence forthcoming in the majority of theatres does not
suffice to fix the date of the proskenion except within very wide
limits, and that the more closely the evidence is examined, the
less confident it is possible to be.

Only a few illustrations can here be given.

2. The theatre at *Eretria*[2] is usually dated, in its original form,
in the last third of the fifth century B.C. The grounds for this are
not very satisfying; but it seems clear that in its earliest period,
whenever it was, there can have been no raised stage, and that

[1] For inscriptional evidence of performances in these see Vitucci in *Dioniso*,
vii (1939), pp. 210 ff., 312 ff.
[2] See esp. Fiechter, *Das Theater in Eretria*, and Bulle, *Untersuch.*, pp. 81 ff.,
266 ff., and above, pp. 23, 70.

plays must have been acted before the skené, probably on a wooden floor raised only one step above the level of the orchestra, and flanked by the projecting paraskenia.[1] But it is disputed, and the evidence is not good enough to settle the dispute, whether after this there were two periods of reconstruction or one. Two changes of great importance were certainly made: (1) The orchestra was lowered by about 11 feet by excavation to its present level, leaving the previously existing skené (which was also probably much altered) as an upper story, above and some way behind the retaining wall which held up the earth at the limit of the excavation. Whether plays were entirely acted henceforth on the new orchestral level, wooden or canvas backgrounds being provided as required[2] in front of the retaining wall, or whether the actors played between the old skené and the top of the retaining wall, i.e. 11 feet above the orchestra, is much disputed. The date of the excavation is conjecturally placed about 300 B.C., but without any conclusive evidence. (2) A marble proskenion (Pr in Fig. 64) was erected at some distance in front of the retaining wall, supporting a logeion running back to the retaining wall. When this happened—the skené itself probably being rebuilt at the same time nearer to the top of the retaining wall—the action must necessarily have been on the new logeion. (The marble proskenion itself, having only one door in its façade, would not have sufficed as a background of action.) But as to when this proskenion was built there is no agreement; one scholar makes it contemporary or almost contemporary with the excavation, another dates it a century or so later; and there is no decisive evidence.

3. With regard to the theatre at *Megalopolis*[3] there are equally strong differences of opinion. The orchestra was laid out and the auditorium constructed in front of the Thersilion or Council Hall in the fourth century. Whether at first plays were acted there at all is uncertain. But, probably in the first half of the third century, there came into use the so-called *scaena*

[1] See above, p. 70. The position of this step is marked L in Fig. 64.
[2] The retaining wall, to the south of the excavated orchestra, would have been quite inadequate as a background by itself. The scene of action would be bounded by P1 and P2 in Fig. 64.
[3] See D.R., pp. 133 ff.; Fiechter, *Das Theater in Megalopolis*; Bulle, *Untersuch.*, pp. 97 ff., and *Das Theater zu Sparta*, pp. 24–7; von Gerkan, *Gnomon*, 1938, pp. 232 ff., &c.

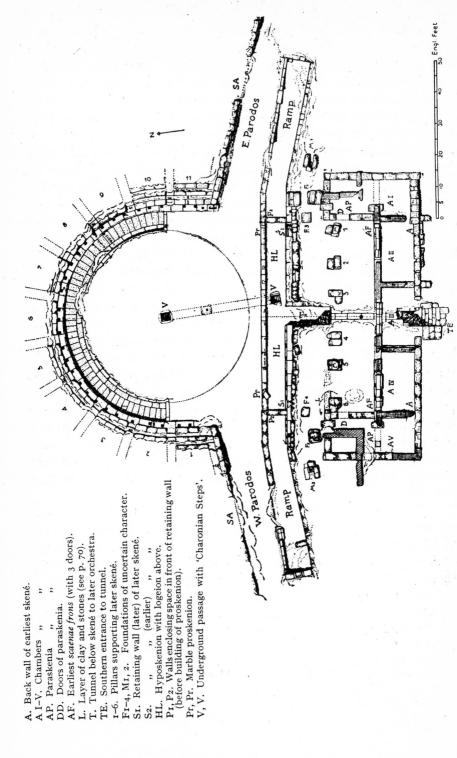

A. Back wall of earliest skené.
A I–V. Chambers   ,,   ,,
AP. Paraskenia   ,,   ,,
DD. Doors of paraskenia.
AF. Earliest *scaenae frons* (with 3 doors).
L. Layer of clay and stones (see p. 70).
T. Tunnel below skené to later orchestra.
TE. Southern entrance to tunnel.
1–6. Pillars supporting later skené.
Fr–4, M1, 2. Foundations of uncertain character.
Sr. Retaining wall (later) of later skené.
S2.   ,,   ,,   (earlier)   ,,
HL. Hyposkenion with logeion above.
P1, P2. Walls enclosing space in front of retaining wall
    (before building of proskenion).
Pr, Pr. Marble proskenion.
V, V. Underground passage with 'Charonian Steps'.

Fig. 64. Plan of Theatre at Eretria

Fig. 65. View of remains of Theatre at Eretria

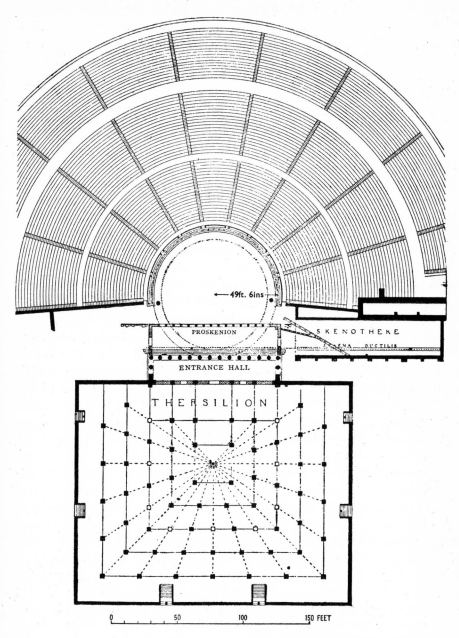

FIG. 66. Plan of Theatre at Megalopolis (restored)

The labels within the figure read:

49ft. 6ins

PROSKENION

SKENOTHEKE

SCENA DUCTILIS

ENTRANCE HALL

THERSILION

0   50   100   150 FEET

ductilis[1]—a stage rolled along in front of the orchestra from the *skenotheké* in which it was housed. It was certainly not a high stage, and there is no certain evidence of such a stage before the erection of a marble proskenion, perhaps about the middle of the second century.

4. At *Priene*,[2] at the time of the original construction, which may have been between 350 and 330 B.C.[3]—roughly speaking, the date of the Lycurgean reconstruction at Athens—the action was probably on the ground-level in front of the skené (as we have reason to think it was at Athens). But the date of the proskenion and the logeion remains quite uncertain. Von Gerkan makes them part of the theatre as originally constructed, but his argument is unconvincing. He also supposes that, whenever the proskenion was constructed, the action nevertheless took place in front of it, and not on the logeion, down to about 160 B.C. His conclusion depends (1) on the correctness (which is very doubtful) of his reconstruction of the skené, which would make action on the logeion difficult, because there would not be enough ways of access on to it, (2) on the assumption that the only use of decorative pinakes, such as those of which he finds evidence in the proskenion front, can have been to serve as a background for drama—which is quite unproved.[4] Von Gerkan further thinks that the modification (which he dates in the second half of the second century B.C.) of the *scaenae frons* into a background consisting largely of wide thyromata, the removal of the prohedria from the front row of the auditorium to the fifth, and the erection of statues in the orchestra against the proskenion, indicate that that was the time when action was transferred to the logeion. (As regards the last two points, Dörpfeld rightly notes that the prohedria was *not* removed, though additional seats of honour were provided on a higher level, and that the statues, the dates of which are not quite certain, were placed where they would not interfere with the action or the spectators' view of it, even if the action were still in the orchestra.) But even if the

---

[1] An unfortunate name. The *scaena ductilis* referred to by Servius on Virg. *Georg.* iii. 24 was a part of the *scaenae frons* which could be drawn aside to disclose an interior. See p. 237.

[2] See esp. von Gerkan's fine monograph; also Dörpfeld, *Ath. Mitt.* xlix, 1926, pp. 50–101; Bulle, *Untersuch.*, pp. 250 ff.

[3] This seems more probable than 300 B.C. (von Gerkan's date).　　[4] Cf. pp. 187–9.

FIG. 67. View of remains of Theatre at Megalopolis

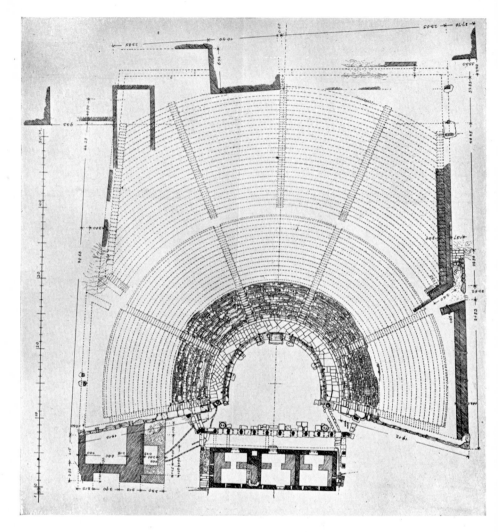

Fig 68. Plan of Theatre at Priene

Fig. 69. View of remains of Theatre at Priene

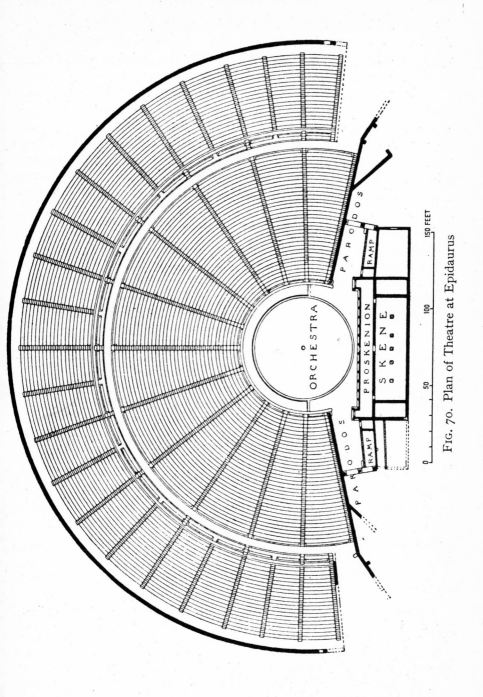

PARODOS

RAMP

PROSKENION

SKENE

150 FEET

100

ORCHESTRA

50

PARODOS

RAMP

0

FIG. 70. Plan of Theatre at Epidaurus

date of the thyromata-background is correct, as it well may be, there is no reason why action on the logeion should have waited till then. It doubtless coincided with the construction of the proskenion, and it is the date of that which cannot be determined.

5. In three theatres—those of Epidaurus,[1] Oropos,[2] and Sikyon[3]—there were ramps leading up to the logeion, which was above and behind the proskenion, and it seems highly probable that in these the action was on the logeion from the first. The theatre at *Epidaurus* dates from the latter part of the fourth century, and it may have been the first theatre built from the outset for action on a raised stage—perhaps mainly with comedy in view, though it is only a conjecture that tragedy was never performed there.[4] The actual proskenion, of which the remains are still in position, seems to belong to the third or second century, but the lines of the front and the height of the logeion must have been very much the same from the first. The stone circle in the orchestra enclosing the domain of the chorus comes right up to the proskenion, and at least suggests that the actors did not perform where they would necessarily be trespassing on that domain. If the ground in front of the proskenion was the actors' territory, the stone circle would hardly have been brought so far forward.

The theatre at *Oropos* dates from some time in the third century B.C., that at *Sikyon* probably between 303 and 251 B.C., and there is no difficulty in supposing that it was on the logeion to which the ramps led up that the dramatic action took place.[5]

It is obviously natural to suppose that where there were ramps leading up to each end of the proskenion roof or logeion, and lying in the same line as it, they were used by actors coming on to the stage, such as messengers or persons arriving from the country or from abroad. The ramps would thus supplement the ordinary entrances from the skené, and the difficulty, put forward by Dörpfeld, of timing entrances by the ramps exactly (the ramps being in full view of the audience) is one which a very moderate

[1] See D.R., pp. 120–33; Bulle, *Untersuch.*, pp. 167–74, &c.
[2] See esp. Fiechter, *Das Theater in Oropos*; von Gerkan, *Gnomon*, 1933, pp. 145 ff.; Bulle, op. cit., pp. 255–6, and also Dörpfeld, *Ath. Mitt.* xlix (1924), pp. 90, 91.
[3] See esp. Fiechter, *Das Theater in Sikyon*; Bulle, op. cit., pp. 192–9; von Gerkan, *Gnomon*, 1933, pp. 145–58.   [4] See p. 197.
[5] This is disputed by von Gerkan, loc. cit., but not very convincingly and mainly on theoretical or *a priori* grounds.

FIG. 71. View of Theatre at Epidaurus

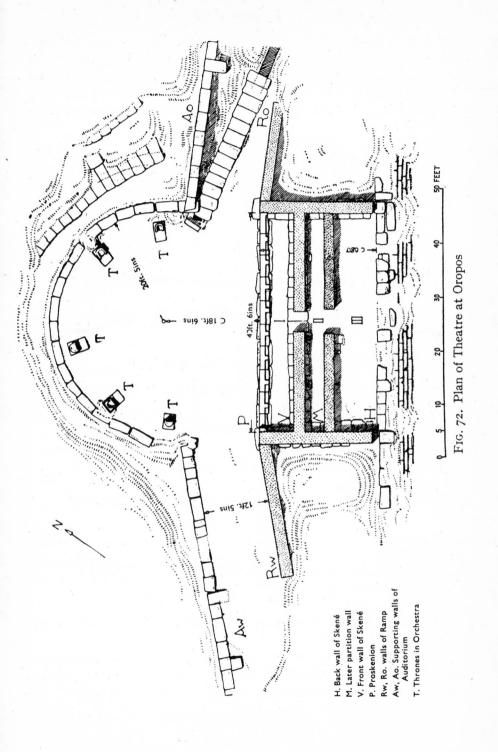

FIG. 72. Plan of Theatre at Oropos

H. Back wall of Skené
M. Later partition wall
V. Front wall of Skené
P. Proskenion
Rw, Ro. walls of Ramp
Aw, Ao. Supporting walls of Auditorium
T. Thrones in Orchestra

amount of rehearsal would get over. His own suggestion is that they were used for the chariots needed for the appearance of gods (when they came in chariots, for most frequently they did not), or for machines required for use in connexion with the theologeion or upper story.[1] But this rare or occasional use

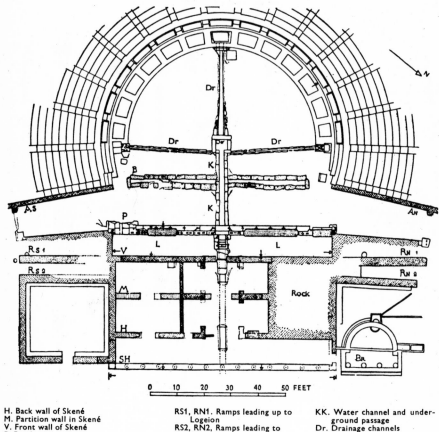

H. Back wall of Skené	RS1, RN1. Ramps leading up to	KK. Water channel and under-
M. Partition wall in Skené	Logeion	ground passage
V. Front wall of Skené	RS2, RN2, Ramps leading to	Dr. Drainage channels
P. Proskenion	interior of Skené	SH. Stoa behind Skené
B. Front of Roman stage	AS, AN. Supporting walls of	Br. Fountain-house
L L. Logeion with Hyposkenion beneath	Auditorium	

FIG. 73. Plan of Theatre at Sikyon

seems to be a very inadequate explanation of such substantial permanent structures.

6. A reliable history of the theatre at *Delos* is made almost impossible by the looseness with which the most important terms— σκηνή, προσκήνιον, παρασκήνια, λογεῖον—seem to be used in the

―――――――――
[1] *Ath. Mitt.* xxiii, 1898, p. 350.

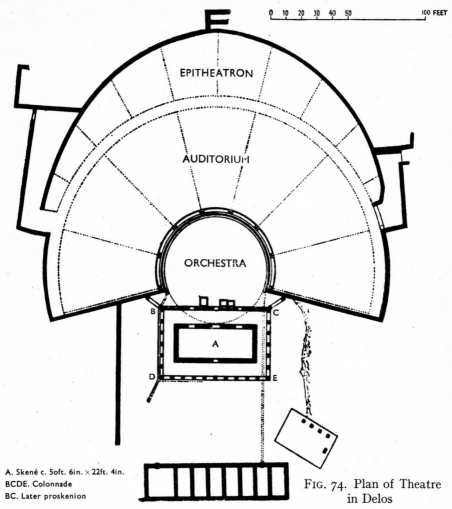

A. Skené c. 5oft. 6in. × 22ft. 4in.
BCDE. Colonnade
BC. Later proskenion

FIG. 74. Plan of Theatre in Delos

extant records. These records consist of a long series of inscriptions,[1] dating from the first building of the theatre about 300 B.C., or possibly a few years earlier, and recording payments for constructive and decorative operations of all kinds. One of the earliest of these payments (probably very soon after 300 B.C.) was

---

[1] *I.G.* xi. 2, 142 to 291, being the records of the ἱεροποιοί of Delos; see Chamonard, *B.C.H.* xx (1896); D.R., pp. 144–9; Vallois (refs. below); Puchstein, pp. 53 ff.; Fiechter, *Baugesch.*, pp. 23 ff.; Bulle, *Untersuch.*, pp. 174 ff., 279 ff. The present discussion is directed only to the evidence as regards a raised stage, and does not touch the many problems of great interest which this theatre presents.

made τοῖς τὴν σκηνὴν ἐργολαβήσασι καὶ τὸ προσκήνιον, and in 282 B.C. there are payments for making and painting wooden πίνακας εἰς τὸ προσκήνιον. In 279 B.C. a beam 18 feet long was purchased εἰς τὸ λογεῖον τῆς σκηνῆς, but λογεῖον is in fact a restoration of a defective word in the inscription which is not accepted by some scholars (though it seems quite probable), nor is the meaning of the word agreed. Other inscriptions show that this earliest theatre (which may have been mainly of wood) had παρασκήνια, which were also provided with πίνακες (as well as with doors), though these παρασκήνια were probably not projecting wings, but the portions of the *scaenae frons* to right and left of the central part. If the words προσκήνιον and λογεῖον (supposing the reading to be correct) are used in their common meanings, this earliest theatre must have had a raised stage supported by a προσκήνιον (including painted πίνακες) at some distance in front of the σκηνή, which would thus be two-storied at least, and there is no convincing reason why this should not have been so.[1]

The inscriptions which follow[2] record the reconstruction of the theatre in stone by several stages, the work continuing from 274 B.C. onwards for nearly thirty years. The rebuilding of the skené in two or possibly three stories[3] was probably completed by 250 B.C., but work was still going on in the auditorium for some years later. The proskenion (in the ordinary sense), of which the traces are still to be seen, is of still later date, possibly of the second century B.C., and it was too low, in all probability, to serve as a background for action without ludicrous effects, nor is it certain that it had more than one door; this implies that the actors performed on a logeion above it. But this proskenion must have been a modification of, or a substitute for, an earlier one, the change being made to bring the proskenion into conformity with a colonnade which was built round the whole skené at some time in the Hellenistic period. An inscription of much later date[4] speaks of the κατασκευὴ τῶν πινάκων ἐπὶ τὸ λογεῖον in

---

[1] But some suppose that προσκήνιον = *scaenae frons*, or else a screen drawn, when required for dramatic purposes, in front of the skené—the whole being on the ground-level.

[2] In these inscriptions there is no mention of προσκήνιον or λογεῖον.

[3] See Vallois, *Nouvelles archives des missions scientifiques*, 1920, pp. 213–17, and *Rev. Ét. anc.* 1928, pp. 171–9.   [4] *B.C.H.* xviii, p. 165, No. 11.

FIG. 75. View of Theatre in Delos

FIG. 77. Relief in Naples

180 B.C., but it is not certain[1] whether this inscription refers to the theatre at all.

7. The date of the first proskenion and logeion at *Oiniadai*[2] may be in the third century or later. At *New Pleuron*[2] it is also uncertain whether the proskenion was part of the late third-century building. At *Ephesus*[3] also, where the Roman building has wholly or partly destroyed most of the evidence as regards the earlier periods in the history of the theatre, it is disputed whether the marble proskenion belonged to the building of the early third century or not.

8. The brief accounts here given may suffice to illustrate the present condition of our knowledge. The examination of many other theatres[4] yields equally unsatisfactory results. All that can be said is that there is some reason for thinking that in certain theatres the action of the plays may have been on the raised logeion from the first, i.e., roughly speaking, from the latter part of the fourth century (at Epidaurus) or a little later (e.g. at Oropos and Sikyon, and possibly at Delos at the beginning of the third century); that elsewhere, for whatever reasons, the change may have been made later, but that it is not legitimate to draw inferences from these facts as to the history of the Dionysian theatre at Athens, where the conditions may have been quite different. The assumptions of most German scholars and archaeologists that all changes must have been initiated at Athens, and that all theatres must have changed their structure almost simultaneously, are more characteristic of German mentality than they are probable, when we have to think of a large number of independent cities; and we are left with a possibility that Athens may have continued contentedly to perform plays on the orchestral level for many years after Epidaurus and other theatres had been

[1] D.R., p. 301.

[2] Fiechter, *Die Theater von Oiniadai u. Neu-Pleuron*; Bulle, op. cit., 91 ff., 242 ff.; Arias, *Il Teatro Greco fuori di Atene*, pp. 46–57; von Gerkan, *Das Th. von Priene*, pp. 89, 90.

[3] Heberdey und Wilberg, *Forschungen in Ephesos*, ii (1912); Dörpfeld in *Jahrb. Arch.* 1913, *Anz.*, cols. 38 ff.; von Gerkan, op. cit., pp. 90–3.

[4] A very convenient summary of the facts as regards a large number of theatres is given in the little book of Arias named above, and he gives references to all the more important discussions of each down to 1934. Some similar work, brought up to date and extended so as to cover some other theatres, would be a great advantage to English students.

doing otherwise. It must also be remembered that while at Athens the performance of tragedy and comedy continued to be the most important purpose of the theatre, and there were other buildings for other purposes, it was not always so outside Attica in places where, in all probability, the drama was only one, and not necessarily the most important, of the objects which theatre-builders had in view.

9. Two remarks may be added:

(1) The argument that the underground passages leading from the skené into the orchestra in certain theatres—as at Eretria, Sikyon, and Segesta—imply that the action took place in the orchestra is a very unsafe one. In fact the date and history of these passages is very uncertain (the earliest appears to be that at Eretria, which may belong to the third century B.C.), and they may not have anything to do with drama at all. In any case no one can suppose that there was any passage like these at Athens.[1]

(2) In one or two theatres it appears that statues were placed in the Hellenistic period in front of the proskenion, and it is sometimes argued from this, that the proskenion cannot have been the background of dramatic action. It is better, however, not to support what appears to be a good case by a bad argument. At Priene (as has already been noted) the statues stood quite near the ends of the proskenion and left all the centre free. Of the statues at Delos too little is certain to afford any reliable argument; their date is unknown, and probably is relatively late; and in any case it is not safe to argue from Priene and Delos to Athens.

VII

1. The attempt is sometimes made to ascertain a probable date for the introduction of a raised stage by reference to the scholiasts, who in their comments on Aristophanes and other poets have obviously in mind a theatre with a λογεῖον, a raised structure

---

[1] See above, pp. 51, 65, 146. At Segesta the opening of the passage was not in the middle of the orchestra, but close to the corner of the auditorium, and this, as Bulle (*Untersuch.*, p. 293) points out, illustrates Pollux iv. 132 Χαρώνιοι κλί-μακες, κατὰ τὰς ἐκ τῶν ἐδωλίων καθόδους κείμεναι, τὰ εἴδωλα ἀπ᾽ αὐτῶν ἀναπέμ-πουσιν. But under what circumstances such ghosts appeared we do not know. Pollux also names the ἀναπιέσματα or lifts, of which τὸ μέν ἐστιν ἐν τῇ σκηνῇ ὡς ποταμὸν ἀνελθεῖν ἢ τοιοῦτόν τι πρόσωπον, τὸ δὲ περὶ τοὺς ἀναβαθμούς, ἀφ᾽ ὧν ἀνέβαινον Ἐρινύες, but no one knows what plays, if any, he had in mind.

contrasted with the ὀρχήστρα. It is, indeed, admitted that they were wrong in supposing that such an arrangement, which was doubtless invariably present in theatres of their own day, existed in the fifth century B.C.[1] But, it is suggested,[2] their comments are mainly derived from scholars of the Alexandrian age—from the third to the first centuries B.C.—and therefore it is presumed that these scholars also believed that there was a raised stage in the fifth century, and it is further presumed that they must have been right. Further, it is argued that the chief authority used by Pollux, who clearly assumes throughout his work a theatre with a high stage, was the θεατρικὴ ἱστορία of Juba (late first century B.C. and early first century A.D.), who had been closely connected with Alexandria, and must therefore have been right. The looseness of these arguments, however, is obvious, and even if on some subjects different scholiasts explicitly quote Aristophanes of Byzantium and Aristarchus, there is no reason to suppose that these were their only authorities on the theatre, so that it is going much too far to claim (with Haigh) that 'the testimony of Pollux and the scholiasts is really testimony of the third century B.C.' Nor were the Alexandrians themselves necessarily right.[3] They were literary critics, not archaeologists, and need not have been acquainted with the Athenian theatre as it was two or more centuries before their time, though intimate with the literature. If, however, they were mistaken, this would be the more intelligible if the theatre at Alexandria with which they were familiar in the second century B.C. were of the type which had a logeion; and this consideration, for what it is worth, may be used to reinforce the probability, based on the remains of theatres in many parts of the Greek world, that it was in the late third and in the second centuries B.C. that a raised stage, and action on the stage and not on the level of the orchestra, became common, while in a few theatres, such as those at Epidaurus, Oropos, and Sikyon, it may, as we have seen, have been earlier still. When once this had happened, commentators and writers of all kinds—Alexandrians possibly, scholiasts and lexicographers, Plutarch, Pollux—almost unconsciously assumed that it had

---

[1] See above, pp. 69–74.   [2] e.g. by Haigh, *Attic Theatre*[3], pp. 149, 150.
[3] We have seen (p. 24) that Didymus almost certainly misinterprets a theatrical term in Demosthenes on the assumption that the theatre of Demosthenes' time was like that of his own day.

been so always, and used the language appropriate to contemporary conditions.

2. The word λογεῖον, which all these late writers use freely of the high stage, first appears in the Delian inscription of 279 B.C. (if it is correctly read there).[1] Whether in the later Delian inscription of 180 B.C. it refers to the theatre at all is disputed, as has already been mentioned. It is not found again before Vitruvius,[2] who gives it as a synonym of *pulpitum*—the Roman stage —and applies it to the higher stage of 'Greek theatres'.

There is no evidence that will bear inspection that it was first used of the orator's platform. All that is adduced consists of passages of Aeschines[3] showing that orators spoke ἐν τῇ τοῦ Διονύσου ὀρχήστρᾳ—which of course proves nothing to the point; the orators may have stood on the step of the central θυμέλη as flute-players probably did—and passages of writers who are too late to give any help.[4] Plutarch and scholiasts use it in reference to the theatre of the fifth and fourth centuries, but this, as has already been explained, is because they assume for earlier times the same constructions as those of their own day. If in fact the name, referring to the raised stage in the theatre, came into existence in the third or second centuries B.C. it may be because the thing itself came into common use first in that period. But unfortunately the only evidence of the use of the word before the time of Vitruvius consists of the two Delian inscriptions, and from them no certain inference can be drawn.[5]

---

[1] See p. 208. The term was sometimes applied by late writers to the orchestra (e.g. Anon. *De Com.* vii, &c.) ; and this corresponds to the occasional converse use of ὀρχήστρα for the stage of the Roman theatre, which encroached on what had been the orchestra.   [2] v. vii. 2.   [3] *In Ctes.*, §§ 156, 176.

[4] Plut. *Praec. ger. rep.*, p. 823 b. The χρηστὸς ἀνήρ is described as οὐ μικρὸν ἡμέρας μέρος ἐπὶ τοῦ βήματος ἢ τοῦ λογείου πολιτευόμενος—where βῆμα probably has reference to meetings elsewhere than in the theatre with its λογεῖον (where assemblies were often held). Müller also cites Timaeus, *Lex. Plat.*, p. 190 R (? 3rd or 4th cent. A.D.), where verses are quoted which Rohde (on no evidence) assigns to Helladius (? 4th cent. A.D.), s.v. ὀκρίβας· πῆγμα τὸ ἐν θεάτρῳ τιθέμενον, ἐφ᾽ οὗ ἵστανται οἱ τὰ δημόσια λέγοντες· θυμέλη γὰρ οὔπω ἦν. λέγει γοῦν τις· 'λογεῖόν ἐστι πῆξις ἐστορεσμένη | ξύλων᾽, εἶτα ἑξῆς ' ὀκρίβας δ᾽ ὀνομάζεται '. Without dates it is impossible to tell what is referred to.

[5] The suggestion that λογεῖον was only an abbreviation of θεολογεῖον and therefore means the speaking-place of gods and not of ordinary characters can hardly be taken seriously. Pollux clearly regards the two words as standing for two different things.

3. Vitruvius (before 14 B.C.) ascribes the raised stage to 'the Greeks', but gives no help as to the date at which it came into vogue; he is obviously thinking of a type of theatre which was being built and was likely to be built in his own day.[1] His *Theatrum Graecorum* is one which has a larger orchestra than the Roman, a *scaena* farther away from the audience, and a narrower *logeion*, because 'tragici et comici actores in scaena[2] peragunt, reliqui autem artifices suas per orchestram praestant actiones, itaque ex eo scaenici et thymelici Graece separatim nominantur.' (He seems to have neglected the tragic and comic choruses entirely; they could hardly be included among *reliqui artifices*, nor were they ever spoken of as *thymelici*.) The fact that no known Roman theatre exactly accords with his rules for the Roman theatre suggests that he was prescribing rules for two ideal types, a Greek and a Roman, the features of which were not taken exactly from any existing theatre and cannot be assumed to have been carried out exactly in any theatre after him.[3] The essential difference between them was not that in the one dramatic actors performed on the stage, for they did this in both types, but that in the Greek type, where the stage was 10 or 12 feet high,[4] performances of other kinds took place in the orchestra, whereas in the Roman all performances were on the stage. But as regards the questions now under consideration—how long such a high stage had been in vogue, and how long dramatic actors had performed on it—he gives us no help.

4. We are left therefore, as before, with the possibility that action on a raised stage may go back to the end of the fourth century in some theatres, as at Epidaurus, and the probability that the practice came into vogue gradually afterwards, coincid-

---

[1] e.g. v. vii, § 1 'In Graecorum theatris non omnia isdem rationibus *sunt facienda*'; § 2 'eius logei altitudo non minus *debet esse* pedum x, non plus xII', and 'gradationes scalarum *dirigantur*', &c. Roman architects, for whom he is writing, might quite well be employed in Greece, as Cossutius was for the Olympieum.

[2] *in scaena* must here mean 'on the *logeion*': cf. v. vi, § 3, where, in the Roman theatre, 'omnes artifices in scaena dant operam'.

[3] Such as the Graeco-Asiatic theatres, often referred to as embodying his principles. The measurements recorded by Fiechter, *Baugesch.*, p. 70, for a number of theatres illustrate this.

[4] These were Roman feet. The corresponding English figures would be 9 ft. 8½ in. and 11 ft. 6½ in.

ing with the construction of high proskenia, and that it was normal in theatres in which there was only one door in the proskenion. The construction or reconstruction of theatres, giving them high proskenia, seems to have been common in the second century B.C.;[1] with regard to the first century we have very little information, but the theatres already existing doubtless continued in use as they were until the date of the Roman reconstructions and of the erection in the early centuries A.D. of theatres of the Graeco-Asiatic pattern.[2] As for Vitruvius' 'Theatre of the Greeks', we can name no theatre which was actually built or reconstructed in his own day, and scholars are still prepared to argue that some Hellenistic theatres such as those of Delos and Priene[3] correspond more nearly in their measurements to his prescription than some Graeco-Asiatic theatres; but if he was, as has been suggested, drawing two ideal types, both roughly represented in his own day, and both likely to be followed more or less by the builders for whom he was writing, it seems idle to attempt to tie him down either to Hellenistic or to later models; he was prescribing, not recording or copying. (There is no need to discuss here Dörpfeld's belief that the *theatrum Graecorum* of Vitruvius was based on the theatre of Mytilene, as copied, with some increased magnificence and the insertion of a Roman stage, by Pompeius in his theatre at Rome. His argument involves assumptions about both theatres which are not easily substantiated.[4])

5. It is to be feared that our knowledge of the theatre of Dionysus between the Lycurgean and the Roman periods amounts to very little. At some time in this period (possibly in the first half of the second century B.C.) the great change was made—

---

[1] e.g. probably at Eretria, Megalopolis, Athens (see above), the Peiraeus, Magnesia, Thera, and many other places; but dates are disputed in almost every instance.

[2] A good discussion of the passages of Vitruvius will be found in Flickinger, *Greek Theater*[4], pp. 75 ff. One of Vitruvius' requirements, viz. that the skené of the Greek theatre should be as high as the covering erected over the back of the auditorium, seems to be fulfilled much better in the later theatres of the Graeco-Asiatic type than (e.g.) in Athens, Epidaurus, Delos, Priene, &c., in the Hellenistic period; and either he may have influenced their builders, or he may himself have been influenced by a practice just coming into vogue in his own day.

[3] Cf. von Gerkan, op. cit., p. 117.

[4] His view is summarized in *Ath. Mitt.* xlix (1924), pp. 95 ff., and references to earlier discussions are given there.

the erection of a stage with a columned proskenion to support it;[1] this concealed from the audience the ground floor of the skené, and the upper story became the background of the action, but of the appearance of this upper story we have no direct information at all. Doubtless it had three principal doors—possibly five, and possibly with arrangements for περίακτοι, though there is no actual evidence of their employment at Athens. There was probably a way on to the stage from each side of the skené, and above the three or five doors a higher (or third) story (of wood or stone), with, perhaps, some arrangement for the appearance of gods on its roof. Whether the three principal doorways (and the others, if there were any) were broad *thyromata*, capable either of being closed by painted scenery or curtains, or of being thrown open to reveal interiors, we do not know. Such things existed in some other theatres, and they may have existed at Athens.[2] The defectiveness of our knowledge is very tantalizing, but it is better to be honest about it than to furbish up speculations with arguments which will not bear criticism.

Note on Terminology

It has already been made clear that scholiasts and lexicographers and other late writers often use such terms as ὀρχήστρα, θυμέλη, σκηνή, προσκήνιον, λογεῖον, κτλ. in more than one sense, and that popular usage in regard to these terms either changed or became very loose. With regard to σκηνή, the brief account on pp. 72–3 may almost suffice. The word

---

[1] Dörpfeld (*Ath. Mitt.* xlix (1924), p. 90) dates the proskenion about the time of Sulla (86 B.C.), but will not admit a stage for acting before the time of Nero, and then only doubtfully; he is not certain that there was one before Phaedrus (see p. 259). We have seen reason to think that the date of the Athenian proskenion may more probably have been about 160 B.C. (see above, pp. 182, 198, &c.).

[2] The difficulty of inferring from other theatres the structure of the theatre at Athens appears as soon as we ask, *which* theatres? Thus in the third and second centuries some theatres (e.g. at New Pleuron and Thera) had projecting paraskenia; many others had not. Of the latter, some had three openings in the *scaenae frons*, some five, the theatre at Ephesus seven; the history and structure of the proskenion, though not always determinable with certainty, varied greatly in different theatres (see Bulle, *Untersuch.*, pp. 297 ff.); so did the arrangements for entrances and exits at the side of the skené; so also did the dimensions of the thyromata, or broad openings in the *scaenae frons*, which existed in several late Hellenistic theatres, and so on. Every attempt to range all the Greek theatres in one line of continuous chronological development does violence to the facts.

denotes primarily the building forming the background, but came also to
refer to the 'scene of action' as a whole (e.g. schol. Aristoph. *Ran.* 181 ἐνταῦθα
δὲ τοῦ πλοίου ὀφθέντος ἠλλοιῶσθαι χρὴ τὴν σκηνήν), and, comparatively late,
to the raised stage. The latter, at least, is possibly but not certainly the
case in Polybius ap. Athen. xiv, p. 615 d καὶ πύκται τέσσαρες ἀνέβησαν ἐπὶ
τὴν σκηνήν, and almost certainly in Pollux iv. 127 εἰσελθόντες δὲ κατὰ τὴν
ὀρχήστραν ἐπὶ τὴν σκηνὴν ἀναβαίνουσι διὰ κλιμάκων—though even here the
strict meaning *may* be 'to the front of the stage building'—which was only
visible above the λογεῖον or raised stage. There is the same uncertainty in
the phrase ἀναβιβάσαι ἐπὶ τὴν σκηνήν which occurs in Lucian, *Jupp. trag.* 41
and *Tox.* 9; and in *Philops.* 29 αὗται δὲ (sc. αἱ θύραι) πρὸς τὴν εὐθεῖαν
τοῦ θεάτρου πλευρὰν ἀνεῴγεσαν, οὗ καὶ ἡ σκηνὴ καὶ τὸ προσκήνιόν ἐστιν;
and also in Pollux iv. 123 ἐπὶ τῆς σκηνῆς ἀγυιεὺς ἔκειτο βωμός. The uses
of ἐπὶ (τῆς) σκηνῆς and ἀπὸ (τῆς) σκηνῆς have been discussed at the end of
Chapter II; cf. also p. 168.

The term προσκήνιον has been briefly discussed in Chapter IV (pp. 158-9)
in connexion with certain passages of Plutarch and a fragment of Douris,
where it was shown to be at least probable that in the fourth century B.C.
it referred to a decorative screen or curtain drawn immediately in front of
the σκηνή and varied as circumstances required. In the inscriptions of the
early third century at Delos the προσκήνιον was apparently distinct from
the σκηνή, and was furnished with painted πίνακες, but the position of this
early προσκήνιον (as distinct from the later one, forming part of the colonnade surrounding the σκηνή) cannot be certainly determined. Other
inscriptions (of later date) at Oropos and Kalymna similarly distinguish
the προσκήνιον (which at Oropos bore πίνακες) from the σκηνή, and the
προσκήνιον (as probably at Delos) seems to mean an erection some way in
front of the σκηνή, such as is usually denoted by the word in modern discussions of the theatre. But very few, if any, passages in which the word
is used are really decisive as to the meaning. Philologically speaking it
could mean either the space before the σκηνή or anything which filled that
space (cf. πρόθυρον), and it may sometimes mean the stage (= λογεῖον) and
not merely the wall erected to support the stage in front. In most passages
it could mean either. The Latin *proscaenium* sometimes means the stage
on which actors performed, sometimes even the theatre as a whole, including the auditorium, and it is not surprising that from the beginning of
the Roman period in theatrical history the use of the word should fluctuate
in Greek as in Latin. (The few passages in which the word occurs are
quoted in Müller, op. cit., pp. 35-49, but his attempts to fix the meaning
in each are not always convincing.) Similarly the word ὑποσκήνιον
sometimes means the chamber underneath the λογεῖον, sometimes it is
equivalent to προσκήνιον in one of its senses—e.g. in Pollux iv. 124 τὸ δ᾽
ὑποσκήνιον κίοσι καὶ ἀγαλματίοις ἐκεκόσμητο πρὸς τὸ θέατρον τετραμμένοις,

ὑπὸ τὸ λογεῖον κείμενον—where it is plainly the front supporting wall of the λογεῖον.

APPENDIX I

On Pinakes, &c. in the Proskenion

In the theatre of Dionysus and in the theatre in the Peiraeus the columns of the proskenion were full columns without any devices for holding pinakes. Other forms of support for the proskenion roof are known from

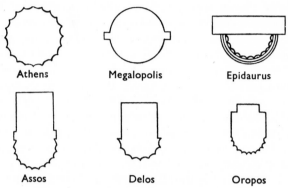

Athens   Megalopolis   Epidaurus

Assos   Delos   Oropos

FIG. 76. Varieties of Proskenion column

other theatres. At Megalopolis, for instance, the stylobate, which may perhaps be dated about 150 B.C., carried full columns with slight projections designed for the retention of pinakes. In a large number of theatres there were half-columns, the other half being replaced by a rectangular pillar, or half-columns set against broader pilasters, and in some of these there are projections, grooves, or other devices which would serve to keep pinakes in place. In some, as at Epidaurus, there are half-columns with no such devices; at Epidaurus they apparently rested, not against pilasters, but against sections of a closed wall. The accompanying illustration gives some of the forms (Fig. 76).

Puchstein assumes that the simple full columns must be earlier than full columns with special projections for fastening pinakes, and these in turn earlier than half-columns, and so on, and constructs a chronology of theatres on this assumption. But it is very unsafe in any case to construct a chronology on a supposed development in a straight line (or a logical order) as between theatres in widely separated places. It would be quite easy for a city to erect full columns in its proskenion even after others had experimented with reduced or modified columns, and (it may be added) to erect proskenia without pinakes or provision for them, if they preferred an open colonnade. The assumption that when once a theatre had used a particular form of decoration for its proskenion, all other theatres must have followed suit or made changes in the same direction, is not valid;

still less is the assumption that because a particular form of decoration—pinakes or any other—is found in various theatres at particular dates it must have existed at Athens before such dates. There was probably much more local variety and freedom than such assumptions allow. From the third century onwards Athens was by no means the only important literary and artistic centre; provincial architects were as free to experiment then as now, and provincial producers to adapt their productions to the conditions of a particular place in ways which might have been shocking at Athens. Even therefore if columns (or modified columns) with devices for holding pinakes were in vogue in the second century or earlier at Megalopolis, it does not follow that pinakes must have been used earlier in Athens, or that the full columns at Athens must have been earlier than the modified columns in other places. It is an equally probable interpretation of the facts to suppose that the use of modified columns with pinakes was the earlier experiment, and that these and the use of pinakes for the decoration of a proskenion front were gradually given up or did not extend at all to some theatres, so that at Athens and the Peiraeus, and in the later phases of the theatres at Sikyon and Megalopolis, there were full columns and, at least in some of these, no pinakes;[1] and if, as is contended in this chapter, the erection of a proskenion coincided with the transference of the action to the stage (or proskenion roof), pinakes would not be required as a scenic background for drama. If the intercolumnia were filled up in various ways, as they appear to have been in some theatres, a single central door—such as is found in nearly all proskenia[2]—would suffice for any communication that might be necessary between the ground floor of the skené and the orchestra through the hyposkenion.

There is really no evidence for Bulle's conjecture[3] that votive dedications after victory may have formed the subject of painted pinakes included in the proskenion when the action was transferred to the logeion.

APPENDIX II

On the evidence of certain Reliefs

Dörpfeld and Reisch attempt to confirm their general view of the proskenion by the evidence of certain reliefs depicting scenes from the New Comedy, or from its Roman imitations. The most important of these are:

[1] This view is also taken by von Gerkan, *Das Theater von Priene*, p. 124.
[2] Priene is an exception; Dörpfeld's 'discovery' of three doors in the proskenion at Delos is very uncertain. There was possibly no door at all in the proskenion at Megalopolis, and in other theatres the central door is narrow for the door (e.g.) of a palace or temple or even of a rich house, e.g. 4 feet at Epidaurus, 3 ft. 8 in. at Oropos, 3 ft. 3 in. at Delos. [3] *Das Theater zu Sparta*, pp. 91 ff.

(1) A marble relief in the Naples Museum (Fig. 77)[1] of uncertain date, in which the background includes a large doorway, raised by one step above the level of the actors, and part of the background is covered by a curtain. This seems to stand in no discernible relation to the Athenian theatre; its relation to the Roman is not for discussion here.

(2) A terra-cotta relief in the Campana collection in Rome, copies or

FIG. 78. Relief from Campana Collection

variants of which are in other museums. In the Campana relief itself there is only one (central) door behind the three actors, but in a version of the same scene in relief in Hanover the back wall includes three doors— a larger and two small—each with its own gable and with vases between the gables. In both versions there are six Corinthian columns in front of the wall, in three pairs. (In the Hanoverian version, the central

---

[1] D.R., p. 327, Fig. 81; Bieber, *Denkm.*, Taf. 89; cf. Bulle, *Untersuch.*, p. 264, who connects it with what he terms the *Magnesiatypus* of late Hellenistic theatres. For the curtain, see below, p. 233.

interval is larger than the others.) The figure (Fig. 78) here given is Puchstein's combination[1] of the Campana and Hanover versions. A fragment in the Kircherian Museum in Rome showing the same scene (Fig. 79) also gives the three-gabled façade, with vases standing between the gables, and what looks like a tall decorative erection behind the gables, but is, according to Dörpfeld,[2] part of the general decoration of the relief and has nothing to do with the proskenion represented on it. In some variants the middle door is very small. The actors are much taller than the doors and as tall as the pillars, and though Dörpfeld may be right in thinking that this may be due to a crude attempt at perspective, it is clear that the whole scene and the decorations are in accordance with the conventions of sculptured reliefs and are a very unsafe guide as regards actual theatrical structures. Moreover, the reliefs are, at best, of early Imperial date, and the fact that the façade of the building is straight only in the middle and oblique on each side shows that, if any theatres are copied, it is those of the Roman epoch. It is, however, worth while to notice that the back wall consists of solid rectangular blocks, without a sign of pinakes.

The Roman habit of using stage scenes (based on the Roman theatre) for the purpose of decoration in relief is illustrated by the monument (Fig. 80) of P. Numitorius Hilarus (about the end of the first century B.C.). The relief represents the death of Astyanax (the figures being those of Odysseus, Andromache, Astyanax, and two attendants), and may be reminiscent of the *Astyanax* of Accius.

(3) A marble in the Museo delle Terme in Rome (Fig. 81), of late Hellenistic or, more probably, early Imperial date, showing three doors set in a wall of rectangular blocks. This may be suggested by the theatre, but it is very doubtful if it is at all exact as a reproduction of any.

APPENDIX III
On the evidence of various works of Art

It may be convenient to notice here certain other works of art which have been supposed to illustrate the Hellenistic theatre.

1. *A painted terra-cotta relief from St. Angelo* (Fig. 82). This presents a two-storied façade. The lower half includes three doors and four Ionic columns; the upper story has four shorter Corinthian columns, set more towards the centre than the columns below. The pediment above these has a bust in the middle and a circular decoration at the top and on each side. The whole is flanked by two small towers, each with a door in front. Both the date and the subject of the relief are disputed. Reisch[3] thinks

---

[1] See Puchstein, *Die gr. Bühne*, pp. 26, 27, Fig. 4. He gives an outline showing the plan of the epistyle.   [2] D.R., p. 330.

[3] D.R., pp. 332–3. Cf. Dörpfeld, *Ath. Mitt.* xlix (1924), p. 93, who notes that if it represents a *scaenae frons*, it is unlike any known one, e.g. in the narrowness

Fig. 79. Terra-cotta from Museo Kircheriano

Fig. 80. Monument of Numitorius

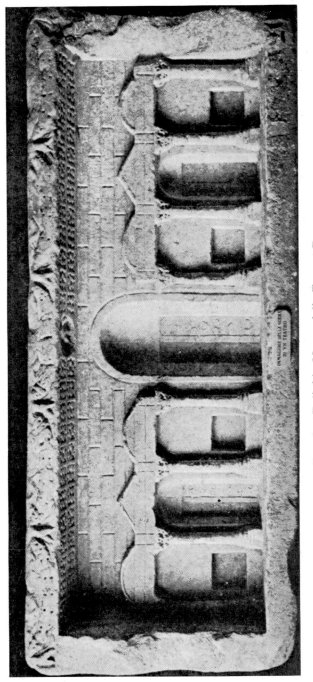

FIG. 81. Relief in Museo delle Terme, Rome

Fig. 83. Vase of Assteas

Fig. 82. Terra-cotta relief, St. Angelo

that it depicts, not a theatre, but a gateway in a city wall, but no parallel for such a gateway can be found, and there is a strong preponderance of opinion in favour of the view that what is presented is a theatre. But of what date? Bulle,[1] following the opinions of Macchioro and Langlotz, dates the relief in the second half of the fourth century B.C., chiefly on the ground of the special rose colour used by the painter (though in view of the state of preservation of the colours this does not seem very conclusive); and on the strength of this Bulle claims the relief as proving the existence of a two-storied and gabled *scaenae frons*, flanked by paraskenia, at that date. (He argues that the theatre at Segesta shows the same constructional elements, including the circular akroteria; but these features appear to be at least a century later there than the date to which he ascribes the relief.) Most other archaeologists[2] regard it as a work of the first century B.C., representing the *scaenae frons* of a Roman theatre, mounted on a low podium of the regular Italian pattern, and, if so, it throws no light on the Hellenistic theatre. It is impossible to say how exactly it represents any theatre.

2. *A vase-painting* (Figs. 83 and 84) from Magna Graecia by *Assteas*, who painted in the fourth century B.C. The painting represents the Madness of Herakles, who is about to throw one of his children on to a bonfire fed with various articles of domestic furniture. There is a sloping roof supported—or at least flanked—in front by a slender column on each side, and at the back there is a kind of loggia, the front wall of which, rising breast-high, seems to be solid, though a single column stands against it near the left-hand side; above this breast-high wall are four openings separated by short columns, and in three of the openings the figures of Mania, Iolaos, and Alkmene (mother of Herakles). On the right-hand side of the picture is a half-opened double door, above a single step, and Megara (wife of Herakles) is about to flee through it. If the scene is a theatrical one at all, the door might be one opening into one of the paraskenia, as on some other Italian vases,[3] and Dr. Bieber points out the resemblance between the loggia here and that which appears on a mosaic (perhaps of the 1st cent. B.C.) from Pompeii, depicting the rehearsal of a· satyr chorus.[4]

of the interval between the three doors and the construction of the upper story; but this may only be an indication of careless work.

[1] Op. cit., pp. 225–6.

[2] Cf. Dörpfeld, *Jahrb. Arch.* xvi (1901), pp. 22–37; Fiechter, *Baugesch.*, p. 102; von Gerkan, op. cit., p. 112 (who is not certain whether it represents a theatre at all). Most scholars are agreed in rejecting Bethe's interpretation of the relief as representing a Hellenistic *scaenae frons* (*Jahrb. Arch.* xv (1900), pp. 59 ff.).

[3] See above, pp. 170–2, Figs. 55–8.

[4] Bieber, *Denkm. zum Theaterwesen*, Abb. 49. (The resemblance is not really very close.) The loggia cannot possibly be a theologeion, as some have supposed,

But it is extremely unlikely that a scene from the theatre is represented at all. Scenes of murder were not presented to the spectators of a play, and the present scene is supposed to be taking place either in the interior of the house,[1] or, more likely, in a courtyard,[2] with persons looking out from a columned hall on the far side of it. (The roof is that of this hall, and the two front columns have nothing to do with it, but belong to the nearer

FIG. 84. Vase of Assteas

side of the courtyard.) The painter appears to be following his favourite practice of filling the upper part of his vase-painting with busts of human beings. The scene does not give the impression of being a kind of burlesque (as some have supposed it to be) in spite of the gorgeous plumes of Herakles' helmet (which have been compared to those of Lamachus in the *Acharnians*) and of the fact that the bonfire is fed with such incombustible articles as vases. (After all, Herakles was mad!) The

since two of the persons who appear in it are mortals. On the mosaic, see below, p. 223, and Fig. 98.

[1] So Dörpfeld (*Jahrb. Arch.* xvi (1901), pp. 22–37), who notes that there is no door in the back scene; Fiechter's view (*Baugesch.*, p. 41) that the door through which Megara flees is really intended to be in the back wall seems to be refuted by looking at the picture.

[2] See von Gerkan, op. cit., p. 109. (He says also that Robert has proved that the scene cannot be a theatrical one, in *Deutsch. Litztg.* 1915, p. 1172, and 1919, p. 869, which I have not been able to consult.)

architectural setting is very like that of some wall-paintings at Pompeii, depicting scenes of which some are based on tragedy.[1]

3. *The Mosaics of Dioskorides* (Figs. 85 and 86). These two pictures, each about 18 inches long, form part of a mosaic floor in the so-called 'Villa of Cicero' at Pompeii. They represent respectively three street-musicians playing and three women in conversation; in the latter an attendant is shown as a small subsidiary figure, in the former a dwarf. The conversation picture is regarded by several scholars as representing the consultation of an extremely ugly 'wise woman' or φαρμακεύτρια by two women, as in the Φαρμακεύτρια of Theocritus; cf. especially l. 1 πᾷ μοι ταὶ δάφναι; φέρε, Θεστυλί· πᾷ δὲ τὰ φίλτρα; and ll. 90–1 καὶ ἐς τίνος οὐκ ἐπέρασα | ἢ ποίας ἔλιπον γραίας δόμον, ἅτις ἐπᾷδεν; On this interpretation the objects on the table in the picture are a laurel-twig and vessels which might hold φίλτρα, love-charms. This scene is one which might conceivably be taken from real life, but the three women appear to be wearing masks, and this suggests a scene from comedy.[2] A quite different explanation is offered by F. Marx,[3] according to which the women are an aged *lena* and two prostitutes, and what is represented is actually the first scene of Plautus' *Cistellaria*, or rather of its Greek original, which, it is argued, was a play of Menander.[4] The objects on the table could be explained so as to suit such a scene. In either case, we have a scene from comedy, and it is commonly considered that the three women are seated on a podium or platform raised on steps, and fitted into one of the thyromata or broad openings[5] which occupied most of the background on the raised stage of a number of Hellenistic theatres.[6] It is suggested that the colouring of the setting at the sides and at the back of the figures is so graded as to display an interior with a wall at the back. This explanation is very ingeniously worked out in detail by Bulle,[7] though it is not universally accepted, and von Gerkan thinks it impossible to say what the framework and the steps are meant to represent. It is also suggested that the figures were raised up on a podium and steps in order to give the more remote spectators a better view of them.

[1] See below, pp. 230 ff.

[2] A. Körte (*Neue Jahrb.* xlvii (1921), p. 310) thinks they may be merely caricatures and not masked, but the masks seem to be very plain.

[3] *Rhein. Mus.* lxxix (1930), pp. 197 ff.

[4] Menander, fr. 558 (K), from an unknown play, is very close in its language to the *Cistellaria*, 86 ff.; but the incident described was one which may well have been recurrent in comedy, so that the inference, though highly probable, is not absolutely certain.

[5] It is calculated that to accommodate the three women the opening must have been about 6 ft. 6 in. wide.

[6] As at Ephesus, where the openings were much broader; there are strong differences of view as to the date of such a structure at Ephesus.

[7] *Untersuch.*, p. 277 f.

Dörpfeld, who, of course, cannot accept a raised stage, affirms[1] that the steps do not support a podium, but represent only the steps leading from the house-door to the street. No explanation is perfectly satisfactory, and it is impossible to say how much the original painting may have been altered—whether it copied a stage setting or not—in order to embody it in mosaic.

The three musicians—two dancing and playing cymbals and tambourine, the third standing and playing the flute—might also be taken from real life; they, too, appear to be wearing masks, but perhaps of a lighter kind than were usual on the stage[2] and such as might be worn by real street-musicians. Whether drawn from real life or from comedy, they might be μητραγύρται, begging priests of Kybele, and it is known that Menander wrote a Μητραγύρτης. They can, however, hardly represent the kind of chorus which sang or played *intermezzi* in a comedy, being only three in number, and it is not clear what their place in a comedy would be. The musicians are plainly dancing in front of a house, of which the doorway is partly shown. Bulle (very unconvincingly) would fit them into a thyroma, but it is hard to see why such lively action should be so cramped,[3] and it remains doubtful whether we have here a stage scene at all.

Nothing is known of Dioskorides of Samos, who is named as the artist on each of the two mosaics. The lettering of the inscriptions, according to Hiller von Gärtringen, belongs to the period between the end of the second century and the time of Augustus. There is another, though inferior, copy of the picture of the musicians in a wall-painting at Stabiae.[4] It has generally been supposed that Dioskorides was the painter of the two originals, not the maker of the mosaic copies, and that he lived in eastern, not in western Greece, and was contemporary with the theatrical structures supposed to be depicted; but attention has been called[5] to differences in technique between the two pictures, which make it improbable that they were originally from the same hand, and in that case Dioskorides must have been the executor of the mosaics. However this may be, it is obvious that

---

[1] *Woch. Klass. Phil.*, 1918, col. 364.

[2] So Robert, *Die Masken der neueren att. Kom.*, p. 67. He regards the mosaic as presenting a typical Alexandrian street scene. Some have thought that both scenes might be derived from mimes, but the use of masks is against this interpretation.

[3] Bulle attempts also to show that the comic scenes from the Casa dei Dioscuri and the Casa della Grande Fontana can be fitted into thyromata; but it seems most unlikely that the action depicted in each scene was so circumscribed. It would seem obviously to belong to the open stage.

[4] The figures of two of the musicians also resemble those of two terra-cotta figures from Myrrhina. See Bulle, *Untersuch.*, p. 282, and *Jahrb. Arch.* 1895, *Anz.*, col. 122.

[5] Pernice, *Die hellenistische Kunst in Pompeii*, vi, pp. 169 ff.

Fig. 85. Mosaic of Dioskorides (1) from 'Villa di Cicerone', Pompeii

FIG. 86. Mosaic of Dioskorides (2) from 'Villa di Cicerone', Pompeii

the mosaics give no clear or reliable information about the theatre, and none about the theatre of Dionysus at Athens.[1]

4. *Wall-paintings at Pompeii, &c.* Many writers on the theatre believe that the kind of decoration employed in Hellenistic theatres (and therefore, they would say, in the Athenian theatre of the period) can be inferred from wall-paintings of the several styles at Pompeii and elsewhere in Italy. These fall into two groups: (1) the great wall-paintings at Boscoreale, near Pompeii, together with the scenes from the *Odyssey* from the Esquiline in Rome, the House of Livia on the Palatine, and some others; (2) a considerable number of groups of figures in scenes based in part on the Greek drama and set in an architectural framework and background; these are believed by several scholars to be derived from Hellenistic originals, the painters of which are supposed to have copied what they saw in the theatres of their own day.

As regards the first group, the strongest argument is that derived from passages in Vitruvius VII, ch. v. (It is generally considered that the work of Vitruvius was published shortly before 14 B.C.) He is discussing the best way of decorating the interior of large rooms, and he first describes the 'Incrustation Style', which does not immediately concern us here ('ex eo antiqui, qui initia expolitionibus instituerunt, imitati sunt primum crustarum marmorearum varietates et conlocationes, deinde coronarum, †siliculorum, cuneorum inter sese varias distributiones'). The paintings imitated on stucco the appearance of a wall veneered with coloured marbles; but fine mosaic pictures were laid in the floors. This style is commonly thought to have originated in Alexandria in the third century B.C., and traces of it have been found in buildings at Pergamon, Delos, and Priene. It remained in vogue at Pompeii down to the end of the second century, and a little later.

Vitruvius next describes the Second or 'Architectural' Style, which was employed through most of the first century B.C., but had gone out of fashion, to his great distress, by the time at which he was writing. (It is exemplified in the House of Livia on the Palatine, and in paintings transferred from a house near the Tiber to the Museo delle Terme in Rome, as well as in the Esquiline and Boscoreale paintings.) It presented in its landscapes architectural designs such as were not structurally impossible, whereas in his own day the architectural schemes of the painters were fantastic combinations, out of all relation to reality or possibility (the Third or 'Ornate' Style). His words are important:

(§ 2) postea ingressi sunt, ut etiam aedificiorum figuras, columnarum et

---

[1] Discussions of the two mosaics have been innumerable and far more detailed than has been possible here. See especially Bieber and Rodenwaldt in *Jahrb. Arch.* xxvii (1911), pp. 1 ff., Fiechter, *Baugesch.*, p. 49, L. Curtius, *Die Wandmalerei Pompeii's*, pp. 336 ff., in addition to works already cited.

fastigiorum eminentes proiecturas imitarentur, patentibus autem locis, uti exhedris, propter amplitudines parietum *scaenarum frontes tragico more aut comico seu satyrico designarent*, ambulationibus vero propter spatia longitudinis varietatibus topiorum ornarent, ab certis locorum proprietatibus imagines exprimentes; pinguntur enim portus, promuntoria, litora, flumina, fontes, euripi, fana, luci, montes, pecora, pastores. Nonnulli loci item signorum megalographiam habent et deorum simulacra seu fabularum dispositas explicationes, non minus Troianas pugnas seu Ulixis errationes per topia, ceteraque, quae sunt eorum similibus rationibus ab rerum natura procreata. (§ 3) Sed haec, quae ex veris rebus exempla sumebantur, nunc iniquis moribus improbantur. Nam pinguntur tectoriis monstra potius quam ex rebus finitis imagines certae.

For an illustration of this degenerate Third Style, he cites its employment by Apaturius of Alabanda in an assembly hall at Tralles: (§ 5) etenim etiam Trallibus cum Apaturius Alabandeus eleganti manu finxisset scaenam[1] in minusculo theatro, quod ἐκκλησιαστήριον apud eos vocitatur . . . Apaturius was publicly rebuked for his impossible designs by the mathematician Licymnius, and gave way. (§ 7) itaque Apaturius contra respondere non est ausus, sed sustulit scaenam et ad rationem veritatis commutatam postea correctam adprobavit. Utinam dii immortales fecissent, uti Licymnius revivesceret et corrigeret hanc amentiam tectoriorumque instituta.'

It can hardly be denied, in face of Vitruvius' language, that the wall-decorations of the first century B.C. included scenes in some way recalling those presented in tragedy, comedy, and satyric drama; but what he means by this may be inferred from a later passage (v. vi, § 9) from which it appears that a 'tragic' background is one including columns, pediments, and palatial structures; a 'comic', one with a background of ordinary houses, with imitations of windows and balconies; a 'satyric', one with trees, caves, mountains, and country scenes. There are plenty of scenes among the wall-paintings which include all these things, and so far they may have recalled the scenes of the stage, but there is no ground for inferring that the exact forms in which they appear in the paintings are derived from the stage, nor would it be safe to argue from them to the structure of Hellenistic stage buildings without independent evidence.

As regards the scenes from epic poetry on a number of walls painted in the Second Style, it is believed by Fiechter[2] that these were copied from

[1] *scaena* does not necessarily mean a theatrical stage: the word was used in Latin for a 'picture' generally, e.g. in Pliny xxxv. 65, &c. Cf. Müller, *Untersuch. zu den Bühnenalt.*, p. 34, who corrects Reisch (D.R., p. 290) in certain points.

[2] *Baugesch.*, pp. 42 ff. Dörpfeld in *Ath. Mitt.* xlix (1924), pp. 92 ff. finds the originals not in the thyromata of a stage background, but in the intercolumnia of

FIG. 87 (*left*). Scene from Odyssey (from the Esquiline)

FIG. 88 (*left*). Scene from Odyssey (from the Esquiline)

FIG. 87. (*right*) Scene from Odyssey (from the Esquiline)

FIG. 88. (*right*) Scene from Odyssey (from the Esquiline)

landscape scenery inserted in the thyromata of Hellenistic theatres, that as the human figures in the wall-paintings could hardly be in place in the thyromata as a background to real human actors, they must have been inserted by the Pompeian painter, and that the theatrical origin of the paintings is shown by the occurrence in one of the Boscoreale pictures of a door which would otherwise be out of place in a landscape, but was essential in the theatrical background.[1] He even suggests that the landscapes of the Second Style may go back to theatres of the fourth century B.C., when, as he thinks, the *scaenae frons* was divided by pillars even before the introduction of a fixed proskenion, the art of perspective having already been developed by Anaxagoras and Democritus as the result of the work of Agatharchus.[2]

In reply to Fiechter it is perhaps sufficient to say, as regards the landscapes (Figs. 87, 88)[3] of the first century B.C., illustrating the *Odyssey*, that it is almost inconceivable that anyone looking at the pictures should not recognize the intimate connexion between the figures and the landscape, or should imagine that the former were an afterthought and not rather conceived with their setting as a unity. Nor is there any reason to suppose that the thyromata *were* separated and flanked by pilasters, with capitals and architrave, of the type which forms the setting of the landscape pictures; the divisions between the thyromata, so far as anything can be conjectured from the very slight evidence which exists, were, for the most part, flat mural spaces, and did not carry any ornamental architrave.[4] Moreover, Vitruvius (in the passage quoted above) quite clearly distinguishes the illustrations of the *Iliad* and *Odyssey* from the *scaenarum frontes*. The attempt of Fiechter to carry back the *scaenae frons* divided by decorative pillars to the fourth century falls to the ground for lack of evidence. Whatever may be the date of the originals which the Esquiline and other Roman landscape-painters copied, the setting of them tells us nothing about the Greek theatre. Similarly the pillars which divide the several paintings on the walls of the *cubiculo* in the villa (c. 40–30 B.C.) of Fannius Sinistor at Boscoreale (Figs. 89–91) have not, so far as can be told, any parallel in the Hellenistic theatres. One of the paintings themselves (Fig. 91) may indeed represent a cave in the foreground, which may resemble such caves as were seen in the *Ichneutae* and the *Cyclops*, and may so far illustrate the words of Vitruvius, but

a proskenion or in a long background introduced in the form of a *scaena ductilis* or *versilis*. The dark band at the foot represents, he thinks, not, as Fiechter supposes, a stage, but only the place of the action before the skené or proskenion.

[1] There is really nothing incongruous or theatrical about this door, which is a decorative but not abnormal garden entrance. See Fig. 89.   [2] See above, p. 124.

[3] Pfuhl, *Malerei u. Zeichnung*, iii, Figs. 721, 722, and Woermann, *Die antiken Odyssee-Landschaften*, where the colours are finely shown.   [4] Cf. Bulle, op. cit., p. 255.

the rest of the picture is singularly unlike anything which we have any reason to suppose to have been introduced in these or other satyric plays; and there seems to be no reason for regarding the elaborate architectural picture in the same room, with a round temple in the background, as taken from any kind of drama. The scheme seems to be peculiarly Italian. Whether or not it may contain architectural elements comparable with those in the background of the more elaborate *Roman* theatres we cannot tell; even if it were so, they need be no more than parallel examples of the dominant architectural conventions of the time. (The round temple closely resembles the tholos in the Macellum and other round temples where a connexion with the Hellenistic theatre seems to be out of the question.) There is in fact no reason to suppose that the architectural schemes at Boscoreale are 'derived' from anything but the brain of the painter, following and varying at pleasure the decorative conventions of his day. The fact that on these and other walls there are masks—at Boscoreale affixed to the architrave—proves nothing, since masks were used freely as ornaments in many non-theatrical settings. Those set over wall-paintings (such as that of the 'Shrine of Hecate'), which are explained by Fiechter and others as tragic, are frequently masks of Silenus, and can have very little connexion with 'tragic' paintings. They are sometimes set on screens or balconies, as in the *triclinio d'estate* at Boscoreale[1] (Fig. 92), and in a painting in the 'Villa of Diomedes' at Pompeii[2] (Fig. 93), in neither of which can they have any connexion with the theatre. This does not mean that the artists may not have borrowed particular motives or designs from painted theatrical backgrounds;[3] we know, in fact, nothing directly of the paintings in Hellenistic theatres, and in some of them there may have been perspective and other scenes like those in the Italian wall-paintings. It does mean that we can safely infer nothing from these wall-paintings as to the structure or decoration of the theatres, and although we must accept Vitruvius' word for the fact that scenery recalling the three dramatic types appeared *inter alia* in the wall-paintings,[4] we cannot be sure that any extant painting is one of the kind which he mentions, or draw retrospective conclusions from it about theatrical structures. The fresco at Boscoreale of the so-called 'Shrine of Hekate' (Fig. 94), which Bulle[5] claims as an illustration of Vitruvius' *tragicum genus*, seems to have no points of contact with tragedy. It shows a shrine of the goddess sup-

[1] See Barnabei, *Villa Pompeiana di P. Fannio Sinistore*, pp. 64, 65, Fig. 13, &c. On pp. 41 and 46 there are illustrations of masks of a fawn and a silenus which are used purely as ornament.   [2] Pfuhl, op. cit., Fig. 710.

[3] A view very like that maintained here will be found in L. Curtius, *Die Wandmalerei Pompeii's*, pp. 121 ff.

[4] Especially (it is to be noted) in exhedrae, open galleries, &c. (Vitruv. VII. v, § 2).   [5] *Untersuch.*, p. 276.

F‍IG. 89. Wall-painting from *cubiculo* of Villa at Boscoreale

Fig. 90. Wall-painting from *cubiculo* of Villa at Boscoreale

FIG. 91. So-called 'Satyric scene' from *cubiculo* of Villa at
Boscoreale

ported on garlanded pillars and set against a wall, and rising against a background of clear sky. Above it are silver vases and a golden shield, and below the architrave the mask, not of a tragic figure, but (as has already been indicated) of a silenus. In front of the shrine and separated from it by a low wall is a recessed precinct containing an altar and benches, and behind the altar a low doorway surmounted by a row of spikes. The

FIG. 92. From *triclinio d'estate* in villa at Boscoreale

whole scene is framed by the drawing of a column on each side; but the picture looks much more like independent work than like a design derived from the stage. Why should the artist not be independent? The picture in the same room which is supposed to be derived from the New Comedy provides little that can support such a theory beyond the fact that the buildings represented have projecting balconies, as Vitruvius[1] says the comic *genus scaenarum* had; but the comic *genus* had these only because ordinary real houses often had, as the text of Vitruvius indicates, and the painter need not go to the stage to find such things. Why it should be thought that the somewhat elaborate doorway built out from the garden wall which crosses the picture (near the front of the whole scene) could come only from the comic stage, and not from the painter's imagination, passes

[1] v. vi, § 9 'comicae autem aedificiorum privatorum et maenianorum habent speciem prospectusque fenestris dispositos imitatione *communium aedificiorum* rationibus.'

comprehension. Nor is it easy to see any certain traces of theatrical origin in the famous picture of the fall of Icarus :[1] neither the rising ground in the foreground nor the cliffs flanking the view of the sea need have been suggested by theatrical thyromata ;[2] and in fact it seems very improbable that the actors moving in front of theatrical scenery would have had behind them a number of painted human beings, on a different scale of size. The general assumption of the advocates of a theatrical origin for such scenes as those of Boscoreale, that wherever a painting shows different depths in perspective it must be referred to the theatre,[3] appears to be quite gratuitous. The painters of thyromata (of whose work we know little or nothing) and the wall-painters in Italy, or the Hellenistic painters from whom they may have taken some of their subjects, had doubtless some of the same problems to solve, and they may have solved them partly in the same ways and followed the same artistic conventions, but it is going much too far to speak of the dependence of the one on the other. (It should be noticed that the building which Apaturius is said to have painted at Tralles[4] was not a theatre for dramatic purposes, but an assembly hall in the shape of a theatre, and that the wall-paintings in the Little Theatre at Pompeii were also in a building designed for performances of other kinds than drama.)

The same kind of reasoning, *mutatis mutandis*, has to be applied to the paintings of groups of figures taking part in scenes based on the tragic drama, from which Fiechter and others have thought that they could infer what structures were used to fill, or to afford backgrounds within, the thyromata of the theatres. Many of these scenes, it must be observed, cannot have been presented on the stage at all—this is true of all those depicting violence and death, or including a large number of figures. At most they represent what was narrated by a messenger. Many appear to have no connexion in subject with drama at all, but to be illustrations of epic poetry or mythology, in which the painter has given his imagination free play.

A number of these paintings show in the background of the front group of figures a low wall or balustrade, about breast-high, with or without a low door in the centre, and behind this two or more pillars supporting an architrave, often with a curtain draped in front of them. Such is the well-known picture (Fig. 96) of Admetos, Alkestis, and the Messenger, from the House of the Tragic Poet at Pompeii. Behind the low wall, and looking over it, are two human beings and two divinities, keenly interested.

---

[1] Finely reproduced in Pfuhl, *Mal. u. Zeichn.*, Fig. 722 a.

[2] It is claimed that they are derived from the podium and side screens inserted in thyromata.

[3] Cf. Fiechter, *Baugesch.*, pp. 45, 46; Bulle, *Untersuch.*, pp. 275, 283.

[4] See above, p. 226.

But such an arrangement of persons, and particularly the position of the two divinities, is quite inconsistent with what we know of the conventions of Greek tragedy; the conversation seems to be taking place in a furnished room, not on the stage, and the *seated* messenger is quite undramatic. The scene must be the expression of a great painter's reflection on the famous tale; nor need his architectural setting have been determined by the theatre, even though in his treatment of the attitude and facial expression of the persons he may naturally have been influenced by the language of the poets. The complete absence from extant remains of such low walls and pillars set in thyromata might indeed be accounted for by their having been of wood and having therefore perished; but why should it be assumed that they were there at all? The painters had no need to go to the theatre for such things, even if they were to be found there; and the band of dark colour across the foot of several of these paintings need not represent the upper edge of the supporting wall of a stage, but may well be simply a conventional way of finishing off the picture. (Of the curtain something will be said later.) In another version (Fig. 97) of the same scene, from Herculaneum, we have still the two pillars and the curtain (differently draped), but the arrangement of the figures is different, though Apollo still rises in the background, apparently from a slight elevation; no low wall is visible. Evidently the painters were not tied by adherence to any theatrical scheme. A scene comparable with the first of these two pictures is found in the mosaic (Fig. 98), of uncertain date, which depicts the rehearsal for a satyric play, and it is significant, because, though partly dominated by the same conventions, it certainly does not represent a theatre, but a private house;[1] and it seems most likely that the wall-paintings were intended to do the same, and had no need of the theatre as an intermediary. There are many modifications of the convention of a low wall and pillars,[2] which it is not necessary to study in detail here; but there is an interesting class of pictures, the subjects of which are certainly taken from tragedy. In these, behind the figures in the foreground, is a wall in which there is a tall doorway, and, at one side, a kind of window, generally fitted with a curtain; there is often a figure looking out of this to see what is going on.

Such are the two scenes from Pompeii (Figs. 101, 102) depicting Medea

[1] Rehearsals are not known to have taken place in public, as they would, if they were in the theatre.

[2] e.g. the representations of Thetis in the workshop of Hephaistos (Fig. 99), and of Ares and Aphrodite—again with persons looking over the low wall (Fig. 100). These are probably not based on drama at all, and could afford no motive for reproducing dramatic scenery. Another variant of the same scheme is seen on the vase of Assteas (above, p. 222), which also is probably not a reproduction of a dramatic scene.

and her children, and the paintings of Phaedra and her nurse (Fig. 103) and of Paris and Helen (Figs. 104, 105). But there seems no reason to think that the painter was tied to the theatre, and it is very unlikely that in any play the παιδαγωγός was seen eavesdropping, or that an Eros looked on knowingly through the doorway.[1] Closely akin to these in their setting, but based on epic rather than on drama, are the scenes depicting the meeting of Odysseus and Penelope (Figs. 106, 107). On a number of paintings there is in the background (behind the low wall or balustrade, if it is present) the vista of a large hall—as, for instance, in the picture (at Pompeii) of Peirithous receiving the Centaurs (Fig. 108)—a scene which can never have been presented on the stage; or those of Achilles hearing of the death of Patroklos (at Herculaneum) (Fig. 109), where the roofed interior in the background is presumably that of his 'tent'; and of Achilles at Skyros (at Pompeii) (Fig. 110), on which Bulle claims that the palace-front represented by the pillared background is taken from the stage with its thyromata, apparently on the ground that it is enclosed in such a way as to look like an excerpt from a larger scene. But this framing of the picture may well have been a convention of wall-painting, and we have no evidence that thyromata were in fact divided by pillars constructed like those in the picture. Moreover, the scene depicted is again not one which can ever have been seen on the stage.

In many of these wall-paintings there is a more elaborate architectural background. In the picture at Pompeii (Fig. 111) of the arrival of Jason at the palace of Pelias, there is the view of the palace with a flight of steps leading up to it, and the figures are on two levels. (The subject itself, as depicted, can hardly be from a play.) In four pictures from Pompeii (Figs. 112–15) Orestes and Pylades are below and Iphigeneia upon the steps of the Temple of Artemis.[2] In the 'Theft of the Palladium' and the 'Death of Neoptolemus', both from Pompeii (Figs. 116, 117), the whole background is much more elaborate, and there is nothing in the framing of the picture which requires us to assume that a thyroma, any more than any other restriction of space, is the explanation.

In contrast to these, two pictures (Figs. 118, 119) in which Theseus ap-

[1] The fact that in the second of the 'Medea' pictures the position of the παιδαγωγός is different illustrates the painter's freedom. A technique somewhat similar to that of this group of paintings appears on the stelé of Hedisté from Pagasai (Pfuhl, *Mal. u. Zeichn.*, iii, Abb. 748; Bulle, *Untersuch.*, p. 325, Abb. 27), where there seems to be really no reason to assume the influence of the theatre.

[2] In the fourth painting, published by E. Löwy, *Jahrb. Arch.* xliv (1929), Taf. f., the triple division of the background may have been suggested by the stage, though obviously the architecture is not in detail that of a theatre; but a triple division may just as naturally have been suggested by the subject itself.

Fig. 93. Wall-painting in 'Villa of Diomedes'

FIG. 94. 'Shrine of Hekate' in Villa at Boscoreale

FIG. 95. Wall-painting, the Fall of Icarus, Pompeii

FIG. 97. Admetos and Alkestis (Herculaneum)

FIG. 96. Admetos and Alkestis (House of Tragic Poet, Pompeii)

FIG. 98. Rehearsal of Satyric Play (Mosaic from House of Tragic Poet, Pompeii)

FIG. 99. Thetis and Hephaistos (Pompeii, Reg. IX, Ins. 1, No. 7)

FIG. 100. Ares and Aphrodite (Casa di Frontone, Pompeii)

FIG. 101. Medea (Pompeii, Reg. IX, Ins. 5, No. 18)

FIG. 103. Phaedra (Pompeii, Reg. IX, Ins. 5, No. 18)

FIG. 102. Medea (Casa dei Dioscuri, Pompeii)

FIG. 104. Paris and Helen (Pompeii, Reg. IX,
Ins. 5, No. 18)

FIG. 105. Paris and Helen (Casa dei Amorini Dorati, Pompeii)

Fig. 106. Odysseus and Penelope (Macellum, Pompeii)

FIG. 107. Odysseus and Penelope (Casa dei Cinque Scheletri, Pompeii)

FIG. 108. Peirithous and Centaurs (House of Gavius Rufus, Pompeii)

Fig. 109. Achilles hears of Death of Patroklos (Herculaneum)

Fig. 110. Achilles at Skyros (Casa dei Dioscuri, Pompeii)

FIG. III. Jason and Pelias (Pompeii, Reg. IX, Ins. 5, No. 18)

Fig. 112. Iphigeneia in Tauris (Casa Citarista, Pompeii)

Fig. 114. Iphigeneia in Tauris (Casa Centenario, Pompeii)

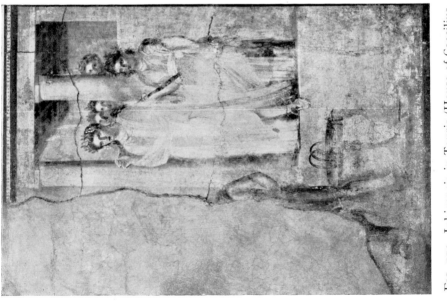

Fig. 113. Iphigeneia in Tauris (House of Caecilius Iucundus, Pompeii)

FIG. 115. Iphigeneia in Tauris (Pompeii)

FIG. 116. The Theft of the Palladium (Pompeii, Reg. I, Ins. 2, No. 6)

FIG. 117. The Death of Neoptolemus (Casa di Frontone, Pompeii)

Fig. 118. Theseus victorious over Minotaur (House of Rufus, Pompeii)

Fig. 119. Theseus and Ariadne (Casa di Frontone, Pompeii)

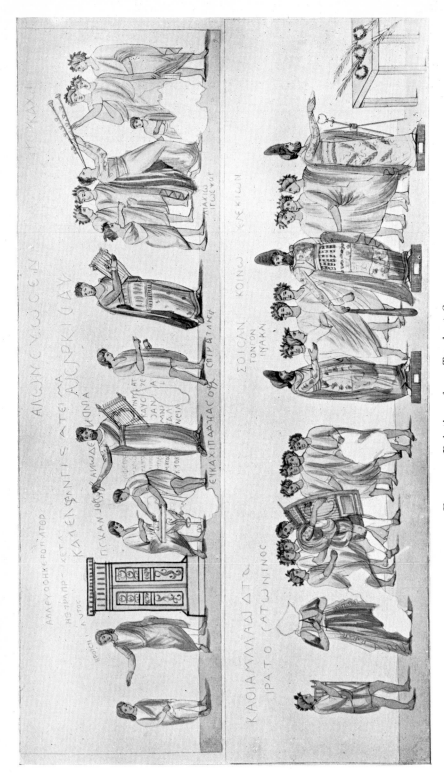

FIG. 120. Paintings from Tomb at Cyrene

FIG. 121. The Orchestra in the Roman period

pears outside the cave of the Minotaur—in one with Ariadne, who gives him the guiding threads, in the other after his victory—have a very simple background, and, speaking generally, it seems that the painters, while sometimes working within conventional patterns, could be entirely free in regard to the setting and framing of the picture, and that where they are restricted in scope by limitations of space, it is not necessarily or probably because they are copying the thyromata of the theatre, of the treatment of which we have no knowledge, but only conjectures. It may be that they sometimes copy and are often influenced by great paintings of the Hellenistic epoch, and that the original painters themselves were inspired by the great dramatic poets in the treatment of their human subjects, just as vase-painters were; but this is no reason for supposing that the setting and framework of the pictures were those of the stage, and we can draw no inferences from the former as to the latter. Bulle indeed distinguishes very interestingly a number of periods in the technical development of the treatment of space in the pictures; but where he is unconvincing is in his association of each of these with different types of theatrical stage, and if his conjectures as to the Lycurgean stage or the theatre at Segesta and other places are not accepted (and some of them seem to be more than doubtful), the whole structure of his theory breaks down. It is to be noticed that in none of these wall-paintings are the figures masked—a clear indication that the painters, like the painters of vases, were not just imitators of what they saw in the theatre. They need no more be supposed to have copied the stage setting than to have copied the costumes—which they certainly did not do. So also a modern painter of a scene based on *Hamlet* does not reproduce the stage setting of his own or any other period, but gives as a background his own conception of the castle of Elsinore.

The illustrations show that in a considerable number of paintings, especially in those where the background represents a low wall or balustrade with pillars behind it, or a wall with a high door and a window, there is a curtain draped over or above the pillars, or across a portion of the window. Some have supposed that this is copied from the use of curtains on the Hellenistic stage, and Bulle[1] speaks of curtains in the thyromata as predecessors of the *siparia* of the Roman stage. Whether we know anything at all of curtains in the thyromata is in the highest degree uncertain; but is it an outrageous suggestion that the *real* houses (or 'palaces') of Greece or Rome may have been provided with curtains which could be draped over the openings between rooms and courtyards, or over windows? and that their introduction into the paintings may have helped the painter in designing his colour-scheme? In any case it is hard to see any connexion between these curtains and the curtain shown in the relief at Naples,[2] on which a scene from the New Comedy is presented, and

[1] *Untersuch.*, p. 285.   [2] See above, p. 219, Fig. 77.

a curtain is roughly draped over one division of the background, evidently to put it 'out of action' for the purpose of the particular play. To assert, as Bulle does,[1] on the strength of the tiny corner of the background which is left uncovered, that what the curtain concealed was a view of buildings like one of the architectural scenes at Boscoreale, seems to be more than fanciful.[2]

APPENDIX IV

περίακτοι

Among the devices of which the use is well attested for the Roman, and therefore, in all probability, for the later Hellenistic period, were the περίακτοι, of which mention has already been made[3] in order to point out the lack of evidence for their use in the classical age. They now demand a somewhat fuller discussion.[4] They are described by Vitruvius, who is clearly speaking of his own day, and by Pollux, who has in mind a theatre with a high stage:

Vitruv. v. vi, § 8 'ipsae autem scaenae suas habeant rationes explicatas ita uti mediae valvae ornatus habeant aulae regiae; dextra ac sinistra hospitalia; secundum autem spatia ad ornatus comparata, quae loca Graeci περιάκτους dicunt ab eo quod machinae sunt in eis locis versatiles trigonoe, habentes singulae tres species ornationis, quae cum aut fabularum mutationes sunt futurae, seu deorum adventus cum tonitribus repentinis, versentur mutentque speciem ornationis in frontes; secundum ea loca versurae sunt procurrentes, quae efficiunt una a foro altera a peregre aditus in scaenam.'

Pollux. iv. 126–7 and 130–1 παρὰ ἑκάτερα δὲ τῶν δύο θυρῶν τῶν περὶ τὴν μέσην, ἄλλαι δύο εἶεν ἄν, μία ἑκατέρωθεν, πρὸς ἃς αἱ περίακτοι συμπεπήγασιν, ἡ μὲν δεξιὰ τὰ ἔξω πόλεως δηλοῦσα, ἡ δ' ἑτέρα τὰ ἐκ πόλεως, μάλιστα τὰ ἐκ λιμένος· καὶ θεούς τε θαλαττίους ἐπάγει καὶ ὅσα ἐπαχθέστερα ὄντα ἡ μηχανὴ

---

[1] *Untersuch.*, p. 284.

[2] No attempt is made here to follow the arguments drawn from mural paintings into all their ramifications. Bulle's interpretation of the well-known pictures (briefly referred to above, p. 224) of scenes from comedy at Pompeii (*Untersuch.*, pp. 280 ff.) seems very doubtful, and his argument from Plautus' *Rudens* to the stage in the theatre of Lycurgus (even if there was a stage) even more so. Enough has been said to indicate a belief that the assumptions of nearly all such arguments are unwarranted, and are no substitute for the direct evidence which is lacking for the theatres of the Hellenistic age. For a small selection out of the vast literature on the subject in general, see Bibliography, p. 278. See also n. on p. 246.   [3] Above, pp. 126–7, 215.

[4] I am particularly indebted to the discussions by Prof. P. Gardner, *J.H.S.* 1889, pp. 260 ff. and Prof. W. Beare, *Class. Quart.* 1938, pp. 205 ff.; I do not here enter into the question in which the latter is particularly interested, whether the Roman convention was identical with the Greek.

φέρειν ἀδυνατεῖ. εἰ δ'ἐπιστραφεῖεν αἱ περίακτοι, ἡ δεξιὰ μὲν ἀμείβει τόπον,[1]
ἀμφότεραι δὲ χώραν ὑπαλλάττουσιν· τῶν μέντοι παρόδων ἡ μὲν δεξιὰ ἀγρόθεν
ἢ ἐκ λιμένος ἢ ἐκ πόλεως ἄγει· (127) οἱ δ' ἀλλαχόθεν πεζοὶ ἀφικνούμενοι
κατὰ τὴν ἑτέραν εἰσίασιν .... (130) κεραυνοσκοπεῖον δὲ καὶ βροντεῖον· τὸ μέν
ἐστι περίακτος ὑψηλή· τὸ δέ βροντεῖον ὑπὸ τῇ σκηνῇ, ὁπόθεν ἀσκοὶ ψήφων
ἔμπλεοι διωγκωμένοι φέρονται καὶ χαλκωμάτων. (131) ... καταβλήματα δὲ
ὑφάσματα ἢ πίνακες ἦσαν ἔχοντες γραφὰς τῇ χρείᾳ τῶν δραμάτων προσ-
φόρους· κατεβάλλετο δ' ἐπὶ τὰς περιάκτους ὄρος δεικνύντα ἢ θάλατταν ἢ
ποταμὸν ἢ ἄλλο τι τοιοῦτον.

The general picture which Vitruvius gives is quite clear—the *scaenae frons* included a central door of some magnificence, and a more modest door on each side of it; beyond these doors, on each side, was a portion of the front in some way connected with the περίακτοι, and beyond each of these portions (at each extremity of the *scaenae frons*) was a side entrance opening towards the front; one of these was for persons coming from the market-place (i.e. from the town itself in which the scene was laid), the other for persons from 'abroad'. Apparently the name περίακτοι was known to be applied by the Greeks both to the machines described and to the part of the *scaenae frons* in which they operated, and this would be natural enough, if the side of the triangular periaktos which was turned forward formed for the time part of the background, and was in a straight line with the rest of the background. What was effected by the use of the περίακτοι was (1) a change of scene, when required, between one play and the next, (2) 'the arrival of gods with sudden thunder'. The latter is best discussed after we have considered the statement of Pollux.

Pollux has the same general picture (§ 124) of a *scaenae frons* with three doors in the *frons* and an entrance at each extremity of the stage, with a περίακτος close to each. The turning of both περίακτοι indicated a change of scene or country (χώρα) such as would take place between one play and another. (This corresponds to Vitruvius' *fabularum mutationes*.) The turning of only one indicated a change of τόπος, i.e. a change from one part of a χώρα to another. If, e.g., an actor were supposed to be coming from the sea (or harbour), a turn of the περίακτος would indicate the fact by presenting a surface bearing perhaps a line of waves or a dolphin or a ship; if he were coming from the country—or indeed if the scene were laid in the country—the περίακτος might show a mountain or a river, and so on. This was done by means of καταβλήματα—hangings or boards draped or hung on the περίακτος. So much is fairly clear and is consistent with what Vitruvius says, though which side was 'right' and which was 'left' is not explained by either author.

But what does the reference to sea-gods and thunder mean? Clearly the ordinary method of arrival employed by gods was by the μηχανή.

[1] A certain emendation of MS. τὸ πᾶν.

But Poseidon in his chariot might be too heavy for this, and, despite Aeschylus, sea-gods, not coming from heaven, might not be entitled to the use of the μηχανή. Accordingly a sea-god would come in by the entrance at the end of the stage, beyond a περίακτος, and the περίακτος would indicate the nature of the new-comer by displaying, e.g., the sea, while the βροντεῖον would thunder appropriately, and possibly the upper part of the περίακτος would depict a brilliant flash of lightning. (The κεραυνοσκοπεῖον may have been a special kind of revolving prism, raised high up, with a metal surface flashing in the sun.) This solution seems better than to suppose (with Haigh) that the heavy god was accommodated on a ledge on the περίακτος and then rolled round into view. What other objects might be too heavy for the μηχανή must be left to the imagination.[1] (Bulle may be right in thinking that at this late period αἰῶραι were in use which were lighter than the γέρανος or μηχανή of old days.) There is no evidence on these points. None, however, of our authorities speaks of these objects as being *carried by* the περίακτοι, but only of the περίακτοι being used when such objects were introduced.

There is no satisfactory reconciliation of the words of Vitruvius indicating that one of the outermost entrances gave access *a foro*, the other *a peregre*, with the statements of Pollux that one of the περίακτοι displayed or indicated (δηλοῦσα) τὰ ἔξω πόλεως, the other τὰ ἐκ πόλεως, μάλιστα τὰ ἐκ λιμένος. The words τὰ ἔξω πόλεως might correspond to *a peregre*, if the περίακτος gave indications of some foreign object; and τὰ ἐκ πόλεως, μάλιστα τὰ ἐκ λιμένος might correspond roughly to *a foro*, assuming that the harbour and market-place were both part of the πόλις, though one would think that persons coming *a peregre* would naturally come from the harbour.[2] But what can then be made of the statement which follows, that the right parodos gave access from country or harbour or city, the left from 'elsewhere'? There is some confusion, which has not been cleared up, and which may have been in the mind of Pollux himself. The convention of the chorus, which is likely to have been in agreement with that of the actors, was that, if coming from the country, the chorus entered from the right; if from the city, from the left.[3] It is commonly supposed that 'right' and 'left' are used in this reference from the point of view of the audience and correspond (at Athens) to west

---

[1] Nilsson, *Die alte Bühne und die Periakten*, p. 19, suggests that Pollux may be thinking of the *Prometheus*, and that the chariot of the Okeanids may have been represented by a painting on the περίακτος. Like P. Gardner, he imagines the περίακτοι to have been used in the Classical period, on the ground that so crude a device must have been primitive. See above, p. 126.

[2] Beare (l.c., p. 207) concludes that in the Κιθαριστής of Menander the entrances from the harbour and from the market-place must have been on opposite sides.

[3] Dindorf, *Proleg. de Com.*, p. 36 (Vit. Aristoph.) καὶ εἰ μὲν ἀπὸ τῆς πόλεως ἤρχετο ἐπὶ τὸ θέατρον, διὰ τῆς ἀριστερᾶς ἁψῖδος εἰσῄει, εἰ δὲ ὡς ἀπὸ ἀγροῦ, διὰ τῆς δεξιᾶς.

and east, and in Pollux from that of the actors, but as Pollux gives access from both country and city by the same parodos, the difficulty is not solved, and we have to be content with the general probability that the periaktoi, placed near the side entrances, gave indications in some conventional manner of the place from which newly arriving persons came.[1] It may be that they were used solely or principally in those theatres which had five doorways in the *scaenae frons* and that the two outermost were actually occupied by the periaktoi, which revolved in the door-space. The remains of some of the later theatres are consistent with this, but as regards Athens all information is lacking.

A reference to the periaktoi is found by some writers in Servius' commentary on Virgil's *Third Georgic*, l. 24 'scaena quae fiebat aut versilis erat aut ductilis erat. versilis tum erat cum subito tota machinis quibusdam convertebatur et aliam picturae faciem ostendebat.' The reference must be to late Hellenistic or Roman theatres; but if the *scaena versilis* is the same as the periaktoi, and not (as may well be the case) some different mechanical device altogether, the passage attributes to the periaktoi a far greater change in the background than can be extracted from the notices of Vitruvius and Pollux.[2] Nor is it clear exactly what picture Virgil himself has in mind in the words on which Servius is commenting, *vel scaena ut versis discedat frontibus.* He seems to be speaking of a background which is made to part asunder by the turning round of portions of it, which presumably closed up again and presented a new scene. This too is a change on a much larger scale than seems to be indicated by the notices of περίακτοι. Neither Virgil nor Servius helps us to know what the περίακτοι really were.

Nor is much help to be derived from Plutarch,[3] who is imagining a parade of Athenian poets: βούλεσθε τοὺς ἄνδρας εἰσάγωμεν αὐτοὺς τὰ σύμβολα καὶ τὰ παράσημα τῶν ἔργων κομίζοντας, ἰδίαν ἑκατέρῳ πάροδον ἀποδόντες; ἔνθεν μὲν δὴ προσίτωσαν ὑπ' αὐλοῖς καὶ λύραις ποιηταὶ λέγοντες καὶ ᾄδοντες ... καὶ σκευὰς καὶ προσωπεῖα καὶ βωμοὺς καὶ μηχανὰς ἀπὸ σκηνῆς περιάκτους καὶ τρίποδας ἐπινικίους κομίζοντες; The reference must here be to some portable models of the περίακτοι as employed on the stage. The interest of the passage is that it shows that περίακτοι were regarded as a characteristic

---

[1] K. Rees in an article 'On the significance of the parodoi in the Greek Theater' at least shows that the text of Pollux does not make sense either in itself or in relation to the plays so far as we know them. He discusses various emendations.

[2] It should be noticed that Servius does not (as some modern commentators assume) attribute to Virgil a reference to *both* the *scaena ductilis* and the *scaena versilis*. Virgil is clearly referring only to the latter. For the *scaena ductilis* see pp. 200–2, 227.

[3] *De glor. Athen.* 348 d, e. He imagines also a counter-parade of Athenian generals, the subject of the treatise being πότερον Ἀθηναῖοι κατὰ πόλεμον ἢ κατὰ σοφίαν ἐνδοξότεροι;

property of the stage in Plutarch's day, and it is possible that he refers to them in another (obviously untechnical) passage[1]—τὴν μεγάλην καὶ μυστηριώδη . . . ἀρχὴν τοῦ δόγματος ὀκνῶ μὲν ἔτι τῷ λόγῳ κινεῖν, ὥσπερ ναῦν ἐν χειμῶνι ναύκληρος ἢ μηχανὴν αἴρει ποιητικὸς ἀνὴρ ἐν θεάτρῳ σκηνῆς περιφερομένης.

It may be added that the suggestion of Dörpfeld[2] that the paraskenia at Epidaurus were occupied (on the ground-level) by περίακτοι is not more than a guess, and one which assumes that the action there was on the ground-level, and Bulle is probably right in contending that the space would not have been sufficient for περίακτοι. Such evidence as there is suggests that περίακτοι were a device of the late Hellenistic and Roman periods, and had their place (at least in Graeco-Asiatic theatres) on the level of the logeion.

Other devices for changing the scenery or introducing special scenic effects are mentioned by Pollux: (1) the ἡμικύκλιον, which may have been a semicircular revolving structure, instead of a triangular one, inserted in one of the thyromata; but its description by Pollux has never been satisfactorily explained—ἡ δὲ θέσις κατὰ τὴν ὀρχήστραν, ἡ δὲ χρεία δηλοῦν πόρρω τινὰ τῆς πόλεως τόπον ἢ τοὺς ἐν θαλάττῃ νηχομένους, 'Its position is *in the orchestra*,[3] and its use is to display some place far from the city, or persons swimming in the sea.' (2) The στροφεῖον, ὃ τοὺς ἥρως ἔχει τοὺς εἰς τὸ θεῖον μεθεστηκότας, ἢ τοὺς ἐν πελάγει ἢ πολέμῳ τελευτῶντας—the meaning of which is equally obscure. Bulle conjectures that a revolving machine depicted the hero on one side as a man, on the other as a god; but how persons dying at sea or in battle came into a Greek play is still unexplained. (3) The ἡμιστρόφιον, which is only mentioned,[4] but not described.

Note on the function of the three doors

Vitruvius and Pollux make statements about the use of the three doors in the back scene which must be true, if at all, of the drama of the Hellenistic period. They are certainly not true—at least not generally—of the classical period. They are as follows:

Vitruv. v. vi. ipsae autem scaenae suas habent rationes explicatas ita uti mediae valvae ornatus habeant aulae regiae, dextra ac sinistra hospitalia.

Pollux iv. 124. τριῶν δὲ τῶν κατὰ τὴν σκηνὴν θυρῶν ἡ μέση μὲν βασίλειον ἢ σπήλαιον ἢ οἶκος ἔνδοξος ἢ πᾶν τοῦ πρωταγωνιστοῦ τοῦ δράματος, ἡ δὲ δεξιὰ τοῦ δευτεραγωνιστοῦντος καταγώγιον· ἡ δὲ ἀριστερὰ τὸ εὐτελέστατον

[1] *De esu carnis*, p. 996 a.

[2] D.R., pp. 126, 270; cf. Bethe, *Gött. Gel. Anz.* 1897, p. 723; Puchstein, op. cit., p. 21; Bulle, *Untersuch.*, p. 171.

[3] Bulle, *Untersuch.*, p. 289 makes a lame attempt to explain this, but evidently does not believe in it himself.　　　　[4] Pollux iv. 127.

ἔχει πρόσωπον ἢ ἱερὸν ἐξηρημωμένον ἢ ἄοικός ἐστιν. ἐν δὲ τραγῳδίᾳ ἡ μὲν
δεξιὰ θύρα ξένων ἐστίν, εἱρκτὴ δὲ ἡ λαιά. τὸ δὲ κλεισίον ἐν κωμῳδίᾳ παράκειται
παρὰ τὴν οἰκίαν παραπετάσμασι δηλούμενον, καὶ ἔστι μὲν σταθμὸς ὑπο-
ζυγίων, καὶ αἱ θύραι αὐτοῦ μείζους δοκοῦσι, καλοῦμεναι κλεισιάδες, πρὸς τὸ καὶ
τὰς ἁμάξας εἰσελαύνειν καὶ τὰ σκευοφόρα. ἐν δὲ Ἀντιφάνους Ἀκεστρίᾳ καὶ
ἐργαστήριον γέγονεν.

As regards tragedy, Vitruvius' statement is much too rigid for the fifth
century, though the central door, when the scene was a palace, would
naturally be the grand entrance; and Pollux must be generalizing (as he
often does) from particular plays; there is no reason to think that at any
period of tragedy one door was always a 'prison'. It would be wrong to
suppose that the protagonist always used the central door or that the
deuteragonist was lodged behind a side door. As Haigh pointed out, Kreon
the tyrant in the *Antigone* and Clytemnestra in Sophocles' *Electra* were
deuteragonists, and Antigone and Electra protagonists, and neither Kreon
nor Clytemnestra was likely to have entered otherwise than centrally.
Nor is Pollux' account of the κλεισίον or shed, which might be a stable
or an entrance for vehicles, &c., or a workshop, at all clear, as it is not
known to what plays he refers, or even to what period, or what the
vehicles were doing on the stage.

APPENDIX V

Dithyrambic Contests

Wilamowitz put forward a theory (*Gött. Gel. Anz.* 1906, p. 614) that the
tribal contests for the prize for Dithyramb ceased early in the third
century B.C. His reason is the fact that the great didascalic inscription
I.G. ii. 972 = *I.G.* ii–iii². 2319, which was probably erected soon after
280 B.C., does not mention either choregi or dithyrambs, and he assumes
that the dithyrambic contest must have ceased soon after the abolition of
choregia about 315 B.C. This is not conclusive, as the intention of the
compiler of the list cannot be absolutely determined; he does not mention
choregi or dithyrambic contests even in the parts of the list covering
periods when both were certainly in existence; and the assumption of
Wilamowitz that the compiler, knowing that there was no contemporary
interest in such things, omitted them for the earlier period also, is far from
convincing. His record may never have been intended to include them,
and so he omits them, later as well as earlier. Wilamowitz thinks that the
reason for the cessation of tribal contests was that amateurs, such as the
tribal choruses must have been, were not equal to the highly elaborate
music of the day; that the flute-player, the virtuoso, brought his own
troupe of singers with him, and that the Athenian Διονύσου τεχνῖται, who
were professional, did not work on tribal lines. But highly elaborate music

was in vogue a century earlier, when the tribal contests were certainly regular. In Aristotle's day they were quite as important as tragedy and comedy. Dithyrambs certainly continued to be performed, whether in competition or not. If Wilhelm is right (*Urkunden*, p. 90), the inscription *I.G.* ii. 1264 records a tribal victory about 270 B.C.—it might well be a little earlier; but both the restoration and the date of the inscription are too conjectural to justify reliance upon it as evidence. Performances, however, of choruses in which the tribe was interested seem to be proved for the Athenian Dionysia at least down to about A.D. 100. The earliest definite evidence of their abandonment (though the performances went on without the competition) is somewhat later. See *Dithyramb, Tragedy, and Comedy*, pp. 79, 80; and below, p. 245.

APPENDIX VI

Theatrical Performances outside Athens from the Third Century B.C.

An inscription[1] from Ptolemais enumerating the members of the Guild of Artists of Dionysus in the reign of Ptolemy Philadelphus (283–247 B.C.) speaks of two τραγῳδιῶν ποιηταί, two κωμῳδιῶν ποιηταί, one τραγῳδός, six κωμῳδοί, four συναγωνισταὶ τραγικοί, one χοροδιδάσκαλος, and an αὐλητὴς τραγικός—implying some kind of choral tragedy, but telling nothing of the relation between chorus and actors, nor whether the chorus sang or only danced. Tragedies were composed at Alexandria by Alexander Aetolus (fl. *c*. 280 B.C.), and no less than twenty by Lycophron, one of which, the Κασσανδρεῖς, had a contemporary subject. Later in the third century Machon appears to have produced comedies in Alexandria.

An important series of inscriptions[2] refers to the performances at the Soteria at Delphi. The festival was probably instituted in, or soon after, 276 B.C.[3] It commemorated the defeat of the invading Gauls in the year 279–278 B.C. The inscriptions belong to various dates down to 225 B.C. In the earliest, which different scholars ascribe to dates ranging from 275 to 255 B.C., the performers include seven comic choreutae, but no tragic. The natural interpretation would seem to be that while some kind

---

[1] *B.C.H.* ix (1885), pp. 133–4. Körte (*Neue Jahrb.* iii (1900), p. 86) may be right in thinking that the lacuna of 7 lines after the name of the χοροδιδάσκαλος contained the names of 7 comic choreutae, as in the inscriptions relating to the Delphic Soteria.

[2] Dittenberger, *Sylloge*³, Nos. 424, 489, 509, 690.

[3] Pomtow in *Klio*, xiv (1914), pp. 265 ff. The precise chronology and early history of the festival are much disputed; see Ferguson, *Hellenistic Athens*, p. 164 and *Am. J. Phil.* 1934, pp. 318 ff.; also Flacelière in *B.C.H.* lii, pp. 256 ff.; Tod, *J.H.S.* 1931, pp. 230–1, and refs. there given; Kolbe, *Hermes*, 1933, pp. 440–56, and Kahrstedt, ibid. 1937, pp. 368 ff.

of comic dances persisted—whether with or without words, and whether as interludes, or as independent parts of the programme—there were no tragic choruses, and that the τραγῳδοί, the actors, presented scenes from plays, without a chorus. The tragedy thus performed apparently had an αὐλητής, who may have accompanied the τραγῳδός in his singing or recitation of lyrics. There seem to be no solid grounds for the conjecture[1] that tragic choreutae were supplied from the dithyrambic ἄνδρες χορευταί mentioned (along with παῖδες χορευταί) earlier in the inscription. The comic choruses performed by the seven must have been very different from those performed by twenty-four in the fifth century. In an inscription[2] more than a century later (before 130 B.C.) the comic dancers are reduced to four χορευταί κωμῳδοί. An inscription from Tegea[3] already referred to, in honour of an actor who evidently specialized in the performance of old tragedies, includes among his victories one gained at the Soteria with the *Herakles* of Euripides: Διονύσια ἐν ταῖς Ἀθήναις Ὀρέστῃ Εὐριπίδου, Σωτήρια ἐν Δελφοῖς Ἡρακλεῖ Εὐριπίδου . . . ταίῳ Ἀρχεστράτου, Ἡραῖα Ἡρακλεῖ Εὐριπίδου, Ἠλέκτρᾳ (?) Εὐριπίδου, Ναῖα ἐν Δωδώνῃ Ἀχελῴῳ Εὐριπίδου, Ἀχιλλεῖ Χαιρήμονος. The inscription, the date of which cannot be determined, except that it must be later than 276 B.C., is interesting as evidence of the continued vogue of Euripides, but does not tell us how much of each play the τραγῳδός presented, nor whether he had a chorus.

From Delos there is a series of inscriptions[4] ranging from 284 to 170 B.C. and mentioning contests at the Apollonia and Dionysia of τραγῳδοί and κωμῳδοί (with the formula οἵδε ἐπεδείξαντο τῷ θεῷ or, in 200 B.C., οἵδε τῷ θεῷ ἠγωνίσαντο), and giving the names of the χορηγοί in each contest, and in the later inscriptions those of the victorious χορηγοί. There is nothing to show how far the performances were choral.[5] On this point the only evidence comes from another inscription[6] (one of the series containing the accounts of the Hieropoioi of Delos) recording a payment χορῷ τῷ γενο-μένῳ τοῖς κωμῳδοῖς καὶ τῷ τραγῳδῷ Δράκοντι τοῖς ἐπιδειξαμένοις τῷ θεῷ δᾷδας παρὰ Ἐργοτέλους ⊢⊢⊢, ῥυμοὶ καὶ ξύλα ΙΙΙ. (The materials were probably for use in connexion with sacrifices.)[7] The date of this inscription is 279 B.C., and it strongly suggests that comedy had a chorus and tragedy

---

[1] Körte, l.c.   [2] Dittenb.³, No. 690.

[3] *I.G.* v. 2, No. 118; see above, p. 167.

[4] *I.G.* xi. 2, Nos. 105–16, 118, 120, 122–4, 126, 128, 130, 132, 133. See Brinck, *Diss. Hal.* vii, pp. 187 ff.

[5] In No. 132 occurs the expression (apparently of an αὐλητής) ἐνίκα μετὰ χοροῦ, but this is a distinct entry from those referring to τραγῳδοί and κωμῳδοί.

[6] *I.G.* xi. 2, No. 161 A, l. 86. For this series of inscriptions, see also pp. 206–9.

[7] Körte (l.c.) compares ll. 101 ff. of the same inscription: εἰς τὸν χορὸν τὸν γενόμενον Τιμοστράτῳ τῷ αὐλητῇ, ὅτε ἀπεδείξατο τῷ θεῷ, δᾷδες παρὰ Ἀρχικλέους ⊢⊢⊢ΙΙ, ῥυμὸς ΙΙ. The ῥυμός was perhaps a long pole used as a spit.

had not; and this would be in accordance with our inference from the almost contemporary Delphian inscriptions which never mention tragic choreutae. The materials were supplied to the comic *chorus* and the tragic *actor*; this at least seems as likely an interpretation of the sentence as that the comic chorus also served in tragedy, supporting the tragic actor Drakon.[1] (The fact that the same persons did on occasion serve for both forms of drama in Aristotle's day[2] does not prove that they did so here.)

Evidence as regards the second century B.C. is very scanty. The reference made by Philodemus[3] (quoting Diogenes of Babylon) to the cessation of dancing in tragedy may apply to other theatres besides that of Athens, and it is in keeping with the absence of all mention of tragic choreutae at Delphi and (probably) at Delos, though it is impossible to say whether the lyric portions were omitted or whether they were sung (on the stage or in the orchestra) in some theatres by a few singers. The names of a few tragic poets are known, e.g. Dymos of Iasos,[4] Melanthius of Rhodes (a pupil of the philosopher Carneades[5]), and Lysimachus in Asia Minor.[6] The records of the Soteria at Delphi show (as was noticed above) that about 130 B.C. the number of comic choreutae was only four.[7] Three other inscriptions must be mentioned. In the first[6] the regional guild of Artists of Dionysus for Ionia and the Hellespont promises to send to the people of Iasos, free of charge, in view of their financial difficulties, αὐλητὰς δύο, τραγῳδοὺς δύο, κωμῳδοὺς δύο, κιθαρῳδόν, κιθαριστήν, ὅπως συνάγωσιν τῷ θεῷ τοὺς χοροὺς κατὰ τὰς πατρίους αὐτῶν διαγραφάς . . . τοὺς δὲ νεμηθέντας πάντας ἐπιτελεῖσαι τοὺς τῶν Διονυσίων ἀγῶνας ἐν τοῖς ὡρισμένοις χρόνοις πάντα παρασχόντας ἀκολούθως τοῖς Ἰασέων νόμοις. Unfortunately this gives no clear indication as regards the nature of the 'choruses'. The other two inscriptions are of interest because they include records of satyric drama. One, from Samos,[8] is dated on epigraphical grounds by the late Professor Percy Gardner in the second century: the victors in the Heraea at Samos include poets of new satyric plays, new tragedies, and new comedies. The other[9] is on the base of a statue at Delos,

---

[1] The same Drakon of Tarentum appears as a tragic διδάσκαλος at Delphi.

[2] Ar. *Pol.* iii. 1276 b; see above, p. 161.

[3] See above, p. 195.

[4] *Inscr. in Brit. Mus.* iii. 444 (with full discussion).

[5] Gomperz, *Sitzb. Wien. Akad.* 1890, p. 84 (quoting a papyrus fragment).

[6] Le Bas and Waddington, *Inscr.* iii, No. 281; Lüders, *Dion. Künstler*, p. 181.

[7] Dittenb. *Syll.*[3], No. 690.

[8] *J.H.S.* vii, p. 148 τοὺς ποιητὰς τῶν καινῶν σατύρων (sc. ἐνίκα) Ἀρχένομος Ἑρμία Ῥόδιος· τοὺς ποιητὰς τῶν καινῶν τραγῳδιῶν Σωσίστρατος . . . τοὺς ὑποκριτὰς Δημήτριος Νικαίου Μιλήσιος· τοὺς ποιητὰς τῶν καινῶν κωμῳδιῶν Ἀρίστων Τιμοστράτου Ἀθηναῖος, ὑποκριτὴς Καμναγόρας Στράτωνος Μαλλώτης.

[9] *B.C.H.* xiii (1889), pp. 372 ff. It is very doubtful whether the omission of the article with σατύρων implies that both were included in the same competition

of the date of (about) 112 B.C., and dedicated by a certain Dionysius of Athens: Διονύσιος Δημητρίου Ἀθηναῖος νικήσας τοὺς ποιητὰς τῶν τραγῳδιῶν καὶ σατύρων, ἱερεὺς Ἀπόλλωνος καὶ ἐπιμελητὴς Δήλου γενόμενος, Διονύσῳ καὶ Μούσαις χαριστήριον.

On the borderline between the second and first centuries B.C. are two inscriptions,[1] one probably before, one just after, the beginning of the century, recording the sending of Dionysiac artists from Athens to Delphi. The first mentions κωμῳδοί (probably eight) and τραγῳδοί (probably three) ; the second, two tragic and five satyric poets, two τραγῳδοί with seven συναγωνισταί, and four κωμῳδοί with six συναγωνισταί. This indicates that satyric drama was no unimportant element in the Delphic festivals; but the exact functions of the συναγωνισταί remain uncertain. A remarkable inscription from Rhodes[2] records the victory there of the actor Alkimachos of Athens with four plays of Sophocles, including the satyric *Telephos*. Whether these plays, and particularly the satyric play, might have been acted without a chorus, or with a chorus separated from the actors, or a skeleton chorus on a high stage, it is impossible to say ; but it was an actor's victory and he may only have presented certain scenes.

A series of inscriptions[3] records the victors in the Charitesia and Homoloïa at Orchomenos early in the first century B.C. All include τραγῳδοί and κωμῳδοί, and the third mentions a ποιητὴς σατύρων named Ameinias, as well as poets of tragedy and comedy. (One of the tragic poets is Σοφοκλῆς Σοφοκλέους Ἀθηναῖος.) Another series comes from Oropos,[4] recording victories at the Amphiaräa, and again poets of all three forms of drama are mentioned, as well as actors of both old and new tragedies and comedies. The same is the case in the inscriptions[5] which refer to the Sarapiaia at Tanagra. A record[6] of the Μουσεῖα at Thespiai in the same century also mentions a σατύρων ποιητής, as well as actors of old tragedies and old comedies. An inscription[7] from Akraiphia (in Boeotia) records satyric as well as comic and tragic poets, and so do the lists of poets victorious with new plays at the Ῥωμαῖα—festivals in honour of Rome— at Magnesia on the Maeander, probably in the first half of the first century

---

in face of such expressions as τὴν Μεγαρέων πόλιν καὶ Κορινθίων (Ar. *Pol.* III. ix), which are frequent in Aristotle and others.

[1] Colin, *B.C.H.* xxx (1906), pp. 276 ff., dates them about 128 and 97 B.C.

[2] *I.G.* XII. i. 125. (The date is uncertain, but is said to be scarcely later than the first century B.C.) Ἀλκίμαχος Ἀθ[ηναῖος Πηλ]έα Σοφοκλέους καὶ ᾿Οδυσσέ[α μαινόμενον κ]αὶ ῎Ιβηρας καὶ σατυρικὸν Τήλεφ[ον ἐνίκα] ὑποκρινόμενος ἐν Ῥόδῳ.

[3] *I.G.* vii. 3195, 3196, 3197.

[4] *I.G.* vii. 416, 419, 420.

[5] *I.G.* vii. 540 to 543. The first is dated between 100 and 70 B.C. by the editor.

[6] *I.G.* vii. 1760.

[7] *I.G.* vii. 2727.

B.C.[1] The satyric plays named are the Θύτης and Παλαμήδης of Theodorus, the Αἴας of Polemaeus of Ephesus, and the Πρωτεσίλαος of Harmodius; a satyric poet named Polemon is also mentioned, and it is noticeable that Theodorus and Polemaeus also won victories with their tragedies. The performance of scenes from the *Bacchae* by the actor Jason before the Armenian king after the death of Crassus in 53 B.C.[2] is interesting, but proves nothing as to regular theatrical performances. Three inscriptions from Teos,[3] which may be of about this date, mention victories at the Dionysia of satyric poets and actors, and in particular the victory of the actor Asklepiades of Chalai with a satyric play—'δράματι Πέρσαις'. In a passage of Fulgentius[4] the Muse, speaking of the epoch after Cicero and Varro, appears to refer to satyric drama as well as tragedy and comedy at Alexandria, but the language is not such as to be very good evidence for anything. The composition of satyric drama at Rome in the Augustan age is proved by the attention paid to it by Horace,[5] but we know nothing of the nature of these compositions, nor whether they were intended for performance on the Roman stage or only for reading; it would certainly have been a stage of the Roman pattern, if any, that was in his mind. Later in the Imperial period we find two inscriptions from Samos[6] enumerating victorious choregi and poets. Two inscriptions from Thespiae[7] of the second and early third centuries A.D. mention poets and actors of both old and new tragedies and comedies, and one of them (of the second century) adds σατυρογράφος Μ. Αἰμίλιος Ὑήττιος.[8] An inscription from Aphrodisias[9] records payments to τραγῳδοί and κωμῳδοί. There is an epitaph[10] on a tragic poet Euandridas of Miletus, early in the first century A.D. An im-

---

[1] *Ath. Mitt.* xix (1894), pp. 96 ff. (= Kern, *Inschr. von Magn.* No. 88). Feasts in honour of Rome were also celebrated at Alabanda, Leucophryene, and other towns.　　　　　　　　　　　　　　　　　　　　　　[2] Plut. *Crass.*, ch. 33.

[3] Le Bas and Waddington, *Inscr.* iii, Nos. 91, 92, 93; Lüders, op. cit., p. 180.

[4] *Mythologicon* i. p. 609. Ast ubi me Romuleae arcis conventu bellicus vidu- avit incursus, Alexandriae conciliabula urbis exsulata posseeram, variis dog- matum imbutamentis lasciva Graecorum praestruens corda, postque Catonum rigores Tullianasque severas invectiones et Varroniana ingenia, Pelleae gentis enerves sensus aut satyra luseram aut comoedico phantasmate delectabam aut tragica pietate mulcebam aut epigrammatum brevitate condibam.'

[5] *Ars Poetica*, ll. 220–50.

[6] Brinck, *Diss. Hal.* vii, pp. 211, 212. The date is conjectured by Kirchhoff to fall in the first or second century A.D. An inscription from Teos of the second century A.D. (ibid., p. 213= Boeckh, *C.I.* 9. 3089) is only made to include dramatic performances by uncertain restorations.

[7] *I.G.* vii. 1773 and 1776.

[8] The date of the σατυρογράφος Demetrius of Tarsus mentioned by Diog. Laert. v. 25 is unknown.　　　　　　　　　　　　　　　[9] Boeckh, *C.I.G.* ii. 2758.

[10] Rayet, *Rev. Archéol.* xxvii (1874), p. 113; Kaibel, *Epigr.*, p. x.

portant statement of Dio Chrysostom[1] (already alluded to) appears to
indicate that in performances of tragedies the lyric portions were omitted,
and only selected iambic scenes were acted; but unfortunately he does not
tell us whether this practice was common, and an epigram of Lucillius,[2]
who lived under Nero, at least appears to assume that a τραγῳδός might
be expected to have a chorus and its flute-player with him, though they
may only have danced:

> οὐκ ᾔδειν σε τραγῳδόν, ᾿Επίκρατες, οὐδὲ χοραύλην
> οὐδ᾿ ἀλλ᾿ οὐδὲν ὅλως, ὧν χορὸν ἔστιν ἔχειν.
> ἀλλ᾿ ἐκάλουν σὲ μόνον· σὺ δ᾿ ἔχων χορὸν οἴκοθεν ἥκεις
> ὀρχηστῶν, αὐτοῖς πάντα διδοὺς ὀπίσω.

Plutarch (who lived from about 46 to 120 A.D.) writes[3] as if visits to the
performance of tragedies in the theatre were a normal activity in his
time—for children as well as for their elders.

There is also reproduced in Wieseler's *Theatergebäude* a series of paintings
from a grave of the Imperial period at Cyrene, depicting groups of actors
and musicians; one of these represents three tragic actors (one in the part
of Herakles, another in that of Hermes or a herald) with seven choreutae,
and each of the other groups includes seven choreutae. The drawings were
made by Pacho,[4] who was not an archaeologist, and are obviously in some
respects inexact, but they may imply that a small chorus was employed
at this period in tragedy—of such a size as the broad stage of a theatre of
the Roman pattern could accommodate.

It should be added that there is evidence going down at least to the second
century A.D. of the performances of choruses of boys and of men (παῖδες
αὐληταί and ἄνδρες αὐληταί) in many parts of the Greek world, often at the
same festivals as the performances of tragedy, comedy, and satyric drama.
Such choruses were evidently part of the regular repertoire of the guilds of
Artists of Dionysus; but the number of members of each chorus was much
smaller than that of the dithyramb in classical times at Athens—sometimes, as at the Soteria, only from five to fifteen, and they may have
differed in other ways from the classical dithyramb.[5] The survey which
has been made points to the conclusion that outside Athens, if not in the
city, the producers of drama, and chiefly the Artists of Dionysus, who had
their guilds in very many towns, felt free to adapt tragedy to their needs
at least as regards the size of the chorus and even its retention at all.

---

[1] xix, 487 R. His date is about A.D. 40–114. See above, pp. 195–6.
[2] *Anth. Pal.* xi. 11.
[3] *De amore prolis*, p. 495 a; *de sera num. vind.*, pp. 554 b, 556 a.
[4] *Relation d'un voyage dans la Marmorique, la Cyrénaïque, etc.* (Paris, 1827).
[5] An inscription from Thespiai, *I.G.* vii. 1776, later than A.D. 212, mentions by
name a κύκλιος αὐλητής.

Away from Athens the religious interest of tragedy, which was largely expressed in the fifth century through the chorus, was probably very slight, and the interest in the actor's technique much greater. In comedy the dances and songs of the chorus were part of the fun, and were probably retained as such, though with a greatly reduced number of dancers. Through all the later part of the long period of three centuries or more which we have surveyed it is certain that the plays must have been given in theatres in which there was a raised stage; but the reduction in the numbers of the choruses did not wait until the time when all performers were on the stage and none were in the orchestra—when, of course, the reduction would have become necessary; and unfortunately the evidence does not give any hint of the time when the transference of the action to the stage took place. Given a certain liberty of adaptation, it might have been at any time after the death of Menander; but it need not have been before a date well into the Roman period.

Additional note to pp. 225–34.

I was unable, owing to conditions arising out of the War, to obtain a copy of Dr. H. G. Beyen's most exhaustive treatise, *Die pompeianische Wand-malerei*, i (1938) until the above pages were in proof. It does not alter the opinions I have expressed in any important respect, but this is not the place for the very minute discussion of detail which a consideration of Dr. Beyen's work demands. The only question relevant to my present subject is whether the Italian wall-paintings throw any light on the Theatre of Dionysus at Athens, and I am still convinced that (whatever may be the general relation between the wall-paintings and the theatres of Italy) any inference from them to the Greek theatres of the Hellenistic period would be very hazardous. It also remains true that we do not know enough of the way in which the thyromata in the background of the stage of some Hellenistic theatres were fitted or used to justify us in 'deriving' anything in Italy from them. Dr. Beyen makes a very able attempt to reconstruct the *scaenae frons* of Apaturius at Tralles in close conformity with the wall-paintings, but this building was not a normal theatre. (See pp. 226, 230.)

THE THEATRE IN THE ROMAN PERIOD

1. The history of the theatre after the erection of a permanent stage at some time in the Hellenistic period—whether about 160 B.C., as seems most probable, or after the destruction wrought in Athens by Sulla, as some scholars conjecture—is beset with difficulties and uncertainties, and the points upon which scholars are agreed are few, but it is at least possible to describe the existing remains and to mention some of the competing theories.

Whether King Ariobarzanes II of Cappadocia (63–52 B.C.), to whom the restoration of the Odeum is attributed, was in any way a benefactor of the theatre is unknown; but a part of a column, which Rousopoulos in 1862 found embedded in a late wall of the skené and which now lies near the Later Temple of Dionysus, is engraved with an inscription[1] in his honour, which runs: ὁ δῆμος βασιλέα Ἀριοβαρζάνην Φιλοπάτορα τὸν ἐκ βασιλέως Ἀριοβαρζάνου Φιλορωμαίου καὶ βασιλίσσης Ἀθηναΐδος Φιλοστόργου τὸν ἑαυτοῦ εὐεργέτην ἀνέθηκεν. Further, Fiechter conjectures that an inscription[2] in almost similar terms in honour of Ariobarzanes III (52–42 B.C.), son of the former, may originally have formed part of a similar column of which some remains exist in the theatre.

2. But the principal ruins of the theatre in the Roman period are of the Imperial epoch. In the time of Nero there appears to have been a general reconstruction, affecting the orchestra, the stage, and the stage building. Large fragments remain of an architrave which must have formed part of the central projecting porch or *aedicula* of the *scaenae frons* of the new construction, bearing an inscription[3] which is incomplete, but is by general agreement assigned to the time of Nero. It embodies the dedication of the theatre to Dionysus Eleutherieus (an otherwise unknown variant of the epithet)[4] and, as is practically certain, to

[1] *I.G.* ii–iii². 3427.
[2] *I.G.* ii–iii². 3428. It is not known where this was found.
[3] *I.G.* ii–iii². 3182.
[4] Graindor, *Athènes de Tibère à Trajan*, p. 14, suggests that Ἐλευθεριεύς may have been due to a deliberate assimilation of Ἐλευθερεύς to Ἐλευθέριος used as a complimentary epithet of Nero, who in 66 gave 'freedom' to the Greeks, and in conformity with this he dates the structure not earlier than 66. But this seems very far-fetched.

Nero, though the Emperor's name was chiselled out at a later time when his memory had become odious. The inscription (Fig. 122),[1] so far as it can be certainly restored, runs as follows:

[Διονύσῳ 'Ελ]ευθεριεῖ καὶ [Νέρωνι] Κλαυδίῳ Καίσαρι Σε[βαστῷ

and in the second line:

]δίων ἀνέθηκεν στρατηγοῦντος ἐπὶ τοὺς ὁπλείτας τὸ ·ζ· κ[

At the beginning of the second line ἐκ τῶν ἰδίων has been generally accepted. Other architrave blocks bear the letters MAN,[2]

FIG. 122. Fragments of Architrave of Roman Skené

OY (followed by ΔIABI erased, but still just legible), IK. With the help of these and other slight traces of letters, Bulle conjecturally restores the whole inscription with its upper line running along the architrave of the left, central, and right *aediculae* of the *scaenae frons* and of the two recessed intervening spaces, while the lower line is inscribed on the central *aedicula* and the right-hand space. He reads: Τι. Κλαύδιος Νούϊος Φιλίνου ἐπιμελητὴς τῆς | πόλεως διὰ βίου διὰ βι . . | Διονύσῳ 'Ελευθεριεῖ καὶ Νέρωνι Κλαυδίῳ Καίσαρι Σεβαστῷ Γερ|μανικῷ | τὸ ὑποσκήνιον καὶ τὴν σκηνὴν σὺν τῷ κόσμῳ | ἐκ τῶν ἰδίων ἀνέθηκεν στρατηγοῦντος ἐπὶ τοὺς ὁπλείτας τὸ ζ' καὶ τὸ η' αὐτοῦ Νούϊου.

This restoration is not without its difficulties. The justification given for the name of Ti. Claudius Novius is that it is known[3] that he was general for the eighth time in the year A.D. 61–2, and

---

[1] After D.R., Fig. 27.

[2] Formerly read as ΠΑ, but Bulle (ap. Fiechter, iii, p. 62) seems right in reading MAN.

[3] *I.G.* ii–iii². 1990. The inscription records Nero's 'victory' over the revolting Britons.

although the repeated holding of this office seems to have been
not uncommon in the second century[1] the justification has some
probability, since Novius was plainly one of the most important
men of his time. He had been given Roman citizenship by
Claudius, and the inscription[2] which records his eighth generalship also records that he was (among many other things) high-
priest of Nero and ἐπιμελητὴς τῆς πόλεως for life. The partial
dittography of διὰ βίου could be explained by the carelessness of
the carver, and the epithet *Germanicus* was regularly used in
reciting Nero's titles. Some[3] have felt a difficulty about the
genitive absolute στρατηγοῦντος, if it refers to the same person as
the nominative Νοούϊος. It may be suggested, however, that it is
explained by the regular custom of giving the date by means of
a genitive absolute, usually with ἄρχοντος,[4] and that (particularly
after so many intervening words) the slight grammatical discrepancy would hardly be noticed. The restoration καὶ τὸ η΄
Bulle explains as implying either that the reconstruction took
two years, or (if the strict sense of ἀνέθηκεν, as referring to the
act of dedication, is insisted upon) that the dedication took place
at the moment when Novius' seventh generalship was passing
into his eighth. Neither of these explanations is altogether convincing, and it is not quite satisfactory that αὐτοῦ Νοουΐου should
overrun the central *aedicula* into the right-hand interspace, when
the corresponding place in the left-hand interspace was blank, so
that there seems still to be an opportunity for the ingenious to
rediscover the original termination of the inscription.[5] But perhaps we may provisionally give the credit of the Neronian reconstruction to Novius, and date it in A.D. 61.

3. The account of this reconstruction may conveniently begin

---

[1] See Graindor, *Athènes de Tibère à Trajan*, pp. 14, 39, 77, who suggests the
name of Αἰολίων Ἀντιπάτρου Φλυεύς, who at some time in the second century
was general for the seventh time, but is otherwise almost unknown. He is,
however, right in noting that the ascription to Novius is not proved, however
likely it may be.

[2] *I.G.* ii–iii². 1990. The inscription records Nero's 'victory' over the revolting
Britons.

[3] e.g. Schleif, *Jahrb. Arch.* 1937, *Anz.*, cols. 42, 43.

[4] Dating by στρατηγίαι and in particular by the eighth στρατηγία of Novius is
found in other inscriptions (vide Fiechter, iii, p. 65).

[5] Some other difficulties in points of detail are noted by von Gerkan, *Gnomon*,
1938, pp. 245–6.

with the skené and the *scaenae frons*. Behind the wall (marked
VV in Plan III and Figs. 52 and 59) which was the foundation of
the Lycurgean *scaenae frons* are the foundations of a stròng
Roman wall of limestone blocks, about 82 feet long and from
4 ft. 11 in. to 5 ft. 3 in. wide, marked RV–RV in Plan III. The

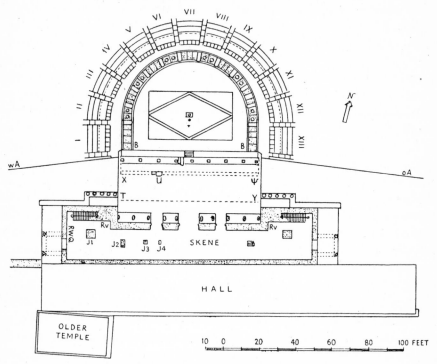

FIG. 123. Sketch-plan of Theatre in Roman period
(For explanation of symbols, see p. 287)

gap in the middle of this wall was not original; excavations have
uncovered traces of the lower stratum of the missing portion.[1]

Similar foundations, but rather wider (wRV and oRV in Plan
III) are found behind each of the paraskenia, lying above the
older breccia foundations, and projecting beyond each paraskenion to west and east respectively. From the west end of
wRV the foundation of a cross-wall RwQ runs southward at
right angles towards the wall H, and along the southern end of
RwQ lies a layer of blue Hymettian marble—the foundation of a
double gateway; the base of the pillar separating the gates is still
in position, and fragments of the round arches of the gateway are

[1] Fiechter, i, p. 36.

among the ruins. Fiechter asserts that this gateway is slightly out of line with the wall, and must therefore be of later date, but both the alleged fact and the inference from it are disputed with some reason,[1] and probably the gateway is contemporary with the Roman walls described, and led, up a few steps and through another doorway, into the main hall of the skené, which was now reduced in width by the breadth of the wall RV. The wall at the east end corresponding to RwQ can no longer be found.

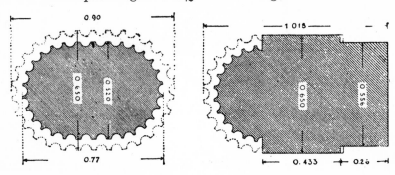

FIG. 124. Columns of Roman Skené

4. The Roman skené thus had a front and paraskenia, but the exact length of the *scaenae frons* is uncertain: Fiechter makes it about 73 ft. 4 in., von Gerkan about 69 feet, Schleif about 67 ft. 5 in.; a definite estimate is impossible,[2] as the nature of the connexions between the *scaenae frons* and the paraskenia is undiscovered, as is also that of the sides of the paraskenia which face each other looking inwards. The reconstruction of the *scaenae frons* itself is also most uncertain. Ziller's plan of the ruins in 1863 (Plan II) marks a wall (T–Y in the plan), of which no trace now remains, fitting closely on to the north side of the Hellenistic proskenion foundation, and farther north another wall (X–Ψ), of which only a few stones survive (marked U in Fig. 123). It is possible that the former of these lost walls served as a foundation for the broken front line of the Roman *scaenae frons*, and V and RV for the back line; but some scholars (among them Fiechter) believe that Ziller's two walls were simply supports of the stage,[3] and that the *scaenae frons* did not extend so far for-

[1] Schleif in *Jahrb. Arch.* 1937, *Anz.*, col. 50.
[2] von Gerkan, l.c., p. 246; Schleif, l.c., col. 48.
[3] The stage in the later Greek theatres was more commonly supported on pillars.

ward. Many fragments of the *frons* are lying about among the ruins (besides the fragments of the architrave bearing the inscription already discussed), and show at least that in its lower story it included three projecting porches or *aediculae* (each corresponding to a door leading into the skené), and, in the upper, two or three, each surmounted by a gable.[1] These *aediculae* were

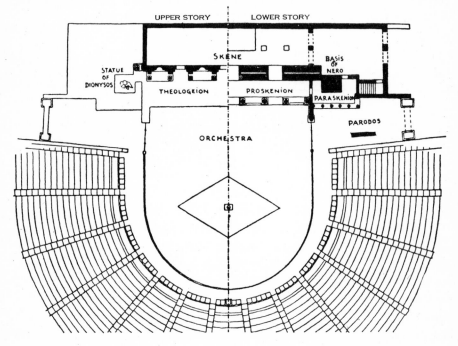

FIG. 125. Plan of Roman Theatre according to Dörpfeld (1935)

supported by columns of which two types exist—one oval and entire,[2] the other semicircular, the back half of the circle being replaced by a rectangular pillar (Fig. 124). Ordinary round columns have also been found.[3] But it is uncertain whether these

[1] If Dörpfeld's latest view is accepted (see below) the term *aediculae* for these projecting structures, at least those in the lower story, would not be strictly correct, though the appearance from the front would be very much that of a projecting porch. Dörpfeld terms the front row of columns a proskenion—believing it to stand on the line of the Hellenistic proskenion and to have served as the background of dramatic action.

[2] Dörpfeld is doubtless right in thinking (D.R., p. 86) that the oval columns stood clear of any wall; they probably composed the front immediately facing the orchestra.   [3] Fiechter, iii, p. 30.

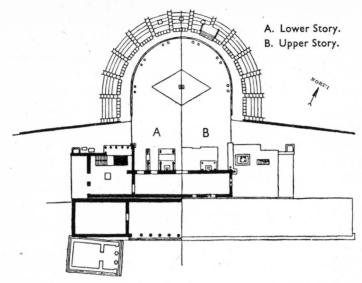

A. Lower Story.
B. Upper Story.

FIG. 126. Plan of Roman Theatre according to Schleif; cf. Fig. 129

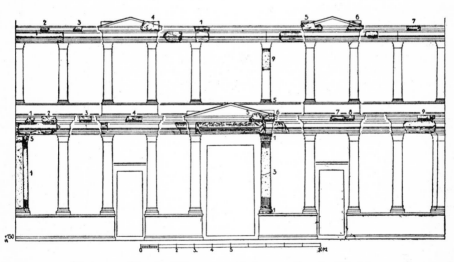

FIG. 127. Skené of Roman period according to Fiechter

aediculae were very shallow, or projected considerably, as they
must have done if Ziller's wall *T–Y* was used to carry the
front line of their columns. So the front line is pictured in
one way by Fiechter (Fig. 127) and in another by Schleif

(Fig. 129),[1] and in Dörpfeld's latest reconstruction (Fig. 128)[2] which Schleif (Fig. 129) partly follows, the front line of columns on their bases is detached from the parallel back line, which in Schleif's version consists of half-columns treated as *antae* terminating short walls projecting at right angles from the wall of the skené, leaving an interval between them and the front line.[3]

According to Fiechter's measurements and calculations the columns of the lower story were about 14 ft. 6 in. high, those of the upper perhaps 11 ft. or a little more. The total height, therefore, of the front, including bases, architraves, and gables, may have been, on a rough calculation, from 38 to 40 feet above the stage (assuming that the bases of the row of columns in front rose from the level of the stage—an assumption denied, in his latest pronouncement, by Dörpfeld and also by Schleif, but very likely correct).[4]

5. It seems clear that the columned Hellenistic fronts of the north ends of each of the paraskenia were still preserved (with some possible modification, such as the loss of a column, at the

[1] See Fiechter, iii, p. 25, whose theory in regard to the *scaenae frons* is followed in Fig. 123; and Schleif, l.c., cols. 46, 47, who criticizes some of the details of Fiechter's reconstruction; von Gerkan, l.c., p. 247 also thinks of the *aediculae* as projecting. For the sake of comparison illustrations are given of the Roman fronts of the skené at Ephesus and at Aspendos (Figs. 130 and 131).

[2] *Mélanges Navarre* (1935), pp. 159–67. (His view was also given in 1927 in the *Verhandlungen der 56 Philol. Versammlung in Göttingen*, p. 47, of which no copy appears to be procurable at present in this country.) There seems to be no justification for setting back the upper story in the manner imagined by Dörpfeld, except his anxiety to include a theologeion, the demand for which in Roman times was perhaps not very great.

[3] Dörpfeld and Schleif support their views by a comparison with structures of Imperial times found at Sparta and at Stobi in Macedonia; but there is no real parallelism between the columned front at Athens and the high wall with eleven openings, decorated with columns and with statues standing on the top, which was erected across the theatre at Sparta at a very short distance from the corners of the auditorium. Bulle (*Das Theater zu Sparta*, p. 45) is quite right in saying that this could only form the setting for a play if a special stage were erected against it, hiding its lower portion, much as the later stage is imagined by Dörpfeld and Schleif to have hidden the bases of the columns (see below). But it is clear that at Sparta at this period the whole layout of the theatre scarcely took drama into consideration, and at Stobi (as Bulle, ibid., pp. 46–7 makes clear) the arrangements were entirely calculated for gladiatorial combats, animal shows, &c., not for drama at all. These theatres are in no way comparable to that of Athens.　　　[4] See below, p. 257.

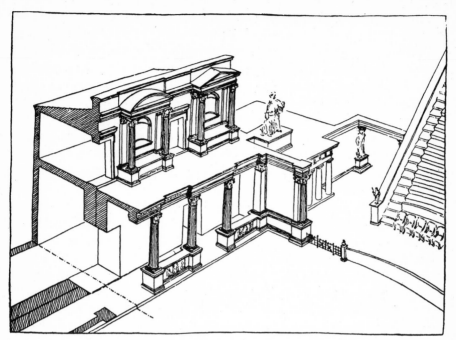

FIG. 128. Skené of Roman period according to Dörpfeld (1935)

FIG. 129. Skené of Roman period according to Schleif

inner extremities), but otherwise the Roman treatment of the paraskenia is quite uncertain.[1] It may be that they were treated as virtually separate structures, forming the bases of colossal statues, somewhat in the manner suggested in the reconstructions of Dörpfeld and Schleif, the space between the paraskenia (and in part beyond them) being enclosed by independent walls some 17 feet long, but this is no more than conjecture.

There may well have been staircases in the paraskenia giving access to the roof of these buildings or to the upper story of the skené, though stairs leading to the latter may have been constructed within the skené itself.

6. There is no clear evidence as to the interior of the skené. Some scholars believe[2] that at some time in the Imperial period, in consequence of the decay of drama proper, the dressing-rooms were done away with, and one continuous hall formed which was used as a promenade and adorned with statues, and that access was given to this by the double gateway in the wall RwQ, with an intermediate doorway at J2.[3] The remains J3 and J4 are conjectured by Fiechter to have been bases for pillars[4] to support the roof of this hall. But it may be argued that the hall, reduced in width by the construction of the wall RV, would not need such supports; and it is perhaps more probable that these bases belong to the Lycurgean skené.[5]

7. It has generally been taken for granted that in front of the *scaenae frons* in the Roman theatre there ran forward a stage (a λογεῖον or *pulpitum*) of the Roman kind, about 5 feet high above the orchestral level, and Dörpfeld in 1896 gave reasons for this

[1] Bulle, op. cit., thinks that as the columns of the Hellenistic paraskenion front which are preserved are not absolutely *in situ* (see above, p. 151), the argument for the continuous preservation of this front into the Roman period is destroyed. The matter must remain uncertain until we know (if ever we shall) what exactly Rousopoulos did about these columns in 1862. (On the whole, it seems most likely that he re-erected them substantially in the proper place.) Bulle adds that the graceful Hellenistic columns would be incongruous with the massive architecture and heavy decorations of the Roman period. But what do we really know of these in connexion with the paraskenia? or of the Romano-Greek sense of congruity? The latter may at least have been not impeccable.

[2] See Bulle, *Untersuch.*, p. 19.

[3] So Bulle, followed by Fiechter, iii, p. 37.

[4] Possibly the pillars shaped as sileni (see p. 264).

[5] See above, p. 149, and Schleif, l.c., col. 41.

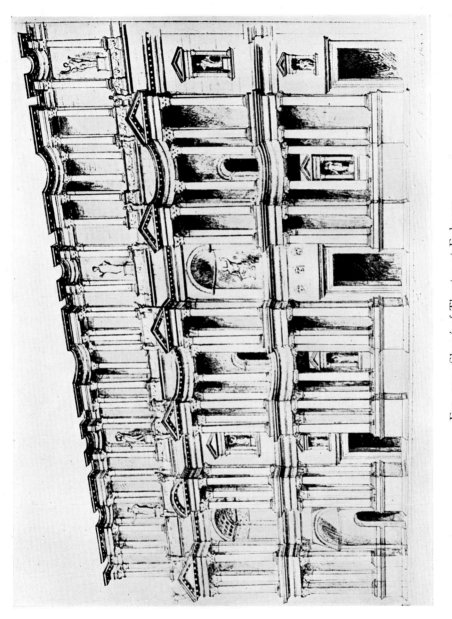

Fig. 130. Skené of Theatre at Ephesus

Fig. 131. Skené of Theatre at Aspendos

FIG. 132. The Bema of Phaedrus (general view)

FIG. 134. Remains of female
figure

FIG. 133. Remains of female figure

FIG. 135. Front of Bema of Phaedrus (1)

FIG. 136. Front of Bema of Phaedrus (2)

belief.[1] A much stronger reason is the improbability of the sup-position that, when reconstructing the theatre on Roman lines as a compliment to Nero, the Athenians should have omitted the stage, which was one of the most important and characteristic elements in all Roman theatres and in Greek theatres influenced by them.[2] But in his last writing on the subject, to which reference has already been made, Dörpfeld's passion for getting rid of the stage everywhere proved too much for him, and Schleif also, his faithful follower, reconstructs the Neronian theatre without one, and with the bases of the front row of columns standing on the level of the orchestra (on the line of the Hellenistic proskenion, strengthened, to bear the additional weight, by the juxtaposition of Ziller's wall T–Y); they suppose that when at some later date a stage was really introduced (of which the north supporting wall was in the position of the bema of Phaedrus) the back of the stage was fitted on to, and of course concealed, the bases on which these columns stood, so that the columns, without their bases, were visible above the stage. But this would have completely destroyed the proportion between the lower and upper stories, nor can it be assumed that this row of columns did in fact run along the line of the Hellenistic proskenion. (The wall T–Y may well have been simply the support of a stage.) Nor does Dörpfeld consider the great improbability of a theatre of the Roman pattern without a stage.

But, assuming that there was such a stage, it cannot be certainly determined whether it at first stretched northwards as far as the line of the later bema of Phaedrus,[3] or only as far as (e.g.) the northern (X–Ψ) of the two walls marked in Ziller's plan. In favour of the latter view is the fact that in the orchestra, reduced in size and surfaced with marble in the course of the Neronian reconstruction, the rhombus of ornamental marbles lies considerably south of the centre of the orchestra as it would be if it

[1] D.R., pp. 86–7. He thinks that the bema of Phaedrus, which is roughly of this height, is likely to have followed the earlier layout in this point; and he argues that the layers of stone forming the inner walls of the paraskenia, which rise above the level of the orchestra, could not possibly have been intended to be seen, and must therefore have been concealed by a logeion. (He may be right in this, but no arguments based on the paraskenia at this period can be considered safe.)

[2] On the two apparent exceptions, Sparta and Stobi, see note on p. 254.

[3] Dörpfeld once thought this probable; see D.R., p. 89.

were bounded by the bema of Phaedrus, and it is hardly likely that it was placed thus uncentrally in the original plan of the reconstruction, whereas, if the orchestra in the Neronian reconstruction ran southwards as far as Ziller's wall (where, it is suggested, the front edge of the stage may have been), the rhombus would have been practically central. In that case the reduction of the orchestra to a semicircle would have been made at some time between Nero and Phaedrus.

The rhombus was decorated with a design of coloured marbles, smaller than those used in the paving of the orchestra generally, and in the middle of the rhombus there is a rectangular slab, with a round depression, probably intended for a small altar.

8. A marble barrier was erected about A.D. 61, or, more probably, somewhat later, round the orchestra, enclosing it completely as far as the parodoi. Its object must have been to protect the spectators of gladiatorial and other shows.[1] At its lowest point, opposite the centre of the front row of thrones, it was 2 ft. 9 in. high, but it rose to about 3 ft. 7½ in. at the points farthest from the prohedria. It was pierced at the foot in places to allow the escape of surface water into the water-channel. This channel was now covered with large marble slabs, which served to enlarge the area of the orchestra; some of them were pierced with rosettes to let water through. A series of small holes, at more or less regular intervals, is found in the pavement edging the orchestra —evidently for the reception of poles, but the date and further purpose of these are unknown.[2]

Various geometrical figures were drawn at some time or other in places on the surface of the orchestra, the most remarkable being a large heptagon overlapping the south-east side of the rhombus. Possibly they were connected with games of some sort.

When at some later date, after the construction of the bema, it was desired to make the orchestra into a watertight basin for

[1] Dio Chrys. xxxi. 121 a speaks of a gladiatorial fight (c. A.D. 100) in which one of the fighters was killed in between the thrones in which the hierophant and others were sitting; cf. Philostratus, *Vit. Apoll.* iv. xxii, where Apollonius is said to have shown his disgust at the popularity of human combats to the death in the theatre. The name κονίστρα as applied to the orchestra (Suid. s.v. σκηνή) may belong to this period; in late Greek writers it is used of the arena in a wrestling school. The barrier round the orchestra can hardly have been there at the time of the incident described by Dio Chrysostom.

[2] Fiechter, i, pp. 60, 61.

'sea-fights', the water-channel was blocked, the rosettes were closed or the slabs through which they were pierced were removed, the holes at the foot of the marble barrier were stopped, and the bema itself made watertight in the manner to be described below.

9. This 'bema of Phaedrus', as it has always been called after the inscription which he erected, is preserved only to the extent of half its length, and in a condition which shows that it has undergone many alterations. As it is, its northern face, which is about 4 ft. 9 in. high, consists of a continuous foundation upon which rests a wall of poros forming the background of four groups of figures in relief, divided by intervals or niches, in one of which a crouching silenus has been forcibly fitted. Above are the remains of a heavy cornice, and the figures in the reliefs have been decapitated to make them fit under this. At the east end of the existing structure (i.e. in the original centre of the front) is a set of four stone steps, of which the uppermost bears an inscription recording the dedication of 'this noble bema' to Dionysus by Phaedrus:

Σοὶ τόδε καλὸν ἔτευξε, φιλόργιε, βῆμα θεήτρου
Φαῖδρος Ζωίλου βιοδώτορος Ἀτθίδος ἀρχός.

Phaedrus is otherwise unknown, and the date of the inscription is doubtful; Dittenberger says that the letters show that it is later than Hadrian, and it is variously placed from the end of the second to the end of the fourth century A.D.

All are agreed that the stone with its inscription did not originally belong to this place, so that the bema which Phaedrus erected was not the bema as it now is, but a predecessor or an earlier state of it. Indeed it seems inconceivable that anyone should claim credit for the erection of a row of decapitated or otherwise mutilated figures. The natural supposition would be that he erected a bema faced by a fine series of reliefs, and that some vandals of a later generation, desiring a somewhat lower structure, cut them all down. The occasion of this mutilation and the rebuilding of the wall was doubtless the enclosure of the orchestra as a watertight basin. In 1862 Rousopoulos[1] found the figures plastered over with cement, and the traces of a reddish cement are still to be seen in places on the wall, as well as beneath

[1] Ἐφ. Ἀρχ., 1862, col. 210.

some immediately adjacent parts of the orchestra. (The marble pavement of the orchestra had already been broken up in front of the wall to facilitate the building of the bema in its first state, and replaced by coarser materials.) The same cement appears on the barrier between the orchestra and the auditorium ; and the barrier was now strengthened for its new purpose.

10. The careful examinations of the bema which have been made—the latest and most thorough by Fiechter—show that it consists of three distinct walls, of which the one carrying the reliefs was later than the middle one. The latter was probably the original, and if the Neronian stage came as far forward as this (which may not have been the case), this wall must have been of Neronian date ; if not, it must belong to some date after Nero. With this middle wall are closely connected a series of nine small shafts of brickwork (indicated in Fig. 123), sunk into the ground and intended for the reception of posts forming part of the apparatus for operating a great curtain, such as was also used in other theatres of the Imperial period.[1] Behind the middle wall (i.e. against its south surface) is a third and later wall, which was evidently intended to strengthen the whole structure when it was required to become watertight and which blocked up the curtain-shafts. (One of the slabs from the orchestral channel, pierced by a rosette, was found built into this wall.)

We can thus with some probability trace three stages in the history of the bema :

(1) The original—now the middle—wall of Neronian or (more probably) post-Neronian date,[2] and with it the brick shafts for use in connexion with the curtain.

(2) The bema of Phaedrus, in which the original wall was hidden by a new wall against which the reliefs stood (probably brought from elsewhere) ; these reliefs being then complete and the whole structure somewhat higher than it is at present (as also the original wall may have been).

---

[1] Fiechter, iii, p. 79, thinks that the space (about 8 feet wide) between the bema and Ziller's wall, the floor of which was lower than the orchestra by about 1 ft. 7 in., and into which the shafts descended, was a channel into which the curtain was lowered when not in use, as in some other theatres, but that it was boarded over when necessary.

[2] von Gerkan, l.c., p. 245 states dogmatically that the brick 'curtain-shafts' cannot possibly be later than Nero, but does not say why.

Of what materials the cornice at this stage was composed it is impossible to say.

(3) The adaptation of the bema to form part of a water-tight basin, the figures being cut down and covered up with cement, and the whole structure lowered to a height of about 4 ft. 9 in. The present cornice was used in front—it can hardly have been the original one—and the back part of the wall was covered at the top with slabs brought from else-where. The small staircase belongs to the same date, the stone bearing Phaedrus' inscription being used as a top step.

The dates and many of the details of these changes remain very obscure; about most of them no two archaeologists agree, and the evidence is too defective to allow of much profitable discussion. Bulle conjures up to his aid an earthquake which, he supposes, shattered the Neronian stage-buildings and caused some of its stones to be used to cover the bema. It would cer-tainly be wrong to connect Phaedrus' employment of the word βῆμα rather than λογεῖον with the decay of dramatic performances such as would require a λογεῖον, and to assume that there was no stage behind the βῆμα. There are a number of instances in which a stage is called βῆμα.[1]

East of the four steps only the foundations of the bema exist, but Fiechter's excavations in front of them showed that the oval basin in which Bulle[2] thought he had traced these never existed. He found, however, in front of the bema various remains of drainage arrangements rendered necessary by the disuse of the channel round the orchestra.

11. The reliefs with which the bema is adorned have been the subject of a special study by R. Herbig,[3] who, after careful examination of the characteristics of the figures and the composi-tion of the groups decides that they are Attic work of about the middle of the second century A.D. The belief held by some scholars that they were of earlier date rested mainly on the quite unproved suggestion of Wolters that the figure on the left hand

---

[1] e.g. Plut. *Phoc.* 34; *C.I.G.* (Boeckh) 2681; Hesych. s.v. βῆμα.

[2] *Untersuch.*, p. 23.

[3] In the second volume of Fiechter's *Das Dionysos-Theater in Athen*. He makes some use of A. B. Cook's study of the reliefs in *Zeus*, vol. i, pp. 708 ff., though not accepting all the latter's restorations. See also Dörpfeld and Reisch, pp. 88–9.

of one group, which has been carefully removed, must have been that of Nero in the guise of Apollo (to whom Nero liked to be compared), and that its removal coincided with the erasure of Nero's name on the *scaenae frons*. Herbig, on the other hand, lays stress on the fact that the slab on which the relief stood was also carefully removed with it—a mere agent of vengeance upon Nero would not have needed to do this—and believes that the figure was taken away by someone who stole it as an artistic treasure at some later date, and that fragments of it are to be found in portions of a draped female figure partly in the National Museum at Athens, and partly among the ruins of the theatre itself (Figs. 133, 134).

The reliefs were, as is generally agreed, brought to the bema from elsewhere, though there is no certainty as to their original use. Svoronos[1] regards them as originally the four sides of an altar, but Herbig gives reason for thinking that they were originally intended to be seen from below and at a greater distance from the eye than the sides of a thymele (Figs. 135 to 138).

The subjects of the four groups appear to be:

I. Zeus seated, Hermes with the infant Dionysus, and two Kouretes (one on each side), who had been present at the infant's birth.

II. Dionysus clad in chiton, panther-skin, and kothornoi; Ikarios, accompanied by his hound, bringing a goat to be sacrificed; his daughter Erigone with a dish of cakes and fruit, and on the other side a satyr.

III.[2] The marriage of Dionysus and the Basilinna at Athens, with Tyche carrying a cornucopia. The left-hand figure, which has been cut away, may have been Eros (as Cook suggests), but not Nero; or it may have been the figure of Figs. 133–4.

IV. Enthronement of Dionysus in the theatre (with the Acropolis rock in the background); his bride, the Basilinna; Theseus, the representative of Athens, and Tyche.

In two of the niches in the bema were huge crouching sileni, which formed a pair: one of them is fairly well preserved; it was obviously not intended for its present position, and the stones on

[1] *Reliefs des Athen. Nat. Mus.* (1908), pp. 232 ff.

[2] Cook, l.c., p. 709, gives good reasons against earlier explanations of III and IV.

which and against which it rests were cut away to admit of its being forced into place. It is uncertain what they carried on their shoulders in their unmutilated condition and original position.

12. The history of the *Auditorium* in the Imperial epoch is affected by the uncertainty which besets that of the rows of thrones which form its most striking feature. Reasons have been given in Chapter IV for thinking that these, or some of the most remarkable of them, are copies, made from the first century B.C. onwards, of fourth-century originals, and some of these, like the inscriptions on them, probably date from Imperial times. A number of special seats or thrones for officials or benefactors were erected from time to time in different parts of the auditorium, as well as statues, of which several of the bases are preserved. One, behind the throne of the priest of Dionysus, bore a statue of Hadrian, who attended the Dionysia in A.D. 126, and another and smaller basis on the east side of the auditorium also bears an inscription describing him as Αὐτοκράτορα Καίσαρα Θεοῦ Τραϊανοῦ. Dedications also exist to Trajan and Marcus Aurelius. The purpose of a large erection, which seems to be some kind of platform, with a special set of steps leading to it, to the east of the throne of the priest of Dionysus, is unknown. A number of inscriptions reserving seats for priests of the several emperors are preserved.

It appears that awnings supported on wooden posts were erected to shelter the front rows from the heat of the sun; two parallel rows of sockets for these posts can be traced. The awnings may (as Dörpfeld suggests) have been steeply sloped, so as not to interrupt the view of the orchestra and stage from the rows of seats above them.

13. The remains of a number of statues or sculptured figures of imperial date have been found among the ruins of the theatre. Perhaps the most striking are those of a pair of statues which Bulle regards as Muses, Herbig, with some probability, as personifications of Tragedy and Comedy (Figs. 139 and 140). There are remains of three other colossal draped figures,[1] the correct reconstruction of which and their original position in the theatre

---

[1] Fiechter[2] (Herbig), p. 33. Dörpfeld, *Mélanges Navarre*, p. 160, speaks of colossal statues of Dionysus and Nero as having been found to right and left of the proskenion and having probably stood on the paraskenia, but it is not clear upon what evidence.

are uncertain. (Bulle[1] conjectures that two of them stood in the parodoi.) There is part of a colossal silenus in the attitude of Atlas, which is variously dated from the fourth century B.C.[2] to the time of Hadrian.[3] A date in Imperial times seems most likely. Besides another relic of a colossal weight-carrying silenus, there are remains of series of from four to eight smaller sileni (Fig. 141), which may be of Neronian date, but may be of the Hadrianic or Antonine periods. Herbig[4] conjectures that there may have been several pairs of similar figures included in this series. What were the burdens which the weight-carrying figures bore is quite unknown.[5]

14. Of the history of the theatre after the reconstruction of the bema and the conversion of the orchestra into a pond—perhaps late in the third or early in the fourth century—there is little to be said. It fell gradually into disuse and decay. In the Middle Ages even its site was unknown, and it was not rediscovered before Chandler's visit in 1765. In the nineteenth century the Turks built a fortification-wall across it, using many of the stones of the theatre for the purpose.[6] It was not until 1862 that serious excavations were undertaken; these were suspended after about three years; a little more was done in 1877, and in 1886 Dörpfeld began his great work, which he continued from time to time until his death. But in spite of all that has been done by Bulle, Fiechter, and others, there is still much that requires a thorough-going examination, and such examination may well modify many of the views expressed in this volume.

---

[1] *Untersuch.*, p. 18.　　　　　　[2] e.g. by Bulle, op. cit., pp. 238–9.
[3] Herbig in Fiechter, ii, p. 9.　　　[4] Herbig, l.c., pp. 11–13, 35.
[5] It is impossible to say how far the practice of erecting statues of poets in the theatre was continued into the Roman period. We have seen that in the fourth century statues were erected of Aeschylus, Sophocles, Euripides, and Astydamas, and early in the third century a statue of Menander was added—the work of Kephisodotos and Timarchos, sons of Praxiteles (I. G. ii, 1370). The statues of Sophocles and Euripides were seen by Pausanias (i. xxi. 1), as well as those of other tragic and comic poets, mostly undistinguished; of the comic poets none of the more famous was represented except Menander; cf. also Dio Chrys. xxxi. 116.
[6] Rousopoulos, l.c., col. 214.

FIG. 137. Front of Bema of Phaedrus (3)

FIG. 138. Front of Bema of Phaedrus (4)

Fig. 139. Statues of Tragedy and Comedy (?) (2)

Fig. 140. Statues of Tragedy and Comedy (?) (1)

FIG. 141. Silenus of Roman period

VII

SUMMARY

THE reader who has persevered so far may be glad of a summary of the principal results of the preceding chapters.

1. The history of the theatre of Dionysus at Athens begins with an orchestra placed on a terrace banked up on its south side by a curved wall, of which only the fragment SM 1 remains. Below this terrace wall and between it and the Older (but then comparatively new) Temple of Dionysus a curving road or path led up to the western edge of the orchestra. The spectators of performances at first stood or sat on the same level as the orchestra itself, or took advantage of the slope of the hill above it; but by the beginning of the fifth century it is probable that wooden stands carried seats for them. An accident to these stands—or possibly to similar erections in the agora—probably early in the century, caused the Athenians to replace these by earthen embankments accommodated to the hill-side, though still with wooden seats or benches, and these continued to suffice for them for many years. At first there was no skené or 'stage building', and the stage properties were of the simplest—an altar, a tomb, a plain background with a single doorway; but the later plays of Aeschylus and the plays of Sophocles, who began to produce some years before Aeschylus' death, called for something more elaborate, and it is probable that at least by about 460 B.C. backgrounds representing a palace or a temple were provided in stock sets, mainly of wood and canvas, and that these were terminated at either end by projecting wings or paraskenia. At the same time some amount of scene-painting came into vogue; the name of Agatharchus is connected with this. Conventional backgrounds must also have been provided for satyric drama and comedy.

2. The latter half of the fifth century, from the time of the building of the Odeum of Pericles onwards, appears to have been a time of great activity in connexion with the theatre. It appears that the orchestra was moved northwards, and the front lines of the auditorium were correspondingly retracted; the auditorium was banked up afresh, with a steeper slope, and its eastern boundary adapted to the western side of the Odeum. Probably

arrangements for the drainage of the orchestra and auditorium were made at the same time. The seats for the spectators were still for the most part of wood, though a partial use of stone in the auditorium cannot be entirely ruled out. The steeper auditorium required strong stone walls to contain it, and these were apparently executed by degrees; the building of the double wall on the western side may have been spread over many years; of the south walls, the westernmost (a A in the Plans) was not quite symmetrical with that to the east of the centre, but appears not to have been altered until some date in the next century. The 'Periclean' period also saw the replacement of the old curved terrace wall behind the orchestra by a new, long, and straight wall, calculated to hold up the mass of earth constituting the extended terrace. This wall was probably low at first, but in its northern surface were grooves for the reception of strong wooden posts, which were doubtless of great service (together with others, of which all traces have now disappeared, at a convenient distance to the north of them) in upholding an improved skené or stage building of wood. It may safely be conjectured that all the scenic arrangements were now made more elaborate, as the plays of Sophocles, Euripides, and Aristophanes and their contemporaries demanded, though we have no indication of their actual character except from the plays themselves. These suggest the existence of a series of conventional 'sets', at the same time admitting of considerable variation for the different kinds of play. There can be little doubt that there were projecting paraskenia enclosing the actors' domain on either side, but the evidence for a prothyron or porch, standing out in front of the central doorway and regularly found in backgrounds representing a palace or temple, breaks down on examination. Frequent use was made of what seem now to be somewhat crude devices, such as the μηχανή and γέρανος, for transporting gods and heroes through the air, but it is very uncertain whether what was termed the ἐκκύκλημα—a platform on wheels, rolling out of a doorway to show either an interior scene or its consequences— belongs to this period. The evidence of the plays is strongly against the supposition that a raised stage was employed in the Classical age, though temples, palaces, and altars would naturally stand above one or two broad steps, of which advantage would be taken for dramatic purposes.

The plays suggest that the stage building in the set representing a palace or houses was normally of two stories, and that the upper may have been slightly set back and may have afforded room for actors to pass in front of it and round its sides. The set representing a temple as its central feature may well have had a gabled pediment. In either set the appearance of gods above the roof may have been contrived by means of a special θεολογεῖον, though there is nothing to show exactly what it was like, nor how much of the platform composing it, as distinct from the figure or figures on it, was visible.

The 'Periclean' reconstruction was completed—though by what date is uncertain—by the building of a hall or stoa, with an open colonnade on its south side, along the whole length of the terrace wall, and with free access between the skené and the hall by a staircase leading from the former (which was on the level of the orchestra) to the floor of the latter about 8 feet below. The terrace wall and the hall ran parallel to the Later Temple of Dionysus, which dates probably from the last third of the fifth century. It seems evident that these buildings all belong to the same plan.

3. It is not improbable that the reconstruction of the greater part of the theatre which is commonly associated with the name of Lycurgus had been going on for many years before he completed it, probably about 330 B.C. (Attempts to limit the period during which this would have been possible on the ground of political conditions and military necessities are not convincing; Athenian statesmen spent money in any ways which they thought would please the people, and the importance attached to the payment of 'theoric money' is some indication that the theatre was a very popular institution.) The special work of Lycurgus may have been the building, or completion, of the stone auditorium, large portions of which are still to be seen to-day; and, as connected with this, the removal of the orchestra a short distance farther northward, and the rebuilding of the westernmost of the two south walls of the auditorium on the line marked wA in our Plans. The double supporting wall of the auditorium on the western side, with its buttresses, was probably completed as part of the same series of operations. The drainage of the orchestra by means of the existing circular channel and the paving of the passage between the channel and the front row of

seats must also belong to this time, and it is likely that the seats of honour, or 'thrones', which are still to be seen, had their predecessors (probably very like them) in the Lycurgean theatre.

Of equal importance, and possibly prior in time to the building of the auditorium, was the building of a permanent skené in stone in place of the movable wooden buildings with which the Periclean age had been content. The breccia foundations of this and of the paraskenia which projected some 16 ft. 6 in. from the front line of the skené at either end are easily traceable, but there is little agreement as to the character either of the interior of the skené, or of the *scaenae frons* (the façade of the skené), except that this façade must have been pierced by three doorways. It is probable that the northern end and the inner sides of the paraskenia were columned, and that two of the columns are those which are still partly preserved, though not in their original position. What exactly was the nature of the buildings which flanked the paraskenia on their outer sides is very uncertain. The attempt to prove that there was at this period a proskenion of wood, at some distance to the north of the *scaenae frons* and supporting a wooden stage, must be pronounced unsuccessful, and plays doubtless continued to be acted on the orchestral level before the *scaenae frons*, which was adapted for the needs of special plays by the use of screens, curtains, and other devices, to any of which the name προσκήνιον may have been applied.

4. But the time came when the intimate association of the chorus with the action of the play, both in tragedy and in comedy, was weakened and came to an end; and there was no longer any reason to refuse the actors, on whom the interest of the audience was now wholly concentrated, the advantage of a stage raised above the level of the orchestra, or to refuse the audience (and particularly the spectators in the more remote seats) the improved conditions of vision which were negligible when the chorus in the orchestra was important and the auditorium was smaller. (In some of the theatres which, from the latter part of the fourth century onwards, were springing up all over the Greek world, there may have been a raised stage for actors from the first.) So there came into existence the Hellenistic theatre at Athens, in which there was a high stage, supported in front by the columned stone proskenion of which the foundation is still traceable. The northern façade of the paraskenia was retracted by over 6 feet,

so that they projected only slightly in front of the proskenion and incidentally left room for wider parodoi, giving better access to the auditorium. Henceforth the play was acted on the stage (with or without choral interludes in the orchestra), the *scaenae frons* being so far modified that what for dramatic purposes was the ground story, with three or more doorways, rose from the back of the stage, and a second story was (or could be, if required) erected above this. Of the details of the *scaenae frons* and the interior of the skené in the Hellenistic theatre at Athens there is no evidence. In some other theatres during this period there appear to have been five or even more broad openings or thyromata in the background, some of which could be filled with painted scenery[1] or could afford a view into the interior of the building, where the play required it, and the familiar resources for the purpose of scenic variation, the use of screens, curtains, &c., doubtless continued to be available, while new devices, such as the περίακτοι, came into use in some theatres. (Nothing is explicitly said about their use at Athens.)

About the date when the all-important change, the introduction of the raised stage, was made, whether at Athens or elsewhere, there is no agreement; but there is at least some probability that at Athens the change is to be placed not long before the middle of the second century B.C., a date which may be considerably later than that at which action on a high stage had become the practice in some other Greek theatres. There is no sufficient reason for thinking that at Athens the play was ever acted (after the erection of such a stage) in front of the proskenion —except possibly in some revivals of choral tragedy, and even this is very uncertain—or that the proskenion itself was made into a scenic background, as some have supposed, by the fitting into it of movable pinakes or painted panels. At Athens itself there is no trace of any provision for the fixing of these, and elsewhere they may have carried geometrical and purely decorative, rather than scenic, designs. Moreover, even if at Athens the proskenion was high enough to serve as a scenic background without ludicrous or improbable effects, there are very few other theatres in which it was so. It is impossible to form any detailed

---

[1] But the attempt to infer the nature of this scenery and the structure of the Hellenistic *scaenae frons* from wall-paintings in Rome and Pompeii is not successful.

picture of the performances of tragedy, comedy, and satyric drama, or of scenes from each, by the 'Artists of Dionysus', whose companies, local and travelling, appear to have monopolized the theatres of the Greek world in the Hellenistic age; but they were evidently very different from the fully choral performance of the Classical epoch.

5. The conjecture that the invasion of Sulla, which resulted in the destruction of the Odeum and its rebuilding some twenty years later by Ariobarzanes of Cappadocia, may have in some way affected the theatre, appears to have no solid support, and there is no definite evidence of reconstruction before the time of Nero, when the skené and the stage were rebuilt, probably by Ti. Claudius Novius; the work was completed in A.D. 61. In the preceding two hundred years there may have been many changes, but they have left no trace. The foundations of the Neronian skené and paraskenia exist, and they indicate that the Lycurgean building (with the possible exception of some parts of the paraskenia adjacent to them) was entirely removed; the new *scaenae frons* was probably somewhat longer than the old, and included two stories decorated with porch-like structures projecting to a distance which cannot be exactly determined, but less ornamental than in many theatres of the Roman period.[1] In front of this there was a stage of the Roman type, perhaps about five feet high, and extending northwards at least as far as the wall marked X–Ψ in Ziller's plan. The orchestra, which probably met the stage at this point and was relaid in marble with ornate designs, was smaller than that of the Lycurgean and Hellenistic theatre, and later was still further curtailed (and the stage probably extended) by the erection between the corners of the auditorium of the wall which, after an interval estimated at from one and a half to three centuries, developed into the bema of Phaedrus. At some period in its history this bema came to include arrangements for the raising and lowering of a great curtain, as in many Roman theatres. The building of a marble barrier round the orchestra at some time in the Roman period was doubtless designed to protect the occupants of the thrones from accidents arising out of the more violent types of performance by which the orchestra had now come to be desecrated.

Then there came a time when it was desired to convert the

[1] Of the internal structure of the skené nothing certain can be known.

orchestra, when required, into a watertight basin for the presentation of sea-fights. The outlets of water into the circular channel were closed, and the bema of Phaedrus strengthened and cemented over and its fine reliefs mutilated and covered with cement.

In the course of the Roman Imperial epoch various minor changes had taken place in the auditorium. Some of the existing thrones belong to this period, though they may reproduce with little alteration the work of the fourth century B.C. New seats of honour were added and monuments dedicated to popular emperors. But there is no sign of any great structural changes. After about the beginning of the fourth century A.D. the history of the theatre is virtually blank until the nineteenth century, and much of it still remains to be rediscovered.

BIBLIOGRAPHY

This Bibliography does not profess to be complete, and I have omitted many writings which appeared to contribute little of value to the discussion of questions raised in this volume. The entries are grouped roughly according to their subjects, but no exact classification is possible. I have not as a rule gone further back than 1896, when the great work of Dörpfeld and Reisch was published, which is the necessary starting-point of all modern discussions of the Greek Theatre. A brief account of the literature from 1896 to 1930 is given by Fensterbusch in Bursian's *Jahresbericht*, Bd. 227 (1930), pt. iii, pp. 1–95.

A

E. A. GARDNER, *Ancient Athens*. 1902.

W. JUDEICH, *Topographie von Athen*, ed. ii. 1930.

P. GRAINDOR, *Athènes de Tibère à Trajan*. 1931.

B

A. S. ROUSOPOULOS, *Ἐφημερὶς Ἀρχαιολογική*, 1862. A series of articles on excavations in the theatre.

A. MÜLLER, *Lehrbuch der griechischen Bühnenalterthümer*. 1886.

W. DÖRPFELD und E. REISCH, *Das griechische Theater*. 1896.

E. BETHE, *Prolegomena zur Geschichte des griechischen Theaters*. 1896.

A. MÜLLER, *Untersuchungen zu den Bühnenaltertümern*. 1899.

O. PUCHSTEIN, *Die griechische Bühne*. 1901.

A. MÜLLER, *Das attische Bühnenwesen*. 1902.

E. BODENSTEINER, *Das antike Theater*. 1902.

A. E. HAIGH, *The Attic Theatre* (revised and partly rewritten by A. W. PICKARD-CAMBRIDGE). 1907.

O. NAVARRE, art. 'Theatrum' in Daremberg et Saglio, *Dict. des Antiquités*, v. i, pp. 178–205. 1913.

E. FIECHTER, *Die baugeschichtliche Entwicklung des griechischen Theaters*. 1914. (Review by C. Robert, *Deutsch. Littztg.* xxx (1915), cols. 1164–75.)

F. NOACK, *Σκηνὴ Τραγική*. 1915.

A. FRICKENHAUS, *Die altgriechische Bühne*. 1917.
> (Reviews by W. Dörpfeld in *Woch. Klass. Phil.*, 1917, and by A. Körte in *Götting. gelehrt. Anzeigen*, 1920.)

J. T. ALLEN, *The Greek Theater of the Fifth Century*. 1919.

M. BIEBER, *Denkmäler zum Theaterwesen im Altertum*. 1920.

O. NAVARRE, *Le Théâtre grec*. 1925.

A. FRICKENHAUS, art. 'Skene' in Pauly–Wissowa, *Real-Encycl.* III A, i. 1927.

J. T. ALLEN, *Stage Antiquities of the Greeks and Romans and Their Influence.*
1927.

H. BULLE, *Untersuchungen an griechischen Theatern.* 1928.

C. FENSTERBUSCH, *Das Theater im Altertum.* 1930.

TH. BIRT, *Die Schaubauten der Griechen und die attische Tragödie.* 1931.

C. FENSTERBUSCH, art. 'Theatron' in Pauly–Wissowa, *Real-Encycl.* v, A ii.
1934.

E. FIECHTER, *Das Theater in Athen,* i, ii, iii. 1935–6.
(Review by A. von Gerkan in *Gnomon* xiv (1938), pp. 236–46.)

R. FLICKINGER, *The Greek Theater,* ed. iv. 1936.

H. SCHLEIF, 'Die Baugeschichte des Dionysostheaters in Athen', in *Jahrb.
Arch.* lii (1937), *Anz.,* cols. 26–51.

M. BIEBER, *History of the Greek and Roman Theater.* 1939.

C

The articles grouped together in this section belong mostly to the contro-
versial literature provoked by the work of Dörpfeld and Reisch (1896).

B. GRAEF, review of Dörpfeld and Reisch in *Woch. Klass. Phil.* 1897,
cols. 816–30.

E. BETHE, ditto, in *Gött. gel. Anz.* 1897, pp. 704–28.

A. MÜLLER, ditto, in *Berl. Philol. Woch.* 1897, cols. 1089–100, 1121–31.

C. ROBERT, 'Zur Theaterfrage', in *Hermes* xxxii (1897), pp. 421–53.

W. DÖRPFELD, 'Das griechische Theater Vitruvs', in *Ath. Mitt.* xxii
(1897), pp. 439–62.

E. BETHE, 'Das griechische Theater Vitruvs', in *Hermes* xxxiii (1898),
pp. 313–23.

W. DÖRPFELD, 'Das griechische Theater Vitruvs', in *Ath. Mitt.* xxiii
(1898), pp. 326–53.

F. GROH, 'Beiträge zur Geschichte des griechischen Theaters', in *Woch.
Klass. Phil.* 1897, cols. 1073–5; 1898, cols. 236–8, 549–50.

W. DÖRPFELD, 'Die optischen Verhältnisse des griechischen Theaters', in
Ath. Mitt. xxiv (1899), pp. 310–20.

A. MÜLLER, 'Noch einmal die Sehverhältnisse im Dionysos-Theater', in
Philolog. xii (1899), pp. 329–43.

F. NOACK, 'Das Proskenion in der Theaterfrage', ibid., pp. 1–24.

E. BETHE, 'Die hellenistische Bühne und ihre Dekorationen', in *Jahrb.
Arch.* xv (1900), pp. 59–81.

W. DÖRPFELD, 'Die vermeintliche Bühne des hellenistischen Theaters',
ibid. xvi (1906), pp. 22–37.

A. FURTWÄNGLER, 'Zum Dionysostheater in Athen', in *Sitzber. Bayr.
Akad. München* (1901), pp. 411–16.

J. Frei, *De certaminibus thymelicis.* 1900.

E. Bethe, 'Thymeliker und Skeniker', in *Hermes* xxxvi (1901), pp. 597–601.

W. Dörpfeld, 'Thymele und Skene', ibid. xxxvii (1902), pp. 249–57.

W. Dörpfeld, 'Die griechische Bühne', in *Ath. Mitt.* xxviii (1903), pp. 383–436.

K. Weissmann, *Die szenischen Anweisungen in den Scholien.* 1896.

R. Flickinger, *The Meaning of ἐπὶ τῆς σκηνῆς in Writers of the Fourth Century.* 1902.

——, *Plutarch as a Source of Information on the Greek Theater.* 1904.

O. Scherling, *De vocis σκηνή quantum ad theatrum pertinet significatione et usu.* 1906.

L. Pschor, Σκηνὴ μὲν ὑποκριτῶν ἴδιον, ἡ δὲ ὀρχήστρα τοῦ χοροῦ. 1908.

R. Flickinger, 'Scaenica', in *Trans. Amer. Phil. Ass.* xl (1910), pp. 109–20.

C. Fensterbusch, 'Σκηνή bei Pollux', in *Hermes* lx (1925), p. 112.

E. Petersen, 'Nachlese in Athen, IV. Das Theater des Dionysos', in *Jahrb. Arch.* xxiii (1908), pp. 33–44.

F. Versakis, 'Das Skenengebaüde des Dionysos-Theaters', ibid. xxiv (1909), pp. 194–224.

W. Dörpfeld, 'Zum Dionysos-Theater in Athen', ibid., pp. 224–6.

——, 'Über das Theater in Ephesos', ibid. xxviii (1913), *Anz.*, cols. 37–42.

——, 'Zur baugeschichtlichen Entwicklung des antiken Theatergebäudes', ibid. xxx (1915), *Anz.*, cols. 93–105.

Bijvanck, 'De theatro antiquo' in *Mnemosyne* xlviii (1920), pp. 122–51.

J. T. Allen, *The Key to the Reconstruction of the Fifth-century Theater at Athens.* 1918.

——, *The Orchestra Terrace of the Æschylean Theater.* 1922.

——, *Problems of the Proskenion.* 1923.

W. Dörpfeld, 'Das Theater von Priene und die griechische Bühne', in *Ath. Mitt.* xlix (1924), pp. 50–101.

——, 'Die im Januar 1925 im Dionysos-Theater in Athen untergenommenen Ausgrabungen', in Πρακτικά (1925), pp. 25–32.

R. Flickinger, 'Some Problems in Scenic Antiquities', in *Philol. Quarterly* v (1926), pp. 97–113.

K. Lehmann-Hartleben, 'Zum griechischen Theater', in *Jahrb. Arch.* xlii (1927), pp. 30–40.

W. Dörpfeld, in *Verhandlungen der 56. Philol. Versammlung in Göttingen,* 1927, pp. 47 ff.

C. Fensterbusch, 'Die baugeschichtliche Entwicklung des athenischen Dionysos-Theater im V. Jahrhundert', in *Philolog.* lxxv (1930), pp. 229–42.

W. Dörpfeld, 'Das Proskenion Kaisers Nero im Dionysos-Theater', in *Mélanges Navarre* (1935), pp. 159–67.

D

E. Capps, 'The Greek Stage according to the Ancient Dramas', in *Trans. Amer. Phil. Ass.* xxii (1891), pp. 5 ff.

N. Terzaghi, *Fabula*. 1911.

R. Engelmann, *Archäologische Studien zu den Tragikern*. 1900.

E. Petersen, *Die attische Tragödie als Bild- und Bühnenkunst*. 1915.

C. Robert, 'Die Szenerie des Aias, der Eirene und des Prometheus', in *Hermes* xxxi (1896), pp. 530 ff.

J. Hampel, *Was lehrt Aischylos' Orestie für die Theaterfrage?* 1899.

L. Bolle, *Die Bühne des Aischylos*. 1906.

F. Weise, *Zur Frage der Bühnenaufführung des äschyleïschen Prometheus*. 1908.

E. Bethe, 'Der Spielplatz des Aischylos', in *Hermes* lix (1924), pp. 108–17.

W. Schmid, *Untersuchungen zum gefesselten Prometheus*. 1929.

R. Flickinger, 'The Theater of Æschylus', in *Trans. Amer. Phil. Ass.* lxi (1930), pp. 80–110.

T. Musenides, *Aischylos und sein Theater*. 1937.

L. Bolle, *Die Bühne des Sophokles*. 1902.

W. J. Woodhouse, 'The Scenic Arrangements of the Philoctetes', in *J.H.S.* xxxii (1912), pp. 241–9.

T. von Wilamowitz-Moellendorff, *Die dramatische Technik des Sophokles*. 1917.

A. Müller, 'Szenisches zu Euripides' Kresphontes', in *Berl. Phil. Woch.* (1900), cols. 187–9.

J. W. White, 'The Stage in Aristophanes', in *Harvard Studies* ii (1891), pp. 159–205.

K. Zacher, 'Die erhöhte Bühne bei Aristophanes', in *Philolog.* lv (1896), pp. 181–5.

A. Müller, 'Szenisches zu Aristophanes' Wolken', in *Berl. Phil. Woch.* (1900), cols. 923–5.

E. F. Krause, *Quaestiones Aristophaneae Scaenicae*. 1903.

C. Fensterbusch, *Die Bühne des Aristophanes*. 1912.

A. Müller, 'Der Schauplatz ·in Aristophanes' Wespen', in *Philolog.* lxxii (1913), pp. 442–4.

W. Schmid, 'Bemerkungen zu Aristophanes' Froschen', ibid. lxxvi (1920), pp. 220–4.

R. Flickinger, 'The Staging of Aristophanes' Pax', in *Mélanges Navarre* (1935), pp. 191–205.

P. E. Legrand, *Daos*. 1910.

R. GRAF, *Szenische Untersuchungen zu Menander*. 1914.

C. O. DALMAN, *De aedibus scaenicis Novae Comoediae*. 1929.

A. LESKY, 'Die Theophoroumene und die Bühne Menanders', in *Hermes* lxxii (1937), pp. 123–7.

E. CAPPS, 'The Chorus in the Later Greek Drama, with reference to the Stage-question', in *Amer. J. Arch.* x (1895), pp. 287–325.

A. KÖRTE, 'Das Fortleben des Chors im griechischen Drama', in *Neue Jahrb.* (1900), pp. 81–9.

K. J. MAIDMENT, 'The Later Comic Chorus', in *Class. Quart.* 1935, pp. 1–24.

[Discussions of problems connected with the staging of plays are to be found in the most important editions of many plays.]

E

P. GARDNER, 'The Scenery of the Greek Stage', in *J.H.S.* xix (1899), pp. 252–64.

A. S. GOW, 'On the Meaning of the Word Θυμέλη', ibid. xxxii (1912), pp. 213–38.

A. KÖRTE, 'Die Exostra des griechischen Theaters', in *Rhein. Mus.* lii (1897), pp. 333–7.

C. EXON, 'A New Theory of the Ekkyklema', in *Hermathena* xi (1900), pp. 132–43.

E. BETHE, 'Ekkyklema und Thyroma', ibid. lxiii (1934), pp. 21–38.

M. P. NILSSON, 'Die alte Bühne und die Periakten', in *Från Filologiska Foreningen i Lund.* 1908.

K. REES, 'The Significance of the Parodoi in the Greek Theater', in *Amer. J. Phil.* xxxii (1911), pp. 377–402.

——, 'The Function of the Prothyron in the Production of Greek Plays', in *Class. Phil.* x (1915), pp. 117–38.

W. W. MOONEY, *The House Door of the Ancient Stage*. 1914.

A. FRICKENHAUS, art. 'ἰκρίον', in Pauly–Wissowa, *Real-Encycl.* ix, i. 1914.

O. BRONEER, 'The ΟΧΕΤΟΣ in the Greek Theater', in *Class. Studies presented to E. Capps*, pp. 29–41. 1936.

A. B. COOK, *Zeus* i, pp. 708–11. (On the Bema of Phaedrus.)

A. PHILADELPHEUS, 'Ἀνασκαφὴ παρὰ τὸ Λυσικρατεῖον μνημεῖον', in 'Εφημ. 'Αρχ. 1921, pp. 85–97.

P. KASTRIOTIS, 'Περικλεῖον ᾠδεῖον', ibid. 1922, pp. 25–38.

G. WELTER, 'Die Tripoden-Strasse in Athen', in *Ath. Mitt.* xlvii (1922), pp. 72–7.

J. T. ALLEN, *On the Odeum and the Periclean Reconstruction of the Theater.* 1941.

W. DÖRPFELD, 'Das choregische Denkmal des Nikias', in *Ath. Mitt.* xxxvi (1911), pp. 60–7.

G. WELTER, 'Das choregische Denkmal des Thrasyllos', in *Jahrb. Arch.* liii (1938), *Anz.*, cols. 33–68.

F

Corpus Inscriptionum Graecarum (Boeckh). 1828–77.
Inscriptiones Graecae (Vols. i–xiv), 1877–90.
Inscriptiones Graecae, Editio Minor (in progress, 1924–   ).
W. DITTENBERGER, *Sylloge Inscriptionum Graecarum*, ed. iii. 1915–24.
P. LE BAS et W. H. WADDINGTON, *Inscriptions grecques et latines recueillées en Grèce et en Asie Mineure.* Tome iii. 1870.
A. WILHELM, *Urkunden dramatischer Aufführungen in Athen.* 1906.
O. LÜDERS, *Die dionysischen Künstler.* 1873.
P. FOUCART, *De collegiis scaenicorum artificum apud Graecos.* 1873.
E. REISCH, *De musicis Graecorum certaminibus.* 1885.
A. BRINCK, 'Inscriptiones graecae ad choregiam pertinentes', in *Diss. philol. Halenses* (1886), pp. 71–274.
A. SCHNEIDER, art. 'Σκηνικοὶ ἀγῶνες' in Pauly–Wissowa, *Real-Encycl.* iii, A i. 1927.

G

G. LIBERTINI, *Il teatro antico e la sua evoluzione.* 1910.
P. A. ARIAS, *Il teatro greco fuori di Atene.* 1934.
A. FOSSUM, C. L. BROWNSON, E. CAPPS, and T. W. HERMANCE, 'Excavations in the Theater at Eretria', in *Amer. J. Arch.* vii (1891), pp. 253–80; x (1895), pp. 338–46; xi (1896), pp. 317–31.
E. FIECHTER, *Das Theater in Eretria.* 1937.
E. A. GARDNER, W. LORING, G. C. RICHARDS, and R. W. SCHULTZ, 'Excavations at Megalopolis' (*J.H.S.* Suppl. No. 1). 1892.
E. FIECHTER, *Das Theater in Megalopolis.* 1931.
   (Review by A. von Gerkan, *Gnomon* xiv (1938), pp. 232–6.)
G. E. RIZZO, *Il Teatro greco di Siracusa.* 1923.
E. FIECHTER, *Das Theater in Oropos.* 1931.
——, *Das Theater in Sikyon.* 1931.
——, *Das Theater in Oiniadai und Neu-Pleuron.* 1931.
   (Review of these three by A. von Gerkan, *Gnomon* ix (1933), pp. 145–57.)
H. BULLE, *Das Theater zu Sparta.* 1937.
TH. WIEGAND und H. SCHRADER, *Priene.* 1904.
A. VON GERKAN, *Das Theater von Priene.* 1921.
W. DÖRPFELD, 'Das Theater von Priene und die griechische Bühne', in *Ath. Mitt.* xlix (1924), pp. 50–101.
A. VON GERKAN, 'Die Datierung der Statuenbasen vor dem Proskenion in Priene', ibid. xlix (1924), pp. 225–30.
J. CHAMONARD, 'Théâtre de Délos', in *B.C.H.* xx (1896), pp. 251–318.

W. Dörpfeld, 'Le théâtre de Délos et la scène du théâtre grec', ibid. xx (1896), pp. 563–80.

R. Vallois, articles on Delos in *Nouvelles Archives des Missions Scientifiques* xxii (1921), pp. 213 ff., &c.

——, 'Les théâtres grecs: skené et skenai', in *Rev. Études Anc.* xxviii (1926), pp. 171–9.

Y. Béguignon et J. Replat, 'Le tracé du théâtre de Délos', in *B.C.H.* (1927), pp. 401–22.

R. Heberdey, G. Niemann und W. Wilberg, 'Das Theater in Ephesos', in *Forschungen in Ephesos*, Bd. ii. 1912.

H

C. Robert, *Bild und Lied*. 1881.

——, *Archäologische Hermeneutik*. 1919.

J. H. Huddilston, *Greek Tragedy in the light of the Vase-paintings*. 1898.

R. Engelmann, *Archäologische Studien zu den Tragikern*. 1900.

L. Séchan, *Études sur la tragédie grecque dans ses rapports avec la céramique*. 1926.

A. Furtwängler und K. Reichhold, *Griechische Vasenmalerei*. 1900–32.

F. Messerschmidt, 'Bühnenbild und Vasenmalerei', in *Röm. Mitt.* xlvii (1932), pp. 122–51.

H. Philippart, *Iconographie de l' Iphigénie en Tauride*. 1925.

——, *Iconographie des Bacchantes d'Euripide*. 1930.

E. Löwy, 'Iphigenie in Taurien', in *Jahrb. Arch.* xliv (1929), pp. 86–103.

H. Bulle, *Eine Skenographie*. 1934.

M. Bieber und G. Rodenwaldt, 'Die Mosaïken des Dioskurides von Samos', in *Ath. Mitt.* xxvi (1911), pp. 1–23.

P. Herrmann. *Denkmäler der Malerei des Altertums*. 1901–31.

E. Pfuhl, *Malerei und Zeichnung der Hellenen*. 1923.

A. Mau, *Geschichte der dekorativen Wandmalerei in Pompeii*. 1882.

G. Rodenwaldt, *Komposition der pompeianischen Wandmalerei*. 1909.

A. Ippel, *Der dritte pompeianische Stil*. 1910.

F. Barnabei, *Villa Pompeiana di P. Fannio Sinistore*. 1901.

E. Pernice, *Die hellenistische Kunst in Pompeii*. 1926.

L. Curtius, *Die Wandmalerei Pompeiis*. 1929.

H. G. Beyen, *Die pompeianische Wanddekoration*, I. 1938.

INDEX

Acharnae, theatre at, 198.

Actors: importance of, at different periods, 71, 197, 246; law of Lycurgus concerning, 138, 162; visibility of (*see also* Visibility, conditions of), 70.

Acts, division of play into, 165.

aediculae, 80–100, 252–5, 270.

Aeschines, 162, 163, 212.

Aeschylus:

Scenic arrangements required by, 10, 30–47, 76.

Use of scene-painting? 46; paraskenia? 40, 43, 44; high stage? 33, 36, 42, 45–7; Horace's statement, 72; prothyron? 44, 76 (*and see s.v.*); ekkyklema? 44, 106–8; (*and see s.v.*), θεολογεῖον or upper story, 39–42, 46, 68; περίακτοι? 126; curtain? 128–30.

Changes of scene (in *Eumenides*), 45.

Size of chorus, 32.

Scenery of special plays: *Aegyptii*, 32; *Agamemnon*, 42–4, 68, 106; *Choëphoroe*, 43, 76, 106–7, 131; 'Ηδωνοί, 46; *Eumenides*, 43–6, 81, 84, 107–8, 126; *Europa*, 100; 'Ιέρειαι, 46; *Kares*, 100; *Lycurgeia*, 82; *Memnon*, 37; *Myrmidones*, 37, 130; *Nereïdes*, 37, 130; *Niobe*, 36, 83, 130; *Oresteia*, 10, 42–6; *Persians*, 10, 35–6; *Phorkides*, 46; Φρύγες ἢ ῞Εκτορος Λύτρα, 37, 47; *Prometheus Vinctus*, 37–42, 56, 68, 166; *Pr. Unbound*, 128–9; *Pr.* Πυρφόρος, 42; *Psychostasia*, 39, 42, 46, 68, 127–8; *Seven against Thebes*, 10, 36–7; *Suppliants*, 10, 31–6; *Threïssai*, 37.

Collapse of ἰκρία during play of Aesch., 12–14.

Agatharchus, 37, 124–5, 227, 265.

Agathon, 71, 72.

Agen (satyric play), 161.

ἀγκυρίς, 127.

ἀγῶνες Διονυσιακοί in Agora, 12.

Agonothetes, appointment of, 167.

Agora, plays and seats in, 11–13.

Agyieus, 42.

αἴγειρος, 11, 12.

Αἰολίων, 259.

αἰῶραι, 127, 236.

Aixone, choregi at, 167; theatre at, 198.

Akraiphia, performances at, 243.

Alexander Aetolus, 240.

Alexandria, performances at, 108, 240, 244.

Alexandrian scholars, 211, 240.

Alexis (plays and passages), 78, 157, 164, 173.

Alkamenes, 4, 16, 17, 28.

Alkimachus, 243.

Allen, J. T., 6, 8, 17, 19, 60, 80, 150.

Altar in Orchestra, 9, 10, 34, 40, 71, 131–2, 147, 168, 212; before skené, 36, 47, 53, 64, 66, 68, 105–6, 131–2; see also κοινοβωμία.

Ameinias, 243.

Amphiaräa, 243.

Amphis, 157.

ἀναβάδην, 103–4.

ἀναβαίνειν, 60, 66, 69, 72.

Anaxagoras, 124, 227.

Anaxilas, 157.

Andokides, 1.

Anonymus de Comoedia, 132–3.

Antiphanes, 128, 164.

Apaturius, 226, 230.

Aphrodisias, performances at, 244.

Apollodorus, 124.

Arias, P. A., 209.

Ariobarzanes II, 1, 247, 270.

Ariobarzanes III, 247.

Aristarchus, 211.

Aristeides, 170.

Aristias, 14.

Aristion, 180.

Aristophanes (of Athens):

Scenic arrangements of special plays: *Acharnians*, 59, 101–4, 115; *Birds*, 59, 65; *Clouds*, 59, 60, 73, 78, 104, 129, 130; *Ekklesiazousai*, 59, 67, 103, 190; *Frogs*, 59, 66; *Knights*, 59, 60; *Lysistrata*, 58, 59, 65; *Peace*, 59, 61–5, 68; *Plutus*, 59, 68, 163; *Thesmophoriazousai*, 59, 66, 102–6, 115, 123; *Wasps*, 59, 60, 76, 129, 130.

Use of scene-painting, 65; paraskenia? 60, 61, 66, 67; high stage? 60, 64, 69; prothyron? 76, 78–80; ekkyklema? 101–6, 115; distegia or upper story, 61 ff., 67.

Changes of scene, 59–64, 67.

Aristophanes of Byzantium, 100, 111–12, 211.

Aristotle: on actors, 71, 197; on Megarian comedy, 123; on chorus, 160–2, 242; on μηχανή, 56, 128; on scenes laid in Hades, 99; on scene-painting, 124; on choregia, 167; use of ἐπὶ τῆς σκηνῆς, &c., 73.

ἅρπαξ, 127.

'Artists of Dionysus', 167, 197, 240–5, 270.

Asklepiades, 244.

Aspendos, theatre at, 254.

Assos, theatre at, 191, 217.

Assteas, Vase of, 172, 221–3, 231.

Astydamas, 86, 134–6, 147, 161.

Athenaeus, 118, 157, 162, 168.

Attalus II, 182.

Index

παρεπιγραφή, 105, 117.
πάροδοι, Parodoi, 21, 58, 69, 147–8, 159, 175.
Pausanias, 2, 3, 4, 28, 137, 180, 264.
πέδον, 76, 113.
Pegasos, 4.
Peiraeus, theatre at, 139, 144, 181, 183, 198, 217–18.
Peisistratus, 4.
Pergamon, theatre at, 191, 225.
περίακτοι, 123, 126–7, 188, 215, 234–8.
Pericles, 1, 2, 15, 17.
Pernice, E., 224.
Petersen, E., 22, 160, 180.
Pfuhl, E., 227, 230, 232.
Phaedrus (*and* Bema of Phaedrus), 257–63.
Philippi, theatre at, 51.
Philochorus, 138.
Philodemus, 195, 242.
Philostratus, 117–19, 258.
Philoxenus, 189.
Phlya, theatre at, 198.
Phormos, 122–3.
Pillar (and Column), forms of, 217, 251–2, 256.
Pinakes, 184–9, 202, 208, 217–18.
Plato (comicus), 162.
Plato (philosophus), 13, 72, 127, 141.
Plautus, 77, 164, 173, 193–4, 223, 234.
Plutarch, 29, 46, 108, 127, 137–8, 158–9, 167, 211–12, 237, 245.
Polemaeus, 244.
Polemon, 244.
Pollux, 19, 32, 46–7, 54–6, 68, 77, 115–16, 118–20, 126–8, 131, 139, 170, 188, 210–13, 216, 234–9.
Polybius, 118, 158, 216.
Polygnotus, 123–4.
Pompeii: theatre at, 230; wall-paintings at, 188, 223–34.
Pratinas, 12–14, 168.
Priene, theatre at, 131, 187, 189, 191–2, 202, 210, 214, 218, 225.
Proagon, 73.
Proclus, 132.
'Properties', *see* Altar, Statues, Tombs, &c.
Propylaeum, 1–3.
προσκήνιον, meaning of word, 157–9, 206, 208, 216–17, 268.
Proskenion, προσκήνιον, *proscaenium*: in Lycurgean theatre? 156–60, 172–4, 185; in Hellenistic theatre, 175–90, 193, 216–18, 269; in non-Athenian theatres, 198–9, 202–10, 216; in Roman period? 252.
Prothyron, 44, 56, 75–100, 108, 112–13, 174, 266.
πτερνοκοπεῖν, 19.
Ptolemy Philadelphus, 162.
Puchstein, 138, 150, 152–3, 155, 187, 217, 220, 238.
pulpitum, 72, 78, 212, 256.
Python, 161.

Radermacher, L., 67.
Ramps (in theatres), 204–6.
Rees, K., 77–81, 108, 112, 237.
Reisch, E., 29, 33–4, 67, 69, 108, 128, 158, 188–9, 194, 226; *see also* Dörpfeld.
Reliefs, evidence of, 196, 218–21.
Religious interest of tragedy, 71.
Rhamnus: inscriptions from, 167; theatre at, 198.
Rhinthon, 172.
Rhodes, performances at, 243.
Ῥωμαῖα (at Magnesia, &c.), 243–4.
Ridgeway, Sir W., 45.
Risom, S., 143–4.
Rizzo, G. E., 131.
Robert, C., 9, 42, 53, 85, 87, 130, 222, 224.
Rohde, E., 212.
Rome, wall-paintings at, 225, 227.
Roof (or Upper Story), scenes on, 39, 42, 51, 55, 60–2, 67, 103–4, 186, 190, 267; *see also* διστεγία, θεολογεῖον).
Rousopoulos, A. S., 151, 247, 256, 259, 264.

Salamis, theatre at, 198.
Samos, performances at, 242, 244.
Sannio, 162.
Sarapiaea, 243.
Satyric plays (and scenery): in 5th century, 46, 50, 54; in Lycurgean period, 121, 161–2; in later periods, 185, 189, 196, 226–8, 242–4.
Satyr-reliefs, 196.
scaena, meaning of word, 226; *see also* σκηνή.
scaena ductilis, 199, 202, 227, 237.
scaena versilis, 227.
Scene, changes of, 45, 49, 59, 60, 67, 122–3, 234–8.
Scenery: earliest, 10, 22–3, 32–7; scene-painting, 10, 23, 30, 37, 49, 51–2, 54, 65, 68, 121–7, 133, 188, 215, 265–6, 269–70; degree of realism expected (in theatre), 31, 53, 123, 125–7; scenes in Hades, 54, 99, 124, (on vases), 94–9.
Schleif, H., 16, 23, 26, 156, 249, 251, 253–7.
Schmid-Stählin, 195.
Scholiasts (as authorities), 11, 49, 55, 73, 103–11, 114, 116–21, 132, 210–12, 216.
Schultz, R. W., 141.
Sea-fights in theatre, 258–9.
Sea-gods in theatre, 234–6.
Seats, *see* Auditorium, ἰκρία.
Seats, struggle for, 12.
Séchan, L., 81, 99.
Segesta, theatre at, 51, 171, 210, 221, 233.
Servius, 237.
Sharpley, H., 65.
Sikyon, theatre at, 51, 190, 192, 193, 204, 206, 209–11, 218.
Sileni in theatre, 262, 264; masks of, 228–9.

PLANS I AND III

(*and Figures 7, 46, 51, 52, 59, 123 in Text*)

EXPLANATION OF LETTERS AND NUMBERS

I–XIII. Position of thirteen blocks of seats (κερκίδες).

aA–aA. South wall of Auditorium, western half ('Periclean').

wA–wA. South wall of Auditorium, western half ('Lycurgean').

oA–oA. South wall of Auditorium, eastern half.

b1, b2. Foundations of monuments of uncertain nature (see p. 15).

b3. Basis of late Roman Epoch.

b4, b5, b7. Bases of Roman Epoch.

b6. Basis of pre-Roman date.

b8, b9. Pre-Roman foundations (purpose unknown).

b10. Basis of late date.

B–B. Bema of Phaedrus (see also a b c in Plan II).

U. Wall of Roman period (Remains of X–Ψ in Plan II).

wPa. West Paraskenion (see Figs. 46, 47).

oPa. East Paraskenion (see Fig. 51).

P–P. Foundation of Hellenistic Proskenion (see Fig. 60).

WE. West end of continuation of P–P.

RV–RV⎫
wRV ⎬ Foundations of Roman period.
oRV ⎭

RwQ, RoQ. Roman (western and eastern) cross-walls.

SM1. Supporting wall of earliest Orchestra Terrace (see p. 5).

SM2. Fragment of an old supporting wall.

SM3. Fragment of 6th-cent. supporting wall (see p. 8.)

SM4. ?Fragment of supporting wall of west parodos.

SM5. Fragment of supporting wall, Roman period.

SM6. Fragment of breccia wall.

J1–J4. Foundations of uncertain date and purpose (see pp. 7, 149, 256).

K–K. Water-channel, leading from channel round Orchestra.

H–H. Supporting wall of 'Periclean' Orchestra Terrace, and double north wall of long hall.

T. Foundation projecting from 'Periclean' Terrace wall (see p. 21).

S1–10. Vertical grooves in 'Periclean' Terrace wall (see p. 21).

wQ, mQ, oQ. West, middle, and east cross-walls of hall.

SH–SH. South wall of hall (foundations of steps and colonnade).

Z1, Z2. Breccia foundations of disputed dates.

NOTE. Many of the letters are explained by the German words naturally employed by Fiechter, e.g. wA = west-Analemma, oA = ost-Analemma, wE = west-Ende, SM = Stütz-Mauer, S = Schlitze, Q = Querwand, &c. It seemed better to keep his lettering throughout than to create confusion by a partial substitution of letters representing English words, as his plans may well hold the field for a long time to come.

PLAN I

THE PRECINCT OF DIONYSUS

Plan I does not represent the Theatre as it was at any one moment, but is a sketch-plan of the extant remains, which should enable the reader to assign the structures indicated in the various special plans, figures, and descriptions to their place in the general lay-out. The details of the central portion, as it now is, are given with greater accuracy and completeness in Plan III. In Plan I the dark cross-hatched portions represent roughly the lines of breccia foundations, and the simple hatching the remains of Roman work; the stippled work in the lower part of the Plan indicates modern buildings.

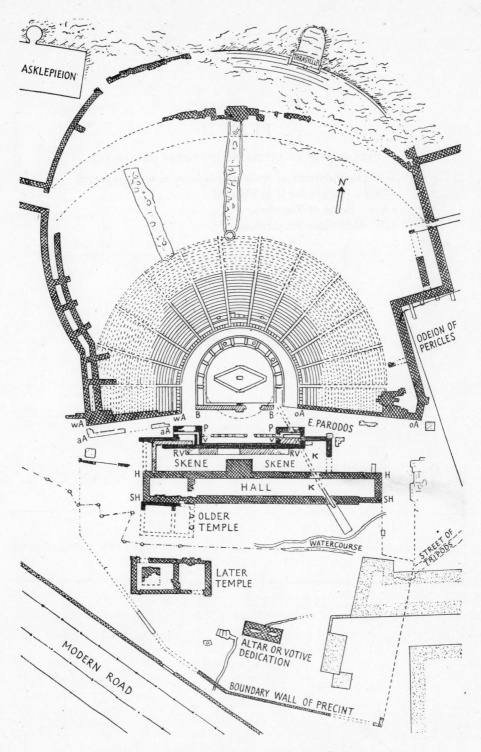

ASKLEPIEION

THRASYLLUS

N

ODEION OF
PERICLES

wA   wA   B   B   oA
aA   aA   P   P   oA   E. PARODOS
                      RV   RV   K
                      SKENE   SKENE
                    H   H
                 SH   HALL   K   SH

OLDER
TEMPLE

WATERCOURSE

LATER
TEMPLE

STREET OF
TRIPODS

ALTAR OR VOTIVE
DEDICATION

MODERN ROAD

BOUNDARY WALL OF PRECINT

PLAN I. THE PRECINCT OF DIONYSUS

PLAN II

EXPLANATION OF LETTERING (SO FAR AS NECESSARY)

X-Ψ } Foundations of walls which have now disappeared
T-Y } (except for U in Plan III).

a b c. Bema of Phaedrus.

α β. Hellenistic Proskenion.